...ing of

THE WISE QUR'AN

THE ETERNAL BOOK OF GUIDANCE

Translated into plain English
by
Dr. Sahib Mustaqim Bleher
with a Brief Index of Subjects

IDCI
Islamic Dawah Centre International

1st Edition printed 2018.

A catalogue record for this book is available from the British Library

ISBN 978-1-910432-03-7

Translated by Dr. Sahib Mustaqim Bleher

Published by IDCI
Islamic Dawah Centre International
Tel: 0121 327 2277 | Web: www.idci.co.uk
Registered Charity No. 1092139

Typeset, cover design and Index compilation by Abdul-Majid Zameer
Printed by Avea Basim - Mega Print, Istanbul, Turkey

Table of Contents

Translator's preface

Why another attempt at translating the Qur'an? The Qur'an is a book of guidance, which can only be followed if properly understood. Language continually develops, and the language of yesterday can prove a barrier to understanding for the reader of today. Most translators have in the past tried to enhance the esteem of the Qur'an by choosing a distinguished, learned and complicated language. The result has been that the message was lost on the ordinary reader. Furthermore, translators have been at pain to achieve the greatest possible accuracy. This being a worth-while objective, even more so when dealing with the divine word, it very often destroyed the clarity of expression as a result by keeping the translation too literal. It is my belief that those who would like to explore the fine details of the Qur'anic text best do so by learning Arabic as it is entirely impossible to consistently mirror in another language the full richness and detail of the original.

In any case it is a fallacy that there should only be one authoritative translation into a given other language. Since a full understanding, and thus transferring, the complete content of the book of Allah is not given to any human, perfection being a prerogative of the divine, there must by necessity be several translations, some focusing on the meaning, some on the literary and poetic style, for example. Furnishing another translation does not imply that existing ones are inadequate, but simply that they are unsuitable for the intended purpose.

My attempt at translating the Qur'an is therefore not a scholarly exercise, but an effort to make these words of guidance and wisdom reach as large an audience as possible and enable them to act upon it by absorbing the meaning of the divine address and the images it contains in a language they can relate to as their own. The Qur'an states that it was revealed in "clear (or plain) Arabic". For its meaning to be transferred to another language, in this case English, one must equally strive for the same clarity of expression which speaks directly to the soul without requiring the mind to engage in complicated decoding first.

An important condition for translating the Qur'an is that one's own interpretation does not overtake the wider meaning. Language is open to interpretation, and interpretations differ in accordance with time and culture. For that reason, the Qur'an cannot be correctly implemented without reference to the life example of the prophet Muhammad, peace be with him, who not only transmitted the Qur'an but also demonstrated its practicability and viability. To include this dimension, classical writings on Tafsir (Qur'anic exegesis), predominantly amongst them the very detailed work of Al-Qurtubi, were extensively consulted when preparing this translation.

Yet, one must also avoid the mistake of making the translation of the Qur'an itself into a commentary by substituting words in order to force their interpretation. The Qur'an speaks for itself, and as far as possible the words and phrases chosen by the Creator should remain unchanged. Adaptations are, however, required where a literal translation of the Arabic sentence would violate the syntax of the English and thus sound outlandish.

To illustrate the approach described above I would like to give a few examples of the choices made when completing the translation.

As for clarity of expression being achieved by not adhering unnecessarily closely to the word sequence in the original, the phrase "did you not see the water which you drink" is appropriately rendered as "take a look at your drinking water". Likewise, the single letter word "wa", meaning "and", is often used in the same way as a comma in English and when it occurs in a list, the repetitive insertion of "and" will make the sentence difficult to follow.

Another example is prepositions which differ between languages, and to use the same preposition just to "stay close to the original" actually distorts it. Previous English translations of the Qur'an describe the gardens of paradise "underneath which rivers flow", conjuring the image of some kind of sewage system. The Arabic word "below" is used in connection with rivers because the river bed is below the earth surface, but in English rivers flow "through" the land, since different cultures have different concepts of space and time. Thus in English children, for example, play "in the street", which does not mean the inside of it but the inside of the space between buildings which is defined by the street. In German, on the other hand, they play "on the street", the street here being defined as the actual road surface. Likewise, when we are told in the Qur'an to travel "in" the earth, we use "on" the earth in English.

Another difficulty when translating between languages belonging to distant geographical environments is that it is not always possible to use the same equivalent of a word throughout. On the one hand, Arabic has a multitude of names for an object, for example a camel, for which English only has one or two. On the other hand, the reverse is also often the case, and the same Arabic word needs to be represented by a different English word dependent on context. A "kafir" is, for example, both the one who rejects the truth and the one who rejects the blessings he received. In the latter case he needs to be described as ungrateful. So in the Qur'anic statement "if you were to count the blessings of Allah you could not enumerate them - man is unjust and ungrateful" it would be wrong to use "disbelieving" instead.

I have avoided the word "disbelief" and used "rejection" instead, because the concept is of somebody who rejects the truth after having been exposed to it. As for "abd", literally a slave, I have used "servant", although man is not just in the service of Allah but also owned by Him. I have made this choice not only because of the tarnished image of slavery but because it allows to retain the correlation between the noun and the verb, so Allah's "servant" is somebody who "serves" Him, rather than just "worships"

Him, as the concept of worship in the Qur'an is much more extensive than the English word implies.

If this translation were aimed exclusively at Muslims who are already familiar with key Arabic terms, then it would be legitimate to leave many such terms in Arabic without translating them, but because I want this translation to make the Qur'an more accessible not only to Muslims but also those who have not previously encountered the message of Islam, I decided to opt for a translation of terms wherever possible, even if such a translation is not always adequate to convey the complete meaning, for example, I have rendered Salah as prayer in spite of the different associations various cultures attach to this word. Whilst the Qur'an is the foundation of Islam, it is not possible to learn everything about Islam exclusively from the Qur'an, less so from a translation, and an exploration of the meanings of key Islamic terms will need to be pursued elsewhere.

I have made an exception from this rule of translating key technical terms of Islam in two cases in particular: Zakat and Injil. A simple translation does not do justice to the concept of Zakat which forms the third pillar of Islam. Zakat is a specified share of surplus wealth to be redistributed to a specified group of disadvantaged members of society. Due to its obligatory nature it is more than charity, yet it is not a tax, because it can, and preferably should, be given directly to the recipients without the involvement of the state. So in this case I have left the Arabic term without further explanation. I have also left Injil as the revelation given to 'Isa (Jesus), because it is not equivalent to the Gospel, the latter representing third party accounts about his life rather than the actual revelation he received.

A particular difficulty in translation is posed by idioms and metaphors. Where there is a direct correlation, the familiar idiom should be used. For example, the woman who untwists her thread after having spun it is, in fact, the woman who undoes her knitting after completing it, and to cling to the literal wording means losing the power of this well-known expression. Other idioms have become common but are based on earlier incorrect translations, so for example, the "camel fitting through the eye of a needle" is based on a mistranslated Biblical metaphor. Etymologically the term "jamal" used in the Qur'an, which also means camel, here means a thick rope, and the expression makes a lot more sense with this meaning, so in spite of everybody having heard the camel version, I chose to move away from it.

Finally, there is the issue of tense: Many future events are described in the Qur'an in the past tense, because in the knowledge of Allah they have already happened, and present tense is used to convey a sense of regularity or immediacy also for events of the past. Whether this appeared equally strange to Arab listeners at the time of first revelation we do not know, but in order to make the text more approachable, all those who have previously translated the Qur'an into English have substituted those tenses with the ones one would normally expect in a continuous narrative.

These are not always ideal choices. As a result of settling for one option above another, some of the depth of the meaning of the original will be lost, especially where the Arabic word has layers of meaning. Here, only the dominant meaning can be conveyed, and to access the fine nuances of alternative interpretations the reader would have to consult a book of Tafsir. Similarly, when legal rulings are derived from the Qur'an, these cannot be based on a translation but require full consideration of the original wording and its context. Where it is possible, however, to leave an ambiguity in place, it is best to do so. A day in the Qur'anic text often means a time period rather than a day, but this inference is also possible in English, so there is no problem in keeping to the six "days" of creation, for example. Ultimately, every translation of a perfect text such as the Divine revelation will be a compromise, and I pray that I will have achieved my aim of introducing the reader of my translation to some of the beauty of the original without diverting from its meaning but, most of all, make it easy to read and comprehend and allow it to speak both to the intellect and the heart.

A number of Qur'an translations add an introductory chapter to each Surah, explaining its background and relevance, as well as footnotes to provide additional explanations to the text. After carefully considering this option I have decided against it as the result is the mixing of divine and human discourse and such interpolated passages distract from the cohesion and flow of the Qur'anic text. A detailed Tafsir (exegesis) of the Qur'an in English may well be of benefit but represents an enormous task which could not be done justice with the occasional interjection of a few interpretative or explanatory notes in this translation in any case. I therefore resolved to let available Arabic books of Tafsir inform my translation but ultimately let the text speak for itself.

I ask Allah to forgive me all the shortcomings in my work and to accept my efforts by making use of my translation to help guide people to the truth. I pray that this translation will open the doors to understanding the message of the Qur'an for many speakers of English who are unable to unlock its treasures in the original Arabic and, maybe, even encourage them to learn Arabic in order to discover the much greater depth and beauty of the original word of Allah.

Completed by the grace of Allah in the month of Rajab 1439 (2018).

Sahib Mustaqim Bleher

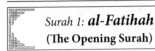

Surah 1: **al-Fatihah**
(The Opening Surah)

1. *In the name of Allah,*
the Owner and Giver of Mercy

2. Allah is praised, the Lord of all worlds

3. The Owner and Giver of Mercy

4. The King of the Day of Repayment

5. We serve only You and ask only You for help

6. Guide us on the straight path

7. The path of those You have favoured, Not of those deserving anger, Nor of those who lose their way.

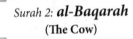

Surah 2: **al-Baqarah**
(The Cow)

In the name of Allah,
the Owner and Giver of Mercy

1. *Alif, Lam, Mim.*

2. This Book contains without doubt a guidance for those who beware (of Allah).

3. Those who believe in what is hidden, and keep up prayer, and spend from what We have provided for them.

4. And those who believe in what has been revealed to you, and in what had been revealed before you, and are certain about the Hereafter.

5. They are the ones who follow the guidance from their Lord, and they are the ones who will succeed.

6. Those, however, who reject (the truth), it makes no difference to them whether you warn them or warn them not, they will not believe.

7. Allah has sealed their hearts and their hearing and placed a blindfold over their eyes, and severe punishment awaits them.

8. There are also those kind of people who say, we believe in Allah and the Last Day, but they believe not.

9. They try to cheat Allah and the believers, but cheat only themselves, without realising.

10. There is an illness in their hearts, and Allah increases that illness for them, and painful punishment awaits them because of their lying.

11. And when they are told: do not cause corruption on earth, they say, we are only making things better.

12. Oh no, they are the corrupters, but they realise it not.

13. And when they are told: believe as ordinary people do, they say, should we believe as the fools do? - oh no, they are the fools, but they know it not.

14. And when they meet those who believe, they say: we believe, but when they are alone with their devils, they say: we are with you, we are just making fun of them.

15. Allah makes fun of them, and lets them get lost in their rebellion.

16. Those are the ones who have traded error for guidance, and their trade will not prosper, and they are not going to be guided.

17. Their example is like someone who lights a fire, and when it lights up his surroundings, Allah takes their light away and leaves them in darkness unable to see.

18. Deaf, dumb and blind - so they cannot return.

19. Or like a rain cloud from the sky with darkness, thunder and lightning in it; they put their fingers in their ears out of mortal fear of the lightning strike, and Allah surrounds those who reject (the truth).

20. The lightning almost takes away their eyesight; whenever it lights up for them, they walk with it, and when it becomes dark for them, they stop. If Allah wished, He would have taken away their hearing and their eyesight. Allah has the power to do anything.

21. Oh people, serve your Lord who created you and those before you, so that you beware of Him.

22. He who made the earth spread out for you, and the sky a cover, and sent water down from the sky, with which He makes fruit grow as provision for you. So do not knowingly set up partners for Allah.

23. And if you have doubts about what We have revealed to Our servant (Muhammad), produce a similar Surah with the help of anyone you like besides Allah, if you are truthful.

24. But if you don't do that - and you can never do it - then beware of the fire promised for those who reject (the truth), which is fuelled by people and stones.

25. And announce to those who believe and do good work that they will have gardens with rivers in them; whenever they are given provision of fruit from it they will say, this is

what we were provided with before - and they will be given what is similar to it - and they will have purified partners in there and they will remain there forever.

26. Allah is not shy to use a fly, or even something smaller, as an example. Those who have faith will say this is the truth from their Lord, whereas those who reject (faith) will say: what's the point of Allah giving this example. He leads many astray with it, and He guides many with it, and He only leads those astray with it, who are sinful.

27. The ones who break their agreement with Allah after it has been entered into and who cut off what Allah commanded to be kept together and who cause corruption on earth - those are the losers.

28. How can you reject (faith in) Allah when you were dead and He brought you to life? Then He makes you die again, then He brings you to life again to return to Him.

29. He alone created for you everything on earth, then He turned to the heaven and shaped it into seven heavens, and He knows everything.

30. When your Lord said to the angels, "I am going to place a representative on earth", they said, "Are you going to place someone there who will cause corruption and spill blood, whilst we (already) sing your praise and glorify you?" He said, "I know what you don't know."

31. And He taught Adam all the names and then presented (things) to the angels and said: "tell me the names of these if you are right."

32. They said: "Glory be to you, we have no knowledge except what You have taught us. You are the knowledgeable and wise."

33. He said: "Oh Adam, tell them their names." And when he told them their names, He said: "Did I not tell you that I know the secrets of the heavens and the earth and that I know what you let on and what you hide?"

34. And when We said to the angels: "Prostrate before Adam", they prostrated except for Iblis (the devil); he refused, was arrogant and rejected (the truth).

35. And We said: "Oh Adam, live with your wife in the garden, and eat from anywhere in it as you please, but do not approach this tree, because then you would be wrongdoers."

36. But the devil made them trip up on this and had them thrown out from their environment, and We said: "Get down as enemies one to another. There will be a place to settle and a limited provision for you on earth."

37. Then Adam received words (of guidance) from his Lord, and He turned back to him, for He is full of acceptance and mercy.

38. We said: "Get down from here, all of you. And when a guidance from Me comes to you, then if you follow My guidance, you shall have no fear nor worry.

39. And those who reject (the truth) and deny Our signs, they will be the inmates of the fire where they will remain.

40. Oh Children of Israel, remember My blessing with which I favoured you, and keep your deal with Me, I will keep My deal with you, and fear only Me.

41. And believe in that which I have sent as confirmation of what you already have and be not the first to reject it, and don't sell the signs of Allah for a small gain, and beware of Me only.

42. And don't cover the truth with falsehood, hiding the truth knowingly.

43. And keep up prayer and give the Zakat, and bow down with those who do.

44. Would you command people to do right and forget about yourselves, whilst you read the book (of revelation)? Don't you think straight?

45. And ask for help, - with patience and prayer -, which is surely difficult except for those who are humble.

46. Those who imagine that they will meet their Lord and return to Him.

47. Oh Children of Israel, remember My blessing with which I favoured you and that I preferred you over everybody else.

48. And beware of a day when no soul will be of benefit to another and no word of support nor any betterment will be accepted from her, and they shall not be helped.

49. And when We rescued you from the family of Pharaoh who afflicted you with bad punishment, slaughtering your sons and sparing your women, which was a tremendous test from your Lord for you.

50. And when We split the sea for you and rescued you, but drowned Pharaoh's people whilst you looked on.

51. And when We arranged a meeting with Musa (Moses) for forty days; then you wrongfully took the calf (as an idol) after he (had gone).

52. Then We forgave you afterwards so that you would be grateful.

53. And when We gave Musa (Moses) the book (of revelation) and the distinction, so that you would be guided.

54. And when Musa (Moses) said to his people: My people, you have wronged yourselves in taking to the calf, so repent to your Maker, and kill your own; that is better for you with your Lord, so that He returns to you: He accepts repentance and is Merciful.

55. And when you said: Oh Musa (Moses), we shall not believe you until we see Allah clearly, and then the lightning struck you whilst you saw.

56. Then We raised you after your death, so that you would be grateful.

57. And We placed you under the shade of a cloud and sent upon you honeydew and quails: eat from the good which We have provided for you. They did wrong not to Us but to themselves.

58. And when We said: Enter this township and eat there freely from where you like, and enter the gate submissive and ask to be accepted, We shall forgive you your shortcomings,

and We shall give more to those who do good.

59. Yet the wrongdoers changed their instructions into something else, so We sent the wrongdoers punishment from the sky because of their excesses.

60. And when Musa (Moses) asked for something to drink for his people, We said: Strike the rock with your stick. Then twelve springs gushed forth from it. All the people straight away knew their drinking places. Eat and drink from the provision of Allah, but do not spread corruption on earth.

61. And when you said: Oh Musa (Moses), we can't bear having just one kind of food, so call your Lord that He produces for us from the herbs and cucumber and lentils and garlic and onions which the earth grows. He said: Do you want to change what is lower for what is better? Go down to Egypt where you will have what you asked for. And humiliation and disgrace were brought upon them and they earned the anger of Allah, because they denied Our signs and killed the prophets without right; because they disobeyed and transgressed.

62. The believers, the Jews, the Christians, and the Sabeans – whoever believes in Allah and the last day and does good work, they will have their reward with their Lord and shall not fear nor worry.

63. And when We made an agreement with you and raised the mountain above you: Take what We gave you with strength and remember its contents so that you will beware (of Allah).

64. Then you turned away afterwards, and if Allah's favour and mercy were not with you, you would have been losers.

65. And you knew of those amongst you who transgressed the Sabbath, and so We said to them: Be despicable monkeys.

66. And We made this a punishment for what lead up to it and what came after and an admonition to those who beware (of Allah).

67. And when Musa said to his people: "Allah commands you to slaughter a cow." They said: "Are you making fun of us?" He said: "I seek refuge in Allah that I should be so ignorant."

68. They said: "Call your Lord for us to explain to us what she is to be like." He said: "He says, she is to be a cow which is not too old nor too young, but middle-aged, so do what you have been commanded."

69. They said: "Call your Lord for us to explain to us what colour she should be." He said: "He says, she should be of an intense yellow colour that is pleasing to look at."

70. They said: "Call your Lord for us to explain to us what she is to be like, for the cows all look the same to us, but if Allah wants we shall be guided."

71. He said: "He says, she is a cow which is not subjugated to plough the earth or water the crops, a healthy cow without any fault." They said: "Now you have come out with the truth." Then they slaughtered her, but had almost not done it.

72. And when you killed someone and then argued about it, and Allah exposes what you want to hide.

73. So We said strike the body with some of (the cow); this is how Allah brings the dead to life and shows you His signs so that you would think.

74. Then your hearts hardened afterwards and became like stone or harder; for even amongst stone there are some from which rivers gush forth, and amongst them are some which break up and water emerges from them, and amongst them are some which fall down out of fear of Allah. And Allah is not unaware of what you do.

75. Do you hope that they will believe you when some of them heard Allah's word before and then knowingly changed it after they had understood it?

76. And when they meet the believers, they say: we believe; and when they are alone amongst each other, they say: are you going to tell them what Allah has decided against you, so that they can use it as an argument against you before your Lord? Don't you think straight?

77. Don't they know that Allah knows what they conceal and what they disclose?

78. And amongst them are unlettered people who know the book only from hearsay and only presume.

79. So woe to those who make up the book themselves and then say this is from Allah, so that they gain a small profit from it. Woe to them for what they make up, and woe to them for what they gain.

80. And they say: the fire shall only touch us a limited number of days. Say: have you got a promise from Allah, for Allah does not break his promise, or do you say about Allah what you don't know.

81. Oh no, whoever does evil, and his sin surrounds him, they belong in the fire (of hell), where they will remain.

82. And those who believe and do good work, they belong in the garden (of paradise), where they will remain.

83. And when We took a promise from the Children of Israel: don't serve anyone but Allah and be good to parents and relatives and the orphans and the poor, and speak well to people, and keep up prayer and give Zakat; then you turned away, except a few of you, and became rebellious.

84. And when We took a promise from you: do not spill each other's blood and do not throw each other out of your homes, then you agreed and were witnesses to it.

85. Then you were the ones killing each other and throwing some of you out of their homes, behaving sinful and showing enmity against them. And when they came to you as captives you would buy them out, when it was unlawful for you in the first place to throw them out. Do you believe only in part of the book and reject the rest? Whoever of you does that, his punishment will only be disgrace in this world, and on the

day of resurrection they will be put through the severest punishment, and Allah is not unaware of what you do.

86. They are the ones who have bought the worldly life for the price of the hereafter, so the punishment shall not be lightened for them, nor shall they be helped.

87. And We gave Musa (Moses) the book before and followed it up by messengers after him, and We gave 'Isa (Jesus) the son of Maryam (Mary) clear proofs and helped him with the Holy Spirit. Do you then become arrogant whenever a messenger comes to you with something you don't like, and you reject some and kill others?

88. And they say: our hearts are sealed. But Allah has cursed them for their rejection, and they believe little.

89. And when a book from Allah comes to them which confirms what they already have, as they were previously asking for victory against the disbelievers, so when that which they recognise comes to them, they reject it, so Allah's curse is upon those who reject (the truth).

90. Bad is what they have sold themselves for, that they reject that which Allah has revealed, envious that Allah favours for His revelation whom He pleases from His servants. So they deserved anger upon anger, and for those who reject (the truth) is a humiliating punishment.

91. And when they are told to believe in that which Allah has revealed, they say: we believe in that which was revealed to us; and they reject that which came after it, although it is the truth which confirms what they have. Say: Why then did you kill the prophets of Allah before, if you were believers?

92. And Musa (Moses) already came with clear proofs to you; then you wrongfully took the calf (for worship) after him.

93. And when We took your promise and raised the mountain above you: take what We gave you with strength and listen. They said: We listen and we disobey, and they let the calf sink into their hearts because of their rejection. Say: Bad is what your faith commands you, if you are believers.

94. Say: If the abode of the hereafter was exclusively for you and not for other people, then you should wish for death if you are truthful.

95. But they shall never wish for death because of the deeds they have sent ahead, and Allah knows the wrongdoers.

96. And you will find them the most greedy of people for life, even more than the idolaters. Each one of them wishes to live a thousand years, but it would not save them from the punishment if they lived that long, and Allah sees what they do.

97. Say: Who is an enemy to Jibril (Gabriel)? We have sent him onto your heart with Allah's permission to confirm that which was revealed before and as a guidance and good news to the believers.

98. If someone is an enemy to Allah and His angels and His messengers and Jibril (Gabriel) and Mika'il (Michael), then Allah is an enemy to those who reject (the truth).

99. And We did send clear proofs to you, and only the sinful reject it.

100. Is it that whenever they make a deal, a group from them throw it out? But most of them believe not.

101. And whenever a messenger from Allah comes to them to confirm what they already have, a group from those who were given the book throw the book of Allah behind themselves as if they did not know it.

102. And they follow that which the devils ascribe to the kingdom of Sulayman (Solomon), yet Sulayman did not reject (the truth), but the devils rejected it, teaching people magic and that which had been revealed to the two angels in Babylon, Harut and Marut; and the two did not teach anyone without saying, "we are a test, so don't reject (the truth)"; so they learn from them how to split a man from his wife, but they cannot harm anybody with it except by Allah's permission; and they learn what harms them and does not benefit them. And they knew already that whoever sells out to it will have no share in the hereafter. Bad is what they sold themselves for if they knew.

103. And if they believed and were aware (of Allah), the reward from Allah would have been better if they knew.

104. Oh you believers, do not say: pay attention to us!, but say: look at us! (drawing attention to yourselves in a polite way) and listen; for those who reject (the truth) there is a painful punishment.

105. Those who reject (the truth) from amongst the people of the Book and the idolaters don't want anything good to come to you from your Lord, but Allah selects for His mercy whom He pleases, and Allah possesses immense favours.

106. We do not replace a sign or cause it to be forgotten without bringing something better or alike. Don't you know that Allah is able to do anything?

107. Don't you know that to Allah belongs the kingdom of the heavens and the earth, and you have besides Allah no protector nor helper?

108. Or would you like to question your messenger like Musa (Moses) was questioned before him? Anyone who replaces belief with denial (of the truth) has already come off the level way.

109. Many from the people of the Book would like to bring you back from your belief into denial, out of jealousy of their own after the truth has become clear to them. So let them be and ignore them until Allah settles the matter; Allah is able to do anything.

110. And keep up prayer and give Zakat. Whatever good you send ahead for yourselves, you will find it with Allah; Allah sees what you do.

111. And they say nobody but a Jew or a Christian will enter the garden (of paradise). Those are their own desires. Say bring your proof, if you are right.

112. Oh no, anyone who submits himself to Allah and does good will have his reward with his Lord and need not fear nor worry.

113. And the Jews say the Christians have no foundation, and the Christians say the Jews have no foundation, but they read the (same) book. Those without knowledge make similar statements to theirs, so Allah will judge between them on the day of resurrection with regard to what they used to differ in.

114. And who is more sinful than one who stops His name from being mentioned in mosques of Allah and hurries to destroy them. Those shall not be permitted to enter them except in fear. They shall have disgrace in this world and severe punishment in the hereafter.

115. And to Allah belongs the East and the West, so wherever you turn, Allah's presence is there, Allah is far-reaching, knowing.

116. And they say Allah has adopted a son. Glory be to Him. But whatever is in the heavens and in the earth is His, and everything is submissive to Him.

117. He is the originator of the heavens and the earth, and when He decides a matter, He simply says to it "Be!", and it is.

118. And those without knowledge say: "Why does not Allah speak to us, or a sign comes to us?" Those before them made similar statements to theirs. Their hearts are alike. We have explained the signs to people who are sure.

119. We have sent you with the truth to bring good news and to warn, and you will not be asked about the inmates of hell-fire.

120. And neither Jews nor Christians shall be pleased with you until you follow their religion. Say: "Allah's guidance is the (only) guidance." If you followed their desires after the knowledge you have received, you would have no protector nor helper from Allah.

121. Those whom We have given the book read it as it should be read: They believe in it. And whoever denies it, they are the losers.

122. Oh Children of Israel, remember My blessing with which I favoured you and that I preferred you over everybody else.

123. And fear a day when no soul will benefit another soul in any way, and no (promise of) justice will be accepted from her, and nobody shall be able to speak in her favour, and they shall not be helped.

124. And when His Lord tested Ibrahim (Abraham) with some words (of instruction) which he fulfilled, He said: I shall make you a leader for mankind. He asked: What about my descendants? He said: My agreement does not stretch as far as the wrongdoers.

125. And when We made the house (Kaaba) a place of return and of safety for the people, and that you should take the position of Ibrahim (Abraham) as a location for prayer. And when We instructed Ibrahim and Isma'il (Ishmael): Purify My house for those who go round it, those who seclude themselves, and those who bow down in prayer.

126. And when Ibrahim (Abraham) said: My Lord, make this land safe and provide its inhabitants with fruit, those of them who believe in Allah and the last day. He said: And those who reject (the truth), I will give them provision for a while, then I will drag them into the punishment of the fire, and it is a bad destination.

127. And when Ibrahim (Abraham) and Isma'il (Ishmael) raised the foundations of the house, (saying:) Our Lord, accept from us, for You are who hears and knows.

128. Our Lord, and make us both submit to You and from our descendants a community who submit to You, and show us our rituals and turn to us (in acceptance), for You are full of acceptance and mercy.

129. Our Lord, and send them a messenger of their own kind to recite Your signs to them and to teach them the book and the wisdom and to purify them, for You are the mighty and wise.

130. And no-one turns away from the religion of Ibrahim (Abraham) but he fools himself. We have chosen him in this world, and in the hereafter he belongs to the righteous.

131. When his Lord said to him: submit!, he said: I have submitted to the Lord of all worlds.

132. And Ibrahim instructed his sons like this, and so did Ya'qub (Jacob): Oh my sons, Allah has chosen a way of life for you, so do not die but in submission to Him.

133. Or were you witnesses when death appeared to Ya'qub (Jacob), when he asked his sons: Whom will you serve after me. They said: we shall serve your god and the god of your fathers Ibrahim (Abraham) and Isma'il (Ishmael) and Ishaq (Isaac), a single god, and we shall submit to Him.

134. They are a community which has gone before. Their earnings are theirs and your earnings are yours, and you will not be asked about what they did.

135. And they keep saying: you have to be Jewish or Christian to be guided. Say: Not at all, the religion of Ibrahim (Abraham), sincerely devoted, for he was not one of the idolaters.

136. Say you all: We believe in Allah and what has been revealed to us, and what has been revealed to Ibrahim (Abraham), and Isma'il (Ishmael), and Ishaq (Isaac), and Ya'qub (Jacob), and the tribes, and what was given to Musa (Moses) and 'Isa (Jesus), and what was given to the prophets from their Lord; we make no difference between any of them, and we submit to Him.

137. Then if they believe in the like which you believe in, they are guided, and if they turn away, then they are the ones ad odds, and Allah will be enough for you, and He listens and knows.

138. The character-imprint of Allah, and who imprints a better character than Allah, and we serve Him.

139. Say: Do you dispute with us about Allah, when He is our Lord and your Lord, and our work is for us, and your work is for you, and we are sincere to Him.

140. Or do you claim that Ibrahim (Abraham) and Isma'il (Ishmael) and Ishaq (Isaac) and Ya'qub (Jacob) and the tribes were Jews or Christians? Say: Do you know better or Allah? And who is more sinful than he who hides an evidence he has from Allah, and Allah is not unaware of what you do.

141. They are a community which has gone before. Their earnings are theirs and your earnings are yours, and you will not be asked about what they did.

142. The fools amongst people will say: What has turned them away from the prayer direction they used to follow? Say: To Allah belongs the East and the West, He guides whom He pleases unto a straight path.

143. In this way We have made you a balanced community, so that you would be witnesses against mankind, and the messenger would be a witness against you. And We only arranged for the prayer direction which you used to follow, so that We could tell the one who follows the messenger from the one who makes a U-turn. And it was surely a big deal except for those whom Allah guided; and Allah won't waste your faith, for Allah is lenient and merciful towards people.

144. We saw you turn your face towards the sky, so We certainly give you a prayer direction with which you will be content. So turn your face towards the sacred mosque, and wherever you may be, turn your faces towards it. Those who received the book know for sure that this is the truth from their Lord, and Allah is not unaware of what they do.

145. And if you gave those who received the book every possible proof, they would not follow your prayer direction, nor do you follow their prayer direction, and they don't even follow each other's prayer direction, and if you followed their desires after the knowledge you have received, you would definitely be a wrongdoer.

146. Those whom We gave the book know it like they know their own children, yet a group of them hide the truth knowingly.

147. The truth from your Lord, so be not amongst the doubters.

148. Everybody has a direction that he turns to, so strive to do good; wherever you are, Allah will bring you all together, for Allah is able to do anything.

149. From wherever you come out, turn your face towards the sacred mosque, and this is the truth from your Lord, and Allah is not unaware of what you do.

150. From wherever you come out, turn your face towards the sacred mosque, and wherever you are, turn your faces towards it, so that people have no argument against you, except for the wrongdoers amongst them – you must not fear them but fear Me -, and so that I can complete My

favour over you and so that you will be guided.

151. Just as we sent to you a messenger from amongst yourselves to recite Our verses to you and to cleanse you and to teach you the book and the wisdom and teach you what you did not know.

152. So remember Me, and I will remember you, and thank Me and don't reject (My guidance).

153. Oh you believers, ask for help, - with patience and prayer -, Allah is with those who have patience.

154. And don't refer to those who have been killed in the way of Allah as dead, for they are alive but you do not realise it.

155. We shall test you with some fear and hunger and loss of property, and life, and fruits; and give good news to the patient,

156. Who when affliction strikes them say: We belong to Allah and to Him we return.

157. Upon them are blessings and mercy from their Lord, and they are the guided.

158. As-Safa and Al-Marwah are signs of worship from Allah, so if someone does Hajj or Umrah to the house it is no sin for him to go to and fro between them, and if someone does good voluntarily, then Allah appreciates and knows.

159. Those who hide the clear proofs and guidance Allah has revealed after We have made it clear for people in the book, Allah curses them and everyone able to do so curses them, too.

160. With the exception of those who repent and make amends and make things clear; I turn back to them, I am the One who accepts repentance and gives mercy.

161. Those who reject (the truth) and die whilst in rejection, the curse of Allah, and the angels and all people is upon them.

162. They shall remain in it; the punishment shall not be lightened for them and they shall not be given time off.

163. Your god is one single god, there is no god but Him, the Owner and Giver of mercy.

164. In the creation of the heavens and the earth, and the change of night and day, and the ship which sails the sea with what benefits people, and the water which Allah sends down from the sky and then revives with it the earth after its death and spreads on it all kinds of creatures, and the turning of the winds and the heavy clouds between the sky and the earth, in this are truly signs for people who understand.

165. And there are people who take other than Allah as alternatives and love them like Allah should be loved; yet the believers are stronger in love for Allah. If only the wrongdoers could see, when the punishment is before them, that all power belongs to Allah and that Allah is strong in punishment.

166. When those who were followed will denounce those who followed them, and they see the punishment and all ties with them are cut off.

167. And those who followed will say: "If only we could return, so we would denounce them just like they denounce us." This is how Allah shows them their work as a lost opportunity, and they shall not escape the fire.

168. Oh people, eat what is permitted and good on earth and do not follow the footsteps of the devil, for he is an open enemy to you.

169. He only commands you evil and indecency and to say about Allah what you do not know.

170. And when they are told to follow what Allah has revealed they say: "No, we follow what we found our ancestors doing." What if their ancestors never understood anything nor were guided?

171. The example of those who reject (the truth) is like the one who depends on something which cannot hear but (the sound of) the prayer and the calling; they are deaf and dumb, and so they understand not.

172. Oh you believers, eat from the good things which We have provided for you and give thanks to Allah if you truly serve Him.

173. He has only forbidden you carrion, blood and pork and whatever has been consecrated for other than Allah. But whoever is forced without (wilful) transgression or habit is not to be blamed: Allah is forgiving and merciful.

174. Those who hide part of the book which Allah has revealed and gain a small price for this will only eat fire into their bellies, and Allah will not speak to them on the day of resurrection nor will He purify them, and painful punishment awaits them.

175. Those are the ones who purchase error instead of guidance, and punishment instead of forgiveness – so how long will they last in the fire?

176. This is because Allah has revealed the book in truth, and those who differ about the book are far away (from the truth).

177. Godliness is not that you turn your faces to the East or the West, but it is to believe in Allah and the last day and the angels and the books and the prophets, and to give wealth out of love for Him to the relatives and the orphans and the poor and the traveller and those who ask and the liberation (of prisoners), and to keep up prayer and give Zakat, and to keep promises once given, and to be patient in adversity and hardship and distress. Those (who do this) are the truthful, and they beware (of Allah).

178. Oh you believers, revenge for killing has been prescribed for you: a free person for a free person, a slave for a slave, a woman for a woman, but whoever is let off by his brother for something, he must obey in a good way and give to him in goodness. This is a relief for you from your Lord and a mercy, so whoever transgresses after that, he deserves a painful punishment.

179. And revenge holds life for you, oh you who have understanding, so that you are careful.

180. It is prescribed for you that when any of you is near death and leaves any goods behind, he must make a will for the parents and relatives in a proper way, a duty for those who beware (of Allah).

181. And if someone changes it after he has heard it, the sin of that will be upon those who change it, Allah hears and knows.

182. But if someone fears from the issuer of the will a mistake or a sin and makes peace between them (the recipients), it is no sin for him, Allah is forgiving and merciful.

183. Oh you believers, fasting has been prescribed for you, like it was prescribed for those before you, so that you become aware (of Allah).

184. A limited number of days, but if one of you is ill or on a journey, then a number of other days, and those who can should compensate by feeding the poor, and whoever does good out of his own accord, it is better for him, and that you fast is better for you if you knew.

185. The month of Ramadan is the one when the Qur'an was revealed as a guidance for mankind and a clarification of the guidance and the distinction (between right and wrong). So if one of you witnesses the month, let him fast it. And if someone is ill or on a journey, then a number of other days. Allah wills ease for you not hardship, and that you should complete the number and exalt Allah for having guided you, so that you should give thanks.

186. And when My servants ask you about Me, I am near: I answer the call of (every) caller, if he calls on Me. So let them respond to Me and believe in Me, so that they go right.

187. It is permitted for you on the nights of the fast to be with your wives, they are a garment for you, and you are a garment for them. Allah knows that you over-burdened yourselves and turned to you in forgiveness and made it lighter for you. So go onto them now and seek what Allah has prescribed for you. And eat and drink until you can distinguish the white thread of daybreak from the black thread, then continue the fast until nightfall. And do not go onto them whilst you seclude yourselves in the mosques. These are the limits of Allah, so do not overstep them. This is how Allah explains His signs to people so that they become aware.

188. And don't consume the wealth of people foolishly amongst yourselves, nor offer it to the judges so that a clique consumes people's wealth sinfully whilst you know it.

189. They ask you about the moon phases, say they are time-markers for people and the pilgrimage. And godliness is not that you enter the houses from their back doors, but godliness is that you beware (of Allah). Enter the houses from their doors and beware of Allah, so that you can be successful.

190. And fight in the way of Allah those who fight you, but do not transgress. Allah does not love the transgressors.

191. And kill them wherever you get hold of them and drive them out from where they drove you out, for corruption is more severe than killing, but do not kill them near the sacred mosque (in Makkah) unless they fight you in there, but if they fight you, kill them. Thus is the reward of those who reject (the truth).

192. But if they stop, then Allah is forgiving and merciful.

193. And fight them until there is no corruption and the religion is completely for Allah, but if they stop, then there should be no enmity except against the wrongdoers.

194. The forbidden month is for the forbidden month, and what is forbidden should be revenged, so if someone transgresses against you, transgress against him in the same way that he transgressed against you, and beware of Allah and know that Allah is with those who beware (of Him).

195. And spend in the way of Allah and do not bring about destruction with your own hands, and do good, Allah loves those who do good.

196. And complete the Hajj (greater pilgrimage) and Umrah (lesser pilgrimage) for Allah, and if you are prevented then send whatever offering is easy, and do not shave your heads until the offering has reached its destination, but if any of you is ill or has an irritation on his head, then he can compensate with fasting or charity or a sacrifice, then when you are safe and well, whoever combines Umrah with Hajj should give whatever offering is easy, but who does not find any should fast three days during Hajj and seven when you return – that is ten altogether. This is for whose family do not live near the sacred mosque. And beware of Allah and know that Allah punishes severely.

197. The Hajj is during known months, and whoever decides to go on pilgrimage in them must abstain from indecent behaviour, mischief and quarrel during the Hajj. Allah knows whatever good you do. And take provision, but the best provision is awareness (of Allah), so beware of Me, oh you who have sense.

198. It is no sin for you to seek favours from your Lord, but when you come out from Arafat, remember Allah at the sacred location and remember Him how He guided you when you were before that amongst those in error.

199. Then come out from where the people come out and seek Allah's forgiveness, Allah is forgiving and merciful.

200. Then, when you have completed your rituals, remember Allah as you would remember your forefathers or more than that. For amongst people is the one who says: Our Lord give us in this world, and he has no share in the hereafter.

201. And amongst them is the one who says: Our Lord give us good in this world and good in the hereafter and guard us from the punishment of the fire.

202. Those will get paid from what they have earned, and Allah is swift in counting.

203. And remember Allah on a number of days: but if someone has to hurry within two days, then it is no sin for him, and if he stays behind, it is no sin for him, as long as he is aware (of Allah), so beware of Allah and know that you will be gathered back to Him.

204. And amongst people is the one whose talk in this world amazes you, and he takes Allah as a witness for that which is in his heart, and he excels in argument.

205. But when he turns away he tries to cause corruption on earth and destroy people's livelihood and continuity, and Allah does not love corruption.

206. And when he is told to beware of Allah, self-importance leads him to sin, so hell is good enough for him, a bad place to be.

207. And amongst people is the one who gives himself fully to seeking the contentment of Allah, and Allah is lenient towards (His) servants.

208. Oh you believers, enter altogether into submission and do not follow the footsteps of the devil, for he is an open enemy to you.

209. And if you step out of line after the clear evidence has come to you, then know that Allah is mighty and wise.

210. Do they just wait for Allah and the angels to come to them in the shade of a cloud and everything is decided? Everything returns to Allah.

211. Ask the Children of Israel how many a clear sign We gave them. But when someone changes the favour of Allah after he has received it, then Allah is severe in retribution.

212. The life of this world appeals to those who reject (the truth) and they mock the believers, but those who beware (of Allah) are above them on the day of resurrection, and Allah provides for whom He pleases without counting.

213. People were one single community; then Allah sent the prophets as bringers of good news and warners and sent with them the book with the truth so that they would judge between people with regard to what they differed in – and they did not differ about it until it was given to them, after the clear proofs had come to them, out of transgression amongst each other – so Allah guided by His permission those who believed towards that of the truth which they differed in, and Allah guides whom He pleases unto a straight path.

214. Or did you count on entering the garden (of paradise) without facing something similar to those who went before you? Adversity and hardship befell them and they shook until the messenger and those with him said: When comes the help from Allah? But no, the help from Allah is close.

215. They ask you what they should spend, say: whatever good you spend, it should be for the parents and relatives and the orphans and poor

and travellers, and whatever good you do, Allah knows of it.

216. Fighting has been prescribed for you although you resent it. It may be that you resent something whilst it is good for you, and it may be that you love something whilst it is bad for you. Allah knows and you do not know.

217. They ask you about fighting during the sacred months, say fighting during them is a big deal, but diverting from the way of Allah – or just to disbelieve in Him – and the sacred mosque, and expelling its people from it, is a bigger deal for Allah: Temptation is worse than killing, and they will not stop fighting you until they bring you back from your religion, if they can manage, and if any of you gives up his religion and dies a rejecter, their work in this world and the hereafter is wasted; they will be the inmates of the fire, where they will remain.

218. Those who believe and those who emigrate and fight in the way of Allah, they desire Allah's mercy, and Allah is forgiving and merciful.

219. They ask you about narcotic drugs and gambling; say: in them is great sin but also some benefit for people, and their sin is greater than their benefit. And they ask you what they should spend; say: what is spare. This is how Allah explains the signs for you to consider.

220. About this world and the hereafter. And they ask you about orphans; say: it is better to treat them well, and if you mix with them, then they are your brothers. Allah knows the one who does bad from the one who does good, and if Allah wanted He could have made it difficult for you; Allah is mighty and wise.

221. And do not marry idolatrous women until they believe, for a believing slave girl is better than an idolatress even if she looks attractive to you; and don't marry idolatrous men until they believe, for a believing slave is better than an idolater, even if he looks attractive to you. They call towards the fire, and Allah calls towards paradise and forgiveness by His permission, and He explains His signs to people so that they remember.

222. And they ask you about menstruation; say: it is an illness, so leave the women alone during menstruation and do not come near them until they have cleansed themselves. Then when they have cleansed themselves, approach them the way Allah has commanded you, for Allah loves those who repent and loves those who keep clean.

223. Your women are for your cultivation, so go to cultivate them as you like, and produce a future for yourselves, and beware of Allah and know that you will meet Him, and give good news to the believers.

224. And do not make your oaths by Allah an excuse not to do good or be god-fearing or make peace between people. Allah hears and knows.

225. Allah does not hold you to account for unintentionally spoken oaths, but He holds you to account for what your hearts intend, and Allah is forgiving and patient.

226. For those who separate from their women is a waiting period of four months, then if they go back, Allah is forgiving, merciful.

227. And if they decide on divorce, then Allah listens and knows.

228. And divorced women must wait for three menstrual cycles, and it is not permitted for them to hide whatever Allah created in their wombs if they believe in Allah and the Last Day. And their husbands are in that case entitled to take them back if they want to make up. And women have similar rights as they have duties, but men are one stage above them, and Allah is mighty and wise.

229. Divorce can be issued twice; then (women) must be kept honourably or let go amicably. You are not allowed to take back anything which you have given them, except if both of them fear that they cannot keep the limits of Allah. So if you fear that they cannot keep the limits of Allah, then there is no sin upon them in what she gives up to release herself. These are the limits of Allah, so do not overstep them. Whoever oversteps the limits of Allah, they are the wrongdoers.

230. So if he divorces her, then she is not lawful for him afterwards unless she has married somebody else, and if he divorces her as well, then there is no sin upon the two that they get back together if they think that they can keep the limits of Allah. These are the limits of Allah which He explains to people who know.

231. And if you divorce women and they reach the end of their waiting period, then keep them honourably or let them go honourably, and do not keep them by force out of spite. Whoever does that wrongs himself. And don't take the signs of Allah as a joke, and remember Allah's favour for you and the book and the wisdom He revealed to admonish you, and beware of Allah and know that He knows everything.

232. And if you divorce women and they reach the end of their waiting period, then do no prevent them from marrying their husbands if they have agreed amongst themselves in the proper way. This is an admonition for each of you who believe in Allah and the Last Day. It is purer and cleaner for you. Allah knows and you don't know.

233. Mothers should breast-feed their children two full years if they wish to complete the breast-feeding, and the father is responsible for their adequate feeding and clothing - no soul shall be burdened beyond her capacity, and neither should a mother come to harm on account of her child nor a father on account of his child, and the same goes for the heir. But if both decide in mutual agreement and consultation to wean (the child) it is no sin on them, and if you decide to give your children away to be breast-fed (by a wet nurse) it is no sin upon you if you pay properly what you promised, and

beware of Allah and know that Allah sees what you do.

234. And if any of you die and leave wives behind, those must wait four months and ten days, then when they have reached the end of their waiting period there is no sin upon you in what they do with themselves within the rules, and Allah is informed of what you do.

235. It is no sin for you to declare a proposal to women or keep it to yourselves. Allah knows that you think of them, but you must not date them secretly and only say what is appropriate, and you must not decide a marriage contract until after the completion of the obligation (of waiting). Know that Allah knows what is within you, so keep Him in mind, and know that Allah is forgiving and patient.

236. It is no sin for you to divorce women whom you have not touched or not yet declared a bridal gift for them, but give them a gift – the well-to-do according to his means, and the constrained according to his means – a gift out of decency, an obligation for those who do good.

237. And if you divorce women before you have touched them but have already declared a bridal gift for them, then pay half of what you have declared, unless they or the one in charge of the marriage arrangements let you off; and it is closer to god-consciousness that you should give it up. And do not forget to be generous amongst yourselves, for Allah sees what you do.

238. Keep up prayers, especially the middle prayer, and stand humbly before Allah.

239. And if you are in fear, then pray standing or travelling, then when you are safe, remember Allah how He taught you what you did not know.

240. And if any of you die and leave wives behind, they must leave a provision behind for their wives for a year without forcing them out (of the home). But if they leave, there is no sin upon you in what they do with themselves within the rules. Allah is mighty and wise.

241. And for divorced women must be an appropriate provision. This is an obligation for those who beware (of Allah).

242. This is how Allah explains His signs for you to consider.

243. What do you make of those who left their homes in thousands trying to avoid death? Allah said to them: die, then he revived them, for Allah is full of generosity towards people, but most people give no thanks.

244. So fight in the way of Allah and know that Allah hears and knows.

245. Who will lend Allah a good loan, so that He will increase it for him manifold? Allah tightens and expands (the provision), and you return to Him.

246. What do you make of the leaders of the children of Israel after Musa (Moses), when they said to their prophet: appoint a king for us and we will fight in the way of Allah. He said: What if fighting is prescribed for you and you don't fight? They said: How should we not fight in the way of Allah when we have been thrown out of our homes and families? But when fighting was prescribed for them they turned away except for a few of them, and Allah knows the wrongdoers.

247. And their prophet said to them: Allah has appointed Talut (Saul) as a king for you. They said: How can he have the kingdom over us when we have more right to the kingdom than he and he hasn't been given enough wealth? He said: Allah has preferred him over you and given him extra knowledge and strength, and Allah gives His kingdom to whom He pleases, and Allah considers everything and knows.

248. And their prophet said to them: A sign of his kingdom is that he will bring you the Ark which contains reassurance from your Lord and a remainder of what the families of Musa (Moses) and Harun (Aaron) left behind; it is carried by angels. In this is a sign for you if you are believers.

249. And when Talut (Saul) departed with the soldiers he said: Allah will test you with a river; so whoever drinks from it, does not belong to me, and who does not taste it, belongs to me, except for one who takes a quick scoop with his hand. But they drank from it except a few of them. So when he and the believers with him crossed over, they said: We have no strength today against Jalut (Goliath) and his soldiers. Those who were sure that they would meet Allah said: How often did a small group overcome a big group with Allah's permission – Allah is with those who are steadfast.

250. And when they faced Jalut (Goliath) and his soldiers they said: Our Lord, fill us with steadfastness and make our foothold firm and help us against the people who reject (the truth).

251. So they defeated them with Allah's permission, and Dawud (David) killed Jalut (Goliath), and Allah gave him the kingdom and the wisdom and taught him whatever He wanted. And if Allah did not make some people drive out others, the earth would be corrupted, but Allah is full of generosity towards the whole world.

252. These are the signs of Allah which We recite to you with truth, and you are one of the messengers.

253. Those are the messengers, We have favoured some of them above others. Amongst them is whom Allah spoke to, and some of them He has raised in stages. We gave 'Isa (Jesus) the son of Maryam (Mary) the clear proofs and helped him with the Holy Spirit. If Allah willed, those after them would not argue once the clear proofs have come to them, but they differ, so that amongst them are those who believe and those who reject (the truth). If Allah willed, they would not argue, but Allah does what He wills.

254. Oh you believers, spend from what We have provided for you before a day will come when there will be no deals nor friendship nor advocacy and the deniers (of truth) will be the wrongdoers.

255. Allah, there is no God but Him, the Living, the Eternal. Neither slumber nor sleep overtake Him. Whatever is in the heavens and on earth is His. Who will intervene in His presence without His permission? He knows what lies before them and behind them, and they don't grasp any of His knowledge except what He permits. His footstool is as wide as the heavens and the earth; maintaining them does not tire Him, and He is the exalted and great.

256. There is no compulsion in religion. Right and wrong are self-evident. One who rejects idols and believes in Allah holds on to a reliable link which cannot break, and Allah listens and knows.

257. Allah is the protector of the believers. He takes them out from all darkness into the light. But the protectors of those who reject (the truth) are the idols. They take them out from the light into all darkness. They are inmates of the fire, where they will remain.

258. What do you make of the one who disputed with Ibrahim (Abraham) about his Lord that Allah had given him the kingdom. When Ibrahim said to him: "my Lord gives life and death", he replied: "I give life and death". Ibrahim said: Allah brings the sun from the East, so bring it from the West. Then the one who rejected (the

truth) was dumbfounded, and Allah does not guide wrongdoing people.

259. Or the one who walked past a town which was abandoned in ruins and said: "How will Allah revive this after its death?" So Allah made him dead for a hundred years and then raised him. He said: "How long did you stay?" He said: "I stayed a day or part of a day." He said: "No, you stayed a hundred years, so look at your food and your drink, it has not gone off, and look at your donkey, and this is to make you a sign for people. And look at the bones, how We place them upon each other and then cover them with flesh." So when it became clear to him, he said: "I know that Allah is able to do anything".

260. And when Ibrahim (Abraham) said: "My Lord, show me how You revive the dead", He said: "Don't you believe?", he said: "Sure, but it would put my heart at ease." He said: "So take four birds and train them on you, then place some of them on each mountain and call them, they will come to you hurriedly. And know that Allah is mighty and wise."

261. The example of those who spend their wealth in the way of Allah is like that of a seed which grows seven ears, each ear containing a hundred seeds, and Allah gives increase for whom He pleases, and Allah is generous and knows.

262. Those who spend their wealth in the way of Allah without following their expenditure with reproach and insult, they will have their reward

with their Lord and shall have no fear nor worry.

263. An appropriate word and forgiveness are better than charity followed by insult, and Allah is rich and gentle.

264. Oh you believers, do not spoil your charity with reproach and insult like the one who spends his wealth to be seen by people and does not believe in Allah and the last day. His example is like that of a rock covered with soil hit by a torrent, which leaves it arid. They have no power over anything they earn, and Allah does not guide ungrateful people.

265. And the example of those who spend their wealth seeking the contentment of Allah and to strengthen themselves is like that of a garden on a hill hit by a torrent, and it gives double its produce, and if it is not hit by a torrent then by a drizzle, and Allah sees what you do.

266. Would any of you like to have a garden with date trees and grape vines with rivers flowing through it, and he has all kind of fruit in it, and old age hits him whilst he has weak children; then a fiery tornado hits it and burns it – This is how Allah explains the signs to you, so that you ponder.

267. Oh you believers spend of the good things you have earned and what We let come out of the earth for you, and do not try to spend the bad of it which you wouldn't want to receive yourselves, and know that Allah is rich and praiseworthy.

268. The devil promises you poverty and commands you indecency, and Allah promises you forgiveness from Himself and abundance, and Allah is generous and knows.

269. He gives wisdom to whom He pleases, and when someone has been given wisdom, he has been given a lot of good, but only those with understanding appreciate it.

270. Whatever you give and pledge, Allah knows it, and the wrongdoers have no helpers.

271. If you give charity openly, then this is excellent, and if you hide it and give it to the poor, that is better for you, and it will undo some of your bad deeds for you, and Allah knows what you do.

272. Their guidance is not up to you, but Allah guides whom He pleases, and any good you spend is for your own selves, and you only spend to seek the presence of Allah, and any good you spend will be repaid to you, and you will not be wronged.

273. For the poor who are constrained in the way of Allah unable to travel on earth; the ignorant considers them to be rich due to (their) modesty, you can tell them by their sign, they do not ask people incessantly, and any good you spend, Allah knows of it.

274. Those who spend their wealth night and day, secretly and openly, they will have their reward with their Lord and shall have no fear nor worry.

275. Those who consume interest will not stand other than the one whom the devil has struck with madness – This is

because they say interest is like trade, yet Allah has permitted trade and forbidden interest. So when someone receives admonition from his Lord and stops, what is in the past remains his, and his affairs belong to Allah, and those who persist are inmates of the fire, where they will remain.

276. Allah destroys interest and gives increase to charity, and Allah does not love anyone ungrateful and sinful.

277. Those who believe and do good work and keep up prayer and give Zakat, they will have their reward with their Lord and shall have no fear nor worry.

278. Oh you believers beware of Allah and abandon what remains in interest if you are believers.

279. And if you don't do that, then take a declaration of war from Allah and His messenger, and if you repent, then your capital sums are yours. Do not wrong and do not be wronged.

280. And if someone is in hardship then wait until he is at ease, and if you give charity it is better for you if you knew.

281. And fear a day when you will return to Allah, then each soul will be given in full what it has earned and they will not be wronged.

282. Oh you believers, if you borrow from each other until a future date, then write it down. And let a scribe amongst you write impartially, and the scribe must not refuse to write as Allah has taught him; so let him write, and let the one who owes dictate and let him beware of Allah, his Lord, and not omit anything of it. And if the one who owes is mentally unable or weak or cannot dictate, then let his guardian dictate impartially. And let two from amongst your men be witnesses, and if there are not two men then one man and two women of those whom you are content with as witnesses, so if one of the two forgets, the other one reminds her. And the witnesses must not refuse to be called. And do not consider it a bother to write it down for the future, whether it be small or big, as that is more just before Allah and more stable in evidence and less likely to cause you doubt. Except when it is an immediate exchange you conduct amongst yourselves, then there is no sin upon you if you don't write it down. And have your trade transactions witnessed and let no harm come to either the scribe or the witness. Should you do that, it would be immoral of you, and beware of Allah, and Allah will teach you, and Allah knows everything.

283. And if you are on a journey and can't find a scribe, then a tangible security, and when you entrust something to each other, then the one who has been entrusted must return what he has been entrusted with, and let him beware of Allah, his Lord, and do not hide the evidence, for the one who hides it has a sinful heart, and Allah knows what you do.

284. To Allah belongs what is in the heavens and what is on the earth, and whether you expose what is within you or hide it, Allah will take

you to account for it. Then He will forgive whom He pleases and punish whom He pleases, and Allah is able to do anything.

285. The messenger believes in what has been revealed to him from His Lord, and so do the believers. They all believe in Allah, His angels, His books, and His messengers – we make no difference between any of His messengers – and they say we listen and we obey, Your forgiveness, oh our Lord, and to You is the journey.

286. Allah does not burden a soul beyond its capacity, in its favour is what it has earned, and against it is what it has appropriated. Our Lord, do not grab us if we forget or make a mistake; our Lord, and do not place upon us a burden like you have placed upon those before us; our Lord and do not burden us beyond our strength; and let us off and forgive us and have mercy on us: Your are our Protector, so help us against the people who reject (the truth).

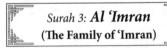

Surah 3: *Al 'Imran*
(The Family of 'Imran)

In the name of Allah,
the Owner and Giver of Mercy

1. Alif, Lam, Mim.

2. Allah, there is no god but Him, He is the Living, the Eternal.

3. He revealed the book to you with the truth, confirming that which came before it, and He revealed the Torah and the Injil.

31

4. An earlier guidance for mankind, and He revealed the distinction (between right and wrong). For those who reject the signs of Allah there is severe punishment, and Allah is mighty and vengeful.

5. Nothing in the earth or the heaven is hidden from Allah.

6. He is the One who shapes you in the wombs as He pleases. There is no god but Him, the mighty, the wise.

7. He is the One who sent to you the book of which there are decisive verses, which are the core of the book, and other ambiguous ones. As for those in whose hearts there is distraction, they follow that of it which is ambiguous in an attempt to cause temptation and seeking a specific outcome, yet no-one knows its outcome but Allah. And those firm in knowledge say: We believe in it, it is all from our Lord. And only those with understanding remember.

8. Our Lord, do not distract our hearts after You have guided us and grant us mercy from You, for You are the one who gives.

9. Our Lord, you will gather all people for a day without doubt, for Allah does not break the promise.

10. Those who reject (the truth), neither their wealth nor their children will benefit them against Allah. They are the fuel of the fire.

11. Like the practice of the family of Pharaoh and those before them, they denied our signs, so Allah seized them on account of their sins. Allah is severe in punishment.

12. Say to those who reject (the truth): You will be overcome and gathered in hell, a bad place to be.

13. There is a sign for you in the two parties who met, one party fighting in the way of Allah and another rejecting (the truth), which outwardly appeared to them to be twice (their strength), yet Allah helps with His victory whom He pleases. In that is a lesson for those who see.

14. The love of desires (aroused) by women and children and accumulated treasures of gold and silver and branded horses and cattle and land appeals to people. That is the provision of this world, and with Allah is the best return.

15. Say: Shall I inform you of better than that. For those who beware (of Allah) there are gardens with their Lord through which rivers flow – they will remain there – and pure partners and contentment from Allah, and Allah sees (His) servants.

16. Those who say, our Lord, we believed, so forgive us our sins and guard us from the punishment of the fire.

17. The patient, the truthful, the humble, the charitable, and those who ask forgiveness at dawn.

18. Allah bears witness that there is no god but Him, and so do the angels and those with knowledge; He upholds justice. There is no god but Him, the mighty and wise.

19. The obligation towards Allah is submission (Islam), and the people of the book only differed out of jealousy amongst each other after having received the knowledge. If someone denies the signs of Allah, Allah is swift in counting.

20. And if they dispute with you say: I have submitted fully to Allah and so have those who follow me. And ask those who were given the book and the unlettered people: Do you submit? Then if they submit, they are guided, and if they turn away, your only duty is to convey, and Allah sees (His) servants.

21. Those who reject the signs of Allah and kill the prophets without justification and kill those who command justice amongst people, announce to them a painful punishment.

22. They are the ones whose work will be wasted in this world and in the hereafter and they have no helpers.

23. What do you make of those who received a portion of the book being called to the book of Allah to judge between them, then a party amongst them turned away in opposition?

24. This is because they say: The fire will only touch us a limited number of days. And their inventions mislead them in their religion.

25. How then when We gather them to a day without doubt and every soul is repaid what it has earned and they will not be wronged?

26. Say: O Allah, King of the kingdom, You give the kingdom to whom You please and take away the kingdom from whom You please, You honour whom You please and humiliate whom You please, the good is in Your hand, You have power over of all things.

27. You blend the night into the day and the day into the night, and You bring out the living from the dead and the dead from the living, and You provide for whom You please without counting.

28. The believers must not take those who reject (the truth) as protectors besides the believers. If someone does so then he has nothing to do with Allah, except if he does so as a precaution against them, and Allah cautions you about Himself, and to Allah is the journey.

29. Say, whether you hide what is inside you or reveal it, Allah knows it. He knows what is in the heavens and in the earth, and Allah has power over all things.

30. On the day when every soul finds all the good she has done present and all the bad she has done, she wishes there was a long distance between it and her. And Allah cautions you about Himself, and Allah is kind to (His) servants.

31. Say: If you love Allah, then follow me and Allah will love you and forgive you your sins. Allah is forgiving and merciful.

32. Say: Obey Allah and the messenger. But if you turn away, then Allah does not love those who reject (the truth).

33. Allah chose Adam and Nuh (Noah) and the family of Ibrahim (Abraham) and the family of 'Imran over everybody else.

34. They are descendants one of the other, and Allah listens and knows.

35. When the wife of 'Imran said: My Lord, I have promised the content of my womb to be devoted to You, so accept it from me, for You are [the One] who listens and knows.

36. So when she delivered it she said: My Lord, I have delivered a female – and Allah knew best what she had delivered, and the male and the female are not alike – and I have named her Maryam (Mary) and I seek refuge in You for her and her descendants from the cursed devil.

37. So her Lord accepted her in the best way and made her grow up well and entrusted her care to Zakariya (Zachariah); whenever Zakariya entered her place of seclusion he found provision with her. He asked: O Maryam (Mary), where did you get this from? She said, it is from Allah, Allah provides for whom He pleases without counting.

38. Upon this Zakariya called His Lord, saying: My Lord, give me a good offspring from You, for You hear the prayer.

39. Then the angels called him whilst he was standing in prayer in the secluded place that Allah gives you good news of Yahya (John) as confirmation of a word from Allah and noble and chaste and a prophet from amongst the righteous.

40. He said: My Lord, how can I have a son when old age has caught up with me and my wife is barren? He said: thus Allah does what He pleases.

41. He said: My Lord, appoint a sign for me. He said: Your sign is that you will not speak to people for three days other than by gestures; and remember your Lord much and give praise in the evening and the morning.

42. And when the angels said: O Maryam (Mary), Allah has chosen you and purified you and chosen you above all the women of the world.

43. O Maryam (Mary), be humble towards your Lord and prostrate and bow down with those who do.

44. This is information We reveal to you from the unseen. You were not amongst them when they drew straws as to who should take care of Maryam (Mary) and you were not amongst them when they argued.

45. When the angels said: O Maryam (Mary), Allah gives you good news of a word from Him whose name shall be the Messiah 'Isa (Jesus) son of Maryam, honoured in this world and amongst those brought close in the Hereafter.

46. He will talk to people whilst in the cradle and in adulthood and will be amongst the righteous.

47. She said: My Lord, how can I have a son when no man has touched me. He said: Thus Allah creates what He pleases. When He decides a matter then He says to it: Be – and it is.

48. And He will teach him the book, the wisdom, the Torah and the Injil.

49. And he will be a messenger to the Children of Israel saying "I have come to you with a sign from your Lord; I will create for you from clay the shape of a bird and breathe into it so that it will be a (real) bird by permission of Allah, and I will heal the blind and the leper, and will bring back to life the dead by permission of Allah, and I will tell you what you eat and what you store in your houses. In that is a sign for you if you are believers.

50. And confirming that which went before me from the Torah and to make lawful for you some of that which was forbidden for you. I have come to you with a sign from my Lord, so beware of Allah and obey me.

51. Allah is my Lord and your Lord, so serve Him. This is a straight path."

52. Then, when 'Isa (Jesus) noticed the denial amongst them, he said: "Who are my helpers towards Allah?" The disciples said: "We are the helpers of Allah, we believe in Allah and be you a witness that we have submitted.

53. Our Lord, we believe in what You have revealed and follow the messenger, so list us amongst the witnesses."

54. And they schemed and Allah schemed, and Allah is the best of schemers.

55. When Allah said: "O 'Isa (Jesus), I will take you away and raise you to Myself and purify you and make those who follow you above those who reject (the truth) until the day of resurrection, then your return will be to Me and I will judge between you with regard to what you used to differ in.

56. As for those who reject (the truth), I will punish them with a severe punishment in the world and the hereafter and they will have no helpers.

57. And as for those who believe and do good work, they will be given their reward. Allah does not love the wrongdoers."

58. This is what We recite to you from the signs and the wise reminder.

59. The likeness of 'Isa (Jesus) with Allah is as the likeness of Adam: He created him from soil and then said to him: Be - and he is.

60. The truth from your Lord, so be not amongst the doubters.

61. So if anyone disputes with you about it after you have received knowledge then say: Come, let us call our children and your children, and our women and your women, and ourselves and yourselves, then we shall pray for the curse of Allah to be brought upon the liars.

62. This is indeed the true story. There is no god but Allah, and Allah is the mighty and wise.

63. Then if they turn away, Allah knows the corrupters.

64. Say, oh people of the Book, come to a common word between us and you that we serve none but Allah and do not associate anything with Him nor take each other as overlords instead of

Allah. Then if they turn away, say: Be witnesses that we have submitted.

65. Oh people of the Book, why do you dispute about Ibrahim (Abraham) when the Torah and the Injil were only revealed after him – don't you think?

66. You are the ones who used to dispute about that which you had knowledge of, so why do you dispute about that which you have no knowledge of? Allah knows and you do not know.

67. Ibrahim (Abraham) was neither Jew nor Christian, he was one dedicated to Allah, submitted to Him (a Muslim), and was not amongst the idolaters.

68. The closest to Ibrahim (Abraham) are surely those who follow him and this prophet and those who believe, and Allah is closest to the believers.

69. A group amongst the people of the Book would love to lead you astray but they only lead themselves astray without realising it.

70. Oh people of the Book, why do you reject the signs of Allah when you witness them?

71. Oh people of the Book, why do you clothe the truth in falsehood and hide the truth knowingly?

72. A group amongst the people of the Book said: Let's believe in that which was revealed to the believers during the day and reject it at the end of it so that they revert.

73. And do not believe anyone unless he follows your religion - Say: the only guidance is the guidance of

Allah - (and do not accept) that he has received something similar to what you have received nor (accept) that he may dispute with you before your Lord. Say: All benefit is in Allah's hand who gives it to whom He pleases, and Allah is far-reaching and knows.

74. He selects for His mercy whom He pleases, and Allah possesses immense favours.

75. Among the people of the book are some who, if you entrust them with a large amount, they will return it to you, and among them are some who, if you entrust them with a single coin, will not return it to you unless you keep constantly at it. This is because they say: There is no redress against us concerning the gentiles; and they speak a lie against Allah knowingly.

76. But no, if someone fulfils his agreements and bewares, then Allah loves those who beware (of Him).

77. Those who sell their agreement with Allah and their oaths for a small gain, they will have no share in the hereafter and Allah will not speak to them nor look at them on the day of resurrection nor will He purify them, and painful punishment awaits them.

78. And amongst them there is a faction who distort the book in their speech so that you consider it to be part of the book when it is not part of the book, and they say it is from Allah when it is not from Allah, and they speak a lie against Allah knowingly.

79. And no person has a right that when Allah gives him the book and sound judgement and prophethood he should say to people be my servants instead of Allah's, but he should say: guide people to your Lord on account of what you know and teach of the book and what you study.

80. Nor would he command you to take the angels and prophets as lords; is he going to command you to reject (the truth) after you have submitted?

81. And when Allah took a promise from the prophets that after I gave you part of the book and the wisdom and then there comes to you a messenger who confirms that which you have, you will believe in him and help him, He said: do you agree and take my covenant on that basis? They said: We agree. He said: Then be witnesses and I shall be a witness with you.

82. Then if anyone turns away afterwards they will be the sinful.

83. Do they then seek a different religion to that of Allah when everything in the heavens and the earth submits to Him (both) obediently and reluctantly and to Him will they be brought back?

84. Say: We believe in Allah and what has been revealed to us and what has been revealed to Ibrahim (Abraham) and Isma'il (Ishmael) and Ishaq (Isaac) and Ya'qub (Jacob) and the tribes and what was given to Musa (Moses) and 'Isa (Jesus) and the prophets from their Lord, we make no difference between any of them, and we submit to Him.

85. And if anyone seeks another religion than Islam (submission), it will not be accepted from him

and he will be amongst the losers in the hereafter.

86. How is Allah going to guide a people who reject (the truth) after they believed and were witnesses that the messenger is truthful and came to them with clear proofs. Allah does not guide wrongdoing people.

87. Their reward will be that that the curse of Allah and the angels and all mankind will be upon them.

88. They shall remain in it; the punishment shall not be lightened for them and they shall not be given time off.

89. Except those who repent afterwards and make amends, for Allah is forgiving, merciful.

90. Those who reject (the truth) after they believed and then increase in rejection, their repentance will not be accepted and those are the ones who have lost their way.

91. Those who reject (the truth) and die in the state of rejection, the weight of the earth in gold would not be accepted from any of them in redemption. Painful punishment awaits those and they will have no helpers.

92. You will not achieve righteousness until you spend from that which you love. And whatever you spend, Allah knows of it.

93. All food was permitted to the Children of Israel except what Israel forbade for himself before the Torah was revealed. Say: bring the Torah and recite it if you are truthful.

94. Therefore, if someone invents a lie against Allah afterwards, then they are the wrongdoers.

95. Say: Allah has spoken the truth, therefore follow the religion of Ibrahim (Abraham), sincerely devoted, for he was not one of the idolaters.

96. The very first house placed for people (to worship at) is that in Bakkah as a blessing and guidance for all the worlds.

97. It contains clear signs, the location of Ibrahim (Abraham), and whoever used to enter it was safe, and Allah obliges mankind to make the pilgrimage (Hajj) to the House if he finds a way to do so, and whoever denies it, Allah is independent of all the worlds.

98. Say: Oh people of the (previously revealed) Book, why do you reject the signs of Allah when Allah is a witness of what you do?

99. Say: Oh people of the book, why do you divert somebody who believes from the way of Allah desiring it to be crooked when you are witnesses and Allah is not unaware of what you do?

100. Oh you believers, if you follow a faction of those who were given the book, they would turn you back to reject (the truth) after your belief.

101. Yet, how should you reject (it) when the signs of Allah are recited to you and His messenger is amongst you. He who holds on to Allah has already been guided on to a straight path.

102. Oh you believers, beware of Allah with the awareness due to Him and do

not die except in submission to Him (as Muslims).

103. And hold on to the connection with Allah altogether and do not break up, and remember Allah's favour upon you when you were enemies and He brought your hearts together and you became brothers by His blessing, and you were at the brink of falling into the fire and He rescued you from it, this is how Allah explains His signs to you so that you may be guided.

104. And there should be amongst you a community who call to what is good and command good conduct and forbid wrongdoing, and those will be the successful.

105. And be not like those who break up and differ after the clear proofs came to them, severe punishment awaits those.

106. On the day when faces will be whitened and faces will be blackened. As for those whose faces will be blackened: Did you reject (the truth) after your belief? Then taste the punishment on account of your rejection.

107. As for those whose faces will be whitened, they are in the mercy of Allah in which they remain.

108. Those are the signs of Allah which We recite to you in truth, and Allah does not will oppression for the worlds.

109. And to Allah belongs whatever is in the heavens and what is on earth, and to Allah return all things.

110. You are the best community brought forth for mankind: you command good conduct and forbid wrongdoing and believe in Allah. If the people of the Book believed, it would have been better for them. Amongst them are believers, but most of them are sinful.

111. They will not harm you except by insult, and if they fight you they will turn to flee and will then not be helped.

112. Humiliation is brought upon them wherever they are found except (when holding on to) the connection to Allah and the connection to the people; and they are burdened with the anger of Allah and misery is brought upon them; this is because they rejected the signs of Allah and killed the prophets without right; this is because they disobeyed and were transgressing.

113. They are not (all) the same. Amongst the people of the Book there is an upright community who read the signs of Allah during part of the night and prostrate.

114. They believe in Allah and the last day and command good conduct and forbid wrongdoing and hasten towards good deeds, and they are amongst the righteous.

115. Whatever good they did will not be denied to them, and Allah knows those who beware (of Him).

116. Those who reject (the truth), neither their wealth nor children will help them the least against Allah, and those are the inmates of the fire where they will remain.

117. The likeness of what they spend in the life of this world is that of a freezing wind which hit the harvest of people who have wronged themselves and destroyed it, and Allah did not wrong them but they wronged themselves.

118. Oh you believers, do not take confidants from outside your own; they will not stop harming you, they love what ruins you, their hatred is already apparent from (what comes out of) their mouths, and what they hide in their chests is more severe. We have already explained the signs to you if you understand.

119. There you are the ones who have affection for them, whereas they have no affection for you, and you believe in all of the book, and when they meet you they say "we believe", and when they are alone they bite their fingers against you out of anger. Say, die from your anger, for Allah knows what is kept inside.

120. When good befalls you, it hurts them, and when harm befalls you they rejoice in it, but if you are patient and beware (of Allah), their deception will not harm you at all, for Allah surrounds what they do.

121. And when you left your home early in the morning to order the believers for battle, and Allah listens and knows.

122. When two groups amongst you tended to despair whilst Allah is their protector, and on Allah should the believers rely.

123. And Allah already gave you victory at Badr when you were few, so beware of Allah in order to be grateful.

124. When you said to the believers: will it not suffice you that your Lord helps you with three thousand angels sent down?

125. More so, if you have patience and beware (of Allah) when they come upon you suddenly, then your Lord will help you with five thousand marked angels.

126. And Allah only gave this as good news for you and to contend your hearts with it, and victory is only from Allah the mighty and wise.

127. So that He cuts off a portion of those who reject (the truth) or subdues them to make them turn back in failure.

128. You have no say in the matter. Or He may turn back to them or punish them because they are wrongdoers.

129. And to Allah belongs what is in the heavens and on earth. He forgives whom He pleases and punishes whom He pleases, and Allah is forgiving and merciful.

130. Oh you believers, do not devour usury multiplied several times and beware of Allah so that you may be successful.

131. And beware of the fire which has been prepared for those who reject (the truth).

132. And obey Allah and the messenger so that you may find mercy.

133. And hurry towards the forgiveness from your Lord and a garden whose width is that of the heavens and the earth, which has been prepared for those who beware (of Allah).

134. Those who spend in ease and hardship and those who restrain their anger and those who are gentle towards people, and Allah loves those who do good.

135. And those who, if they have committed an indecency or wronged themselves, remember Allah and ask forgiveness for their sins - for who forgives sins except Allah? - and did not knowingly persist in what they did.

136. For those the reward is forgiveness from their Lord and gardens through which rivers flow where they will remain; blessed is the reward of those who work.

137. Examples have already passed before you, so travel on the earth and see what the outcome was like for the deniers.

138. This is a clear exposition for mankind and a guidance and admonition for those who beware (of Allah).

139. And do not lose heart nor grieve and you will come out on top if you are believers.

140. If a wound has afflicted you, then a similar wound has also afflicted the people, and we alter these days amongst mankind and for Allah to know those who believe and to take witnesses from you, and Allah does not love the wrongdoers.

141. And for Allah to test those who believe and to destroy those who reject (the truth).

142. Or did you count on entering the garden without Allah knowing those who strive amongst you and knowing the patient?

143. And you already hoped for death before you met it, and you already saw it with open eyes.

144. And Muhammad is only a messenger who was preceded by the messengers, so if he dies or is killed, will you turn back on your heels? And if someone turns back on his heels he will not harm Allah at all. And Allah will repay the grateful.

145. And no soul will die without Allah's permission as a fixed appointment, and if someone wants the reward of this world, We give him of it, and if someone wants the reward of the hereafter, We give him of it, and We will repay the grateful.

146. And how many a prophet was there with whom a large multitude fought, and they did not waver on account of what happened to them in the cause of Allah nor weaken or give in, and Allah loves the patient.

147. And all they said was: Our Lord, forgive us our sins and excesses in our affair and make our foothold firm and help us against people who reject (the truth).

148. So Allah gave them the reward of this world and the best reward of the hereafter, and Allah loves those who do good.

149. Oh you believers, if you obey those who reject (the truth) they will make you turn back and you will turn back as losers.

150. But Allah is your protector, and He is the best of helpers.

151. We shall place fear in the hearts of those who reject (the truth) on account of having associated with Allah that for which He has not sent any authority, and their abode is the fire and miserable is the home of the wrongdoers.

152. And Allah already made His promise come true for you when you rooted them by His permission, until you weakened and argued about the matter and disobeyed after He showed you what you loved - among you are those who want the world and among you are those who want the hereafter; then He turned you away from them in order to test you, and He has already forgiven you, and Allah is full of generosity for the believers.

153. When you ascended and did not stop for anybody whilst the messenger called you from behind you, and additional grieve afflicted you so that you would not worry about what had escaped you nor about what had befallen you, and Allah knows what you do.

154. Then after this grief He sent you a calming safety which enveloped a group amongst you, and another group troubled themselves with improper thoughts about Allah in the manner of the assumptions of (the days of) ignorance, saying do we have any choice in this matter? Say the matter is entirely up to Allah. They hide in themselves what they do not disclose to you, saying that if we had any choice in the matter we would not have been killed here. Say, had you stayed at home, those who were destined to be killed would have come out, and thus Allah tests what you keep inside and purifies your hearts, and Allah knows what is kept inside.

155. Those amongst you who turned to flee when the two troops met, the devil wanted to make them slip on account of some of their deeds, and Allah has already let them off, for Allah is forgiving and gentle.

156. Oh you believers, do not be like those who reject (the truth) and say to their brothers when they travel or attack: if they had been with us they would not have died or been killed, so that Allah makes them feel this as a loss in their hearts, and Allah gives life and death, and Allah sees what you do.

157. And if you were killed in the way of Allah or died, the forgiveness and mercy from Allah would be better than what they amass.

158. And if you died or were killed you would be gathered to Allah.

159. It is out of mercy from Allah that you are lenient towards them. And if you were harsh with an unforgiving heart, they would disperse around you, so let them off and forgive them and consult them in the matter, and when you have decided, then rely on Allah, for Allah loves those who rely (on Him).

160. If Allah helps you, then nobody can overcome you, and if He abandons you, then who is there to help you afterwards? And on Allah let the believers rely.

161. It is not befitting for a prophet to take advantage (of anyone), whoever takes advantage will bring what he has taken advantage of on the day of resurrection, then every soul will be given in full what it has earned and they will not be wronged.

162. Is he who pursues the approval of Allah like him who brings upon himself disapproval from Allah and his refuge is hell, a bad destination?

163. They have (different) stages with Allah, and Allah sees what they do.

164. Allah already bestowed His favours on the believers when He raised amongst them a messenger of their own kind who recites to them His signs and purifies them and teaches them the book and the wisdom, when before that they were in clear error.

165. Or is it that when a misfortune afflicts you after you already afflicted twice as much, you say: Where did this come from? Say: This came from yourselves, for Allah is able to do anything.

166. What afflicted you on the day the two troops met was with the permission of Allah and in order for Him to know the believers.

167. And to know those who pretend, and they were told: Come and fight in the way of Allah or defend yourselves, and they said: Had we known about a fight we would have followed you. They were closer to rejecting belief that day than to believing. They say with their mouths what is not in their hearts, and Allah knows what they hide.

168. Those who say to their brothers, whilst staying behind, if they had followed us they would not have been killed; say: then avert death from yourselves if you are truthful.

169. And don't count those who were killed in the way of Allah as dead, but they are alive and have provision with their Lord.

170. Rejoicing about what Allah has given them from His favours and glad that those behind them who have not met them yet will have no fear nor worry.

171. Glad about the blessing from Allah and favours and that Allah does not waste the reward of the believers.

172. Those who responded to Allah and the messenger after being afflicted by the wound, for those amongst them who did good and bewared there is immense reward.

173. Those to whom the people said: The people have gathered against you, so fear them, and it increased them in faith and they said: Allah is enough for us and most excellent to be relied upon.

174. So they turned around by the favour and generosity of Allah without any harm touching them and pursued the approval of Allah, and Allah possesses immense favours.

175. It is only the devil who scares those who seek his protection, so do not fear him but fear Me, if you are believers.

176. And do not let those who rush to disbelief make you sad, for they will not harm Allah at least, Allah wills to not give them a share in the hereafter and severe punishment awaits them.

177. Those who exchange belief for rejection, they will not harm Allah the least, and painful punishment awaits them.

178. And those who reject (the truth) should not count it as good for them that We give them time; We give them time so that they increase in sin, and humiliating punishment awaits them.

179. Allah would not leave the believers in the state you are in until He would separate the worthless from the good, and Allah would not give you access to the unseen, but Allah chooses from His messengers whom He pleases, so believe in Allah and His messengers, and if you believe and beware, an immense reward awaits you.

180. And do not count that those who withhold what Allah has given them of His favours have the better (deal), but they have the worse (deal), that which they withheld will surround them on the day of resurrection, and to Allah belongs the inheritance of the heavens and the earth, and Allah knows what you do.

181. Allah has heard the talk of those who said Allah is poor and we are rich, We will write down what they said as well as their killing of the prophets without right, and We will say: taste the punishment of burning.

182. This is for the deeds you have sent ahead and that Allah does not wrong (His) servants.

183. Those who said: Allah took a covenant from us that we should not believe in any messenger until he comes with a sacrifice consumed by fire; say: messengers came to you before with clear proofs and with what you said, so why did you kill them if you are truthful?

184. So if they deny you, they already denied messengers before you who came with clear proofs and scriptures and the enlightened book.

185. Every soul must taste death and they will be receiving their rewards on the day of resurrection, so whoever is removed from the fire and entered into the garden is successful, and the life of this world is only a passing provision.

186. You will be tested in your property and your selves and you will hear from those who were given the book before you and from the idolaters much insult, but if you have patience and beware then this is one of the firmest things (to do).

187. And when Allah took a promise from those given the book that you will explain it to the people and not hide it, then they threw it behind their backs and sold it for a small price, so bad is what they buy (with it).

188. Don't count those who rejoice in what they were given and love to be praised for what they did not

do, don't count that they will escape from the punishment, and a painful punishment awaits them.

189. And to Allah belongs the kingdom of the heavens and the earth and Allah is able to do anything.

190. In the creation of the heavens and the earth and the alteration of night and day are indeed signs for those with understanding.

191. Those who remember Allah standing, sitting and on their sides and reflect about the creation of the heavens and the earth: Our Lord, you have not created this without purpose, glory be to You, so guard us from the punishment of the fire.

192. Our Lord, whoever You enter into the fire you have humiliated, and there is no helper for the wrongdoers.

193. Our Lord, we heard a caller call to faith that you should believe in your Lord, so we believed, our Lord so forgive us our sins and reject our bad deeds and make us die with the righteous.

194. Our Lord, and give us what You promised us through your messengers and do not humiliate us on the day of resurrection, for You do not break the promise.

195. So their Lord answered them that I do not waste the work of a worker, be they male or female, one of you belong to another, so those who emigrated and were forced out of their homes and harmed in the way of Allah and fought and killed, I will reject their bad deeds and enter them into gardens through which rivers flow, a reward from Allah, and Allah has the best reward.

196. Let not the movements of those who reject (the truth) in the country mislead you.

197. A short provision, then their abode is hell, a bad place to be.

198. But for those who beware of their Lord there are gardens through which rivers flow where they will remain, a gift from Allah, and what is with Allah is better for the righteous.

199. Yet amongst the people of the book there are those who believe in Allah and what has been revealed to you and what has been revealed to them, humble before Allah, not selling Allah's signs for a small price; those will have their reward with their Lord, and Allah is swift in counting.

200. Oh you believers, have patience and hold out and hold together and beware of Allah so that you may be successful.

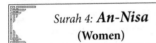

Surah 4: **An-Nisa**
(Women)

In the name of Allah,
the Owner and Giver of Mercy

1. Oh people, beware of your Lord who created you from a single soul and created from it its partner and spread from them both numerous men and women, and beware of Allah through whom you have claims on each other and (respect) relationships, for Allah watches over you.

2. And give the orphans their property and do not exchange bad for good and do not consume their property with your property, for it is a great sin.

3. And if you fear that you cannot do justice to the orphans, then marry from the women permitted to you, two, three and four, and if you fear that you cannot be fair, then one, or one who is in your possession, that is closer to you avoiding transgression.

4. And give the women their (marriage) gifts willingly, but if they make some of it permissible to you themselves, then consume it legitimately and content.

5. And do not give the mentally unable your property which Allah has given you as maintenance, and provide for them and clothe them and say to them appropriate words.

6. And put the orphans to the test until, when they reach (the age of) marriage, if you observe maturity in them, then give them their property, and do not consume it wastefully and in a hurry before they come of age, and whoever is rich, let him abstain, and whoever is poor, let him consume what is appropriate, and when you give them their property, have it witnessed against them, and Allah is sufficient for keeping count.

7. For men there is a share of what parents and relatives leave behind and for women there is a share of what parents and relatives leave behind, be it little or much, a mandatory share.

8. And when the relatives and orphans and poor are present during the division, then provide for them from it and say to them appropriate words.

9. And let them fear for them as if they had left weak offspring behind themselves, and let them beware of Allah and let them speak within the limits.

10. Those who consume the property of the orphans wrongfully, they eat fire into their bellies, and they will reach the blaze.

11. Allah prescribes inheritance for you regarding your children, for a male is the equivalent of the share of two females, and if there are more than two women, then theirs is a third of what he leaves behind, and if there is one, then hers is half, and for his two parents, for each of them is a sixth of what he leaves behind if he has children, and if he does not have children and his parents inherit from him, then for his mother there is a third, and if he has siblings, then for his mother there is a sixth after any will he has made or debt; your parents and your children, you do not know who is of more benefit to you. This is an obligation from Allah, for Allah is knowledgeable and wise.

12. And for you is half of what your wives leave behind if they do not have children, and if they have children, then for you is a fourth of what they leave behind after any will they have made or debt, and theirs is a fourth of what you leave behind if you have no children, and if you have children, then theirs is an eighth of what you leave behind after any will you have made or debt; and if a man or woman leaves inheritance without parents or children and has a brother or sister, then for each of them is a sixth, and if there are several of them, then they share in a third after any will which has been made or debt, without causing harm, a prescriptive inheritance from Allah, and Allah is knowledgeable and lenient.

13. These are the limits of Allah, and who obeys Allah and His messengers, He will enter him into gardens through which rivers flow where they will remain, and that is the ultimate success.

14. And who disobeys Allah and His messenger and transgresses His limits, He will enter him into a fire to remain in it forever and his is a humiliating punishment.

15. And for those of your women who commit adultery, let four from amongst you witness against them, and if they witnessed, then keep them in their homes until death overtakes them or Allah provides a way out for them.

16. And challenge the two who commit it, but if they repent and make amends, then let them be, for Allah is accepting, merciful.

17. Repentance is only accepted by Allah from those who do bad due to ignorance and then repent soon after, Allah accepts it from those, and Allah is knowledgeable and wise.

18. Repentance is not accepted from those who do bad deeds until when death approaches one of them he says: I repent now; nor from those who die whilst rejecting (the truth).

For those We have promised a painful punishment.

19. Oh you believers, it is not permissible for you to inherit women forcibly, and do not prevent them from marrying in order to take away some of that which you have given them, unless they commit evident adultery. And give them appropriate company, and should you resent them, then it may be that you resent something wherein Allah has placed much good.

20. And if you wish to exchange a wife for another, and you have given one of them a treasure, then do not take anything from it; are you going to take it by way of deception and evident sin?

21. And how can you take it when one of you has already spent time with the other and We have taken from you a binding promise?

22. And do not marry women whom your fathers married, except what has gone before, for it is an indecency, abhorrence and bad way.

23. Forbidden to you are your mothers, daughters, sisters, paternal aunts, maternal aunts, brother's daughters, sister's daughters, nursing mothers, nursing siblings, mother-in-laws and the step-daughters from the women in your household with whom you have cohabited, and if you have not cohabited with them, then there is no sin against you, and your daughter-in-laws and that you should keep two sisters (simultaneously), except what has gone before, and Allah is forgiving, merciful.

24. And the chaste women except what is in your possession, a prescription of Allah for you, and anything beyond that is permitted for you to seek out with your wealth, chaste and not through fornication, and give those whom you have made lawful their marital gifts by way of obligation, and there is no sin upon you in whatever you are content with beyond the obligation, for Allah is knowledgeable and wise.

25. And who amongst you does not have the means to marry free believing women, then from amongst what is in your possession of the believing servants, and Allah knows your faith best, you all share a common origin, so marry them with the permission of their family and give them their marital gifts appropriately, as long as they are chaste, not given to prostitution nor fornication, so when they are married and then commit adultery, then their punishment is half that of free women; this if for him amongst you who fears hardship, but to have patience is better for you, and Allah is forgiving and merciful.

26. Allah wills to explain it to you and guide you the paths of those before you and turn back to you, and Allah is knowledgeable and wise.

27. And Allah wants to turn back to you, and those who follow desires want you to stray badly.

28. Allah wants to make it light for you, and man was created weak.

29. Oh you believers, do not consume your wealth between yourselves ignorantly, but it should only be by way of trade you have consented to, and do not kill your own, Allah is merciful with you.

30. And who does so in enmity and oppression, We will soon burn him in fire, that is easy for Allah.

31. If you avoid the major ones which you have been forbidden, We cancel your (minor) bad deeds and give you an honoured entry.

32. And do not wish for what Allah has favoured with some of you above others; for men there is a share of what they have earned and for women there is a share of what they have earned, and ask Allah of His favour for Allah knows all things.

33. And in each case We have assigned somebody to inherit what parents and relatives leave behind, and give to those to whom you have made promises their share, for Allah witnesses everything.

34. Men look after women on account of what Allah has favoured some of them above others and of what they spend from their property, so the righteous women are humble and preserve in absence that which Allah has preserved, and those of whom you fear rebellion, admonish them and ban them from your beds and slap them, and if they obey you then don't seek a way against them, for Allah is elevated and great.

35. And if you fear a break-up between the two, then send a referee from his family and a referee from her family, if the two want reconciliation, then Allah will make them agree, for Allah is knowledgeable and informed.

36. And serve Allah and do not associate anything with Him, and goodness to parents and relatives and the orphans and the poor and the immediate neighbour and distant neighbour and anybody you share company with and the traveller and those in your possession, for Allah does not love one who is arrogant and boastful.

37. Those who are mean and command people to be mean and hide what Allah has given them of His favours, and We have prepared for those who reject (the truth) a humiliating punishment.

38. And those who spend their wealth to be seen by people and do not believe in Allah nor the last day; to whom the devil is an associate - what a bad associate.

39. And what harm would it have done them if they believed in Allah and the last day and spent of that what Allah provided for them, and Allah knows about them.

40. Allah does not wrong by the weight of a tiny speck, and if it is good, he multiplies it and gives an immense reward from Himself.

41. So how will it be when We bring a witness from every community and bring you as a witness against these?

42. On that day those who reject (the truth) and disobeyed the messenger wish for the earth to be flattened with them and they will not hide a word from Allah.

43. Oh you believers, do not come near prayer whilst you are intoxicated until you know what you are saying, and not whilst in a state of sexual impurity until you have showered, except when on a journey, and if you are ill or on a journey or one of you comes from the toilet or you have touched women and you do not find water, then look for clean soil and wipe over your faces and hands, for Allah is lenient, forgiving.

44. What do you make of those who were given a portion of the Book and purchase (with it) error and want you to go astray?

45. Allah knows your enemies best, and Allah is sufficient as protector and Allah is sufficient as helper.

46. Of those who are Jews and twist the meaning of words and say "we listen and disobey" and "listen without being listened to", with smooth tongues whilst attacking the religion, and had they said "we listen and obey" and "listen and pay attention to us" it would have been better for them and more upright, but Allah has cursed them due to their denial and they do not believe but a little.

47. Oh you who were given the book, believe in what We have revealed, confirming that which is with you, before We disfigure faces so they are turned back to front or curse them like We cursed the companions of the Sabbath, and Allah's command will be carried out.

48. Allah does not forgive that anything should be associated with Him and forgives anything else to whom He wants, and who associates anything with Allah has already invented a tremendous sin.

49. What do you make of those who declare themselves pure? and Allah purifies whom He wants and they will not be wronged the least.

50. See how they invent lies against Allah, and that is sufficient as an apparent sin.

51. What do you make of those who were given a portion of the book believing in magicians and fortune tellers and saying to those who reject (the truth) that they are better guided on a way than the believers?

52. Those are the ones Allah has cursed, and whom Allah curses, you will find no helper for him.

53. Or do they own a share in the kingdom; and if so, they wouldn't give people the tiniest bit.

54. Or do they envy people for what Allah has given them from His favours? We gave the family of Ibrahim (Abraham) the book and the wisdom and gave them a mighty kingdom.

55. And amongst them there is he who believes in Him and amongst them there is he who turns away from Him, and hell is sufficient as a fire.

56. Those who reject Our signs, We will burn them in fire; each time their skins are cooked, We will replace them with different skins for them so they taste the punishment. Allah is mighty and wise.

57. And those who believe and do good work, We will enter them into gardens through which rivers flow where they will remain forever, they have purified partners there and We will shade them with (abundant) shade,

58. Allah commands you to return items given in trust to their owners and if you judge between people to judge with justice, beneficial is what Allah admonishes you with, for Allah listens and sees.

59. O you believers, obey Allah and obey the messenger and those placed in authority from amongst you, and if you dispute about something then refer it to Allah and the messenger if you believe in Allah and the last day, that is better and better in outcome.

60. What do you make of those who claim that they believe in what has been revealed to you and what has been revealed before you, wanting to seek judgement from fortune tellers yet were commanded to reject that, and the devil wants to send them far astray.

61. And when it is said to them: come to that which Allah has revealed and to the messenger, you see the pretenders oppose you entirely.

62. So how will it be if an affliction befalls them on account of what they have sent ahead and then they come to you swearing by Allah that we only wanted goodness and reconciliation.

63. Those are the ones of whom Allah knows what is in their hearts, so turn away from them and admonish them and say profound words to them about themselves.

64. And We did not send a messenger except that he be obeyed by Allah's permission, and if they had after wronging themselves come to you and asked Allah for forgiveness and the messenger had asked forgiveness for them, they would have found Allah accepting and merciful.

65. But no, by your Lord, they do not believe until they seek your judgement in what they dispute about between themselves and then do not find within themselves any resentment to what you have decided and submit fully.

66. And if We had prescribed for them to kill your own or to leave your houses, they would not have done it, with the exception of a few of them, but if they had done what they were admonished with it would have been better for them and of greater firmness.

67. And We would then have given them from Us an immense reward.

68. And We would have guided them on a straight path.

69. And whoever obeys Allah and the messenger, those are amongst those whom Allah has favoured from amongst the prophets and the truthful and the martyrs and righteous, and those are excellent companions.

70. This is a favour from Allah, and Allah is sufficient in knowledge.

71. Oh you believers, be on your guard and move out in groups or move out altogether.

72. And among you is the one who stays behind, and if an affliction befalls you he says: Allah has favoured me for not having been a martyr with them.

73. And if generosity from Allah befalls you, he will say - as if there had been no love between you and him: if only I was with them and had achieved a tremendous success.

74. So let those fight in the way of Allah who buy with the worldly life the hereafter, and who fights in the way of Allah and then is killed or overcomes, We will soon give him an immense reward.

75. And what is the matter with you that you do not fight in the way of Allah and for the weak amongst the men and women and children who say: our Lord, take us out from this town of wrongdoing people and assign us a protector from You and assign us a helper from You?

76. Those who believe fight in the way of Allah, and those who reject (the truth) fight in the way of the idols, so fight the allies of the evil one, for the plot of the devil is weak.

77. What do you make of those who were told to hold back and keep up prayer and give Zakat, then when fighting was prescribed for them a group amongst them feared people like the fear for Allah or in greater fear and said: our Lord, why did You prescribe fighting for us, why did You not leave us a little longer? Say: the provision of the world is small, and the hereafter is better for him who bewares (of Allah) and you will not be wronged the least.

78. Wherever you are death will reach you even if you were in fortified

towers, and when good befalls them they say this is from Allah, and when bad befalls them they say this is from you, say: all is from Allah, so what is (wrong) with these people that they hardly understand a word?

79. Whatever good befalls you is from Allah, and whatever bad befalls you is from yourself, and We have sent you to mankind as a messenger and Allah is sufficient as a witness.

80. Whoever obeys the messenger has already obeyed Allah, and whoever turns away, We did not send you as a guardian over them.

81. They say obedience, then when they depart from you a group of them contrive something other than what they say, and Allah writes down what they contrive, so turn away from them and rely on Allah, and Allah is sufficient to be relied upon.

82. Do they not reflect on the Qur'an? If it were from other than Allah, they would have found many contradictions in it.

83. And when a matter regarding security or danger is presented to them, they publicise it, and if they had referred it to the messenger and those placed in authority from amongst them, those who analyse it amongst them would have known it, and if Allah's favour and mercy was not on you, you would follow the devil except for a few.

84. So fight in the way of Allah, you have only been charged with your own self, and encourage the believers, maybe Allah will avert the harm of those who reject (the truth), and Allah is more severe in harm and more severe in repulsion.

85. Whoever encourages a good deed will profit from it, and whoever encourages a bad deed will be burdened by it, and Allah has power over all things.

86. And if you are greeted with a greeting, respond with a better one or return it, for Allah counts everything.

87. Allah, there is not god but Him, He will gather you towards the day of resurrection without doubt, and who is more truthful in speech than Allah?

88. So what is the matter with you that you are two groups concerning the pretenders when Allah has thrown them back for what they have earned. Do you want to guide whom Allah has let go astray? And whom Allah has let go astray, you will not find a way for him.

89. They want you to reject (the truth) like they rejected it so that you would be equal, so do not take allies from them until they migrate in the way of Allah, and if they turn away, then seize them and kill them wherever you apprehend them and do not take from them a protector nor helper.

90. Except those who are connected to people with whom you have a treaty or come to you with no inclination of fighting you or fighting their people, and if Allah wanted He would have given them power over you and they would have fought you. So if they leave you alone and do not fight you and offer peace to you, then Allah does not give you a way against them.

91. You will find others who seek protection from you and seek protection from their people. Each time they return to temptation they fall back into it, so if they do not leave you and offer peace to you and keep off, then seize them and kill them wherever you apprehend them, and Allah has given you clear authority over those.

92. And it is not permitted for a believer to kill a believer except by mistake. And who kills a believer by mistake, then the freeing of a believing prisoner and direct compensation to his family are due unless they cancel it as charity; and if he is from a people who are an enemy to you and he is a believer, then the freeing of a believing prisoner, and if he is from a people with whom you have a treaty, then direct compensation to his family and the freeing of a believing prisoner, and who does not find the means, then fasting of two consecutive months as repentance offered from Allah, and Allah is knowledgeable and wise.

93. And whoever kills a believer deliberately, his reward is hell where he remains forever, and Allah is angry with him and curses him and has prepared for him severe punishment.

94. Oh you believers, when you go out in the way of Allah then make sure and do not say to anyone who offers you peace 'You are not a believer', desiring the offering of this world when with Allah there is plenty of gain; you yourselves were like this before, then Allah bestowed His favours on you, so make sure, for Allah is aware of what you do.

95. Not alike are those who sit back amongst the believers without excuse and those who strive in the way of Allah with their wealth and lives. Allah has set those who strive with their wealth and their lives a stage above those who sit back, and to all Allah has promised good, and Allah has preferred those who strive over those who sit back with an immense reward.

96. Stages from Him and forgiveness and mercy, and Allah is forgiving, merciful.

97. Those whom the angels receive at death whilst they were wronging themselves, saying: what were you up to?, they say: we were weak on earth, they say: was not Allah's earth spacious so you could migrate in it? - the abode of those is hell, a bad destination.

98. Except those who are weak amongst men, women and children and cannot do anything nor find a way.

99. Those Allah may let off, and Allah is lenient, forgiving.

100. Whoever migrates in the way of Allah will find plenty of refuge and facility on earth, and whoever leaves his home migrating towards Allah and His messenger and then death overcomes him, his reward will already be present with Allah, and Allah is forgiving, merciful.

101. And when you travel on the earth it is no sin for you to shorten the prayer if you fear that those who reject (the truth) will harm you, for those who reject are clear enemies to you.

102. And when you are amongst them and lead the prayer for them, then let a group of them stand with you and let them take their weapons, and when they prostrate then let them be behind you and let another group who have not yet prayed pray with you and take their guard and weapons. Those who reject (the truth) would love you to be careless about your weapons and provisions so that they strike you at a single blow. And there is no sin upon you if you are troubled by rain or if you are ill that you lay down your weapons, but be on your guard, Allah has promised to those who reject (the truth) a humiliating punishment.

103. And when you have finished the prayer, remember Allah standing, sitting and lying down, and when you are safe, then keep up prayer, for the prayer is a timed obligation for believers.

104. And do not lose heart when pursuing people, if you are suffering, then they suffer as you suffer, and you look forward to from Allah what they do not look forward to, and Allah is knowledgeable, wise.

105. We revealed to you the book with truth so that you judge between people with what Allah has shown you and do not argue on behalf of those who deceive.

106. And seek forgiveness from Allah, for Allah is forgiving, merciful.

107. And do not dispute on behalf of those who deceive themselves, for Allah does not love the deceiving and sinful.

108. They try to hide from people but cannot hide from Allah and He is with them when they contrive unacceptable statements, and Allah surrounds what they do.

109. Are you the ones who dispute on behalf of them in this world? Then who will dispute on their behalf on the day of resurrection or who will be their representative?

110. And whoever does harm or wrongs himself and then seeks Allah's forgiveness, Allah is forgiving, merciful.

111. And whoever commits a sin, commits it against himself, and Allah is knowledgeable, wise.

112. And whoever commits an error or a sin and then blames it on an innocent person, he is guilty of slander and a tremendous sin.

113. And if Allah's favour and mercy was not with you, a group of them would have attempted to lead you astray, but they only lead themselves astray and they do not harm you at all, and Allah has revealed to you the book and the wisdom and taught you what you did not know, and Allah's favour on you is immense.

114. There is no good in many of their secret meetings except for him who commands charity or good conduct or peace-making between people, and whoever does that seeking the contentment of Allah, He will soon give him an immense reward.

115. And whoever breaks away from the messenger after the guidance has become clear to him and follows a way other than that of the believers, We turn him to where he wants to turn and make him enter hell, a bad destination.

116. Allah does not forgive that anything should be associated with Him and forgives anything else to whom He wants, and who associates anything with Allah has gone far astray.

117. They call only unto idols instead of Him and they call only unto a rebellious devil.

118. Allah cursed him and he said I will take an allocated share of Your servants.

119. I will lead them astray, and I will give them hope, and I will order them to cut off the ears of cattle, and I will order them to alter the creation of Allah; and whoever takes the devil as a protecting friend instead of Allah, he is already in clear loss.

120. He promises them and gives them hope, and the devil only promises them an illusion.

121. The abode of those is hell, and they will not find an escape from it.

122. And those who believe and do good work, We will enter them into gardens through which rivers flow where they will remain forever - a promise from Allah, and who is more truthful in speech than Allah!

123. It is not in accordance with your hopes or the hopes of the people of the Book; whoever does harm will be punished for it and will not find any protecting friend or helper instead of Allah.

124. And whoever does good work, whether male or female, and is a believer, those will enter the garden (of paradise) and will not be wronged the tiniest bit.

125. And who has a better system than who submits his orientation to Allah and does good and follows the religion of Ibrahim (Abraham), sincerely devoted, and Allah took Ibrahim as a friend.

126. And to Allah belongs whatever is in the heavens and what is on earth, and Allah surrounds all things.

127. They seek a ruling from you about women, say Allah will give you a ruling about them and what has been recited to you in the Book about female orphans whom you do not give what has been allocated for them when you want to marry them and about the weak amongst children and that you should treat the orphans with fairness, and whatever good you do, Allah knows of it.

128. And if a woman fears from her husband mistreatment or abandonment, then it is no sin upon them if they make an arrangement between themselves, and an arrangement is better, and selfishness is present in all souls, and if you do good and beware then Allah knows what you do.

129. And you will not be able to act justly between women even if you tried, so be not completely partial leaving her like suspended, and if you make an arrangement and beware, then Allah is forgiving, merciful.

130. And if they both separate, then Allah will enrich each in means, and Allah is full of means, wise.

131. And to Allah belongs whatever is in the heavens and what is on earth, and We already instructed those to whom the Book was given before you and yourselves to beware of Allah, and if you reject (the truth), then to Allah belongs whatever is in the heavens and what is on earth, and Allah is rich and praiseworthy.

132. And to Allah belongs whatever is in the heavens and what is on earth, and Allah is sufficient to be relied upon.

133. If He pleases, oh people, He will take you away and replace you with others, and Allah is capable of doing that.

134. Whoever wants the reward of this world, with Allah is the reward of this world and the hereafter, and Allah listens and sees.

135. Oh you believers, be upright with fairness as witnesses for Allah even if it be against yourselves or your parents and relatives; if either be rich or poor, Allah is nearest to both of them, so do not follow inclination in order to act justly, and if you lean towards or turn away from one, then Allah knows what you do.

136. Oh you believers, believe in Allah and His messenger and the Book which He has revealed to His messenger and the Book which He has revealed before, and who rejects Allah and His angels and His books and His messengers and the last day, he has already gone far astray.

137. Those who believe, then reject (the truth), then believe, then reject (it), then increase in rejection, Allah will not forgive them nor guide them on a way.

138. Announce to the pretenders that for them is a painful punishment.

139. Those who take the rejecters (of the truth) as protecting friends instead of the believers; do they seek strength from them, when all strength belongs to Allah?

140. And He has already revealed to you in the Book that if you hear Allah's signs rejected and made fun of, then do not sit with them until they engage in a different conversation, for you are otherwise like them, for Allah will gather all the pretenders and rejecters in hell.

141. Those who wait what happens to you, and if you have victory from Allah they say: were we not with you?, and if the rejecters have success they say: did we not assist you and protect you against the believers? So Allah will judge between them on the day of resurrection, and Allah will not make way for the rejecters against the believers.

142. The pretenders try to cheat Allah and He cheats them, and when they stand for prayer they stand lazy, wanting to be seen by people, and remember Allah only little.

143. Torn in between, belonging neither to these nor those, and whom Allah has let go astray, you will not find a way for him.

144. Oh you believers, do not take the rejecters as protecting friends instead of the believers, do you want to give Allah clear authority over you?

145. The pretenders are at the lowest level of the fire and you will not find a helper for them.

146. Except for those who repent and do good deeds and hold on to Allah and make their religion sincere for Allah, and Allah will soon give the believers an immense reward.

147. Allah will not bring about your punishment if you are grateful and believe, and Allah appreciates and knows.

148. Allah does not love evil to be talked about except by one who has been wronged, and Allah hears and knows.

149. If you do good openly or secretly or let go of an evil deed, Allah is lenient and powerful.

150. Those who reject Allah and His messengers and want to make a difference between Allah and His messengers and say we believe in some and reject some and want to take a way in between;

151. Those are the true rejecters, and We have promised the rejecters a humiliating punishment.

152. And those who believe in Allah and His messengers and do not make a difference between any of them, He will soon give them their rewards, and Allah is forgiving, merciful.

153. The people of the Book ask you that a book be sent down from the sky for them, and they asked even greater things of Musa (Moses) before and said "show us Allah openly", then the lightning struck them because of their wrongdoing, then they took the calf after clear signs had come to them, then we forgave that and gave Musa (Moses) clear authority.

154. And we raised the mountain above them for their agreement and said to them: "Enter the gate submissively", and we said to them: "Do not violate the Sabbath", and we took a binding agreement from them.

155. And because they fell short on their agreement and rejected the signs of Allah and killed the prophets without right and said: "Our hearts are protected", but Allah sealed them due to their rejection, so they do not believe but little.

156. And because they rejected (the truth) and uttered against Maryam (Mary) a serious slander.

157. And they said we killed the Messiah 'Isa (Jesus), the son of Maryam (Mary), the messenger of Allah, and they did not kill him and did not crucify him, but it appeared to them as if, and those who argue about him are unsure about it, they have no knowledge about it but only follow assumptions, and they did not kill him for sure.

158. But Allah raised him to Himself, and Allah is mighty, wise.

159. And there is none amongst the people of the Book who will not believe in him before his death, and on the day of resurrection he will be a witness against them.

160. And because of the wrongdoing of the Jews we made unlawful for them good provision which was made lawful for them, and because of their frequent diverting from of the way of Allah.

161. And because they took interest when it had been forbidden to them and consumed the property of people without justification, and we promised the rejecters amongst them a painful punishment.

162. However, those amongst them who are grounded in knowledge and are believers who believe in what has been revealed to you and what has been revealed before you and keep up prayer and give Zakat and believe in Allah and the last day, to those we will give an immense reward.

163. We have given revelation to you as We have given revelation to Nuh (Noah) and the prophets after him, and we have given revelation to Ibrahim (Abraham), Isma'il (Ishmael), Ishaq (Isaac), Ya'qub (Jacob) and the tribes and 'Isa (Jesus), and Ayyub (Job), Yunus (Jonah), Harun (Aaron) and Sulayman (Solomon) and gave Dawud (David) the Psalms.

164. And to messengers whom We have told you about before and to messengers We have not told you about, and Allah spoke to Musa (Moses) directly.

165. Messengers bringing good news and warnings so that people would not have an argument against Allah after the messengers, and Allah is mighty, wise.

166. But Allah is a witness that what He revealed to you He revealed with His knowledge, and the angels are witnesses, and Allah is sufficient as a witness.

167. Those who reject (the truth) and divert from the way of Allah have already gone far astray.

168. Those who reject (the truth) and do wrong, Allah will not forgive them nor guide them a path.

169. Except the path to hell where they will remain forever, and that is easy for Allah.

170. Oh people, the messenger has already come to you with the truth from your Lord, so believe, it is better for you. And if you reject (the truth), then to Allah belongs whatever is in the heavens and on earth, and Allah is knowledgeable, wise.

171. Oh people of the book, do not transgress in your religion and do not say anything about Allah except the truth, indeed the Messiah 'Isa (Jesus), the son of Maryam (Mary), is a messenger of Allah and a word He gave to Maryam and a breath of life from Him; so believe in Allah and His messengers and do not say Three, stop, it is better for you, for Allah is one god, glorified is He above having a son, His

is whatever is in the heavens and on earth, and Allah is sufficient to be relied upon.

172. The Messiah is not too proud to be a servant of Allah, nor are the closest angels, and whoever is too proud to serve Him and is arrogant, He will round them all up before Him.

173. Then those who believe and do good work, He will give them their reward in full and give them an increase of His favours, and those who are too proud and arrogant, He will punish them with a painful punishment and they will not find for themselves a protector or helper besides Allah.

174. Oh people, a proof from your Lord has already come to you and We have sent down to you a clear light.

175. So those who believe in Allah and hold on to Him, He will enter them into mercy and favours from Him and guide them on a straight path to Himself.

176. They ask you for a ruling, say Allah gives you a ruling on childlessness, if a man dies and has no child and he has a sister, then for her is half of what he leaves behind, and he inherits from her if she has no child, and if there is two of them (sisters), then for the two of them is two thirds of what he leaves behind, and if there are male and female siblings, then for the male is the share of two females. Allah explains to you so you do not go astray, and Allah knows everything.

Surah 5: **Al-Ma'idah**
(The Table)

In the name of Allah,
the Owner and Giver of Mercy

1. Oh you believers, observe your commitments; lawful for you are domestic cattle except what you have been told, but hunting is not lawful for you whilst you are on pilgrimage, for Allah decides what He wills.

2. O you believers, do not desanctify the rites of Allah, nor the sacred month, nor the offering, nor the traditions, nor those on their way to the house of Allah seeking favour from their Lord and contentment, and when you come out of the state of being a pilgrim, you may go hunting, and do not let the condition of people who want to prevent you from the sacred mosque mislead you to transgress, and help each other in righteousness and awareness (of Allah) and do not help each other in sin and enmity, and beware of Allah, for Allah is severe in retribution.

3. Forbidden to you are carrion, blood, pork and whatever has been consecrated for other than Allah, and what has been strangled, killed by impact, died from falling, died in a fight (between animals), and what has been eaten from by beasts of prey, (and permitted is) only what you have slaughtered correctly, and (forbidden is) what has been sacrificed (to idols) on an altar and that you should divine with arrows, (all) that is an abomination. Today those who reject (the truth) give up on your religion, so do not fear them but fear Me; today I have completed your religion for you and perfected My favour upon you and am content with Islam (submission) as a religion for you, then, whoever is forced from hunger without intending to sin, Allah is forgiving and merciful.

4. They ask you what is permitted for them, say, the good things are permitted for you, and the hunting animals you have trained and teach them what Allah has taught you, eat from what they catch for you and mention the name of Allah over it and beware of Allah, for Allah is swift in counting.

5. Today the good things have been permitted for you, and the food of those who were given the Book before you is permitted for you and your food is permitted for them, and the chaste women amongst the believers and the chaste women of those who were given the Book before you if you gave them their (marital) dues, chaste and not through fornication nor taking girlfriends, and whoever rejects faith, his work is wasted and in the hereafter he is amongst the losers.

6. Oh you believers, when you get up for prayer rinse your faces and your hands up to the elbows and wipe over your heads and your feet up to the ankles. And if you are in a state of sexual impurity, then have a full cleansing. And if you are ill or on a journey or one of you comes from the toilet or you have touched women and you do not find water, then look for clean soil and wipe with it over your faces and hands. Allah wills not to place hardship on you but Allah wills to purify you and to complete His favour upon you so that you are grateful.

7. And remember Allah's favour upon you and His promise He gave you when you said we listen and we obey, and beware of Allah, for Allah knows what is kept inside.

8. Oh you believers be upright for Allah as witnesses with fairness and let not the condition of a people mislead you not to be just; be just, it is closer to awareness (of Allah), and beware of Allah, for Allah knows what you do.

9. Allah has promised those who believe and do good work that for them is forgiveness and immense reward.

10. And those who reject (the truth) and disbelieve Our signs, they will be the inmates of hell-fire.

11. Oh you believers remember the favour of Allah upon you when people tried to get hold of you but He kept them out of reach from you, and beware of Allah, and on Allah let the believers rely.

12. And Allah already took a promise from the Children of Israel and We raised twelve chiefs from amongst them, and Allah said: I am with you; if you keep up prayer and give Zakat and believe in My messengers and assist them and extend to Allah a beneficial loan, I will cancel your bad deeds and enter you into gardens through which rivers flow; and whoever rejects (the truth) after that from amongst you, he has strayed from the level way.

13. Then because they went back on their promise We cursed them and made their hearts remorseless. They twist the meaning of words and forget part of what they had been reminded with, and you will always find betrayal in them except a few of them, so let them be and ignore them, for Allah loves those who do good.

14. And from those who said: we are disciples (Christians), We took their promise, but they forgot part of what they had been reminded with, so We brought about enmity and hatred between them until the day of resurrection, and soon Allah will inform them about what they used to fabricate.

15. Oh people of the book, Our messenger has come to you to clarify for you much of what you used to hide of the book, and much he lets be. A light and clear book has come to you from Allah.

16. By it Allah guides who pursues His approval to the ways of peace and takes them out of darkness to the light by His permission and guides them unto a straight path.

17. Those have already rejected (the truth) who say that Allah is the Messiah, the son of Maryam (Mary); say then who has any power over Allah if He wanted to destroy the Messiah, the son of Maryam, and his mother and all those who are on earth? And to Allah belongs the kingdom of the heavens and the earth and what is between them. He creates what He wills, and Allah is able to do anything.

18. And the Jews and Christians say, we are the children of Allah and His beloved, say then why does He punish you for your sins, but you are humans from amongst His creation, He forgives whom He pleases and punishes whom He pleases, and to Allah belongs the kingdom of the heavens and the earth and what is between them, and to Him is the journey.

19. Oh people of the book, Our messenger has come to you to clarify (the truth) for you, following a break after the (earlier) messengers, in case you might say no bringer of good news nor warner has come to us; so a bringer of good news and warner has come to you, and Allah is able to do anything.

20. And when Musa (Moses) said to his people, oh my people, remember the favours of Allah upon you when He placed prophets amongst you and placed you in charge and gave you what He did not give to anyone else.

21. Oh my people, enter the holy land which Allah has ordained for you and do not turn your backs on it so you would turn out losers.

22. They said, oh Musa (Moses), there are giants in there, and we will not enter it until they leave it, and if they leave it, then we will enter.

23. Two men from those who were fearful, whom Allah had blessed, said enter against them the gate, then when you enter it you will be victorious, and rely on Allah if you are believers.

24. They said, oh Musa (Moses), we will never enter it while they are in it, so go you and your Lord and fight, we will stay here.

25. He said, oh my Lord, I am only in charge of myself and my brother, so differentiate between us and the sinful.

26. He said, so it will be forbidden for them for forty years (during which) they wander the earth, so do not feel sad for the sinful people.

27. Recite to them the true account of the two sons of Adam when they offered a sacrifice and it was accepted from one of them and not accepted from the other. He said 'I shall kill you'; he said 'Allah only accepts from those who beware (of Him).

28. If you stretch out your hand to kill me, I will not stretch out my hand to kill you, for I fear Allah the Lord of all worlds.

29. For I want that you will earn my sin and your sin and will be amongst the inmates of the fire, and that is the reward of the wrongdoers.'

30. Then his self caused him to kill his brother, and he killed him and became of the losers.

31. Then Allah sent a raven who uncovered the earth to show him how to bury the body of his brother. He said, woe to me, am I not able to be like this raven and bury the body of my brother? and he became remorseful.

32. On account of that we prescribed for the Children of Israel that whoever kills a soul other than (in retaliation) for a killing or for a crime on earth, it is as if he had killed all mankind, and whoever revives one, it is as if he had revived all mankind, and Our messengers came to them before with clear proofs, after which many of them were wasteful on earth.

33. For the punishment of those who wage war on Allah and His messenger and strive to cause corruption on earth is that they shall be killed or crucified or have their hands and feet cut off on opposite sides or be banned from the earth. This is a disgrace for them in this world and immense punishment awaits them in the hereafter.

34. Except those who repent before you overpower them, so know that Allah is forgiving and merciful.

35. Oh you believers, beware of Allah and seek to get closer to Him and strive in His way so you may be successful.

36. Those who reject (the truth), if they had all that is on earth and the same again to ransom themselves with it from the punishment of the day of resurrection, it would not be accepted from them and a painful punishment awaits them.

37. They want to escape from the fire but will not escape from it, and a lasting punishment awaits them.

38. As for the male thief and the female thief, cut their hands as a penalty for what they did and a warning from Allah, and Allah is mighty and wise.

39. But whoever repents after his wrongdoing and does good, then Allah accepts it from him, for Allah is forgiving and merciful.

40. Don't you know that to Allah belongs the kingdom of the heavens and the earth, He punishes whom He pleases and He forgives whom He pleases, and that Allah is able to do anything.

41. Oh messenger, let not those sadden you who are quick to reject (the truth) amongst those who say we believe with their mouths whilst their hearts do not believe and of those amongst the Jews who listen to lies and listen to other people who have not come to you, twisting the meaning of words and saying: if you get this, then take it, and if you don't get it, then be wary, and whomever Allah wills to tempt, you will not have control over anything for him regarding Allah. Those are the ones whose hearts Allah does not will to purify; disgrace is theirs in this world and in the hereafter immense punishment awaits them.

42. They listen to lies and consume bribes, and when they come to you, judge between them or turn away from them. And if you turn away from them, then they will not harm you the least, and if you judge between them, then judge between them with justice, for Allah loves the just.

43. And why should they ask you for judgement when they have the Torah containing the judgement of Allah, then they turn away after that, and most of them are not believers.

44. We revealed the Torah containing guidance and light by which the prophets, who submitted to it, judged the Jews, as did the scholars and rabbis with what had been entrusted to them of the book of Allah, and they were witnesses to it. So do not fear people but fear Me and do not sell My signs for a small price, and whoever does not judge with what Allah has revealed, those are rejecters (of the truth).

45. And We prescribed for them in it a life for a life, an eye for an eye, a nose for a nose, an ear for an ear, a tooth for a tooth, and wounds in retaliation, but if someone is charitable about it, then it is an expiation for him, and whoever does not judge with what Allah has revealed, those are the wrongdoers.

46. And We had 'Isa (Jesus) the son of Maryam (Mary) follow into their footsteps, confirming that which came before him of the Torah, and We gave him the Injil containing guidance and light and confirming what came before it of the Torah and a guidance and admonition for those who beware (of Allah).

47. So let the people of the Injil judge with what Allah has revealed in it, and whoever does not judge with what Allah has revealed, those are the sinful.

48. And We revealed to you the Book in truth, confirming what came before it as scripture and preserving it, so judge between them with what Allah has revealed and do not follow their desires away from the truth which has come to you. To each we have given a path and a direction, and if Allah willed, He would have made you a single community but for Him to test you in what He had given you, so pursue what is right, to Allah is your

return altogether, then He will inform you about what you used to differ in.

49. And you must judge between them with what Allah has revealed and not follow their desires and be wary that they do not tempt you away from some of what Allah has revealed to you. And if they turn away, then know that Allah wills to afflict them on account of some of their sins, for many of the people are sinful.

50. Do they desire the judgement of (the days of) ignorance? And who is better in judgement than Allah for people who are sure?

51. Oh you believers, do not take the Jews and the Christians as protecting friends, they are protecting friends of each other, and whoever amongst you befriends them is from amongst them, for Allah does not guide wrongdoing people.

52. Then you see those in whose hearts there is a disease hurrying to be amongst them, saying: we fear that a turn of events will befall us, but maybe Allah will bring victory or some other outcome from Him so that they start regretting what they hid within themselves.

53. And the believers will say: are those the ones who swore by Allah the greatest oaths that they were with you? There deeds were wasted and they have become losers.

54. Oh you believers, if any of you turns away from his religion, soon Allah will bring a people whom He loves and who love Him, humble towards the believers and assertive

towards the rejecters, who fight in the way of Allah and do not fear anybody's criticism, that is a favour from Allah which He gives to whom He pleases, and Allah is generous and knows.

55. For your protecting friend is Allah and His messenger and the believers who keep up prayer and give Zakat and who bow down (in prayer).

56. And whoever seeks the protection of Allah and His messenger and the believers, then the party of Allah are the winners.

57. Oh you believers, do not take those who joke and make fun of your religion from amongst those who were given the book before you nor the rejecters as protecting friends, and beware of Allah if you are believers.

58. And when you call to prayer they joke and make fun of it, that is because they are people who do not understand.

59. Say: oh people of the book, do you resent us for anything other than that we believe in Allah and what He has revealed to us and what He has revealed before and that most of you are sinful?

60. Say: shall I inform you of a worse outcome with Allah? Whom He has cursed, and with whom He is angry, and from whom He made monkeys and pigs and worshippers of the devils, those are in a worse place and further astray from the level way.

61. And when they come to you they say: we believe, whilst they entered in

rejection and left with it, and Allah knows best what they hide.

62. You see many of them hurrying towards sin and enmity and their consumption of bribes, bad is indeed what they used to do.

63. Why do not their scholars and rabbis stop them from sinful talk and consuming bribes, bad is indeed what they used to fabricate.

64. And the Jews say: Allah's hand is tied up. Their hands are tied up, and they are cursed for what they say. Rather, His hands are wide open, He spends how He wills. And what has been revealed to you from your Lord only increases the rejecters amongst them in disobedience and rejection, and We have placed between them enmity and hatred until the day of resurrection. Whenever they ignite a fire for war, Allah extinguishes it, and they hasten to cause corruption on earth, and Allah does not love the corrupters.

65. And if the people of the book believed and bewared (of Allah), We would cancel their bad deeds and enter them into gardens of blessing.

66. And if they upheld the Torah and the Injil and what has been revealed to them from their Lord, they would eat from above and from below; amongst them is a well-meaning community, but what many of them do is bad.

67. Oh messenger, convey what has been revealed to you from your Lord, and if you did not do that, you would not have conveyed His message, and Allah protects you against mankind, for Allah does not guide people who reject (the truth).

68. Say: O people of the book, you have no argument until you uphold the Torah and the Injil and what has been revealed to you from your Lord. And what has been revealed to you from your Lord only increases many of them in disobedience and rejection, so do not worry about the people who reject (the truth).

69. The believers and the Jews, the Sabeans and the Christians – whoever believes in Allah and the last day and does good work, they shall not fear nor worry.

70. And We already took a promise from the Children of Israel and sent to them messengers. Whenever a messenger came to them with what they themselves did not desire, they denied some of them and killed some of them.

71. And they counted on not being tested, so they closed their eyes and ears, then Allah turned back to them, then many of them closed their eyes and ears, and Allah sees what they do.

72. And those have already rejected (the truth) who say: Allah is the Messiah, the son of Maryam (Mary), and the Messiah said: O Children of Israel, serve Allah, my Lord and your Lord, for who associates anything with Allah, Allah has already forbidden the garden (of paradise) for him and his abode is the fire, and the wrongdoers have not helpers.

73. Those have already rejected (the truth) who say: Allah is the third of a

trinity, and there is no god but a single god, and if they do not stop what they are saying, then a painful punishment will afflict those who reject (the truth) amongst them.

74. Are they then not going to repent to Allah and ask Him for forgiveness? And Allah is forgiving and merciful.

75. The Messiah, the son of Maryam (Mary) is only a messenger - messengers have already come before him - and his mother was a truthful woman. They both ate food. See how We explain for them the signs, then see where to they are diverted.

76. Say: do you serve besides Allah what has no power to harm or benefit you, and Allah listens and knows?

77. Say: Oh people of the book, do not transgress in your religion away from the truth and do not follow the desires of people who have already gone astray before and have led astray many and strayed from the level way.

78. Those who reject (the truth) were cursed in the words of Dawud (David) and 'Isa (Jesus) the son of Maryam (Mary) because they disobeyed and transgressed.

79. They did not stop each other from the wrongdoing they committed, bad is indeed what they used to do.

80. You see many of them befriending those who reject (the truth), bad is indeed what they have sent ahead for themselves so that Allah is displeased with them and they will remain in the punishment.

81. And if they believed in Allah and the prophet and what has been revealed to him, they would not have taken them as protecting friends - but many amongst them are sinful.

82. You will certainly find fiercest of people in enmity against the believers the Jews and the idolaters, and you will certainly find most inclined of them to love towards the believers those who call themselves Christians; this is because amongst them are priests and monks and that they are not arrogant.

83. And when they hear what has been revealed to the messenger you see their eyes overflow with tears on account of what they knew of the truth and they say: our Lord, we believe, so list us amongst the witnesses.

84. And how should we not believe in Allah and the truth which has come to us and hope that our Lord will enter us amongst the righteous people?

85. So Allah gave them on account of what they said gardens through which rivers flow where they will remain, and this is the reward of those who do good.

86. And those who reject (the truth) and disbelieve Our signs, they will be the inmates of hell-fire.

87. Oh you believers, do not prohibit the good things which Allah has made lawful for you and do not transgress, for Allah does not love the transgressors.

88. And eat of what Allah has provided you with as lawful and good, and beware of Allah in whom you believe.

89. Allah does not hold you to account for unintentionally spoken oaths, but He holds you to account for oaths you have confirmed, and the compensation (for not keeping them) is to feed ten poor people from the average of what you feed your families or to clothe them or to free a slave, and who does not find (the means), then fasting for three days, that is the compensation for your oaths once you have sworn them, so keep your oaths, this is how Allah explains to you His signs so that you may be grateful.

90. Oh you believers, narcotic drugs and gambling and idolatry and divining are filth from the work of the devil, so shun it in order to be successful.

91. The devil wants to place enmity and hatred amongst you with narcotic drugs and gambling and to divert you from the remembrance of Allah, so will you stop?

92. And obey Allah and the messenger and be wary, and if you turn away, then know that the duty of Our messenger is only to convey clearly.

93. There is no sin for those who believe and do good works in what they used to eat if they bewared (of Allah) and believed and did good works and then bewared and believed and then bewared and did good, and Allah loves those who do good.

94. Oh you believers, Allah will certainly test you with some animals for hunting in reach of your hands and spears, so that Allah knows who fears Him secretly. Then whoever transgresses afterwards, for him is a painful punishment.

95. Oh you believers, do not kill animals by hunting whilst you are on pilgrimage, and whoever of you kills them intentionally, his punishment is equal to what he has killed of the catch, judged by two just people amongst you, as an offering to reach the Ka'bah, or the compensation is to feed poor people or fasting in place of it so that he feels it and comprehends his situation. Allah has forgiven what happened in the past, and whoever returns, Allah will avenge it from him, and Allah is mighty and vengeful.

96. Lawful for you are the animals for hunting on sea and its food as a provision for you and for those on a journey, and forbidden to you are the animals for hunting on land for as long as you are on pilgrimage, and beware of Allah to whom you will be gathered.

97. Allah has made the Ka'bah, the sacred house, a focal point for mankind, and (likewise) the sacred month and the offering and the traditions, this is in order for you to know that Allah knows what is in the heavens and what is on earth and that Allah knows everything.

98. Know that Allah is severe in punishment and that Allah is forgiving and merciful.

99. The duty of the messenger is only to convey, and Allah knows what you let on and what you hide.

100. Say: bad and good are not alike even if the abundance of bad astonishes you, so beware of Allah oh

you who have understanding, in order to succeed.

101. Oh you believers, do not ask about matters which if they were made known to you would trouble you. And if you ask about them at the time the Qur'an is being revealed, they will be made known to you. Allah forgives this, and Allah is forgiving and gentle.

102. People before you asked about them and then started to reject them.

103. Allah has not made any Bahirah, Sa'ibah, Wasilah or Ham (types of cattle exempted from being utilised for food or work due to superstition), but those who reject (the truth) invented a lie against Allah and most of them do not understand.

104. And when they are told to accept what Allah has revealed and the messenger they say: What we found our ancestors doing is sufficient for us. What if their ancestors never knew anything nor were guided?

105. Oh you believers, you are responsible for yourselves, nobody who has gone astray will harm you if you are guided, to Allah is your return altogether, then He will inform you of what you used to do.

106. Oh you believers, evidence between you at the time of making a will, if death comes to any of you, is (provided) by two just men from amongst your own - or two others from people other than your own if you travel on the earth and the affliction of death befalls you. You shall keep them behind after prayer and if you are in doubt they shall swear by Allah that we will not buy any gain for it even if it concerned a relative and we will not hide the evidence given before Allah, as then we would be sinful.

107. And should it be discovered that they committed a sin, then two others from those who were wronged by the first two, who will then swear by Allah that our evidence is more truthful than their evidence and we do not transgress, as then we would be wrongdoers.

108. In this way it is more likely that they will disclose the evidence or fear that their oaths will be opposed by subsequent oaths; and beware of Allah and listen, and Allah does not guide the sinful people.

109. On the day Allah will gather the messengers and say: what reply did you receive? They will say: We have no knowledge, for you are the One who knows the unseen.

110. When Allah will say: Oh 'Isa (Jesus) son of Maryam (Mary), remember My favour upon you and upon your mother when I helped you with the holy spirit and you spoke to people in infancy and as an adult, and when I taught you the book and the wisdom and the Torah and the Injil, and when you created the shape of a bird from clay by My permission and breathed into it and it became a bird by My permission, and you cured the blind and the leper by My permission, and when you brought back the dead by My permission, and when I kept the Children of Israel back from you when you came to them with clear proofs

and those who rejected amongst them said this is only plain magic.

111. And when I inspired the disciples to believe in Me and My messenger and they said: we believe, and be you a witness that we have submitted.

112. When the disciples said: oh 'Isa (Jesus) son of Maryam (Mary), is your Lord able to send down to us a laden table from the heaven? He said: beware of Allah if you are believers.

113. They said: we want to eat from it and put our hearts at ease and know that you have said the truth to us and to be witnesses to it.

114. 'Isa (Jesus) son of Maryam (Mary) said: Oh Allah, our Lord, send down to us a laden table from the heaven to be a feast for the first and last of us and a sign from You, and give us provision, and You are the best who give provision.

115. Allah said: I will send it down to you, then who rejects (the truth) afterwards from amongst you, I will punish him with a punishment with which I will not punish anybody else.

116. And when Allah will say: Oh 'Isa (Jesus) son of Maryam (Mary), did you say to people take me and my mother as gods besides Allah? He will say: glorified are You above that I should say what I have no right to; if I said it, You would already know, You know what is inside me and I do not know what is inside You, for you know all the unseen.

117. I did not say to them except what You commanded me with: that you serve Allah, my Lord and your Lord, and I was a witness against them whilst I stayed amongst them, and when you took me, You were watching over them, and you are a witness over everything.

118. If You punish them, then they are Your servants, and if You forgive them, then You are the mighty and wise.

119. Allah will say: this day their truthfulness will benefit those who were truthful. For them are gardens through which rivers flow where they will remain forever. Allah is pleased with them and they are pleased with Him. That is the ultimate success.

120. And to Allah belongs the kingdom of the heavens and the earth and what they contain and Allah is able to do anything.

Surah 6: *Al-An'am* (The Cattle)

In the name of Allah, the Owner and Giver of Mercy

1. Allah is praised, who created the heavens and the earth and made darkness and light, then those who reject (the truth) turn away.

2. He is who created you from clay then set a term, which is a fixed term with Him, then you express doubt.

3. And He is Allah in the heavens and on earth; He knows your secrets and your pronouncements and He knows what you achieve.

4. And whenever one of the signs of their Lord comes to them, they tend to turn away from it.

5. And they previously denied the truth when it came to them, and soon information of what they made fun of will reach them.

6. Do they not consider how many times before them We destroyed a generation whom We had established on earth more than We established you, and We sent abundant rain from the sky for them and made rivers flow between them, then We destroyed them for their sins and brought about after them another generation.

7. And had We sent down to you a book on paper so they could touch it with their hands, those who reject (the truth) amongst them would have said: this is only plain magic.

8. And they said: why was not an angel sent down to him? And had We sent an angel, the matter would have been decided against them and they would not be given time.

9. And had We made him an angel, we would have made him into a man and would made them wear what they wear.

10. And messengers before you were made fun of, and those who laughed at them were overcome by what they made fun of.

11. Say: travel on the earth, then see what the outcome was like for the deniers.

12. Say: To whom belongs what is in the heavens and on earth? Say: To Allah. He has prescribed for Himself mercy. He will gather you on the day of resurrection without doubt -

those who have lost themselves do not believe.

13. And to Him belongs what exists in the night and in the day and He listens and knows.

14. Say: Should I take other than Allah as protecting friend, the Originator of the heavens and the earth, and He feeds and is not in need of feeding. Say: I have been commanded to be the first to submit and not to be amongst the idolaters.

15. Say: I fear, if I disobeyed my Lord, the punishment of a tremendous day.

16. Whoever is let off on this day, He has been merciful to him, and that is the clear success.

17. And if Allah afflicts you with harm, there is nobody to take it away but Him, and if He afflicts you with good, then He is able to do anything.

18. And He has power over His servants and He is wise and informed.

19. Say: What is greatest in evidence? Say: Allah is a witness between me and you, and this Qur'an has been revealed to me to warn you and whom it reaches. Are you going to witness that there are other gods alongside Allah? Say: I will not witness (this). Say: He is a single god and I am innocent of what you associate (with Him).

20. Those whom We gave the book know it like they know their own children - those who have lost themselves do not believe.

21. And who is more sinful than he who invents a lie against Allah or denies His signs: the wrongdoers will not succeed.

22. And on the day We gather them altogether, then say to the idolaters: Where are the associates whom you claimed?

23. Then they will try to say: By Allah our Lord, we were not idolaters.

24. See how they lie against themselves, and what they used to invent deserted them.

25. And amongst them is he who listens to you, and We have placed a cover over their hearts, so they do not understand it, and a weight upon their ears, and if they see every sign, they will not believe it until when they come to you arguing, the rejecters say these are only stories of old.

26. And they boycott him and keep away from him, and they only destroy themselves without realising it.

27. And if you could see when they are placed in the fire and they say: If only we could return without denying the signs of our Lord and could be of the believers.

28. But what they concealed previously will become apparent to them, and if they were to return, they would go back to what they were prohibited from and they are certainly liars.

29. And they say, there is only this worldly life of ours and we will not be resurrected.

30. And if you could see when they are placed before their Lord, He will say: is this not true? They will say: Sure, by our Lord. So taste the punishment because you used to reject (the truth).

31. Those are already lost who deny the meeting with Allah until when the hour comes upon them suddenly, they say: how unfortunate where we have ended up, and they carry their burden on their backs. Bad is what they carry.

32. And the life of this world is only play and pastime, and the abode of the hereafter is better for those who beware (of Allah) - don't you think?

33. We know that what they say saddens you, yet they do not deny you, but the wrongdoers dispute the signs of Allah.

34. Messengers before you were already denied, and they endured denial and harm until Our help reached them, and the words of Allah will not be changed, and information of the messengers has already reached you.

35. And if their opposition weighs heavy on you, then if you can, find a passage into the earth or a stairway into the sky to bring them a sign, and if Allah willed, He would have united them on the guidance, so be not of the ignorant.

36. Only those who listen respond, and the dead, Allah will resurrect them, then they return to Him.

37. And they say, why is not a sign from his Lord sent down to him? Say: Allah is able to send a sign, but most of them don't know.

38. And there is not a creature on earth nor a bird flying on its wings except that they are communities just like you. We have not left anything out in the book. Then they are gathered to their Lord.

39. And those who deny Our signs are deaf and blind in darkness. Whom Allah wills, He lets go astray, and whom He pleases He leads on to a straight path.

40. Say: Have you considered if the punishment of Allah reaches you or the Hour comes upon you, do you call on other than Allah if you are truthful?

41. But you call on Him, then He removes what you called for if He wills, and you forget what you associated (with Him).

42. And We sent (messengers) to communities before you, then took them with adversity and hardship so that they would humble themselves.

43. So why do they not humble themselves when Our adversity reaches them, but their hearts hardened and the devil made appealing to them what they did.

44. And when they forgot what they were reminded with, We opened for them the doors of everything until when they rejoiced in what they had been given, We took them suddenly and then they were left with nothing.

45. Then the wrongdoing people were uprooted, and Allah is praised, the Lord of all worlds.

46. Say: Have you considered if Allah took away your hearing and your sight and sealed your hearts, what god other than Allah would give them to you?

See how We spell out the signs and then they turn away.

47. Say: Have you considered if Allah's punishment reached you suddenly or expectedly, would any but the wrongdoing people be destroyed?

48. And We only send the messengers to bring good tidings and warnings, so whoever believes and does good, they shall not fear nor worry.

49. And those who deny Our signs, the punishment will afflict them on account of their excesses.

50. Say: I am not telling you that I have the treasures of Allah, nor that I know the unseen, nor am I telling you that I am an angel, I only follow what has been revealed to me. Say: Are the blind and the seeing alike? Don't you reflect?

51. And warn with it those who fear that they will be gathered to their Lord, they have no protecting friend nor advocate besides Him, so that they will beware.

52. And do not dismiss those who call their Lord in the mornings and evenings seeking His presence. Their reckoning is not your concern and your reckoning is not their concern, so if you were to dismiss them you would be of the wrongdoers.

53. And this is how We test some of them by others so that they say: Are these the ones Allah has bestowed His favours on from amongst us. Does not Allah know best who is grateful?

54. And when those who believe in Our signs come to you, say: peace be with you, your Lord has prescribed mercy for Himself so that if any of you does evil ignorantly, then repents afterwards and does good, He is forgiving, merciful.

55. And like this We explain the signs and in order for you to clearly see the path of the offenders.

56. Say: I have been forbidden to serve those you call besides Allah. Say: I do not follow your desires, otherwise I would have gone astray and would not be guided.

57. Say: I follow a clear sign from my Lord and you deny it. I do not have that which you want expedited. The judgement is with Allah alone, He tells the truth and He provides the best explanation.

58. Say: If I had that which you want expedited, the matter would have been decided between me and you, and Allah knows the wrongdoers best.

59. With Him are the keys of the unseen which nobody but Him knows, and He knows what is on land and on sea, and no leaf falls except with His knowledge, and there is no seed in the darkness of the earth nor anything wet or dry except that it is in a clear book.

60. And He is who takes you away at night and knows what you do during the day, then He brings you back to complete a fixed term, then your return is to Him, then He makes clear to you what you used to do.

61. And He has power over His servants and sends a guardian over you until when death comes to any of you, Our messengers take him away, and they do not miss.

62. Then they are returned to Allah their true master, His is the judgement and He is the fastest in taking account.

63. Say: Who rescues you from the darkness of the land and sea when you call Him in hardship and fear that if You rescue us from this we will be of the grateful?

64. Say: Allah rescues you from it and from every distress, then you associate (others with Him).

65. Say: He is able to send upon you a punishment from above or from below you or turn you into factions and make some of you taste the harm of others. See how We spell out the signs so that they understand.

66. And your people denied it whilst it is the truth. Say: I am have not been put in charge of you.

67. For every information there is an outcome and you will soon know.

68. And when you see those who converse disputing Our signs, then turn away from them until they engage in a different conversation, and if the devil makes you forget, then do not sit with the wrongdoing people after having remembered.

69. And those who beware (of Allah) are in no way responsible for their reckoning but for reminding them so that they beware.

70. And leave those who take their religion as play and pastime whilst the life of this world has deluded them, and remind (them) of the fact that a soul will be destroyed by what it has earned, it will not have any protecting friend or advocate besides Allah, and if it offered any kind of compensation it would not be accepted from it; those are the ones who are destroyed by what they earned, they will have a drink of boiling water and a painful punishment on account of having rejected (the truth).

71. Say: Should we call besides Allah that which does not benefit us nor harm us and should we reverse our course after Allah has guided us, like the one whom the devils have tempted into confusion? He has companions calling him to the guidance: come with us! Say: The guidance of Allah, that is the guidance, and we were commanded to submit to the Lord of all worlds.

72. And (saying): keep up prayer and beware, and He is the One to whom you will be gathered.

73. And He is the One who created the heavens and the earth in truth, and on the day He says "Be", it is. His word is the truth and His is the kingdom on the day the horn is blown, He knows the unseen and the apparent and He is wise and informed.

74. And when Ibrahim (Abraham) said to his father Azar: Do you take idols as gods, I sure see you and your people in clear error.

75. And thus We showed Ibrahim (Abraham) the kingdoms of the heavens and the earth so that he would have certainty.

76. And when the night fell upon him he saw a star. He said: This is my Lord. And when it set, he said: I do not love those who set.

77. And when he saw the moon rising, he said: This is my Lord. And when it set, he said: if my Lord does not guide me, I will be from the people who lose their way.

78. And when he saw the sun rising, he said: This is my Lord, this is the greatest. And when it set, he said: Oh people, I am free of what you associate (with Allah).

79. For I have turned my face to the originator of the heavens and the earth, sincerely devoted, and I am not of the idolaters.

80. And his people disputed with him. He said: do you dispute with me about Allah when He has already guided me? And I do not at all fear what you associate with Him unless my Lord wills, my Lord's knowledge extends to everything, do you not then reflect?

81. And how should I fear what you associate when you don't fear that you associate with Allah what He has not sent to you any authority for? Which of the two factions then has more right to safety if you knew?

82. Those who believe and do not cover their belief with wrongdoing, for those is safety and they are guided.

83. And this is the argument we gave to Ibrahim (Abraham) against his people. We raise whom We will in stages, for your Lord is wise and knows.

84. And We gave him Ishaq (Isaac) and Ya'qub (Jacob), each We guided, and We had guided Nuh (Noah) before, and from amongst his descendants are Dawud (David), Sulayman (Solomon), Ayyub (Job), Yusuf (Joseph), Musa (Moses) and Harun (Aaron), and this is how We reward those who do good.

85. And Zakariya (Zacharia), 'Isa (Jesus) and Ilyas (Elias), each were from the righteous.

86. And Isma'il (Ishmael), and Al-Yasa' (Elisha), Yunus (Jonas) and Lut (Lot), each We favoured over everybody else.

87. And from their fathers, descendants and brothers, we selected them and guided them on to a straight path.

88. This is the guidance of Allah by which He guides whom He pleases from amongst His servants. And if they had been idolaters, all they did would have been lost to them.

89. Those are the ones whom We gave the book and sound judgement and prophethood, and if these reject it, then We have entrusted a people with it who will not reject it.

90. Those are the ones whom Allah guided, so follow their guidance. Say: I do not ask you for a reward for it, it is only a reminder for all the worlds.

91. And they do not appreciate the true ability of Allah when they say: Allah has not revealed anything to a human being. Say: Who revealed the book which Musa (Moses) brought as light and guidance for mankind, which you put on paper which you disclose whilst hiding much, and you were taught what neither you nor your fathers knew? Say: Allah. Then leave them to play in their bubble.

92. And this book We have revealed as a blessing and confirming that which came before it and to warn the leading township and those around it, and those who believe in the hereafter believe in it and keep up their prayers.

93. And who is more wrong than he who invents a lie against Allah or who says: I have received revelation when nothing has been revealed to him, and who says: I shall reveal the like of what Allah has revealed, and if you saw the wrongdoers during the hardship of death when the angels stretch out their hands: let go of your souls, today you will be rewarded with a humiliating punishment on account of what you used to say about Allah other than the truth and that you used to be arrogant about His signs.

94. And you will have come to Us alone just as We created you the first time and will have left behind what We had enabled you with, and We do not see with you your mediators you claimed were partners with you, you will be cut off from them and will have lost what you claimed (to have).

95. Allah splits the seed and the kernel, He brings out the living from the dead and is Who brings out the dead from the living, that is Allah for you, so where to are you diverted?

96. He splits the daybreaks and makes the night for rest and the sun and the moon for measure, this

is the arrangement of the mighty and knowing.

97. And He is who made the stars for you to be guided by them in the darkness of the land and the sea; We have already explained the signs for people who know.

98. And He is who brought you into existence from a single soul, then (set) a location and destination; We have already explained the signs to people who understand.

99. And He is who sent down from the sky water, then We make all kinds of plants grow with it and make grow with it greenery from which We bring out stacked seeds, and from the pollen of the palm tree low hanging date clusters, and gardens of grapes and olives and pomegranates, similar and dissimilar; look at their fruit when it grows and ripens - in this are indeed signs for people who believe.

100. And they assign to Allah associates from the Jinn when He created them, and they falsely attribute to Him sons and daughters without knowledge, glorified and exalted is He above what they make out.

101. The originator of the heavens and the earth, how can He have a son and not have a spouse? And He created everything and knows everything.

102. This is Allah, your Lord, there is no god but Him, the creator of everything, so serve Him, and He is a protector of everything.

103. The eyesight cannot reach Him, but He reaches the eyesight, and He is kind and informed.

104. You have already received from your Lord an insight, and he who sees, does so for his own self, and he who is blind, does so against his own self, and I am not a guardian over you.

105. This is how We spell out the signs so that they would say: you studied (them), and so that We clarify it to people who know.

106. Follow that which has been revealed to you from your Lord, there is no god but Him, and turn away from the idolaters.

107. And if Allah willed, they would not have been idolaters, and We did not place you as a guardian over them, and you are no protector over them.

108. And do not insult those they call besides Allah, so they (in turn) insult Allah in enmity without knowledge. This is how for every community We make their deeds appeal (to them), then their return is to their Lord, then He will inform them what they used to do.

109. And they swear by Allah their utmost oaths that if a sign came to them, they would believe in it. Say: The signs are with Allah, and what do you know that if it came to them, they would not believe.

110. And We change their hearts and perception as they did not believe it to start with, and We let them get lost in their rebellion.

111. And if We sent down to them the angels and the dead spoke to them and We would gather everything before them, they would not believe unless Allah willed, but most of them are ignorant.

112. And like this We made for every prophet enemies from the devils amongst the Jinn and mankind who inspire each other with deceptive idle talk, and if your Lord willed, they would not do it, so leave them and what they invent.

113. And so that the hearts of those who do not believe in the hereafter incline to it and are content with it and commit what they were going to commit.

114. Do I then seek other than Allah as judge when He is the One who revealed the book to you in detail? And those who received the book know that it was revealed from your Lord in truth, so do not be of the doubters.

115. And the word of your Lord has been completed in truth and justice, there is no changing His words, and He listens and knows.

116. And if you were to obey most of those on earth they would lead you astray from the way of Allah, for they follow only assumptions and only guess.

117. For your Lord knows best who has strayed from His way and He knows best those who are guided.

118. So eat from that over which the name of Allah has been mentioned if you believe in His signs.

119. And what is the matter with you that you do not eat from that over which the name of Allah has been mentioned, when He has already explained to you what He has forbidden to you, except for that what you are compelled to? And many lead astray with their desires without knowledge. Your Lord knows best those who transgress.

120. And leave what is apparent and what is hidden of sin, for those who commit sin will be rewarded for what they invented.

121. And do not eat from that over which the name of Allah has not been mentioned as it is an abomination, and the devils inspire their allies to argue with you, and if you obey them, then you are idolaters.

122. Is he who was dead, then We brought him to life and gave him light to walk with amongst people, like him who is as in darkness from which he cannot emerge? This is how their deeds are made appealing to those who reject (the truth).

123. And thus we have placed in every town its greatest sinners to plot in it, and they only plot against themselves but do not realise it.

124. And when a sign comes to them, they say: we will not believe until we are given something similar to that which the messengers of Allah were given. Allah knows best where to place His message. Those who sin will be afflicted with humiliation with Allah and a severe punishment on account of what they plotted.

125. And whom Allah wills to guide, He expands his chest towards submission (Islam), and whom He pleases to let go astray, He tightens his chest severely as if he were rising up into the sky; this is how Allah places disgrace on those who do not believe.

126. And this is the straight path of your Lord, We have already explained the signs to people who remember.

127. They will have a place of peace with their Lord, and He is their protector on account of what they did.

128. And on the day He gathers them altogether (He will say): oh congregation of Jinn, you had lots of dealings with mankind; and their allies amongst mankind will say: our Lord, we assisted each other and reached our appointed time which You defined for us; He will say: the fire is your abode where you will remain except for what Allah wills, for your Lord is wise and knows.

129. And in this way We make the wrongdoers turn to each other on account of what they used to commit.

130. Oh congregation of Jinn and Mankind, did not messengers from amongst you reach you and tell you about My signs and warn you of the meeting of this day? They will say: We are witnesses against ourselves, and the life of this world deceived them and they became witnesses against themselves that they rejected (the truth).

131. This is because your Lord never destroyed a township due to wrongdoing whilst its people were unaware.

132. And for everyone are stages on account of what they did, and your Lord is not unaware of what they do.

133. And your Lord is self-sufficient and owner of mercy, if He willed He would remove you and replace you afterwards with what He willed just as He brought you into existence from the descendants of other people.

134. For what you were promised will come and you will not escape.

135. Say: Oh people, do your work as you do, I do my work, then soon will you know who will reach the abode (of the hereafter), for the wrongdoers do not succeed.

136. And they assign for Allah a share of the harvest and the cattle He created and say: this is for Allah, in accordance with their claim, and this is for our idols, and that which was for their idols does not reach Allah, and that which was for Allah, it reaches their idols, bad is how they judge.

137. And likewise to many of the idolaters the killing of their children for their idols appeals to them, so that it ruins them and entangles them in their religion, and if Allah willed, they would not have done it, so leave them and what they invent.

138. And they say: these cattle and harvest are prohibited, nobody but whom we will shall eat from it, in accordance with their claim, and the backs of these cattle are sacred, and there are cattle over whom they do not mention the name of Allah as an invention against Him; He will punish them for what they invented.

139. And they say: what is in the wombs of these cattle is reserved for our males and forbidden to our wives, and if it is dead, then they share in it; He will punish them for their innovation, for He is wise and knows.

140. Lost are those who kill their children ignorantly without knowledge and prohibit what Allah has provided as an invention against Him, they have gone astray and are not guided.

141. And He is the One who brought into existence cultivated and uncultivated gardens and palm trees and plants of various taste and olives and pomegranates, similar and dissimilar; eat from its fruit when it grows and give its due on the day of harvesting, and do not waste, for He does not love those who are wasteful.

142. And from the cattle are those for carrying and those for wool and food. Eat from what Allah has provided for you and do not follow the footsteps of the devil, for he is an open enemy to you.

143. Eight in pairs, two of the sheep and two of the goats - say: are both males forbidden, or both females, or that which the wombs of both females contain? Inform me with knowledge, if you are truthful.

144. And two of the camels and two of the cows - say: are both males forbidden, or both females, or that which the wombs of both females contain? Or were you witnesses when Allah commanded you this? Then who is more wrong than he who invents a lie against Allah to lead people astray without knowledge, for Allah does not guide wrongdoing people.

145. Say: I do not find in what has been revealed to me any food forbidden to eat other than carrion or running blood or pork, for it is unclean, or an abomination consecrated for other than Allah, but if someone is forced without (wilful) transgression or habit, then your Lord is forgiving and merciful.

146. And to the Jews We made unlawful everything with uncleft hooves, and from the cows and small cattle we have forbidden to them their fat, except what is carried on their backs or the offal or the bone marrow. This is how We punished them for their transgression, and We are telling the truth.

147. Then, if they deny you, say: your Lord is full of extensive mercy, and His adversity cannot be averted from sinful people.

148. The idolaters say: had Allah willed, neither we nor our fathers would have been idolaters and we would not have forbidden anything. Likewise those before them denied until they tasted Our adversity. Say: Have you got any knowledge, then produce it for us. You only follow assumptions and only guess.

149. Say: to Allah belongs the ultimate argument, and if He willed, He would have guided you all.

150. Say: bring forward your witnesses who witness that Allah forbade that. Then, if they witness, do not witness with them, and do not follow the

desires of those who deny Our signs and those who do not believe in the hereafter and turn away from their Lord.

151. Say: Come, let me tell you what your Lord has forbidden to you, not to associate anything with him, and goodness towards parents, and not to kill your children out of (fear of) poverty - We provide for them and for you -, and not to come near open or hidden indecency, and not to kill any soul which Allah has forbidden except by right, that is what He orders you for you to consider.

152. And not to approach the wealth of the orphan, except to improve it, until he reaches full strength, and to observe just measure and weight, no soul shall be burdened beyond its capacity, and if you speak, be just, even if it concerns a relative, and observe the agreement with Allah, that is what He orders you for you to take heed.

153. And that this is My straight path, so follow it, and do not follow other paths to divert you from His path, that is what He orders you for you to beware.

154. Then We gave Musa (Moses) the book as a complete (guide) for him who does good and explanation of everything and guidance and mercy so that they would believe in meeting their Lord.

155. And this book We have revealed as a blessing, so follow it and beware (of Allah) so that you may find mercy.

156. In case you might say: the book has been revealed to the two groups before us and we were unaware of their studies.

157. Or you might say: if the book had been revealed to us we would have been more guided than them. So a clear sign has come to you from your Lord and a guidance and mercy, so who is more wrong than the one who denies the signs of Allah and turns away from them? We will punish those who turn away from Our signs with the worst punishment due to having turned away.

158. Do they expect nothing but that the angels should come to them or your Lord should come or some of the signs of your Lord should come? The day some of the signs of your Lord will come, nobody's belief will benefit anyone who has not believed before then or earned good within his belief. Say: wait, we are also waiting.

159. Those who split their religion into factions, you have nothing to do with them; their affair is with Allah, then He will inform them what they used to do.

160. Whoever brings a good deed, for him are ten the like of it, and whoever brings a bad deed, he is not punished except with the like of it, and they will not be wronged.

161. Say: my Lord has guided me to a straight path, an upright system, the religion of Ibrahim (Abraham), sincerely devoted, for he was not one of the idolaters.

162. Say: my prayer, my sacrifice, my life and my death are for Allah, the Lord of all worlds.

163. He has no partner, and this is what I have been commanded, and I am the first to submit (as Muslim).

164. Say: Should I seek other than Allah as Lord when He is the Lord of everything, and every soul's earnings are on its own account, and no-one burdened will carry another's burden, then your return is to your Lord and He will inform you about what you used to differ in.

165. And He is the One who made you successors on the earth and raised some of you above others in stages so He would test you in what He gave you, for your Lord is swift in retribution and He is forgiving and merciful.

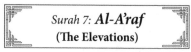

Surah 7: *Al-A'raf*
(The Elevations)

In the name of Allah, the Owner and Giver of Mercy

1. Alif, Lam, Mim, Sad.

2. A book revealed to you, not so you feel distressed on account of it, but to warn with it and a reminder for the believers.

3. Follow that which has been revealed to you from your Lord and do not follow allies besides Him, little do you take heed.

4. And how many towns have We destroyed when Our adversity reached them at night or whilst they rest in the day.

5. Then their only call, when Our adversity reached them, was to say: we were wrongdoers.

6. Then We shall question those who were sent to, and We shall question the messengers.

7. Then We shall tell them with knowledge, and We were not absent.

8. And the weight shall be true that day, so whose weight is heavy, those will be successful.

9. And whose weight is light, those will have lost themselves by doing wrong against Our signs.

10. And already have We established you on earth and given you a livelihood on it, little thanks do you give.

11. And We created you, then shaped you, then said to the angels: prostrate to Adam, and they prostrated except Iblis (the devil) who was not amongst those prostrating.

12. He said: what prevented you from prostrating when I commanded you? He said: I am better than him, You created me from fire and created him from clay.

13. He said: get down from here, you have no right to be arrogant here, so get out, you are from amongst those humiliated.

14. He said: give me time till the day when they are resurrected.

15. He said: you are given time.

16. He said: because You let me go astray, I shall discourage them from Your straight path.

17. Then I shall come to them from in front and from behind and from their right and from their left, and You will find most of them ungrateful.

18. He said: get out of here rebuked and rejected, whoever of them follows you, I will fill hell with you altogether.

19. And oh Adam, live with your wife in the garden, and eat from anywhere as you please, but do not approach this tree, because then you would be wrongdoers.

20. Then the devil whispered to them to disclose to them what had been hidden from them of their bodies and said: your Lord only forbids you from this tree so that you would not be two angels or would be living forever.

21. And he swore to them: I am giving you both sincere advice.

22. So he led them astray with deception, and when they tasted from the tree their bodies became disclosed to them and they began to cover them with leaves from the garden, and their Lord called them: did I not forbid you this tree and tell you that the devil is an open enemy to you?

23. They said: our Lord, we have wronged ourselves, and if You do not forgive us and have mercy on us, we will be lost.

24. He said: get down as enemies one to another. There will be a place to settle and a limited provision for you on earth.

25. He said: you will live on it and die on it and you will be resurrected from it.

26. Oh children of Adam, We have revealed for you clothes to hide your bodies and as ornament, and the clothing of awareness is better;

this is of the signs of Allah so that they remember.

27. Oh children of Adam, let not the devil tempt you like he expelled both your parents from the garden (of paradise), removing from them their clothing to disclose to them their bodies, for he and his tribe see you from where you do not see them. We have made the devils allies for those who do not believe.

28. And when they commit an indecency, they say: we found our fathers doing so and Allah commanded us to do so. Say: Allah does not command indecency; do you say about Allah what you don't know?

29. Say: my Lord commands justice and that you face towards Him wherever you pray and call Him with a sincere religion; as He originated you, you will return.

30. A group He has guided and a group deserves error for they took the devils as allies besides Allah and reckoned that they were guided.

31. Oh children of Adam, use presentable clothing wherever you pray and eat and drink and do not waste, for He does not love those who are wasteful.

32. Say: who has forbidden presentable clothing which Allah brought forth for His servants and good food? Say: on the day of resurrection they are exclusively for those who believed in this world. This is how We explain the signs to people who know.

33. Say: my Lord has forbidden indecency, both open and hidden, and sin and transgression without right and that you associate with Allah that for which He has not sent any authority and that you say about Allah what you don't know.

34. And for every community there is a fixed term, then when its term is up, they will not delay it for an hour nor speed it up.

35. Oh children of Adam, messengers of your own have reached you to relate to you My signs, so who bewares and does good, they shall not fear nor worry.

36. And those who deny Our signs and are arrogant about them, they will be the inmates of the fire where they will remain.

37. Who then is more wrong than him who invents a lie against Allah or denies His signs? Their share of what has been written will come to them until, when Our messengers come to take them away, they will say: where is what you called on besides Allah? They will say: they have abandoned us, and they will be witnesses against themselves that they were rejecting (the truth).

38. He will say: enter the fire with communities who have gone before you of the Jinn and mankind. Whenever a community enters it curses its counterpart until, when they have all arrived there, the last of them will say to the first: our Lord, these have led us astray, so give them double the punishment of the fire. He will say: all will have double, but you don't know.

39. And the first will say to the last: you were no better than us, so taste the punishment for what you used to do.

40. Those who deny Our signs and are arrogant about them, the doors of heaven will not be opened for them and they will not enter the garden (of paradise) until a thick rope fits through the eye of a needle, and this is how We punish the sinners.

41. They will have hell as an abode and as a covering from above them, and this is how We punish the wrongdoers.

42. And those who believe and do good work: We do not task any soul beyond its capability, they belong in the garden (of paradise), where they will remain.

43. And We remove what is within them of ill feeling, rivers flow between them and they will say: Allah is praised who guided us to this, and we would not have been guided had not Allah guided us; the messengers of our Lord came to us with the truth; and it will be announced that this is the garden you have inherited on account of what you used to do.

44. And the inhabitants of the garden will call the inmates of the fire, saying: we found what our Lord promised us to be true, so have you found what your Lord promised you to be true? They will say: yes. And a caller will call from among them that the curse of Allah is upon the wrongdoers.

45. Those who divert from the way of Allah and desire it to be crooked and reject the hereafter.

46. And between them is a barrier, and on its elevations there are men who know each by their signs. And they call the inhabitants of the garden, saying: peace be with you. They haven't entered it yet, but they are hoping.

47. And when their eyes are turned towards the inmates of the fire they say: our Lord, do not place us with the wrongdoing people.

48. And those on the elevations call men whom they know from their characteristics, saying: your grouping together and your arrogance did not benefit you.

49. Are those the ones you swore Allah's mercy would not reach? Enter the garden, no fear shall you have nor shall you worry.

50. And the inmates of the fire call the inhabitants of the garden: pass us of the water or of what Allah has provided you with. They say: Allah has forbidden it to those who rejected (the truth).

51. Those who took their religion as pastime and play and the life of the world deceived them, so today We forget them just as they forgot the meeting of this day and disputed Our signs.

52. And We gave them a book and explained it with knowledge as a guidance and mercy for people who believe.

53. Are they only waiting for its outcome? The day its outcome arrives those who forgot before will say: the messengers of our Lord came to us with the truth, so are there any mediators to speak up for us or will we return to act differently from what we did? They have lost themselves and what they invented has deserted them.

54. Your Lord is the One who created the heavens and the earth in six days, then He rose onto the throne, He makes the night cover the day pursuing it constantly, and the sun and the moon and the stars travel by His command, indeed to Him belongs the creation and the command, exalted is Allah the Lord of all worlds.

55. Call your Lord humble and secretly, for He does not love the transgressors.

56. And do not cause corruption on earth after it has been set right, and call Him in fear and hope, for the mercy of your Lord is close to those who do good.

57. And He is who sends the winds as an advance announcement of His mercy, until when it carries heavy clouds We direct them to dead land and send with them water and with it make all kinds of fruit grow. This is how We bring out the dead so that you take heed.

58. And the good land brings out its fruit by the permission of its Lord, and that which is bad only brings out very little. This is how We spell out the signs for people who are grateful.

59. We previously sent Nuh (Noah) to his people, and he said: oh my people, serve Allah, you have no god other than Him. I fear for you the punishment of a tremendous day.

60. The leaders of his people said: we see you in clear error.

61. He said: oh my people, there is no error with me, but I am a messenger from the Lord of all worlds.

62. I convey to you the messages of my Lord and give you sincere advice and know from Allah what you don't know.

63. Or are you astonished that a reminder reaches you from your Lord through a man from amongst you to warn you and so that you beware (of Him) and find mercy?

64. But they denied him, so We rescued him and those with him in the ship and drowned those who denied Our signs, for they were blind people.

65. And to 'Ad (We sent) their brother Hud, saying: oh my people, serve Allah, you have no god other than Him, do you not beware (of Him)?

66. The leaders of his people who rejected (the truth) said: we see you are foolish and we consider you a liar.

67. He said: oh my people, there is no foolishness with me, but I am a messenger from the Lord of all worlds.

68. I convey to you the messages of my Lord and I am a reliable advisor to you.

69. Or are you astonished that a reminder reaches you from your Lord through a man from amongst you? Remember when He made you successors after the people of Nuh (Noah) and He made you very tall in creation, so remember the blessings of Allah in order to succeed.

70. They said: Have you come to us so we should serve Allah alone and abandon what our fathers served? Then bring us what you have promised us if you are truthful.

71. He said: disgrace and anger from Allah have already fallen upon you. Do you argue with me about names which you and your fathers have given without Allah having sent an authority for it? So wait, I will wait with you.

72. So we rescued him and those with him by Our mercy and uprooted those who denied Our signs and did not believe.

73. And to Thamud (We sent) their brother Salih, saying: oh my people, serve Allah, you have no god other than Him; clear proof has reached you from your Lord: this is Allah's she-camel as a sign for you, so let her eat on Allah's earth and do not harm her or a painful punishment will take you.

74. And remember when He made you successors after 'Ad and accommodated you on earth, whose plains you use for castles and whose mountains you use for dwellings, so remember the blessings of Allah and do not spread corruption on earth.

75. The leaders of his people who were arrogant said to the believers amongst those who were weak: do you know that Salih has been sent from his Lord? They said: We believe in what he was sent with.

76. Those who were arrogant said: We reject that which you believe in.

77. Then they bled the she-camel to death and violated their Lord's command and said: oh Salih, bring us what you promised us if you are a messenger.

78. So the earthquake overtook them and they were found face down in their houses in the morning.

79. So he turned away from them and said: oh my people, I already conveyed to you the messages of my Lord and gave you sincere advice but you do not like those who give sincere advice.

80. And Lut (Lot) when he said to his people: do you bring an indecency no-one in the whole world has preceded you with?

81. For you come to men with lust instead of women, but you are a wasteful people.

82. And the reply of his people was merely that they said: expel them from your town for they are people who want to keep clean.

83. So We rescued him and his family except his wife who was of those who stayed behind.

84. And we sent a downpour on them, so see what the outcome was like for the sinners.

85. And to Madyan (Midian) (We sent) their brother Shu'ayb (Jethro), saying: oh my people, serve Allah, you have no god other than Him. A clear proof has reached you from you Lord, so give full measure and weight and do not short-change people and do not cause corruption on earth after it has been set right. This is better for you if you are believers.

86. And do not block every path threatening and diverting from the way of Allah those who believe in Him and desiring it to be crooked, and remember when you were few and He increased you in number, and see what the outcome was like for the corrupters.

87. And if a party of you believe in that I have been sent with and a party do not believe, then wait until Allah judges between us, and He is the best to judge.

88. The leaders of his people who were arrogant said: we will expel you, oh Shu'ayb (Jethro) and those who believe with you from our town unless you return to our religion. He said: What if we resent it?

89. We would have invented a lie against Allah if we returned to your religion after Allah rescued us from it, and it is not for us to return to it unless Allah, our Lord, wills it; our Lord's knowledge extends to everything, we trust in Allah - our Lord decide between us and our people with truth, and You are the best to decide.

90. And the leaders of his people who rejected (the truth) said: if you follow Shu'ayb (Jethro), you will be losers.

91. So the earthquake overtook them and they were found face down in their houses in the morning.

92. Those who denied Shu'ayb (Jethro), as if they had not prospered

in them, those who denied Shu'ayb (Jethro), they were the losers.

93. So he turned away from them and said: oh my people, I already conveyed to you the messages of my Lord and gave you sincere advice, so how can I be sorry for people who reject (the truth).

94. And We never sent a prophet to a town without afflicting its inhabitants with adversity and hardship so that they would humble themselves.

95. Then We replaced the harm with good, until they recovered and said: hardship and ease previously afflicted our fathers, then We took them suddenly without them realising it.

96. And if the inhabitants of the towns had believed and bewared (of Allah), We would have opened for them blessings from the sky and the earth, but they denied, so We took them on account of what they used to commit.

97. Are then the inhabitants of the towns safe from Our distress reaching them at night whilst they sleep?

98. Or are then the inhabitants of the towns safe from Our distress reaching them in the morning whilst they play?

99. Are they then safe from Allah's scheme? Nobody feels safe from Allah's scheme except people who are losers.

100. Is it not evident to those who inherited the earth after its inhabitants that if We willed We would afflict them on account of their sins? And We imprint upon their hearts so that they do not listen.

101. Those are the towns of whose information We tell you. Our messengers reached them with clear proofs, but they would not believe that which they denied before. This is how Allah imprints on the hearts of the rejecters.

102. And We found most of them without commitment, and We found most of them sinful.

103. Then after them We sent Musa (Moses) with Our signs to Pharaoh and his leaders, but they did not do justice to them, so see what the outcome of the corrupters was like.

104. And Musa (Moses) said: oh Pharaoh, I am a messenger from the Lord of all worlds.

105. It is binding upon me that I do not say about Allah anything but the truth. I have come to you with a clear proof from your Lord, so send the children of Israel with me.

106. He said: if you have come with a sign, then show it if you are truthful.

107. So he threw down his staff and it became a real snake.

108. And he pulled out his hand and it could be seen as white.

109. The leaders of the people of Pharaoh said: this is a knowledgeable magician.

110. He wants to expel you from your land, so what do you command?

111. They said: defer him and his brother and send mobilisers to the cities,

112. To bring you every knowledgeable magician.

113. And the magicians came to Pharaoh saying: for sure we will have a reward if we are the winners?

114. He said: yes, and you will be of the inner circle.

115. They said: oh Musa (Moses), either you throw or we are the ones who throw.

116. He said: you throw, then when they threw, they bedazzled the eyes of people and frightened them and brought tremendous magic.

117. And we inspired Musa (Moses): throw, then it will take over what they invent.

118. Then the truth was established and what they did was cancelled.

119. So they were overcome at this point and turned humiliated.

120. And the magicians fell prostrate.

121. They said: we believe in the Lord of all worlds.

122. The Lord of Musa (Moses) and Harun (Aaron).

123. Pharaoh said: do you believe in him before I have given you permission? This is a scheme you have schemed in the city to expel from it its inhabitants, but soon you will know.

124. I shall cut off your hands and feet on opposite sides, then I shall crucify all of you.

125. They said: we will turn to our Lord.

126. And you only hold against us that we believed in the signs of our Lord when they came to us. Our Lord, grant us patience and take us away whilst having submitted (as Muslims).

127. And the leaders of the people of Pharaoh said: are you going to leave Musa (Moses) and his people to cause corruption on earth and abandon you and your gods? He said: we will kill their sons and spare their women and we have power over them.

128. Musa (Moses) said to his people: seek the help of Allah and be patient, for Allah gives the earth as inheritance to whom He will of His servants, and the outcome is for those who beware (of Him).

129. They said: we were punished before and after you came to us. He said: maybe your Lord will destroy your enemy and make you successors on earth to see how you behave.

130. And We previously afflicted the family of Pharaoh with years of drought and lack of fruit so that they would remember.

131. And when something good reached them, they said: this is for us, and when something bad afflicted them, they ascribed it to Musa (Moses) and those with him. But no, what they ascribe is from Allah but most of them don't know.

132. And they said: whatever sign you bring to bewitch us with it, we will not believe you.

133. So We sent on them the floods, the locusts, the lice, the frogs and the blood as distinct signs, but they were arrogant and were sinful people.

134. And when the punishment fell upon them, they said: oh Musa (Moses), call your Lord for us on account of His agreement with you that if you remove the punishment from us, we will believe in you and send the Children of Israel with you.

135. Then when We removed the punishment from them until a future date set for them, they broke their promise.

136. So We took revenge on them and drowned them in the sea, because they denied Our signs and were careless about them.

137. And We gave to the people who had been oppressed the East and West of the earth which We had blessed as an inheritance, and the good word of your Lord was accomplished for the Children of Israel on account of their patience, and we destroyed the work of Pharaoh and his people and what they had built.

138. And We made the Children of Israel cross the sea and they came to a people devoted to idols of theirs and said: oh Musa (Moses), make us an idol like they have idols. He said: you are foolish people.

139. For what they engage in will be wiped out and what they used to do will be worthless.

140. He said: should I desire any god other than Allah for you when He has favoured you over everybody else?

141. And when We rescued you from the family of Pharaoh who afflicted you with bad punishment, killing your sons and sparing your women, which was a tremendous test from your Lord for you.

142. And We set a time of thirty nights for Musa (Moses) and supplemented it with (another) ten, so the appointment with his Lord was completed in forty nights, and Musa (Moses) said to his brother Harun (Aaron): represent me amongst my people and make peace and do not follow the way of the corrupters.

143. And when Musa (Moses) came for Our appointment and his Lord spoke to him, he said: my Lord, show Yourself to me so I can look at You. He said: you will not see Me, but look at the mountain, and if it stays in its place, then you will see Me. And when his Lord covered the mountain with His glory, He made it crumble and Musa (Moses) fell struck down. Then when he rose up, he said: glorified are You, I repent to you and am first amongst the believers.

144. He said: oh Musa (Moses), I have chosen you above mankind with My messages and speech, so take what I have given you and be of those who are grateful.

145. And We decreed all manner of things for him on the tablets as an admonition and an explanation of everything, so take it with strength and command your people to take of its best (content); I will show you the abode of the sinful.

146. I will turn away from My signs those who are arrogant on earth without right, and when they see each

sign, they do not believe in it, and when they see the path of righteousness, they do not take it as a path, and when they see the path of transgression, they take it as a path, that is because they deny Our signs and are ignorant of them.

147. And those who deny Our signs and the meeting of the hereafter, their deeds are wasted - are they rewarded for anything but what they did?

148. And after he had gone, the people of Musa (Moses) fashioned some of their jewellery into the shape of a calf which had a mooing sound; did they not consider that it did not speak to them nor guide them the way? They fashioned it and were wrongdoers.

149. And when they gave up on it and saw that they had gone astray they said: if our Lord does not have mercy on us and forgive us, we will be lost.

150. And when Musa (Moses) returned to his people angry and sad, he said: bad is what you did in my absence. Do you want to hasten the outcome from your Lord? And he threw the tablets and took his brother by the head and pulled him towards him. He said: son of my mother, the people overpowered me and almost killed me, so do not show enmity towards me and do not place me amongst the wrongdoers.

151. He said: My Lord, forgive me and my brother and enter us into Your mercy and You are the most merciful of all.

152. Those who fashioned the calf, anger from their Lord and humiliation will reach them in this world, and that is how We punish the inventors.

153. And those who do bad deeds, then repent afterwards and believe, your Lord is afterwards forgiving and merciful.

154. And when the anger left Musa (Moses) he took the tablets and within them was guidance and mercy for those who are in awe of their Lord.

155. And Musa (Moses) chose seventy men from his people to meet Us, and when the trembling overtook them he said: My Lord, if you willed, You could have destroyed them and me before, are You going to destroy us on account of what the fools amongst us did? This is only Your test by which You lead astray whom You will and guide whom You will; You are our protector, so forgive us and have mercy on us, and You are the best of those who forgive.

156. And decree good for us in this world and in the next for we repent to You. He said: My punishment, I will afflict with it whom I will, and my mercy extends to everything, so I will decree it for those who beware and give the Zakat and those who believe in Our signs.

157. Those who follow the messenger, the prophet, the unlettered, whom they find described with them in the Torah and the Injil, who commands them good conduct and forbids them wrongdoing and permits them of the good things and prohibits them harmful things and relieves them of their burden and the restrictions which were upon them, so those who

believe in him and support him and help him and follow the light which has been sent with him, those are the successful.

158. Say: oh people, I am the messenger of Allah to all of you, of the One to whom belongs the kingdom of the heavens and the earth, there is no god but Him, He gives life and death, so believe in Allah and His messenger, the prophet, the unlettered, who believes in Allah and His words, and follow him in order to be guided.

159. And from the people of Musa (Moses) is a community who guide with the truth and do justice to it.

160. And We divided them into twelve tribes as communities and revealed to Musa (Moses) when his people asked him for water to strike with your staff the rock, then twelve springs gushed out from it - each people knew their drinking place -, and We shaded the cloud over them and sent to them honeydew and quails: eat from the good things We have provided you with. And We did not wrong them, but they wronged themselves.

161. And when it was said to them: live in this town and eat from it as you please and ask to be accepted and enter the gate submissive, We shall forgive you your shortcomings and shall give more to those who do good.

162. Then the wrongdoers amongst them changed their instructions into something else, so We sent to them a punishment from the sky because of their wrongdoing.

163. And ask them about the town which was near the sea, when they transgressed the Sabbath, when their fish came to them in shoals on their Sabbath day, and on the day they did not observe the Sabbath it did not come to them. This is how We tried them because of their excesses.

164. And when a community from amongst them said: why do you admonish a people whom Allah will destroy or punish severely? They said: as an excuse before our Lord and so that they beware.

165. And when they forgot what they were reminded with, We saved those who prohibited evil and overtook the wrongdoers with a nasty punishment because of their excesses.

166. And when they persisted in what they had been prohibited from, We said to them: be despicable monkeys.

167. And when your Lord announced: I will raise against them until the day of resurrection those who will afflict them with the worst punishment, for your Lord is swift in retribution and He is forgiving, merciful.

168. And We split them on earth into communities, amongst them are the righteous and amongst them are otherwise, and We tested them with good and bad so that they return.

169. Then there were descendants after them who inherited the book; they take from the availability of this lesser world and say: we will be forgiven. And when a similar availability reaches them, they take it. Was not the promise of the book taken

from them that they should not say anything about Allah except the truth, and they studied what it contained? And the abode of the hereafter is better for those who beware (of Allah) - don't you think?

170. And those who hold on to the book and keep up prayer, We do not waste the reward of those who do good.

171. And when We lifted the mountain above them as if it were a cloud cover and they thought it would fall onto them: take what We give you with strength and remember its contents so that you will beware (of Allah).

172. And when your Lord took from the midst of the children of Adam their descendants and made them witness against themselves: Am I not your Lord? They said: Sure, we are witnesses. So that you would not say on the day of resurrection that we were unaware of this.

173. Or that you would say: our fathers were idolaters before and we are descendants after them, are You going to destroy us for what the inventors did?

174. And this is how We explain the signs so that they return.

175. Recite to them the account of the one whom We gave Our signs, then he abandoned them and the devil pursued him, so he was of the misguided.

176. And had We willed We could have elevated him through them, but he wanted to live forever on earth and followed his desire, so his likeness is like that of the dog, if you burden him he pants or if you leave him he pants. That is the likeness of people who deny Our signs, therefore relate the story so that they reflect.

177. Bad is the likeness of people who deny Our signs and were wrongdoers themselves.

178. Whom Allah guides, he is guided, and whom He lets go astray, those are the losers.

179. And already did We create many of the Jinn and mankind for hell. They have hearts with which they do not understand and they have eyes with which they do not see and they have ears with which they do not hear. They are like cattle but more astray. They are the careless.

180. And to Allah belong the most beautiful names, so call Him by them. And leave those who distance themselves from His names, they will be punished for what they did.

181. And from those We have created is a community who guide with the truth and do justice to it.

182. And those who deny Our signs, We gradually pursue them from where they are unaware.

183. And I give them some space, for my plot is firm.

184. Do they not reflect? There is no madness in their companion, he is only a clear warner.

185. Do they not look at the kingdom of the heavens and the earth and what Allah has created and that perhaps their term has already come close?

So in what statement after that do they believe?

186. Whom Allah lets go astray, nobody will guide him, and He lets them get lost in their rebellion.

187. They ask you about the hour, for when is it fixed? Say: knowledge about it is with my Lord, nobody discloses it at its time but He; it is heavy in the heavens and the earth; it does not come upon you but suddenly. They ask you as if you were informed of it. Say: knowledge about it is with Allah but most people do not know.

188. Say: I do not master benefit or harm for myself except for what Allah wills, and if I were to know the unseen I would have abundance of good and bad would not afflict me. I am only a warner and bringer of good news to people who believe.

189. He is who created you from a single soul and produced from it its spouse so that he would find rest in her, and when he covers her she carries a light burden and moves along with it, and when it becomes heavy, they both call on Allah their Lord: if you give us what is healthy we will be grateful.

190. And when He gave them what is good, they assigned partners for it in what He gave them, but Allah is elevated above what they assign as partners.

191. Do they assign as partners what does not create a thing and who are themselves created?

192. And they are unable to help them nor help themselves?

193. And if you call them to the guidance, they do not follow you. It makes no difference to them whether you call them or remain silent.

194. Those you call upon besides Allah are servants just like you, so call them and let them respond if you are truthful.

195. Do they have feet to walk with, or do they have hands to grip with, or do they have eyes to see with, or do they have ears to hear with? Say: call your associates, then plot against me and do not hesitate.

196. For my protector is Allah who has revealed the book and He protects the righteous.

197. And those whom you call upon besides Allah are unable to help you and cannot help themselves.

198. And if you call them to the guidance they do not hear, and you see them gazing at you but they do not see.

199. Accept excuses and command good conduct and turn away from the ignorant.

200. And if you are in any way provoked by the devil then seek refuge in Allah, for He listens and knows.

201. Those who beware (of Allah), when a suggestion from the devil touches them, they reflect and then they see clearly.

202. Whilst their brothers lead them into error, then they do not desist.

203. And if you do not bring them a sign they say: why did you not bring it about? Say: I only follow what has been revealed to me by my Lord. This is clear evidence from my Lord and a guidance and mercy for people who believe.

204. And if the Qur'an is recited, then listen to it and be silent in order to receive mercy.

205. And remember your Lord within yourself humble and secretly and without speaking out in the morning and in the evening and do not be amongst the careless.

206. Those near your Lord are not too arrogant to serve Him, and they glorify Him and prostrate to Him.

Surah 8: *Al-Anfal*
(The Booty)

In the name of Allah,
the Owner and Giver of Mercy

1. They ask you about the booty. Say: the booty is for Allah and the messenger, so beware of Allah and make peace between yourselves and obey Allah and His messenger if you are believes.

2. The believers are those who if Allah is mentioned their hearts become fearful and if His signs are recited to them they increase them in faith and they rely on their Lord.

3. Those who keep up prayer and spend from what We have provided for them.

4. Those are the true believers. For them are stages with their Lord and forgiveness and generous provision.

5. Just as your Lord sent you out from your home with the truth even if a section of the believers resent it.

6. They argue with you about the truth after it has been made clear as if they were driven towards death in plain sight.

7. And when Allah promised you that one of the two parties would be yours and you wished that the one with less sting would be yours and Allah willed to verify the truth with His words and cut off the future of those who reject (the truth).

8. So that He would verify the truth and nullify falsehood even if the sinners resent it.

9. When you asked your Lord for success and He responded to you that I will help you with a thousand angels in succession.

10. And Allah only gave this as good news and to contend your hearts with it, and victory is only from Allah the mighty and wise.

11. When He covered you with a calming safety from Him and sent down to you from the sky water to purify you with and to remove from you the affliction of the devil and to fortify your hearts and make your foothold firm.

12. When your Lord revealed to the angels that I am with you, so make firm those who believe; I will throw fear into the hearts of those who reject (the truth), so strike them on the necks and strike every limb of them.

13. This is because they break away from Allah and His messenger, and whoever breaks away from Allah and His messenger, then Allah is severe in punishment.

14. This is for you, so taste it as for those who reject (the truth) is the punishment of the fire.

15. Oh you believers, when you meet those who reject (the truth) in battle, then do not turn your backs on them.

16. And whoever turns his back that day, except to reposition for fighting or to join a detachment, he has already brought upon himself the anger of Allah and his abode is hell, a bad destination.

17. For you did not kill them, but Allah killed them, and you did not throw when you threw, but Allah threw in order for the believers to be tested by Him in a beautiful manner, for Allah listens and knows.

18. So it was, and Allah always weakens the plot of those who reject (the truth).

19. If you seek victory, victory has already overcome you, and if you stop it is better for you, and if you return, We return and your numbers, however great, will not benefit you, and Allah is with the believers.

20. Oh you believers, obey Allah and His messenger and do not turn away from him whilst you listen.

21. And do not be like those who say we listen, yet they do not listen.

22. For the worst creatures before Allah are the deaf and dumb, those who do not understand.

23. And if Allah knew any good in them, He would have made them hearing, and if He had made them hearing they would turn away in opposition.

24. Oh you believers, respond to Allah and the messenger when he calls you to what revives you, and know that Allah comes between a man and his heart and that you will be gathered to Him.

25. And beware of a corruption which will not only afflict those who do wrong amongst you, and know that Allah is severe in punishment.

26. And remember when you were few and oppressed on earth, fearing that the people would seize you, then He gave you refuge and helped you with His victory and provided well for you so that you would be grateful.

27. Oh you believers, do not betray Allah and the messenger nor betray your trust knowingly.

28. And know that your wealth and children are a test and that with Allah is immense reward.

29. Oh you believers, if you beware of Allah, He will provide a break-through for you and cancel your bad deeds from you and forgive you, and Allah possesses immense generosity.

30. And when those who reject (the truth) plot against you to capture you, kill you or expel you - they plot

and Allah plots, and Allah is the best of plotters.

31. And when Our signs are recited to them, they say we have heard; if we wanted we could say something similar for these are only stories of old.

32. And when they said: oh Allah, if this is the truth from You, then rain upon us stones from the sky or bring us a painful punishment.

33. And Allah was not going to punish them whilst you were amongst them, and Allah was not going to punish them whilst they were seeking forgiveness.

34. And why should Allah not punish them whilst they divert from the sacred mosque when they were not its protectors, for its protectors are only those who beware (of Allah), but most of them do not know.

35. And their prayer near the House was nothing but screaming and clapping, so taste the punishment on account of having rejected (the truth).

36. Those who reject (the truth) spend their wealth to divert from the way of Allah, then they will have spent it after which it will be a loss for them; after that they will be overpowered and those who reject (the truth) will be gathered to hell.

37. In order for Allah to separate the bad and the good and stack up the bad and pile it all up and place it in hell; those are the losers.

38. Say to those who reject (the truth), if they stop, they will be forgiven what went before, and if they return, then the example of old has already passed.

39. And fight them until there is no corruption and the religion is completely for Allah, but if they stop, then Allah sees what they do.

40. And if they turn away, then know that Allah is your protector, the best protector and the best helper.

41. And know that whatever booty you seize, a fifth of it is for Allah and the messenger and the relatives and the orphans and the poor and the traveller if you believe in Allah and what He has revealed to His servant on the day of separation, the day the two troops met, and Allah is able to do anything.

42. When you were on the nearer slope and they were on the more distant slope and the caravan was below you, and had you promised (to fight), you would have disagreed about the promise, but it happened so that Allah would decide a matter which had to be so that whoever was destroyed would be destroyed upon evidence and whoever lived would live upon evidence, and Allah listens and knows.

43. When Allah showed them to you in your sleep as few, and had He shown them to you as many, you would have weakened and disputed about the matter, but Allah gave reassurance, for He knows what is kept inside.

44. And when He showed them to you when you met as few in your eyes and made you look few in their eyes, so that Allah would decide a matter which had to be, and to Allah return all things.

45. Oh you believers, when you meet a detachment, be firm and remember Allah a lot in order to succeed.

46. And obey Allah and His messenger and do not dispute, so that you weaken and your spirit departs, and be patient, for Allah is with the patient.

47. And do not be like those who emerged from their houses proud and to be seen by people and divert from the way of Allah, and Allah surrounds what they do.

48. And when the devil made their deeds appeal to them and said to them, none of the people will overpower you today and I will stand by you, and when the two groups saw each other he turned on his heels and said: I am free of you, I see what you do not see, I fear Allah, and Allah is severe in punishment.

49. When the pretenders and those with a disease in their hearts said, their religion has deceived these, and whoever relies on Allah, Allah is mighty and wise.

50. And if you could see how the angels took away those who reject (the truth), striking their faces and backs and (saying): taste the punishment of burning.

51. This is for the deeds you have sent ahead and that Allah does not wrong (His) servants.

52. Like the practice of the family of Pharaoh and those before them, they rejected the signs of Allah, so Allah seized them on account of their sins. Allah is strong, severe in punishment.

53. This is because Allah never changes a blessing He has blessed a people with until they change what is in themselves, and because Allah listens and knows.

54. Like the practice of the family of Pharaoh and those before them, they denied the signs of their Lord, so He destroyed them on account of their sins and drowned the family of Pharaoh, and they were all wrongdoers.

55. For the worst creatures before Allah are the those who reject (the truth) so do not believe.

56. Those whom you took a promise from, then they break their promise each time, and they do not beware.

57. Then when you capture them in war, frighten with them those behind them so that they will remember.

58. And if you fear from a people treachery, then repudiate them in a fair manner, for Allah does not love the treacherous.

59. And those who reject (the truth) should not count on prevailing, they will not escape.

60. And prepare for them what you can in strength and well-arranged horses to frighten with it the enemy of Allah and your enemy as well as others besides them whom you do not know; Allah knows them. And whatever you spend in the way of Allah, it will be repaid to you and you will not be wronged.

61. And if they incline to peace, then incline to it and rely on Allah, for He listens and knows.

62. And if they want to cheat you, then Allah is sufficient for you, He is the One who aided you with His help and the believers.

63. And He attuned their hearts; if you spent all that is on earth you could not have attuned their hearts, but Allah attuned them, for He is mighty and wise.

64. Oh prophet, Allah is sufficient for you and those amongst the believers who follow you.

65. Oh prophet, encourage the believers to fight; if there are twenty steadfast amongst you, they will overpower two hundred, and if there are a hundred of you, they will overpower a thousand of those who reject (the truth), for they are a people who do not understand.

66. Now Allah has lightened things for you and knows that there is weakness in you, so if there are a hundred steadfast amongst you, they will overpower two hundred, and if there are a thousand, they will overpower two thousand with the permission of Allah, and Allah is with those who are steadfast.

67. It is not fit for the prophet to take captives until he has established himself in the land; you want the offering of the world and Allah wants the hereafter, and Allah is mighty and wise.

68. If there was not a previous decree from Allah, you would have met a severe punishment on account of what you took.

69. Then eat of what you have taken in booty as lawful and good and beware of Allah, for Allah is forgiving and merciful.

70. Oh prophet, say to the captives in your possession: if Allah knows any good in your hearts, He will give you better than what has been taken from you and forgive you, and Allah is forgiving and merciful.

71. And if they want to betray you, then they have already betrayed Allah before, then He took hold of them, and Allah is knowing and wise.

72. Those who believe and have emigrated and fought with their wealth and their lives in the way of Allah, and those who gave refuge and helped, those are mutual protectors of each other, and those who believe but have not emigrated, their protection is not your concern until they emigrate, and if they seek your help in the religion, then it is your duty to help except against a people with a treaty between you and them, and Allah sees what you do.

73. And those who reject (the truth), they are mutual protectors of each other, if you do not do this, there will be corruption and great mischief on earth.

74. And those who believe and have emigrated and fought in the way of Allah, and those who gave refuge and helped, those are the true believers, for them is forgiveness and generous provision.

75. And those who believed afterwards and emigrated and fought with you, those are from amongst you, and relatives are mutual protectors of each other in the book of Allah, for Allah knows everything.

Surah 9: *At-Taubah*
(Repentance)

1. A repudiation from Allah and His messenger for the idolaters with whom you have a treaty.

2. Travel then on earth for four months and know that you cannot defeat Allah and that Allah humiliates those who reject (the truth).

3. And an announcement from Allah and His messenger to the people on the day of the greater pilgrimage (Hajj) that Allah and His messenger repudiate the idolaters, so if you repent it is better for you, and if you turn away, then know that you cannot defeat Allah, and announce to those who reject (the truth) a painful punishment.

4. Except those of the idolaters with whom you have a treaty and who then did not withhold anything from you and did not assist anyone against you, then complete their treaty for them until their (agreed) term, for Allah loves those who beware.

5. Then, when the sacred months have passed, kill the idolaters wherever you find them and capture them and besiege them and intercept them wherever possible, but if they repent and keep up prayer and give Zakat, then let them go their way, for Allah is forgiving and merciful.

6. And if any of the idolaters seeks your protection, then protect him until he has heard the word of Allah, then deliver him to his place of safety; this, because they are people who do not know.

7. How can the idolaters have a treaty with Allah and with His messenger? Except those with whom you entered into a treaty at the sacred mosque - so if they uphold it for you, uphold it for them, for Allah loves those who beware.

8. How (can they), whilst when they gain the upper hand against you they respect neither relationships nor obligations regarding you. They try to please you with their mouths, but their hearts disagree, and most of them are sinful.

9. They have sold the signs of Allah for a small price so that they divert from His way, bad is what they used to do.

10. They respect neither relationships nor obligations regarding a believer, and those are the transgressors.

11. Yet if they repent and keep up prayer and give Zakat, then they are your brothers in religion, and We explain the signs to people who know.

12. And if they break their promises after their treaty and attack your religion, then kill the leaders of rejection, for they keep no promises, so that they stop.

13. Will you not fight a people who broke their promises and strove to expel the messenger when they started against you first? Do you fear them? Then Allah has more right that you fear Him if you are believers.

14. Fight them, Allah will punish them by your hands and humiliate them and help you against them and heal the feelings of believing people.

15. And remove the anger from their hearts, and Allah turns back to whom He pleases and Allah is knowing and wise.

16. Or did you count on being left alone without Allah knowing those who strive amongst you and do not take besides Allah and His messenger and the believers any close friends, and Allah knows what you do.

17. It is not befitting for the idolaters to visit the mosques of Allah bearing witness against themselves of rejection; their deeds are wasted and they will remain in the fire forever.

18. Only those shall visit the mosques of Allah who believe in Allah and the last day and keep up prayer and give Zakat and do not fear other than Allah, and those will likely be amongst the guided.

19. Do you equate the provision of water to the pilgrim and the maintenance of the sacred mosque with someone's belief in Allah and the last day and effort in the way of Allah? They are not the same before Allah, and Allah does not guide wrongdoing people.

20. Those who believe and emigrated and strove in the way of Allah with their wealth and their lives have a higher stage with Allah, and those are the winners.

21. Their Lord gives them good news of mercy from Him and approval and gardens containing lasting blessings for them.

22. They will remain in them forever, for with Allah is immense reward.

23. Oh you believers, do not take your fathers or brothers as protecting friends if they prefer rejection over belief; whoever amongst you seeks their protection, they are wrongdoers.

24. Say: if your fathers and your sons and your brothers and your partners and your relatives and wealth you have acquired and trade whose loss you fear and homes you are content with are dearer to you than Allah and His messenger and to strive in His way, then wait until Allah settles the matter, and Allah does not guide sinful people.

25. Allah has already helped you at many locations and on the day of Hunayn when you were impressed with your multitude, yet it did not benefit you at all, and the earth became tight for you in spite of its vastness, then you turned back.

26. Then Allah sent His reassurance to His messengers and the believers and sent soldiers whom you did not see and punished those who rejected (the truth), and that is the reward of those who reject.

27. Then afterwards Allah turns back to whom He pleases, and Allah is forgiving and merciful.

28. Oh you believers, the idolaters are unclean, so they must not come near the sacred mosque after this year they were given, and if you fear poverty, then soon will Allah enrich you from His favours if He pleases, for Allah is knowing and wise.

29. Fight those amongst the people of the book who do not believe in Allah nor in the last day and do not hold sacred what Allah and His messenger have forbidden and do not observe the true religion until they personally pay the protection tax and are submissive.

30. And the Jews claimed 'Uzayr to be the son of Allah and the Christians claimed the Messiah to be the son of Allah; they say with their mouths what resembles the claims of those who denied (the truth) before - may Allah destroy them, where to are they diverted?

31. They took their rabbis and monks as lords besides Allah and the Messiah, the son of Maryam (Mary), and they were only commanded to serve a single god, there is no god but Him, glorified is He above what they assign as partners.

32. They want to extinguish the light of Allah with their talk, and Allah refuses all but to complete His light even if the rejecters resent it.

33. He is who sent His messenger with the guidance and the religion of truth to make it manifest over all religion even if the idolaters resent it.

34. Oh you believers, many of the rabbis and monks consume the wealth of people by deception and divert from the way of Allah, and those who hoard gold and silver and do not spend it in the way of Allah, announce to them a painful punishment.

35. On the day it will be heated in the fire of hell, then their foreheads and sides and backs will be branded with it: this is what you hoarded for yourselves, so taste what you hoarded.

36. The number of months with Allah is twelve months by the decree of Allah on the day He created the heavens and the earth, four of which are sacred. This is the upright religion, so do not wrong yourselves in them, and fight the idolaters as a whole just like they fight you as a whole and know that Allah is with those who beware (of Him).

37. Substitution is an increase in rejection by which those who reject (the truth) lead astray, making it permissible one year and sacred another in order to preserve the number Allah has made sacred but permit what Allah has prohibited. Their bad deeds appeal to them, and Allah does not guide people who reject (the truth).

38. Oh you believers, what is the matter with you that when you are told to move out in the way of Allah you cling to the earth? Are you content with the life of this world over the hereafter? But the provision of the life of this world is only little compared to the hereafter.

39. If you don't move out, He will punish you with a painful punishment and replace you with other people and you will not harm Him at all, and Allah is able to do anything.

40. If you do not help him, then Allah already helped him when those who reject (the truth) expelled him as one of two, when they both were in the cave and he said to his companion: do not worry, Allah is with us; then Allah sent His reassurance to him and assisted him with soldiers you do not see and made the word of those who reject (the truth) the lowest, and the word of Allah is the highest, and Allah is mighty and wise.

41. Move out, lightly and heavily equipped, and strive with your wealth and your lives in the way of Allah, that is better for you if you knew.

42. Had it been a nearby opportunity and short journey, they would have followed you, but the distance was too far for them, and they will swear by Allah that had we been able we would have gone out with you; they destroy themselves and Allah knows that they are lying.

43. Allah lets you off, but why did you excuse them before those who were truthful were apparent to you and you knew the liars?

44. Those who believe in Allah and the last day do not ask to be excused by you from fighting with their wealth and lives, and Allah knows those who beware (of Him).

45. Only those ask to be excused by you who do not believe in Allah and the last day and their hearts are in doubt and they waver in their uncertainty.

46. And if they wanted to go out, they would have prepared for it, but Allah dislikes dispatching them and prevented them and it was said: stay with those who stay behind.

47. If they went out with you, they would only add disorder and cause disturbance for you, seeking corruption for you, and there are those amongst you who listen to them, and Allah knows the wrongdoers.

48. They already sought corruption before and caused problems for you until the truth came and Allah's command became manifest whilst they resented it.

49. And amongst them is he who says: excuse me and do not tempt me; they have already fallen into temptation and hell surrounds those who reject (the truth).

50. If good befalls you, it hurts them, and if an affliction befalls you, they say: we already took care of our affairs, and they turn away rejoicing.

51. Say: nothing will befall us except what Allah has written for us, He is our protector and on Allah let the believers rely.

52. Say: do you wait for other than one of two good things for us, whereas we wait for you that Allah afflicts you with a punishment from Him or by our hands, so wait, we wait with you.

53. Say: spend obediently or reluctantly, it will not be accepted of you, for you were sinful people.

54. And the only thing which prevented them from their spending being accepted of them is that they rejected Allah and His messenger and do not pray except lazily and do not spend except grudgingly.

55. So do not be amazed by their wealth nor by their children, for Allah wants to punish them with it in the life of this world and let them die whilst rejecting (the truth).

56. And they swear by Allah that they are from amongst you when they are not from amongst you, but they are people who cause division.

57. If they find a refuge or a hide-out or an entry, they will turn to it hastily.

58. And amongst them is who blames you regarding charity, so if they are given of it, they are content, and if they are not given of it, they are annoyed.

59. And if (only) they were content with what Allah and His messenger gave them and said: Allah is enough for us, Allah and His messenger will give us from His favours, we look in hope to Allah.

60. Charity is only for the poor and the needy and those engaged in its administration and those whose hearts are to be reconciled and to free slaves and for those in debt and in the way of Allah and for the traveller, an obligation from Allah, and Allah is knowing and wise.

61. And amongst them are those who insult the prophet and say he listens (to anyone), say: he listens to what is good for you; he believes in Allah and believes the believers and is a mercy to those who believe amongst you. And for those who insult the messenger of Allah is a painful punishment.

62. They swear by Allah to you in order to please you, but Allah and

His messenger have more right to be pleased if they were believers.

63. Did they not know that for whoever opposes Allah and His messengers there is the fire of hell where he will remain, that is the tremendous disgrace.

64. The pretenders are concerned that a Surah should be revealed about them to disclose to them what is in their hearts, say: make fun, for Allah will expose what you are concerned about.

65. And if you asked them, they would say: we were only joking and playing. Say: did you make fun of Allah and His signs and His messenger?

66. Don't make excuses, you already rejected (the truth) after having believed. If We let a party of you off, We will punish another party because they were sinners.

67. The pretenders, men and women, are of one kind, they command wrongdoing and forbid good conduct and are tight-fisted. They abandoned Allah, so He abandoned them. The pretenders are the sinful.

68. Allah has promised the pretenders, men and women, and the rejecters the fire of hell where they will remain, it is enough for them, and Allah has cursed them and for them is a lasting punishment.

69. Like those before you who were stronger than you in power and had more wealth and children, then they enjoyed their share, then you enjoyed your share just like those before you enjoyed their share, and you joked just like they joked; those - their deeds are wasted in this world and the hereafter, and those are the losers.

70. Did not the account of those before them reach them, of the people of Nuh (Noah) and 'Ad and Thamud and the people of Ibrahim (Abraham) and the inhabitants of Madyan (Midian) and the overturned places? Their messengers came to them with clear proofs, so Allah did not wrong them but they wronged themselves.

71. And the believers, men and women, are protectors of each other, they command good conduct and forbid wrongdoing and keep up prayer and give Zakat and obey Allah and His messenger, those - Allah will have mercy on them, for Allah is mighty and wise.

72. Allah has promised the believers, men and women, gardens through which rivers flow, where they will remain, and good habitations in the gardens of Eden, and contentment from Allah is even greater, that is the ultimate success.

73. Oh prophet, fight the rejecters and the pretenders and be tough with them, and their abode is hell, a bad destination.

74. They swear by Allah that they didn't say it, but they already said a word of rejection and rejected (the truth) after their submission (Islam) and were distressed about what they couldn't reach, and they only resented that Allah and His messenger made them rich from His favours, then if they repent it will be better for them, and if they turn away, Allah promises them a painful punishment in this world and the hereafter and they will have no protector or helper on earth.

75. And amongst them is who made a promise to Allah that if He gives us from His favours we will give charity and be of the righteous.

76. Then when He gave them from His favours they withheld it and turned away in opposition.

77. So He rewarded them with pretence in their hearts until the day they meet Him on account of having broken their promise and having been liars.

78. Did they not know that Allah knows their secrets and their secret meetings and that Allah knows the unseen.

79. Those who insult the believers who give generously as well as those who only find the bare minimum, so they make fun of them, Allah makes fun of them, and a painful punishment awaits them.

80. Ask forgiveness for them or do not ask forgiveness for them - if you asked forgiveness for them seventy times, still Allah will not forgive them. That is because they rejected Allah and His messenger and Allah does not guide sinful people.

81. Those who were left behind rejoiced at their idleness in opposition to the messenger of Allah and disliked to strive with their wealth and their lives in the way of Allah and said: do not move out in the heat; say: the fire of hell is more severe in heat, if they only understood.

82. So let them laugh a little and cry a lot as a punishment for what they used to commit.

83. Then when Allah returns you to a party of them and they ask your permission to go out, then say: you will never go out with us and never fight an enemy with me, you were content with sitting idle the first time, so stay with those who are left behind.

84. And never pray over any of them who died and do not stand at his grave, for they rejected Allah and His messenger and died whilst sinful.

85. And do not be amazed by their wealth or their children, for Allah wants to punish them with it in this world and let them die whilst rejecting (the truth).

86. And when a Surah was revealed (saying): believe in Allah and strive with His messenger, the capable amongst them asked to be excused by you and said: leave us to stay with those who stay behind.

87. They were content to be with those left behind and their hearts were sealed so that they do not understand.

88. But the messenger and those who believe with him strove with their wealth and their lives and for those there is all the good and those are the successful.

89. Allah promised them gardens through which rivers flow, where they will remain, and this is the great success.

90. And those who were excused amongst the desert Arabs came to be excused, and those who denied Allah and His messenger stayed behind. A painful punishment will afflict the rejecters amongst them.

91. There is no blame on the weak nor the ill nor those who do not find anything to spend if they are sincere to Allah and His messenger. There is no way against those who do good, and Allah is forgiving and merciful.

92. Nor against those to whom, when they came to be equipped by you, you said: I do not find anything to equip you with. They turned away with their eyes overflowing with tears in sadness that they did not find anything to spend.

93. There is only a way against those who ask to be excused by you whilst they are rich and who were content to be with those left behind, and Allah sealed their hearts, yet they do not know.

94. They offer excuses to you when you return to them, say: do not make excuses, we will not believe you, Allah has already informed us about your affairs, and Allah will see your work, and (so will) His messenger, then you will be returned to the One who knows the unseen and the apparent and He will inform you of what you used to do.

95. They will swear to you by Allah when you return to them so that you leave them alone. Leave them alone, for they are filth and their abode is hell as a punishment for what they used to commit.

96. They swear to you to be content with them, yet if you were content with them, still Allah is not content with sinful people.

97. The desert Arabs are the severest in rejection and pretence and most likely not to know the limits which Allah has revealed to His messenger, and Allah is knowing and wise.

98. And amongst the desert Arabs is he who considers what he spends as a loss and waits for things to change for you; things will change for the worse for them, and Allah listens and knows.

99. And amongst the desert Arabs is he who believes in Allah and the last day and considers what he spends as a means to get closer To Allah and to obtain the messenger's blessings; indeed it is a means of closeness for them - Allah will enter them into His mercy, for Allah is forgiving and merciful.

100. And the earliest of the emigrants and the helpers and those who followed them with good conduct, Allah is content with them and they are content with Him, He has promised them gardens through which rivers flow where they will remain forever, that is the ultimate success.

101. And amongst those desert Arabs around you and amongst the inhabitants of al-Madinah there are pretenders, they persist in pretending, you do not know them, We know them, We will punish them twice, then they will be returned to a severe punishment.

102. And there are others who acknowledge their sins, who have mixed good and bad deeds, maybe

Allah will turn back to them, for Allah is forgiving and merciful.

103. Take charity from their wealth to cleanse and purify them with it and pray for them, for your prayer is a reassurance for them, and Allah listens and knows.

104. Did they not know that Allah accepts the repentance from His servants and receives charity and that Allah is the One who accepts repentance and gives mercy?

105. And say: work, then Allah and His messenger and the believers will see your work, and you will be returned to the One who knows the unseen and the apparent, then He will inform you of what you used to do.

106. And there are others who look forward to Allah's command whether He punishes them or turns back to them, and Allah is knowing and wise.

107. And those who adopted a mosque intending harm and rejection and division between the believers and as a staging post for those who fought Allah and His messenger before - they will swear that we only wanted good, and Allah is a witness that they are liars.

108. Do not ever stand in it (in prayer), for a mosque which was founded on awareness (of Allah) from the first day has more right that you should stand in it; in it are men who love to keep clean and Allah loves those who keep clean.

109. Is not he better who founds his building on the awareness of Allah and for His contentment than he who founds his building on the edge of a falling cliff and it falls into the fire of hell with him, and Allah does not guide wrongdoing people.

110. The building they have constructed will not stop causing unease in their hearts unless their hearts are broken, and Allah is knowing and wise.

111. Allah has bought from the believers their lives and their wealth so that they would have paradise; they strive in the way of Allah and kill and are killed. This is a binding promise upon Him in the Torah and the Injil and the Qur'an. And who keeps His promise better than Allah, so rejoice in the deal you have made, and that is the ultimate success.

112. Those who repent, worship, praise, fast, bow down, prostrate, command good conduct and forbid wrongdoing and observe the limits of Allah, and give good news to the believes.

113. It is not fit for the prophet and those who believe to ask forgiveness for the idolaters, even if they are their relatives, after it has become clear to them that they are inmates of hell-fire.

114. And when Ibrahim (Abraham) asked forgiveness for his father it was only on account of a promise he had given him, then when it became clear to him that he was an enemy to Allah, he renounced it, for Ibrahim (Abraham) was devoted to prayer and gentle.

115. And it is not fit for Allah to let people go astray after He guided them until He has made clear to them what they should beware of, for Allah knows everything.

116. To Allah belongs the kingdom of the heavens and the earth, He gives life and death, and you have besides Allah no protector nor helper.

117. Allah has already turned back to the prophet and the emigrants and the helpers who followed him in an hour of difficulty after the hearts of a group amongst them almost swerved, then He turned back to them, for He is lenient with them and merciful.

118. And to the three who were left behind until the earth became tight for them although it is spacious, and their own selves became tight for them and they considered that there was no refuge from Allah except towards Him, then He turned back to them so that they repent, for Allah is the One who accepts repentance and gives mercy.

119. Oh you believers, beware of Allah and be with the truthful.

120. It is not fit for the inhabitants of al-Madinah or the desert Arabs around them that they should stay behind the messenger of Allah nor that they should consider themselves above him. That is because no thirst nor exhaustion nor hunger afflicts them in the way of Allah nor do they go anywhere to enrage the rejecters (of the truth) nor gain anything from the enemy but a good deed is written for them on account of it, for Allah does not waste the reward of those who do good.

121. Nor do they spend anything small or large in expenditure nor cross a valley but it is written in their favour so that Allah rewards them for the best they did.

122. And the believers should not all move out as one. A party of every group amongst them should keep back to study the religion and warn their people when they return to them so that they are on guard.

123. Oh you believers, fight those of the rejecters who are nearby and let them find you determined and know that Allah is with those who beware (of Him).

124. And when a Surah is revealed there is amongst them he who says: whom does this increase in belief?, but as for the believers it increases them in belief and they rejoice.

125. And as for those in whose hearts is a disease, it increases them in disgrace upon their disgrace and they die whilst rejecting (the truth).

126. Do they not consider that they are being tested every year once or twice, then they do not repent nor remember.

127. And when a Surah is revealed, some look at others: does anybody see you? Then they turn away. Allah turns away their hearts because they are people who do not understand.

128. A messenger from amongst you has already reached you. Your concerns bear heavy on him, he is eager for your benefit and lenient and merciful to the believers.

129. And if they turn away, say: Allah is sufficient for me, there is no god but Him, on Him I rely and He is the Lord of the great throne.

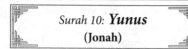

Surah 10: **Yunus**
(Jonah)

In the name of Allah,
the Owner and Giver of Mercy

1. Alif Lam Ra. These are the signs of the wise book.

2. Are people astonished that We revealed to a man amongst them to warn people and give good news to the believers that the truthfulness they have sent before will be theirs with their Lord? The rejecters (of the truth) say: this is a plain magician.

3. For your Lord is Allah who created the heavens and the earth in six days, then He rose to the throne, He manages all affairs, there is nobody who could intercede with Him except after His permission, that is Allah your Lord, so serve Him, do you not take heed?

4. To Him is the return of all of you, a true promise of Allah, for He initiates creation then repeats it in order to reward those who believe and do good work in justice; and those who reject (the truth), for them is a drink of boiling water and a painful punishment on account of having rejected (the truth).

5. He is who made the sun a torch and the moon a light and decreed for it stages so that you know the number of years and counting; Allah only created this with truth, He explains the signs to people who know.

6. For in the alternation of night and day and in what Allah has created in the heavens and earth are signs for people who beware (of Allah).

7. Those who do not look forward to meeting Us and are content with the life of this world and are at ease in it and those who are careless about our signs,

8. Their abode is the fire on account of what they used to commit.

9. Those who believe and do good work, their Lord guides them by their belief; rivers flow amongst them in gardens of blessing.

10. Their call there is glory be to You oh Allah, and their greeting there is peace, and their final call is praised is Allah the Lord of all worlds.

11. And if Allah hastened for people the bad as they ask to hasten the good, their term would have already been decided, so leave those who do not look forward to meet Us to get lost in their rebellion.

12. And if harm afflicts man he calls Us on his side or sitting or standing, then when We remove the harm from him, he moves on as if he never called Us regarding any harm that afflicted him. In this way appeals to the wasteful what they used to.

13. And We already destroyed generations before you when they did wrong and their messengers came to them with clear proofs but they did not believe; this is how we reward sinful people.

14. Then We made you successors on earth after them to see how you behave.

15. And when Our clear signs are recited to them those who do not look forward to meet Us say: bring us a different reading (Qur'an) or change it. Say: It is not fit for me to change it by myself, I only follow what has been revealed to me, for I fear, if I disobeyed my Lord, the punishment of a tremendous day.

16. Say: if Allah willed, I would not have recited it to you nor would He have acquainted you with it, for I already stayed amongst you quite some time before that, so do you not think?

17. So who is more wrong than he who invents a lie against Allah or denies His signs: the sinful will not succeed.

18. And they serve besides Allah what does not harm them nor benefit them and say these are our intercessors with Allah. Say: Are you informing Allah of what He does not know in the heavens and on earth? Glorified and exalted is He above what they assign as partners.

19. And people were a single community, then they differed, and if a word from your Lord had not gone before, it would have been decided between them what they differed on.

20. And they say, why is not a sign sent down to him from his Lord? So say: the unseen is Allah's, so wait, I am waiting with you.

21. And when We make people taste a mercy after harm afflicted them, they have a scheme against Our signs. Say: Allah is faster in scheming, for our messengers write down what you scheme.

22. He is who carries you on land and on sea until, once you are in the ship - and We let them travel with a good wind and they rejoice about it - a strong wind follows it and the waves come to them from everywhere and they think they are surrounded by them, they call Allah with a sincere religion: if You rescue us from this, we will be amongst the grateful.

23. Then when We rescue them, they transgress on earth without right. Oh people, your transgression is against yourselves, the provision of this world, then your return is to Us and We inform you of what you used to do.

24. The likeness of the life of this world is like water which We send down from the sky and the plants of the earth, of which people and cattle eat, absorb it until when the earth has adorned itself and looks appealing and its inhabitants think that they have power over it, Our command comes to it at night or in the day and We make it cut down as it if had not existed the day before. This is how we explain the signs to people who reflect.

25. And Allah calls to the abode of peace and guides whom He pleases to a straight path.

26. To those who do good will be good and more than that and neither impurity nor humiliation will cover their faces. Those are the inhabitants of the gardens where they will remain.

27. And those who committed bad, their reward will be a comparable bad and humiliation will cover them. They will have no protector against

Allah, as if a piece of dark night was wrapped around their faces. Those are the inmates of the fire where they will remain.

28. And on the day We gather them all, then say to the idolaters: stay where you are, you and your idols, then we part them, and their idols say: you did not serve us.

29. Allah is sufficient as witness between us and you that we were unaware of your worship.

30. There catches up with each soul what it left behind and they are returned to Allah their true master, and what they used to invent deserted them.

31. Say: who provides for you from the sky and the earth, or who controls hearing and eyesight, and who brings out the living from the dead and brings out the dead from the living, and who manages all affairs? Then they will say: Allah, so say: will you not then beware (of Him)?

32. For that is Allah, your true Lord, and what is there after the truth except error, so where to are you diverted?

33. This is how your Lord's word about the sinful comes true that they do not believe.

34. Say: is there any amongst your idols who initiates the creation then repeats it? Say: Allah initiates the creation then repeats it, so where to are you deceived?

35. Say: is there any amongst your idols who guides to the truth? Say: Allah guides to the truth. Has then He more right to be followed who guides to the truth or he who cannot guide except if he is guided? So what is the matter with you, how do you judge?

36. And most of them only follow assumptions, but assumptions are of no value compared to the truth, for Allah knows what they do.

37. And this Qur'an has not been invented by someone besides Allah, but it is a confirmation of what came before it and an explanation of the book without doubt from the Lord of all worlds.

38. Or do they say he invented it? Say: bring a comparable Surah and call on whomever you can besides Allah if you are truthful.

39. But they deny what they do not grasp in knowledge and whose outcome has not yet reached them. Likewise those before them denied, so see what the consequence was like for the wrongdoers.

40. And amongst them is he who believes in it, and amongst them is he who does not believe in it, and your Lord knows the corrupt best.

41. And if they deny you, then say: for me is my work and for you is your work, your are free of what I do and I am free of what you do.

42. And amongst them are those who listen to you, can you make the deaf hear even if they do not understand?

43. And amongst them are those who look at you, can you guide the blind even if they do not see?

44. Allah does not wrong people at all, but people wrong themselves.

45. And on the day He gathers them as if they had stayed only an hour of the daytime, acknowledging each other; those will have already lost who denied the meeting with Allah and were not guided.

46. And whether We let you see some of what We promise them or take you away, to Us is their return, then Allah is a witness of what they do.

47. And every community has its messenger, then when their messenger comes, it is decided between them in justice and they are not wronged.

48. And they say: when will this promise happen if you are truthful?

49. Say: I do not master harm for myself nor benefit except for what Allah wills. For every community is a fixed term; then when its term is up, they will not delay it for an hour nor speed it up.

50. Say: Have you considered if His punishment reached you at night or in the day, what of it would the sinful be in a hurry for?

51. Are you then going to believe in it when it happens? Now, but you were already in a hurry for it?

52. Then will be said to the wrongdoers: taste the punishment of eternity. Are you being rewarded for anything but what you committed?

53. And they ask you: is this true? Say: Sure, by my Lord, this is true and you will not escape.

54. And if every wrongdoing soul had what is on earth, it would give it up, and they start regretting when they see the punishment, and it will be decided between them in justice and they will not be wronged.

55. For sure to Allah belongs whatever is in the heavens and on earth, for sure Allah's promise is true, but most of them don't know.

56. He gives life and death and to Him you are returned.

57. Oh people, an admonition has already reached you from your Lord and a healing for what is within you and a guidance and mercy for the believers.

58. Say: Let them rejoice with the favours of Allah and His mercy, that is better than what they amass.

59. Say: Have you considered the provision Allah has sent you, then you turn it into forbidden and lawful. Say: Did Allah give you permission or did you invent against Allah?

60. And what do those who invent a lie against Allah think about the day of resurrection? Allah is full of generosity towards people, but most of them give no thanks.

61. And there is no condition you are in nor do you recite any of the Qur'an nor do you carry out any work except We are witnesses when you engage in it; and not the weight of a tiny speck on earth nor in the sky escapes your Lord, and there is nothing smaller or greater than that but it is in a clear book.

62. For sure the allies of Allah shall have no fear nor worry.

63. Those who believe and constantly beware (of Allah).

64. For them is good news in the life of this world and the next; Allah's words will not be changed - that is the ultimate success.

65. And do not worry about what they say. All power belongs to Allah, He listens and knows.

66. For sure to Allah belongs whoever is in the heavens and whoever is on earth, and those who call on associates besides Allah only follow assumptions and only guess.

67. He is who made the night for you to rest in and the day to see. In that are signs for people who listen.

68. They say Allah has adopted a son. Glory be to Him. He is self-sufficient. To Him belongs whatever is in the heavens and on earth. Do you have any authority for this or do you say about Allah what you don't know?

69. Say: Those who invent a lie against Allah will not succeed.

70. A provision in this world, then their return is to Us, then We make them taste the severe punishment on account of having rejected (the truth).

71. And recite to them the account of Nuh (Noah) when he said to his people: oh my people, if it burdens you that I stand here and remind you of the signs of Allah, then I rely on Allah, so agree on your affairs and your associates, then let not your affairs

trouble you, but bring it to me and do not hesitate.

72. And if you turn away, then I do not ask any reward from you, for my reward is only upon Allah and I was commanded to be amongst those who submit (as Muslims).

73. Then they denied him, so We rescued him and those with him in the ship and left them behind and drowned those who denied Our signs, see then what the consequence was like for those who had been warned.

74. Then We sent messengers afterwards to their people and they came to them with clear proofs, but they were not going to believe in what they denied before; this is how we imprint on the hearts of the transgressors.

75. Then We sent afterwards Musa (Moses) and Harun (Aaron) to Pharaoh and his leaders with Our signs, but they were arrogant and were a sinful people.

76. And when the truth from Us reached them they said: this is only plain magic.

77. Musa (Moses) said: do you say about the truth when it reaches you that this is magic? The magicians do not succeed.

78. They said: did the two of you come to tempt us away from what we found our fathers doing and you have supremacy on earth? We are not going to believe you.

79. And Pharaoh said: Bring me every knowledgeable magician.

80. And when the magicians came, Musa (Moses) said to them: throw what you can throw.

81. Then when they threw, Musa (Moses) said: what you have brought is magic, Allah will nullify it, for Allah does not make good the work of the corrupters.

82. And He verifies the truth with His words even if the sinners resent it.

83. And nobody believed Musa (Moses) except descendants of his people, out of fear that Pharaoh and their leaders would harm them, for Pharaoh exalted on earth and was amongst the wasteful.

84. And Musa (Moses) said: oh my people, if you believe in Allah then rely on Him if you have submitted (as Muslims).

85. So they said: We rely on Allah, our Lord, do not make us a target for the wrongdoing people.

86. And rescue us by Your mercy from the people who reject (the truth).

87. And We revealed to Musa (Moses) and his brother: dedicate houses in Egypt for your people and make them a prayer location and keep up prayer and give good news to the believers.

88. And Musa (Moses) said: Our Lord, You have given Pharaoh and his leaders adornments and wealth in the life of this world, our Lord, so that they lead astray from Your way. Our Lord, destroy their wealth and harden their hearts, so they do not believe until they see the painful punishment.

89. He said: the prayer of you both has already been answered, so be steadfast and do not follow the way of those who do not know.

90. And We made the Children of Israel cross the sea, then Pharaoh and his soldiers followed them full of envy and enmity, until when he came to drown he said: I believe that there is no god except the one the Children of Israel believe in and I am of those who submit (as Muslims).

91. Now, when you disobeyed before and were of the corrupters?

92. So today we rescue your body to be a sign for those after you, and many people are careless about Our signs.

93. And We provided a good place of settlement for the Children of Israel and provided well for them, and they did not differ until knowledge had reached them. Your Lord will decide between them on the day of resurrection with regard to what they used to differ in.

94. And if you are in doubt about what We have revealed to you, then ask those who read the book before you. The truth from your Lord has already come to you, so be not amongst the doubters.

95. And be not amongst those who deny the signs of Allah, for then you would be of the losers.

96. Those upon whom the word of your Lord has come true do not believe.

97. Even if each sign came to them, until they see the painful punishment.

98. And why was there not a town who believed and its belief benefited it? Except the people of Yunus (Jonah), when they believed We removed from them the punishment of disgrace in this world and gave them provision for a limited time.

99. And if your Lord had willed, everyone on earth would have believed, so are you going to compel people until they believe?

100. And no soul will believe without the permission of Allah, and He places disgrace on those who do not understand.

101. Say: look at what is in the heavens and on earth, but the signs and warnings do not benefit a people who do not believe.

102. So do they wait for anything else but the days of those who passed before them? Say: then wait, I will wait with you.

103. Then We will rescue Our messengers and those who believed; the rescue of the believers is thus a duty upon Us.

104. Say: Oh people, if you are in doubt about my religion, then I do not serve those whom you serve besides Allah but serve Allah who will take you away (in death), and I have been commanded to be of the believers.

105. And to turn your face to this religion sincerely devoted and be not amongst the idolaters.

106. And do not call besides Allah on what does not benefit you nor harm you, for if you did that, you would be amongst the wrongdoers.

107. And if Allah afflicts you with harm, then nobody can remove it but Him, and if He wills good for you, then nothing prevents His favour; He gives it to whom He pleases of His servants, and He is the forgiving and merciful.

108. Say: oh people, the truth has reached you from your Lord, so who wants to be guided, then he is guided for his own good, and who goes astray, then he goes astray against himself, and I am not a guardian over you.

109. And follow what has been revealed to you and be patient until Allah judges, and He is the best of judges.

Surah 11: **Hud**

In the name of Allah, the Owner and Giver of Mercy

1. Alif Lam Ra. A book whose verses have been pronounced, then explained, by One wise and informed.

2. That you should serve none but Allah, for I am a warner and bringer of good news to you from Him.

3. And that you should ask your Lord for forgiveness, then repent to Him, He will provide you with a good provision until a fixed date and gives everyone who gives favours His favours. And if you turn away, then I fear for you the punishment of a great day.

4. To Allah is your return and He is able to do anything.

5. But they bend over to hide from Him, yet when they wrap around their clothes He knows what they conceal and what they disclose, for He knows what is kept inside.

6. And there is no creature on earth but its provision is upon Allah, and He knows its place of rest and its destination, everything is in a clear book.

7. And He is who created the heavens and the earth in six days and His throne was upon water, so that He would test you as to who of you is best in work, and if you say: you are going to be raised after death, those who reject (the truth) will say: this is only plain magic.

8. And if We delayed the punishment for them to a fixed term, they would say: what holds it back? For sure, on the day it reaches them, it will not leave them and that which they used to make fun of will overcome them.

9. And if We make man taste mercy from Us, then take it away from him, he is despondent and ungrateful.

10. And if We make him taste a blessing after a harm touched him, he would say: the bad things have left me, for he rejoices and brags.

11. Except those who are patient and do good work, for those is forgiveness and a great reward.

12. So should you abandon some of what has been revealed to you and be uptight because they say: why has not a treasure been sent down to him or did an angel come with him? You are only a warner, and Allah is guardian over everything.

13. Or do they say he invented it? Say: bring ten comparable invented Surahs and call on whomever you can besides Allah if you are truthful.

14. Then if they do not respond to you, know that it has been revealed with the knowledge of Allah and that there is no god but Him, so will you submit (as Muslims)?

15. Whoever wants the life of this world and its adornment, We fully repay them their work in it and they will not be short-changed in it.

16. Those are the ones who have nothing but the fire in the hereafter and whatever they have produced is wasted and what they did is futile.

17. Unlike him who follows a clear proof from his Lord, recited by a witness from Him, and before it the book of Musa (Moses) as a guide and mercy. Those believe in it, and whoever rejects it of the allies, the fire is his abode. So do not be in doubt about it, it is the truth from your Lord, but most people do not believe.

18. And who is more wrong than he who invents a lie against Allah? They will be presented before their Lord and the witnesses will say: these lied about their Lord, may Allah's curse be upon the wrongdoers.

19. Those who divert from the way of Allah and desire it to be crooked and they reject the hereafter.

20. Those will not escape on earth and will not have any protectors besides Allah. The punishment will be multiplied for them. They were unable to listen and unable to see.

21. They are the ones who have lost themselves, and what they used to invent deserted them.

22. Without fail they will be the losers in the hereafter.

23. Those who believe and do good work and are humble before Allah, they belong in the garden (of paradise), where they will remain.

24. The likeness of the two groups is like the blind and deaf and the seeing and hearing, are they alike? Do you not take heed?

25. And We already sent Nuh (Noah) to his people that I am a clear warner for you.

26. That you should serve none but Allah, for I fear for you the punishment of a painful day.

27. And the leaders who rejected (the truth) from his people said: we see in you only a human like us and we see that apparently only those most despised by us follow you, and we do not see any superiority of you over us but think you are liars.

28. He said: oh my people, have you considered that I am following a clear proof from my Lord and He has given me mercy from Him and you are blind to it? Are we going to impose it on you whilst you resent it?

29. And oh my people, I do not ask you for any wealth for it, for my reward is only upon Allah, and I am not going to send away those who believe, for they will meet their Lord , but I see you as an ignorant people.

30. And oh my people, who will help me against Allah if I were to send them away? Do you not reflect?

31. And I do not say to you that I have the treasures of Allah nor that I know the unseen, nor do I say that I am an angel, nor do I say to those who are despicable in your eyes that Allah will not give them any good - Allah knows best what is within them - for then I would be amongst the wrongdoers.

32. They said: Oh Nuh (Noah) you have argued with us and extended the argument with us, so bring us what you promise us if you are truthful.

33. He said: Allah will bring it to you if He wills, and you will not escape.

34. And my advice will not benefit you if I wanted to advise you if Allah wills to let you go astray; He is your Lord and to Him you return.

35. Or do you they say he has invented it? Say: if I invented it, then my sin is upon me and I am free of your sins.

36. And it was revealed to Nuh (Noah) that none of his people would believe besides who already believed, so do not be sad about what they do.

37. And construct the ship under Our supervision and in accordance with Our revelation and do not plead with Me about the wrongdoers, for they will drown.

38. And he constructed the ship, and each time leaders of his people passed him, they made fun of him. He said: if you make fun of us, then we will make fun of you like you made fun of us.

39. Then soon will you know whom a humiliating punishment will reach and who will deserve a lasting punishment.

40. Until when Our command came and the earth burst open We said: carry on it a pair of each kind and your family, except on whom the word has gone before, and those who believe, and only a few believed with him.

41. And he said: ride on it; in the name of Allah be its journey and arrival, for my Lord is indeed forgiving and merciful.

42. And it sailed with them on waves like mountains, and Nuh (Noah) called his son who was at a distance: oh my son, ride with us and do not be with those who reject (the truth).

43. He said: I will seek shelter on a mountain to protect me against the water. He said: there is no protection today against the command of Allah except for whom He has mercy. And the wave came between them and he was of those drowned.

44. And it was said: oh earth, swallow your water, and oh sky, desist, and the water receded and the matter was decided and it came to rest on Judi, and it was said: away with the wrongdoing people.

45. And Nuh (Noah) called his Lord and said: my Lord, my son is of my family and Your promise is true and You are the wisest of judges.

46. He said: oh Nuh (Noah), he is not of your family for his deeds are not good, so do not ask Me of what you have no knowledge of, I admonish you not to be of the ignorant.

47. He said: my Lord, I seek refuge in You that I should ask you what I have no knowledge of, and if You do not forgive me and have mercy on me, I will be of the losers.

48. It was said: oh Nuh (Noah), disembark with peace from Us and blessings upon you and on the communities which are with you; and there are communities whom we will give provision and then a painful punishment will touch them from Us.

49. This is information We reveal to you from the unseen, neither you nor your people knew it before, so be patient, the outcome is for those who beware (of Allah).

50. And to 'Ad (We sent) their brother Hud, saying: oh my people, serve Allah, you have no god other than Him, you are only inventing things.

51. Oh my people, I do not ask you for a reward for it, for my reward is only upon the One who originated me, do you not understand?

52. And oh my people, ask forgiveness from your Lord, then repent to Him, He will send abundant rain from the sky for you and increase your existing strength, and do not turn away sinful.

53. They said: oh Hud, you have not brought us a clear proof, and we are not going to abandon our idols on your say so, and we do not believe you.

54. We can only say that some of our idols have harmed you with evil. He said: I have Allah as a witness, so do witness that I am free of what you associate,

55. Besides Him, so plot altogether against me, then do not hesitate.

56. For I rely on Allah, my Lord and your Lord. There is no creature which He does not control, for my Lord is on a straight path.

57. Then if you turn away, then I have already conveyed what I was sent to you with, and my Lord will replace you with another people and you will not harm Him at all, for my Lord is keeper of everything.

58. And when Our command came, We rescued Hud and those who believed with him through mercy from Us and rescued them from an unrelenting punishment.

59. And that is 'Ad, they disputed the signs of their Lord and disobeyed His messengers and followed the command of every obstinate tyrant.

60. And they are followed by a curse in this world and on the day of resurrection, indeed 'Ad rejected their Lord, so away with 'Ad the people of Hud.

61. And to Thamud (We sent) their brother Salih, saying: oh my people, serve Allah, you have no other god than Him, He brought you into existence from the earth and established you on it, so ask Him for forgiveness, then repent to Him, for my Lord is near and responding.

62. They said: oh Salih, we had hopes for you before that; are you stopping us from serving what our fathers served whilst we are in severe doubt of what you call us to?

63. He said: oh my people, have you considered that I follow a clear proof from my Lord and He has given me mercy from Him? Then who will help me against Allah if I disobey Him, so you would only increase me in loss.

64. And oh my people, this is the she-camel of Allah as a sign for you, so let her eat on Allah's earth and do not touch her with harm or a nearby punishment will take you.

65. Then they bled her to death, so he said: enjoy your homes for another three days, that is an unfailing promise.

66. Then when Our command came, We rescued Salih and those who believed with him through mercy from Us from the disgrace of that day, for your Lord is strong and mighty.

67. And the roar overtook them and they came to lie prostrate in their homes.

68. As if they had not prospered in them, indeed Thamud rejected their Lord, so away with Thamud.

69. And Our messengers came to Ibrahim (Abraham) with the good news, saying: peace. He said: peace, and did not hesitate to bring a roasted calf.

70. Then when he saw that their hands did not reach for it he became weary of them and felt afraid of them. They said: fear not, we were sent to the people of Lut (Lot).

71. And his wife was standing there and laughed, so We gave her good news of Ishaq (Isaac) and after Ishaq Ya'qub (Jacob).

72. She said: woe to me, am I to give birth whilst I am an old woman and this my husband is an old man? This is strange.

73. They said: are you astonished by the command of Allah? The mercy of Allah and His blessings be upon you members of the household, for He is the owner of praise and glory.

74. Then when the fright left Ibrahim (Abraham) and he received the good news, he argued with Us about the people of Lut (Lot).

75. For Ibrahim (Abraham) was gentle, devoted to prayer, repenting.

76. Oh Ibrahim (Abraham), leave it, your Lord's command has already come and a punishment will reach them which cannot be averted.

77. And when Our messengers reached Lut (Lot), he was concerned and uneasy about them and said: this is a troublesome day.

78. And his people came rushing to him and had before been doing bad deeds. He said: oh my people, here are my daughters, they are purer for you, so beware of Allah and do not disgrace me with my guests, is there not a righteous man amongst you?

79. They said: you know that we have no right to your daughters and you know what we want.

80. He said: If only I had strength over you or could resort to a strong support.

81. They said: oh Lut (Lot), we are messengers of your Lord, they will not get to you, so travel with your family part of the night and let not any of them look back, except your wife, what afflicts them will afflict her. Their promised time is the morning. Is not the morning near?

82. And when Our command came We turned them upside down and rained upon them hardened stones in quick succession.

83. Embossed by your Lord; and it is not far from (these) wrongdoers.

84. And to Madyan (Midian) (We sent) their brother Shu'ayb (Jethro), saying: oh my people, serve Allah, you have no god other than Him, and do not give short measure and weight, for I see you are doing well, and I fear for you the punishment of a day surrounding all.

85. And oh my people, give full measure and weight in fairness and do not withhold from people their rights and do not spread corruption on earth.

86. What Allah leaves you is better for you if you are believers, and I am not a guardian over you.

87. They said: oh Shu'ayb (Jethro), does your prayer command you that we should abandon what our fathers served or that we should do with our wealth as we please? You are indeed the gentle and righteous.

88. He said: oh my people, have you considered that I follow a clear proof from my Lord and He has provided me with good provision from Him? And I do not want to differ from you in what I have forbidden you, I only want improvement as much as I can and my success is only from Allah, I have relied on Him and repent to Him.

89. And oh my people, let not disagreement with me mislead you so that the like of what afflicted the people of Nuh (Noah) or the people of Hud or the people of Salih afflicts you, and the people of Lut (Lot) are not far from you.

90. And ask forgiveness from your Lord, then repent to Him, for my Lord is merciful and loving.

91. They said: oh Shu'ayb (Jethro), we do not understand much of what you say and we see that you are weak amongst us, and if it were not for your clan, we would have stoned you, and you have no power over us.

92. He said: oh my people, is my clan more powerful to you than Allah and you have already turned your backs on Him? My Lord surrounds what you do.

93. And oh my people, do your work as you do, I do my work. Soon you will know whom a humiliating punishment will reach and who is the liar. Wait and see, I am waiting with you.

94. And when Our command came, We rescued Shu'ayb (Jethro) and those who believed with him through mercy from Us, and the roar overtook the wrongdoers and they came to lie prostrate in their homes.

95. As if they had not prospered in them, so away with Madyan (Midian) as Thamud have been done away with.

96. And We sent Musa (Moses) with Our signs and a clear authority.

97. To Pharaoh and his leaders who followed Pharaoh's command, and Pharaoh's command was not righteous.

98. He leads his people on the day of resurrection and delivers them to the fire, what a bad delivery location.

99. And they are followed by a curse in this world and on the day of resurrection, what a bad gift to receive.

100. This is information from the towns We tell you about, some (still) stand and some have been knocked down.

101. And We did not wrong them but they wronged themselves, and their idols whom they served besides Allah did not benefit them at all when the command of your Lord came, and they only increased them in ruin.

102. That is how your Lord's grasp was when He overtook the towns whilst they did wrong, for His grasp is painful and severe.

103. In that is indeed a sign for whoever fears the punishment of the hereafter. That is a day when all people will be gathered and that is a day which will be witnessed.

104. And We only delay it for a limited term.

105. On the day it comes, no soul will speak except with His permission, and amongst them will be the distressed and the happy.

106. As for those who are distressed, they will be in the fire. In it will be sighing and wailing for them.

107. They will remain in it as long as the heavens and the earth last except for what your Lord wills, for your Lord does what He wills.

108. And as for those who are happy, they will be in the garden (of paradise) where they will remain as long as the heavens and the earth last except for what your Lord wills, a gift which will not diminish.

109. So have no doubt about what these serve: they only worship like their fathers worshipped before, and We will pay them their full share unreduced.

110. And We already gave Musa (Moses) the book, then they differed about it, and if a word from your Lord had not gone before, it would have been decided between them, and they are indeed in severe doubt about it.

111. And your Lord will pay each in full for their work, for He is informed of what they do.

112. So continue straight as you were commanded, together with whoever repents with you, and do not transgress, for He sees what you do.

113. And do not lean towards those who do wrong, so the fire would touch you and you would not have any protector besides Allah, then you would not be helped.

114. And keep up prayer at the ends of the day and a part of the night, for

good deeds take away bad deeds, that is a reminder for those who pay heed.

115. And be patient, for Allah does not waste the reward of those who do good.

116. So why were there not amongst the generations before you those who insisted on prohibiting corruption on earth, except a few amongst them whom We rescued? Those who did wrong pursued the luxury they had and were sinful.

117. And your Lord would not destroy a town due to wrongdoing whilst its inhabitants improve.

118. And if your Lord willed, He would have made all people a single community, but they will not stop differing.

119. Except those whom your Lord has mercy on, and for that He created them, and the word of your Lord has come to pass that I will fill hell with Jinn and people altogether.

120. And in each case We tell you information about the messengers to strengthen your heart with it, and in this the truth and an admonishment and reminder for the believers has reached you.

121. And say to those who do not believe: do your work as you do, we are working.

122. And wait, we are waiting.

123. And to Allah belongs the unseen of the heavens and the earth and all affairs return to Him, so serve Him and rely on Him, and your Lord is not unaware of what you do.

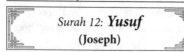

Surah 12: **Yusuf**
(Joseph)

In the name of Allah,
the Owner and Giver of Mercy

1. Alif Lam Ra. These are the signs of the clear book.

2. We revealed it as an Arabic Qur'an so that you might understand.

3. We tell you the most beautiful of stories We have revealed to you in this Qur'an, whilst you were unaware before.

4. When Yusuf (Joseph) said to his father, oh my father, I saw eleven stars and the sun and the moon, I saw them prostrate to me.

5. He said: oh my son, do not tell your dream to your brothers, so they will plot against you, for the devil is an open enemy to man.

6. And this is how your Lord will choose you and teach you of the interpretation of meanings and complete His favours upon you and upon the family of Ya'qub (Jacob) just as He completed it upon your fathers before, Ibrahim (Abraham) and Ishaq (Isaac), for your Lord is knowing and wise.

7. In Yusuf (Joseph) and his brothers there are signs for those who enquire.

8. When they said: Yusuf (Joseph) is dearer to our father than us whilst we are a large group. Our father is indeed in clear error.

9. Kill Yusuf (Joseph) or drive him away to some (distant) land, after which your father will only look at you and you will be righteous people.

10. A speaker amongst them said: do not kill Yusuf (Joseph) but throw him into the depth of the well, some caravan will pick him up, if you have to do it.

11. They said: oh our father, what is the matter with you that you do not trust us with Yusuf (Joseph) whilst we are sincere to him?

12. Send him with us tomorrow to enjoy himself and play and we will look after him.

13. He said: It worries me that you should take him and I fear the wolf will eat him whilst you are careless about him.

14. They said: If the wolf should eat him and we are a large group, then we would be losers.

15. And when they took him and agreed to place him in the depths of the well, We revealed to him that you will inform them of this affair of theirs when they will not realise.

16. And they came to their father in the evening crying.

17. They said: oh our father, we went ahead and left Yusuf (Joseph) with our provisions, then the wolf ate him. And you will not believe us even if we are truthful.

18. And they brought false blood on his shirt. He said: but you have made something up yourselves, so (I will have) beautiful patience and ask Allah for help against what you make out.

19. And a caravan came, so they sent their water carrier and he lowered his bucket. He said: good news, there is a boy, and they hid him as merchandise, and Allah has knowledge of what they do.

20. And they sold him for the price of only a few Dirham in order to get rid of him.

21. And the one who bought him from Egypt said to his wife: look after him well. Perhaps he will benefit us or we will adopt him as a son. This is how We plotted for Yusuf (Joseph) on earth and in order to teach him of the interpretation of meanings, and Allah prevails in His affairs but most people don't know.

22. And when he attained his full strength We gave him the ability to judge and knowledge, and this is how We reward those who do good.

23. And she in whose house he was desired him and locked the doors and said: come here! He said: Allah forbid, my master has provided me with excellent lodgings and the wrongdoers will not succeed.

24. And she was attracted to him and he was attracted to her had he not considered the evidence of his Lord. This was so that We would turn evil and indecency away from him, for he was of Our sincere servants.

25. And they ran to the door and she tore his shirt from behind and they found her master near the door. She said: what other punishment is there for him who wants bad for your family

except that he should be imprisoned or some other painful punishment?

26. He said: she desired me, and a witness of her family gave evidence that if his shirt is torn from the front then she is telling the truth and he is lying.

27. And if his shirt is torn from behind, then she is lying and he is telling the truth.

28. Then when they saw his shirt torn from behind he said: this is one of your plots, the plots of you women are enormous.

29. Yusuf (Joseph), let go of this, and you (woman) seek forgiveness for your sin, for you are guilty.

30. And some women in the town said: the wife of the governor desired her male servant, he has infatuated her with love, we consider her clearly astray.

31. Then when she heard of their plot she sent for them and prepared for them couches and gave each of them a knife and said: come out to them. Then when they saw him they praised him and cut their hands and said: Allah save us, this is not a man but this is a noble angel!

32. She said: so that is what you blamed me about and I did desire him but he resisted, and if he does not do what I command him, he will be imprisoned and will be of those humiliated.

33. He said: my Lord, prison is dearer to me to what they call me to, and if You do not divert their plot from me, I will give in to them and be of the ignorant.

34. So his Lord responded to him and diverted their plot from him, for He hears and knows.

35. Then it seemed right to them after seeing the signs that they should imprison him for some time.

36. And two male servants entered the prison with him. One of them said: I saw myself press wine, and the other said: I saw myself carry bread on my head of which the birds ate. Tell us its interpretation for we consider you amongst those who do good.

37. He said: I will tell you its interpretation before your provision of food will come to you. This is of what my Lord has taught me, for I left the religion of people who do not believe in Allah and who reject the hereafter.

38. And I followed the religion of my fathers Ibrahim (Abraham), Ishaq (Isaac) and Ya'qub (Jacob). We would not associate anything with Allah. That is of the favours of Allah upon us and upon mankind, but most people give no thanks.

39. Oh my companions in prison, are different masters better or Allah, the one and dominant?

40. You only serve besides Allah names which you have invented, you and your fathers. Allah has not sent any authority for it. The judgement is Allah's alone, He has commanded that you serve only Him, that is the upright religion but most people do not know.

41. Oh my companions in prison, as for one of you, he will pour wine for his master, and for the other, he will be crucified and the birds will eat from his head. Decided is the matter about which you asked.

42. And he said to the one of them who thought he would be saved: mention me to your master, but the devil made him forget to make mention to his master, so he stayed in prison a number of years.

43. And the king said: I saw seven fat cows being eaten by seven skinny cows and seven green ears of grain and another dried batch. Oh leaders, explain me my visions if you understand visions.

44. They said: confused dreams, and we do not know the interpretation of dreams.

45. And the one of the two who was saved and remembered after some time said: I will inform you of the interpretation of it, so send me.

46. Yusuf (Joseph), oh you truthful one, explain to us seven fat cows being eaten by seven skinny ones and seven green ears of grain and another dried batch, so that I can return to the people so that they will know.

47. He said: sow for seven years and what you harvest, leave it on its ear but for a little which you eat.

48. Then seven severe years will come after that which will consume what you have stored up for them but for a little which you keep safe.

49. Then a year will come after that during which people receive rain and press (grapes and oil).

50. And the king said: bring him to me, and when the messenger came to him he said: go back to your master and ask him about the women who cut their hands, for my master knows their plots.

51. He said: what do you women have to say about when you desired Yusuf (Joseph)? They said: Allah save us, we do not know any bad about him. The wife of the governor said: now the truth has come out, I desired him and he is telling the truth.

52. This so that that he would know that I did not deceive him secretly and that Allah does not guide the plot of the treacherous.

53. And I do not call myself blameless, for the soul commands evil except when my Lord has mercy, for my Lord is forgiving and merciful.

54. And the king said: bring him to me, I will keep him for myself, and when he spoke to him he said: you are influential and safe with us today.

55. He said: place me over the storehouses of the earth, for I am a knowledgeable keeper.

56. And this is how We established Yusuf (Joseph) on earth to settle wherever he liked. We grant Our mercy to whom We will and do not waste the reward of those who do good.

57. And the reward of the hereafter is even better for those who believe and beware (of Allah).

58. And the brothers of Yusuf (Joseph) came and entered upon him, and he recognised them whilst they did not recognise him.

59. And when he issued them with their supplies he said: bring me your brother from your father, do you not see that I give full measure and am one of the best hosts?

60. But if you do not bring him, then you will have no measure with me and you shall not come close.

61. They said: we will implore our father, we will certainly do that.

62. And he said to his male servants: place their merchandise in their luggage so that they find it when the return to their family so that they come back.

63. Then when they got back to their father they said: oh our father, measure has been denied to us, so send our brother with us, we will obtain measure and we will look after him.

64. He said: shall I entrust him to you like I entrusted his brother to you before? But Allah is the best keeper and the most merciful of all.

65. And when they opened their provisions they found their merchandise had been returned to them. They said: oh our father, what more do we want? This our merchandise has been returned to us, and we will provide for our family and add the measure of a camel, that will be an easy measure.

66. He said: I will not send him with you until you give me a promise by

Allah that you will bring him back unless you are surrounded. Then when they gave him their promise he said: Allah is a guardian over what we say.

67. And he said: oh my children, do not enter from a single gate but enter from different gates, and I will not benefit you in any way against Allah, for the judgement is only for Allah, on Him I have relied, and on Him let all those rely who want to rely on something.

68. And when they entered from where their father had commanded them, it did not benefit them in any way against Allah but was a need within Ya'qub (Jacob) which he discharged, and he had much knowledge of what We taught him, but most people don't know.

69. And when they entered upon Yusuf (Joseph), he took his brother in his care and said: I am your brother, so don't be sad about what they used to do.

70. Then when he issued their supplies he placed the drinking cup in his brother's luggage, then a caller announced: oh you travellers, you are thieves.

71. They said, whilst they approached them: what are you missing?

72. They said: we are missing the king's measuring cup, and whoever brings it will have a camel's load, and I am going to claim it.

73. They said: by Allah, you know that we did not come to cause corruption on earth and that we are not thieves.

74. They said: and what is the punishment if you are lying?

75. They said: the punishment is that whoever it is found in his luggage, he will be the punishment, this is how we punish the wrongdoers.

76. Then he started with their bags before the bag of his brother, then he took it out of the bag of his brother. This is how We plotted for Yusuf (Joseph): he could not have taken his brother under the king's rule unless Allah willed. We raise in stages whom We will, and above everybody with knowledge is He who knows.

77. They said: if he stole, then his brother stole before, but Yusuf (Joseph) kept it inside and did not disclose it to them. He said: you are in a bad situation, and Allah knows best what you make out.

78. They said: oh governor, he has a very old father, so take one of us in his place, we consider you of those who do good.

79. He said: Allah forbid that we take except him whom we found our belongings with, otherwise we would be wrongdoers.

80. And when they gave up on him, they drew apart to consult. Their eldest said: don't you know that your father has already taken your promise by Allah and how you abandoned Yusuf (Joseph)? So I will not leave this land until my father gives me permission or Allah judges for me and He is the best of judges.

81. Go back to your father and say: oh our father, your son has stolen, and we only witness that which we know and we are not keepers of the unseen.

82. So ask the town we were in and the caravan that we came with, and we are telling the truth.

83. He said: but you have made something up yourselves, so (I will have) beautiful patience. Maybe Allah will bring them all to me, for He is knowing and wise.

84. And he turned away from them and said: oh my grief over Yusuf (Joseph), and his eyes turned white from suppressed worry.

85. They said: by Allah, you will not stop remembering Yusuf (Joseph) until you ruin your health or will be destroyed.

86. He said: I only disclose my anguish and worry to Allah and I know from Allah what you do not know.

87. Oh my sons, go and look for Yusuf (Joseph) and his brother and do not despair of relief from Allah, for only people who reject (the truth) despair of relief from Allah.

88. And when they entered upon him they said: oh governor, hardship has afflicted us and our family and we have come with meagre merchandise, but give us full measure and give us charity, for Allah rewards those who give charity.

89. He said: Do you know what you did with Yusuf (Joseph) and his brother when you were ignorant?

90. They said: are you actually Yusuf (Joseph)? He said: I am Yusuf (Joseph) and this is my brother. Allah has bestowed His favours on us, for if someone bewares (of Allah) and is patient, then Allah does not waste the reward of those who do good.

91. They said: by Allah, Allah has preferred you over us and we were guilty.

92. He said: you will not be blamed today, may Allah forgive you, and He is the most merciful of all.

93. Go with this shirt of mine and throw it onto my father's face, he will become sighted (again), and come to me with all your family.

94. And when the caravan broke up (on arrival) their father said: I notice the scent of Yusuf (Joseph) even if you contradict me.

95. They said: by Allah, you are in your old aberration.

96. Then when the bringer of good news came, he threw it over his face and he became sighted again. He said: did I not say to you that I know from Allah what you do not know?

97. They said: oh our father, ask forgiveness for our sins, for we were guilty.

98. He said: I will ask my Lord for forgiveness, for He is the forgiving and merciful.

99. And when they entered upon Yusuf (Joseph) he took care of his parents and said: enter Egypt safely if Allah wills.

100. And he raised his parents on to the throne and they fell prostrate before him, and he said: oh my father, this is the outcome of my earlier dream, Allah has made it come true and He was good to me when He brought me out of prison and brought you from the desert after the devil came between me and my brothers, for my Lord is kind to whom He pleases, for He is the knowing and wise.

101. My Lord, you have given me a kingdom and taught me the interpretation of meanings, originator of the heavens and the earth, You are my protector in this world and the hereafter, take me away whilst having submitted (as Muslim) and join me with the righteous.

102. This is of the information of the unseen which We reveal to you, and you were not with them when they agreed on their affairs and schemed.

103. And most people do not believe even if you are eager.

104. And you do not ask them for a reward for it, for it is only a reminder for all the worlds.

105. And how many signs in the heavens and on earth do they pass by and turn away from them?

106. And most of them do not believe in Allah without being idolaters.

107. Are they then safe that a disaster from the punishment of Allah reaches them or the hour reaches them suddenly without them realising it?

108. Say: this is my way, I call to Allah based on my understanding - I and those who follow me, and glorified is Allah, and I am not of the idolaters.

109. And before you We did not send anything else but men from the people of the towns to whom We revealed. Do they not travel on the earth so they see what the outcome was like for those before them? And the abode of the hereafter is better for those who beware (of Allah), do you not understand?

110. Until when the messengers gave up and thought they had already been denied, Our help reached them, so We rescue whom We will, and Our distress is not averted from the sinful people.

111. In their story is a lesson for those with understanding. It is not an invented tale but a confirmation of what came before it and an explanation of everything and a guidance and mercy for people who believe.

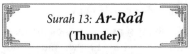

Surah 13: *Ar-Ra'd*
(Thunder)

In the name of Allah,
the Owner and Giver of Mercy

1. Alif Lam Ra. These are the verses of the book, and what has been revealed to you from your Lord is the truth but most people do not believe.

2. Allah is who raised the heavens without visible support, then He rose to the throne and subjugated the sun and the moon, each floats for a fixed term, He manages all affairs, He explains the signs so that you would be certain about meeting your Lord.

3. And He is who expanded the earth and placed on it stabilisers and rivers and placed pairs of every fruit on it; He makes the night cover the day, indeed in this are signs for people who reflect.

4. And on earth there are continuous sections and gardens of grapes and grain and palms, with and without clusters, which are fed from the same water, and We made some taste better than others. In that are signs for people who understand.

5. And if you are astonished, then astonishing is their saying: when we are dust, shall we be in a new creation? Those are the ones who reject their Lord and those are the ones with cuffs around their necks and those are the inmates of the fire where they will remain.

6. And they ask you to hasten the bad before the good, and examples have gone before them, and your Lord is full of forgiveness to people in spite of their wrongdoing, and your Lord is severe in punishment.

7. And those who reject (the truth) say: why has not a sign been sent to him from his Lord? But you are only a warner, and for every people is a guide.

8. Allah knows what every female carries and what the wombs retain less or longer, and everything is measured with Him.

9. The One who knows of the unseen and the apparent, the great and elevated.

10. It makes no difference whether any of you keeps his speech secret or proclaims it and whether he hides at night or is visible in the day.

11. He is accompanied ahead of him and behind him by those who guard him by the command of Allah, for Allah does not change the condition of a people until they change their own condition, and if Allah wants harm for people, then it cannot be averted, and they have no protection besides Him.

12. He is who shows you the lightning in fear and hope and makes the heavy clouds grow.

13. And the thunder glorifies His praise and the angels out of fear of Him, and He strikes down with it whom He pleases, yet they argue about Allah and He is severe in response.

14. He has the right to be called, and those whom they call besides Him do not answer them any more than someone who stretches out his hands to the water will thereby make it reach his mouth, and the calling of those who reject (the truth) is only in error.

15. And to Allah prostrates whoever is in the heavens and on earth obediently and reluctantly as well as their shadow in the mornings and afternoons.

16. Say: who is the Lord of the heavens and the earth? Say: Allah. Say: So do you take protectors besides Him who have no power to benefit or harm themselves? Say: Are the blind and the sighted alike or are the darkness and the light alike? Or do they assign to Allah associates who created like His creation so that the creation looks similar to them? Say: Allah is the creator of everything and He is the one and dominant.

17. He sends water down from the sky and its force makes it flow through channels, then the torrent carries a foam on top, and of what they melt in the fire to fashion into jewellery or utensils there is a similar foam, this is how Allah points out truth and falsehood. So as for the foam, it is carried away as useless, and as for what benefits people, it remains on the ground; this is how Allah coins examples.

18. For those who respond to their Lord is good, and those who do not respond to Him, even if they had all that is on earth and the like again, they would give it up. For those is a bad reckoning and their abode is hell, a bad place to be.

19. Is then the one who knows that what has been revealed to you from your Lord is the truth like the one who is blind? Only those with understanding remember.

20. Those who uphold their agreement with Allah and do not break their promise.

21. And those who keep together what Allah commanded to keep together and fear their Lord and are afraid of a bad reckoning.

22. And those who are patient seeking the presence of Allah and keep up prayer and spend of what We have provided them with secretly and openly and repel a bad deed with a good one, for those is the final abode.

23. The gardens of Eden which they and whoever of their parents and partners and children who were righteous will enter and, the angels will enter upon them from every gate.

24. Peace be with you on account of your patience, so blessed is the final abode.

25. And those who break their agreement with Allah after it has been entered into and who cut off what Allah commanded to be kept together and who cause corruption on earth - those will be cursed and theirs is a bad abode.

26. Allah expands the provision for whom He pleases and tightens it, and they rejoice in the life of this world, yet the life of this world is only a short provision compared to the hereafter.

27. And those who reject (the truth) say: why has not a sign been sent down to him from his Lord? Say: Allah lets go astray whom He pleases and guides to Him who turns (to Him).

28. Those who believe and their hearts find reassurance in the remembrance of Allah, for in the remembrance of Allah do hearts find reassurance.

29. Those who believe and do good work, for them are delights and a good return.

30. This is how We sent you to a community which was preceded by other communities to recite to them that which We revealed to you, yet they reject the Merciful. Say: He is my Lord, there is no god but Him, on Him I rely and to Him I repent.

31. And even if it were a Qur'an by which the mountains were moved or the earth was cut up or the dead would speak - but all affairs belong to Allah. Do not the believers know that if Allah willed He could have guided all of mankind? But those who reject (the truth) will continue to be afflicted by misfortune on account of what they have produced or it will get close to them until Allah's promise comes, for Allah does not break His promise.

32. And messengers before you were made fun of, so I gave those who reject (the truth) some time, then I overtook them, and how was My punishment!

33. So who maintains every soul in line with what it has earned? And they assign to Allah associates. Say: name them! Or will you inform Him of what He does not know on earth, or is it just talk? But their scheming and diversion from the way of Allah appeals to those who reject (the truth), and when Allah lets somebody go astray, there is no guide for him.

34. Theirs is a punishment in this world, and the punishment of the hereafter is even heavier and they have no defence against Allah.

35. The likeness of the garden (of paradise) promised to those who beware (of Allah): rivers flow through it, its food and shade are permanent. This is the outcome for those who beware, and the outcome for those who reject (the truth) is the fire.

36. And those whom We have given the book rejoice in what Allah has revealed to you. And of the allies are those who dislike some of it. Say: I have been commanded to serve Allah and not to associate anyone with Him. I call on Him and repent to Him.

37. And this is how We revealed to you wisdom in Arabic, and if you were to follow their desires after the knowledge you have received, you would have neither protector nor defence against Allah.

38. And We sent messengers before you and gave them wives and children, and no messenger was able to bring a sign except by permission of Allah. Everything is ordained in time.

39. Allah obliterates or confirms what He wills, and with Us is the original book.

40. And whether We show you some of what We have promised them or take you away, your duty is the delivery (of the message) and Ours the reckoning.

41. Do they not consider how We reduce the earth from its ends? And Allah judges, there is no appeal against His judgement, and He is swift in counting.

42. And those before them already schemed, and with Allah is all their scheming, He knows what every soul earns, and those who reject (the truth) will know for whom the final outcome is.

43. And those who reject (the truth) say: you are no messenger. Say: Allah is sufficient as a witness between me and you as well as those who have knowledge of the book.

Surah 14: **Ibrahim**
(Abraham)

In the name of Allah,
the Owner and Giver of Mercy

1. Alif Lam Ra. A book which We have revealed to you to bring people out of darkness to the light by permission of their Lord - onto the path of the mighty and praiseworthy;

2. Allah, to whom belongs what is in the heavens and what is on earth, and woe to those who reject (the truth) due to a severe punishment.

3. Those who prefer the life of this world over the hereafter and divert from the way of Allah and desire it to be crooked, those are in extensive error.

4. And We always sent each messenger with the language of his people to make things clear to them, then Allah lets go astray whom He pleases and guides whom He pleases, and He is the mighty and wise.

5. And We previously sent Musa (Moses) with Our signs: take your people out from darkness to the light and remind them of the days of Allah, for in that are signs for everyone who is patient and grateful.

6. And when Musa (Moses) said to his people: remember the blessing of Allah upon you when He rescued you from the family of Pharaoh who afflicted you with bad punishment and slaughtered your sons and spared your women, which was a tremendous test from your Lord for you.

7. And when your Lord announced: if you are grateful, I give you increase, and if you reject, then My punishment is severe.

8. Musa (Moses) said: if you and all those who are on earth reject (the truth), then Allah is independent and praiseworthy.

9. Did not the account of those before reach you, the people of Nuh (Noah), 'Ad and Thamud and those after them? Only Allah knows them. Their messengers came to them with clear proofs but they bit on their hands and said: we reject what you have been sent with and we are in severe doubt about what you call us to.

10. Their messengers said: are you in doubt about Allah, the originator of the heavens and the earth who calls you to forgive you your sins and give you respite until a fixed date? They said: you are only humans like us. You want to divert us from what our fathers served, so bring us a clear authority.

11. Their messengers said to them: we are only humans like you but Allah blesses whom He pleases of His servants, and we cannot bring you an authority except with the permission of Allah, and on Allah let the believers rely.

12. And how could we not rely on Allah when He has already guided us our ways? And we will endure what you harm us with, and on Allah let all those rely who want to rely on something.

13. And those who rejected (the truth) said to their messengers: we will drive you out of our land unless you return to our religion. Then their Lord revealed to them: We will destroy the wrongdoers.

14. And We will let you live in the land after them. That is for him who fears My presence and fears My promise.

15. And they asked for a decision, and every obstinate tyrant was brought down.

16. After that there is hell and he is given repulsive water to drink.

17. He gulps it down and it is hard to swallow, and death reaches him from everywhere but he does not die, and after that there is an unrelenting punishment.

18. The likeness of those who reject their Lord: their works are like ash stirred up by the wind on a stormy day, they have no control over anything they obtained, that is the extensive error.

19. Do you not see that Allah created the heavens and the earth in truth? If He wills He will remove you and bring a new creation.

20. And that is not difficult for Allah.

21. And they are all presented to Allah, then the weak will say to those who were arrogant: we followed you, so will you avert any of Allah's punishment from us? They will say: if Allah had guided us we would have guided you. It is the same for us whether we are anxious or patient, there is no escape for us.

22. And the devil will say when the matter is decided: Allah promised you a true promise and I promised you but betrayed you, and I had no authority over you except to call you and you responded to me, so do not blame me but blame yourselves, I cannot assist you and you cannot assist me, I already rejected that which you associated me with, for the wrongdoers there is a painful punishment.

23. And those who believed and did good work will be entered into gardens through which rivers flow where they will remain by the permission of their Lord. There greeting in it is peace.

24. Have you not considered how Allah coins the example of a good word like a good tree with its roots firm and its branches into the sky?

25. It produces its fruit every season with the permission of its Lord, and Allah coins the examples for people so that they reflect.

26. And the example of a bad word is like a bad tree with its roots exposed above the earth that has not got established.

27. Allah strengthens the believers with firm speech in this world and the hereafter, and Allah lets the wrongdoers go astray, and Allah does as He pleases.

28. Have you not considered those who replaced the blessing of Allah with rejection and lead their people to the abode of ruin?

29. Hell, which they will enter, a bad place to stay.

30. And they set up partners for Allah to lead astray from His way. Say: enjoy for a while, for your journey is to the fire.

31. Tell My servants who believe to keep up prayer and spend of what We have provided them with secretly and openly before a day reaches them on which there is neither trade nor friendship.

32. Allah is who created the heavens and the earth and sent down water from the sky with which He makes fruit grow as provision for you, and He made the ship of service to you to sail on the sea by His command, and He made the rivers of service to you.

33. And He made the sun and the moon of service to you, both in constant motion, and has made the night and the day of service to you.

34. And He gave you of whatever you asked Him for, and if you were to count the blessings of Allah you could not enumerate them - man is unjust and ungrateful.

35. And when Ibrahim (Abraham) said: my Lord, make this land safe and prevent me and my children from serving idols.

36. My Lord, they have lead many people astray. So if someone follows me he belongs to me, and if he disobeys me, then You are forgiving and merciful.

37. Our Lord, I have settled some of my children in a valley without vegetation near Your sacred house, our Lord, so that they keep up prayer. So make the hearts of people incline to

them and provide them with fruit so that they may be grateful.

38. Our Lord, You know what we conceal and what we disclose, and nothing on earth nor in the sky is concealed from Allah.

39. Allah is praised who granted me in old age Isma'il (Ishmael) and Ishaq (Isaac), for my Lord hears the call.

40. My Lord, make me keep up prayer and my children, our Lord, and accept my call.

41. Our Lord, forgive me and my parents and the believers on the day the reckoning takes place.

42. And don't count on Allah being unaware of what the wrongdoers do, We only give them time until a day when the eyes will be fixed in a stare.

43. Stretching their necks and raising their heads, but they see nothing, and their hearts are feeble.

44. And warn people of a day when the punishment will reach them and those who did wrong will say: our Lord, give us a little bit more time, we will respond to Your call and follow the messengers. Did you not swear previously that there would be no end for you?

45. And you lived in the homes of those who wronged themselves and it was clear to you how We dealt with them and We coined examples for you.

46. They previously came up with their scheme and their scheme is with Allah, even if their scheme would make the mountains disappear.

47. So do not count on Allah breaking His promise to His messengers, for Allah is mighty and vengeful.

48. On the day the earth will be replaced with another earth, and the heavens, and they are presented to Allah the one and dominant.

49. And you see the sinful on that day tied in cuffs.

50. Their clothes are made of tar and the fire covers their faces.

51. So that Allah rewards every soul in line with what it has earned, for Allah is swift in counting.

52. This is a declaration for mankind to be warned with and so that they know that He is one single god, and so that those with understanding remember.

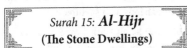

Surah 15: *Al-Hijr*
(The Stone Dwellings)

In the name of Allah,
the Owner and Giver of Mercy

1. Alif Lam Ra. These are the signs of the book and a clear reading (Qur'an).

2. It may happen that those who reject (the truth) wish they were Muslims (who submit).

3. Leave them to eat and enjoy and entertain hope, for soon they will know.

4. Whenever We destroyed a town, there was a known decree for it.

5. No community precedes its fixed term nor do they delay it.

6. And they say: oh you whom the reminder has been revealed to, you are possessed.

7. Why don't you bring us the angels if you are truthful?

8. We only send the angels with the truth, and then they will not be spared.

9. For We have revealed the reminder and We guard it.

10. And before you We sent to the earliest communities.

11. And whenever a messenger came to them, they made fun of him.

12. This is how We let it pass through the hearts of the sinful.

13. They do not believe in it, and the example of the earliest communities has already gone before.

14. And even if We opened a door of heaven for them so they could climb up through it,

15. They would say: our eyesight has been fooled, no we have been bewitched as people.

16. And We place constellations in the sky and made it appealing to look at.

17. And We guarded them against every cursed devil.

18. But if one tries to listen secretly, then a visible shooting star pursues him.

19. And We expanded the earth and placed on it stabilisers and made grow on it of everything in proportion.

20. And We placed on it a livelihood for you and those for whom you don't provide.

21. And whatever there is, its reserves are with Us, and We only send it down with a known measure.

22. And We sent the pollinating wind, then sent down from the sky water to give you to drink from it and it is not you who keep its reserves.

23. And indeed We give life and give death and We are the inheritors.

24. We already know those of you who go ahead and those who stay behind.

25. And your Lord is who will gather them, for He is wise and knows.

26. And We created man from a cement of altered mud.

27. And the Jinn We created before from dry hot fire.

28. And when your Lord said to the angels: I am creating a human from a cement of altered mud.

29. Then when I have fashioned him and breathed into him of My spirit, fall prostate before him.

30. Then all the angels prostrated.

31. Except Iblis (the devil), he refused to be with those who prostrated.

32. He said: oh Iblis, what is the matter with you that you were not with those who prostrated.

33. He said: I am not going to prostrate to a human whom You created from a cement of altered mud.

34. He said: then get out of here, for you are cursed.

35. And the curse will be upon you until the day of repayment.

36. He said: my Lord, then give me time till the day when they are resurrected.

37. He said: then you are given time.

38. Till the day of the time known.

39. He said: my Lord, because You allowed me to stray I shall make it appealing for them on earth and lead them all astray.

40. Except Your sincere servants amongst them.

41. He said: this is a straight path for Me.

42. You have no authority over My servants except those who follow you of the misguided.

43. And hell is the abode for all of them.

44. It has seven gates, for each gate a portion of them will be assigned.

45. Those who beware (of Allah) will be in gardens and springs.

46. Enter safely with peace.

47. And We remove what is within them of ill feeling, they accept each other happily as brothers.

48. No hardship afflicts them there and they will not be expelled from there.

49. Inform My servants that I am the forgiving and merciful.

50. And that My punishment is a painful punishment.

51. And inform them of the guests of Ibrahim (Abraham).

52. When they entered upon him and said: peace. He said: we are afraid of you.

53. They said: don't be afraid, for we give you good news of a knowledgeable boy.

54. He said: do you give me good news after old age has afflicted me? On what account do you give me good news?

55. They said: we give you good news based on the truth, so do not be of those who despair.

56. He said: and who would despair of the mercy of his Lord except those in error?

57. He said: So what have you come for, oh messengers?

58. They said: we were sent to the sinful people.

59. Except the family of Lut (Lot), we will rescue all of them.

60. Except his wife, we have decided that she is of those who stay behind.

61. Then when the messengers came to the family of Lut (Lot),

62. He said: you are unfamiliar people.

63. They said: but we have come to you with what they were in doubt of.

64. And we have reached you with the truth and we tell the truth.

65. So travel with your family part of the night and follow behind them and let not any of them look back and go to where you have been commanded.

66. And We decided for him in this matter that the remainder of these will be cut off in the morning.

67. And the people of the town came rejoicing.

68. He said: these are my guests, so do not dishonour me.

69. And beware of Allah and do not disgrace me.

70. They said: did we not forbid you contact with everybody else?

71. He said: these are my daughters if you have to do it.

72. By your life, they were blind in their intoxication.

73. Then the roar overtook them at sunrise.

74. Then We turned them upside down and rained upon them hardened stones.

75. In this are indeed signs for those who observe.

76. And they are on an established route.

77. In this is indeed a sign for the believers.

78. And the inhabitants of the woodlands were wrongdoers.

79. So we took revenge on them and they are clearly visible ahead.

80. And the inhabitants of the stone dwellings denied the messengers.

81. And they brought them Our signs, but they turned away from them.

82. And they carved out safe homes from the mountains.

83. Then the roar overtook them in the morning.

84. And what they had gathered did not benefit them.

85. And We did not create the heavens and the earth and what is between them except with truth, and the hour will come, so leave them nicely alone.

86. For your Lord is the knowledgeable creator.

87. And We gave you seven of the repeated (verses) and the great Qur'an.

88. Do not extend your eyes to the enjoyment We have given some couples of them and do not worry about them and give comfort to the believers.

89. And say: I am the clear warner.

90. Like We sent to those who like to cause division.

91. Those who are selective about the Qur'an.

92. By your Lord, We will ask them all.

93. About what they used to do.

94. So declare what you have been commanded with and turn away from the idolaters.

95. We suffice you against those who mock you.

96. Those who claim there is another god with Allah, they will soon know.

97. And We know that what they say makes you uptight.

98. So glorify the praise of your Lord and be of those who prostrate.

99. And serve your Lord until the inevitable reaches you.

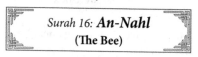

Surah 16: **An-Nahl**
(The Bee)

In the name of Allah,
the Owner and Giver of Mercy

1. Allah's command has come, so do not be in a hurry for it, glorified and exalted is He above what they assign as partners.

2. He sends the angels with the revelation by His command to anyone He pleases of His servants: issue a warning that there is no god but I, so beware of Me.

3. He created the heavens and the earth in truth, exalted is He above what they assign as partners.

4. He created man from a sperm, then he argues openly.

5. And the cattle He created which provide warmth and benefits for you and you eat of them.

6. And there is beauty in them for you when you bring them in and take them out to graze.

7. And they carry your burden to a land you could not have reached without personal exertion, for your Lord is lenient and merciful.

8. And the horses, the mules and the donkeys for you to ride and as an adornment, and He creates what you do not know.

9. And Allah directs the way, and some deviate from it, and had He willed, He would have guided all of you.

10. He is who sent water from the sky which produces drinking water and trees amongst which you let them graze.

11. With it He makes grain grow for you and olives, palms and grapes and every kind of fruit; in that is a sign for people who reflect.

12. He made the night and day of service to you, and the sun, moon and stars are put into service by His command; in that are signs for people who understand.

13. And what He has spread for you on earth in different colours; in that is a sign for people who remember.

14. And He is who made the sea of service so that you eat fresh meat from it and extract from it jewellery which you wear. And you see the ship cut through it, so that you seek of His bounty and so that you would be grateful.

15. And He placed stabilisers on earth so it does not shake you up, and rivers and pathways for you to be guided.

16. And as signposts, and by the stars they are guided.

17. Is then He who creates like he who does not create? Do you not reflect?

18. And if you were to count the blessings of Allah you could not enumerate them, for Allah is forgiving and merciful.

19. And Allah knows what you conceal and what you disclose.

20. And those they call besides Allah do not create anything and are themselves created.

21. They are dead, not alive, and they have no idea when they will be raised.

22. Your god is one single god, and those who do not believe in the hereafter, their hearts are averse and they are arrogant.

23. Without fail Allah knows what they conceal and what they disclose, and He does not love the arrogant.

24. And when they were asked what did your Lord reveal, they said: stories of old.

25. So that they carry their burden in full on the day of resurrection and of the burden of those whom they lead astray without knowledge; bad is what they carry.

26. Those before them schemed, then Allah shook their building from its foundations and the roof fell on them from above and the punishment reached them from where they did not realise.

27. Then on the day of resurrection He will humiliate them and say: where are My associates on whose behalf you were in opposition? Those with knowledge will say: today disgrace and troubles is upon those who rejected (the truth).

28. Those whom the angels take away whilst they wronged themselves, and they offer peace, saying: we didn't do anything wrong, but no, Allah knows what you did.

29. So enter the gates of hell to remain there, and bad is the home of the arrogant.

30. And it will be said to those who bewared (of Allah), what did your Lord reveal, they will say: that which is good. There is good for those who did good in this world, and the abode of the hereafter is (even) better, and blessed is the home of those who beware.

31. The gardens of Eden which they will enter; rivers flow through it and they have there whatever they wish. This is how Allah rewards those who beware (of Him).

32. Those whom the angels take away whilst they are good, saying: peace be with you, enter the garden on account of what you used to do.

33. Do they wait that the angels will come to them or the command of your Lord will come? This is what those before them did, and Allah did not wrong them but they wronged themselves.

34. Then their bad deeds caught up with them and what they used to make fun of overcame them.

35. And the idolaters say: if Allah willed we would not have served anything besides Him, neither us nor our fathers, and we would not have sanctified anything besides Him. This is what those before them did, so are the messengers tasked with anything but to convey clearly?

36. And We sent amongst every community a messenger saying: serve Allah and shun the idols. Then amongst them are those whom Allah guides and among them are those for whom error comes true, so travel on the earth, then see what the outcome was like for the deniers.

37. You may desire their guidance, but Allah does not guide those who lead astray, and they have no helpers.

38. And they swear their utmost oaths by Allah that Allah will not raise the dead, but no, it is a binding

promise upon Him, but most people don't know.

39. So that He explains to them what they differed in and so that those who rejected (the truth) will know that they were liars.

40. For whenever We want something, We say to it: Be, then it is.

41. And those who migrate for Allah after having been wronged, We will arrange for them good in this world and the reward of the hereafter will be greater, if they only knew.

42. Those who were patient and relied on their Lord.

43. And before you We only sent men to whom We gave revelation, so ask those who keep the reminder if you don't know.

44. With clear proofs and the scriptures, and We revealed to you the reminder to explain to mankind what has been revealed to them so that they reflect.

45. Are then those who scheme evil safe that Allah should not make the earth swallow them up or bring them the punishment from where they do not realise?

46. Or overtake them whilst they move about, then they will not escape?

47. Or take things away from them? For your Lord is lenient and merciful.

48. Do they not see that whatever Allah created, its shadow turns submissively to the right and left in prostration to Allah?

49. And to Allah prostrates whatever creature is in the heavens and on earth and the angels, and they are not arrogant.

50. They fear their Lord above them and do as they are commanded.

51. And Allah stated: do not take two gods, for He is one single god, so fear only Me.

52. And to Him belongs whatever is in the heavens and on earth, and His is the lasting religion, so would you beware of other than Allah?

53. And whatever blessing you have, it is from Allah, then, when hardship afflicts you, you pray to Him.

54. Then, when He removes the hardship from you, a group of you assign partners to their Lord.

55. So that they reject that which We gave them, then enjoy it for a while, you will soon know.

56. And they assign a share of what We have provided them with to that which they do not know. By Allah, you will be asked about what you invented.

57. And they assign daughters to Allah, glorified is He, and for them is what they desire?

58. And when any of them is given news of a female, his face darkens and he is upset.

59. He hides from the people on account of the news he received: should he keep it in shame or bury it in the ground? Bad is how they judge.

60. For those who do not believe in the hereafter have evil attributes and

Allah has the highest attributes, and He is mighty and wise.

61. And if Allah held people to account for their wrongdoing, He would not leave a single creature (on earth), but He gives them time until a fixed date, then when their date comes, they will not delay it for an hour nor speed it up.

62. And they assign to Allah what they dislike, and their tongues invent lies that they will have the best, without fail they will have the fire and they will be abandoned.

63. By Allah, We sent to communities before you, then the devil made their deeds appeal to them, so he is their protector today, and theirs is a painful punishment.

64. And We only revealed the book to you to explain to them that in which they differed and as a guidance and mercy for people who believe.

65. And Allah sent down from the sky water then revived with it the earth after its death, in that is a sign for people who listen.

66. And there is a lesson for you in the cattle, We give you pure milk to drink from their bellies, originating in between the waste matter and blood, pleasant to drink.

67. And of the fruit of the palm tree and grape vine you obtain intoxicants and good provision, in that is a sign for people who understand.

68. And your Lord inspired the bee to adopt houses in the mountains and the trees and in what they construct.

69. Then eat of every fruit and travel on the paths made available by your Lord. From its belly emerges a syrup of different colours in which there is healing for people. In that is a sign for people who reflect.

70. And Allah created you, then He takes you away, and amongst you is he who is returned to most feeble old age, so that he knows nothing after having had knowledge, for Allah knows and is able.

71. And Allah preferred some of you over others in provision, and those who were preferred do not reject their provision in favour of those in their possession so that they would be equal in it. Do they then dispute Allah's blessings?

72. And Allah gave you partners from amongst yourselves and gave you from your partners children and grandchildren and provided well for you. Do they then believe in falsehood and reject the blessings of Allah?

73. And they serve besides Allah that which does not have control of any provision for them from the heavens or the earth nor could they.

74. So do not coin likenesses for Allah, for Allah knows and you don't know.

75. Allah coins the likeness of a wholly owned slave unable to do anything and him whom We have provided with good provision of which he spends secretly and openly - are they the same? Allah is praised, but most of them don't know.

76. And Allah coins the likeness of two men, one of them dumb, unable to do anything and useless to his master, wherever he directs him, he does not do any good - is he the same as the one who commands justice and is on the straight path?

77. And to Allah belongs the unseen of the heavens and the earth, and the Hour will happen in the blink of an eye or is even closer, for Allah is able to do anything.

78. And Allah brought you out of the wombs of your mothers when you knew nothing and gave you hearing and eyesight and hearts, so that you would be grateful.

79. Do they not consider the birds held suspended in the air of the sky. Only Allah holds them up, for in that are signs for people who believe.

80. And Allah gave you dwellings in your houses and gave you houses from the skins of cattle which are lightweight on the days you depart and camp, and of their wool and fur and hair you obtain furnishings and provision for a while.

81. And Allah gave you shade from what He created and gave you shelter in the mountains and gave you clothing to protect you against the heat and clothing to protect you against harm. Like this He completed His favours for you, so that you would submit (as Muslims).

82. But if they turn away, then your duty is only to convey clearly.

83. They know the favours of Allah, then they negate them and most of them are rejecters (of the truth).

84. And on the day We raise a witness of every community, no excuses will be accepted from those who rejected (the truth) nor will they be allowed redress.

85. And when those who did wrong see the punishment it will not be lightened for them and they will not be spared.

86. And when the idolaters see their idols, they will say: our Lord, these are our idols on whom we called besides You, but they respond to them: you are liars.

87. And that day they will offer submission to Allah and what they used to invent deserted them.

88. Those who reject (the truth) and divert from the way of Allah, We increase the punishment manifold for them because of their corruption.

89. And on the day We raise in every community a witness against them from amongst themselves and bring you as a witness against these - and We revealed to you the book as an explanation of everything and a guidance and a mercy and good news for those who submit (as Muslims).

90. Allah commands justice and goodness and to give to relatives and forbids indecency, wrongdoing and transgression; He admonishes you so that you take heed.

91. And observe your promise to Allah when you have promised and do not violate your oaths after confirming them when you have made Allah a guarantor over you, for Allah knows what you do.

92. And do not be like the woman who completely undoes her knitting after it has been put together, using your oaths as a means of gaining an advantage between you when one community is stronger than the other, for Allah tests you with it in order to explain to you on the day of resurrection what you used to differ in.

93. And had Allah willed, He would have made you a single community, but He lets go astray whom He pleases and guides whom He pleases, and you will be asked about what you did.

94. And do not use your oaths to gain an advantage between you, derailing things after they were established, so you will experience hardship because you diverted from the way of Allah and you will have a severe punishment.

95. And do not sell your promise to Allah for a small price, for what is with Allah is better for you if you knew.

96. What is with you vanishes and what is with Allah remains, and We will give those who have patience their reward in line with the best of what they did.

97. Whoever does good work, male or female, and is a believer, We let them live a good life and give them their reward in line with the best of what they did.

98. And when you read the Qur'an seek refuge in Allah from the cursed devil.

99. For he has no authority over those who believe and rely on their Lord.

100. He only has authority over those who befriend him and who take him as an associate.

101. And when We replace one verse with another, and Allah knows best what He reveals, they say: you invented it. But most of them don't know.

102. Say: the holy spirit revealed it from your Lord in truth to strengthen those who believe and as a guidance and good news for those who submit (as Muslims).

103. We know that they say: a man taught him. The language of the one they refer to is foreign and this is a clear Arabic language.

104. Those who do not believe in the signs of Allah, Allah does not guide them and theirs is a painful punishment.

105. The ones who invent lies are those who do not believe in the signs of Allah, and they are the liars.

106. Whoever rejects Allah after having believed, except for one who has been compelled whilst his heart is content with belief, but whoever openly shows rejection, upon them is anger from Allah and theirs is a severe punishment.

107. This is because they prefer the life of this world to the hereafter and that Allah does not guide people who reject (the truth).

108. Those are the ones whose hearts, hearing and eyesight Allah has sealed, and those are the careless.

109. Without fail they will be the losers in the hereafter.

110. Then your Lord is forgiving and merciful to those who migrated after having been persecuted, then they fought and were steadfast.

111. On the day when every soul will come arguing on its own behalf and every soul will be given in full what it has worked for and they will not be wronged.

112. And Allah coins the likeness of a town which was safe and content, with its provision reaching it freely from everywhere, but they rejected the blessings of Allah, so Allah made them taste the garment of hunger and fear on account of what they used to fabricate.

113. And a messenger from amongst them had previously come to them, but they denied him, so the punishment overtook them whilst they were wrongdoers.

114. So eat of what Allah has provided you with as lawful and good and be grateful for the blessings of Allah if you serve Him.

115. He has only forbidden you carrion, blood and pork and whatever has been consecrated to other than Allah. But whoever is forced without (wilful) transgression or habit, then Allah is forgiving and merciful.

116. And do not state from your own fabrications that this is lawful and this is forbidden in order to invent a lie against Allah, for those who invent a lie against Allah will not succeed.

117. They will have a short provision and a painful punishment.

118. And to the Jews We made unlawful what We previously told you about, and We did not wrong them, but they wronged themselves.

119. Then your Lords is forgiving and merciful to those who do bad out of ignorance, then repent and do good.

120. Ibrahim (Abraham) was a humble leader, sincerely devoted to Allah, and was not of the idolaters.

121. He was grateful for His blessings, and He chose him and guided him on a straight path.

122. And We gave him good in this world, and in the hereafter he is amongst the righteous.

123. Then we revealed to you to follow the religion of Ibrahim (Abraham), sincerely devoted, for he was not one of the idolaters.

124. The Sabbath was imposed on those who differed about it, and your Lord will judge between them on the day of resurrection with regard to what they used to differ in.

125. Call to the way of your Lord with wisdom and beautiful admonition and argue with them through that which is better, for your Lord knows best who strays from His way and He knows best those who are guided.

126. And if you punish, then punish with the like of what you were afflicted with, and if you have patience, then it is better for those who have patience.

127. And be patient, and your patience is only through Allah, and do

not worry about them and do not be uptight about what they are scheming.

128. For Allah is with those who beware (of Him) and those who do good.

Surah 17: *Al-Isra'*
(The Night Journey)

In the name of Allah,
the Owner and Giver of Mercy

1. Glorified is He who took His servant on a journey by night from the sacred mosque (the Ka'bah) to the furthest mosque (al-Aqsa), whose surroundings We blessed, to show him of Our signs, for He listens and sees.

2. And We gave Musa (Moses) the book and made it a guidance for the Children of Israel, (saying): do not take any protector besides Me.

3. They were descendants of those We carried with Nuh (Noah), for he was a grateful servant.

4. And We decreed for the Children of Israel in the book: you will cause corruption on earth twice and will display great arrogance.

5. Then when the first of the promises came We raised against you servants of Ours with terrifying strength and they devastated your homes and it was an accomplished promise.

6. Then We returned to you the advantage over them and helped you with wealth and children and increased you in numbers.

7. If you do good, you do good for your own souls, and if you do bad, then against them; then when the second of the promises came for them to strike your faces and to enter the temple as they had done the first time and to completely destroy what they conquered:

8. Maybe your Lord will have mercy on you, but if you do it again, We will do it again, and we have made hell a prison for those who reject (the truth).

9. This Qur'an guides to that which is more upright and gives good news to the believers who do good that they will have a great reward.

10. And that We have prepared for those who do not believe in the hereafter a painful punishment.

11. And man calls for bad as much as he calls for good, and man is always in haste.

12. And We made the night and the day as two markers and We erased the marker of the night and made the marker of the day visible for you to seek the favours from your Lord and so that you know the number of years and counting, and We arranged everything in detail.

13. And We attached every man's destiny to his neck and produce a book for him on the day of resurrection which he finds laid open.

14. Read your book, it will suffice as your own account against you today.

15. Whoever wants to be guided is guided for his own good and who goes astray, goes astray only against himself, and no-one burdened will carry another's burden, and We never punish until We send a messenger.

16. And if We want to destroy a town, We give authority to its affluent people, then they act immorally in it, so it deserves the decree, and We annihilate it completely.

17. And how many a generation after Nuh (Noah) did We destroy, and your Lord is sufficient to know and see the sins of His servants.

18. Whoever wants the immediate life, We hasten for whoever We please whatever We please in it, then We arrange hell for him in which he burns condemned and rejected.

19. And whoever wants the hereafter and makes an effort for it and is a believer, their effort will be acknowledged.

20. To all of them We extend the gifts of your Lord, and the gifts of your Lord are not held back.

21. See how We prefer some over others, and the hereafter will have even greater grading and preferment.

22. Do not place another god with Allah or you will be left condemned and abandoned.

23. And your Lord decreed that you should serve none but Him and show kindness to parents. If one or both of them reach old age with you, then do not say words of irritation to them nor scold them but speak to them with respect.

24. And give them comfort in humility out of mercy and say: my Lord, have mercy on them as they looked after me when I was little.

25. Your Lord knows best what is within you. If you are righteous, then He is forgiving to those who repent.

26. And give relatives their due and the poor and the traveller and do not be wasteful.

27. For the wasteful are the brothers of the devils, and the devil was ungrateful to his Lord.

28. And if you turn away from them seeking mercy from your Lord which you look forward to, then say words of ease to them.

29. And do not keep your hands tied to your neck nor stretch them out completely, so that you would be left regretful and destitute.

30. For your Lord expands the provision for whom He pleases and tightens it, for He knows and sees His servants.

31. And do not kill your children due to fear of poverty, We provide for them and for you. Killing them is a great sin.

32. And do not go near fornication, for it is indecency and a bad way.

33. And do not kill a soul, which Allah has forbidden, except with right. And if somebody was killed wrongfully, We have given authority to his successor, but let him not be excessive in killing, for he will be helped.

34. And do not approach the wealth of the orphan, except to improve it, until he reaches full strength, and keep promises, for promises will be asked about.

35. And always give full measure and weigh with a level balance, that is better and better in outcome.

36. And do not support anything of which you have no knowledge, for the hearing and eyesight and hearts all will be asked about.

37. And do not walk triumphant on earth, for you cannot cut through the earth nor reach the mountains in height.

38. The evil of all that is disliked by your Lord.

39. This is of the wisdom your Lord revealed to you, and do not place another god with Allah, so that you will be thrown regretful and rejected into hell.

40. Does your Lord then select sons for you and take females from amongst the angels? You make some great claim!

41. We have repeatedly explained things in this Qur'an so that they would reflect, but it only increases their disagreement.

42. Say: if there were other gods with Him as you say, then they would try to contest the owner of the throne.

43. Glorified and exalted is He greatly above what they say.

44. The seven heavens and the earth and whoever is within them glorify Him, and there is nothing which does not glorify His praise, but you do not understand their glorification, for He is gentle and forgiving.

45. And when you read the Qur'an We place between you and those who do not believe in the hereafter a protective barrier.

46. And We place a cover over their hearts, so they do not understand it, and a weight upon their ears, and if you mention your Lord alone in the Qur'an, they turn away in disagreement.

47. We know best what they listen to when they listen to you and when they talk secretly, when the wrongdoers say: you only follow a deranged man.

48. See how they coin likenesses for you and go astray and can't find a way.

49. And they say: when we are bones and dust, are we going to be raised as a new creation?

50. Say: even if you were stones or iron,

51. Or some creation which seems greater to you. Then they will say: who will bring us back? Say: the One who originated you the first time. Then they will shake their heads at you and say: when will it be? Say: maybe it will be soon.

52. On the day He will call you and you will respond with His praise and think that you only stayed a little while.

53. And tell My servants to speak nicely as the devil causes provocation between them, for the devil is a clear enemy to man.

54. Your Lord knows best about you. If He pleases, He has mercy on you or, if He pleases, He punishes you, and We did not send you as a guardian over them.

55. And your Lord knows best who is in the heavens and on earth, and We have favoured some prophets over others and gave Dawud (David) the Psalms.

56. Say: call on those whom you claim besides Him, then they will have no power to remove harm from you nor change it.

57. Those on whom they call compete (themselves) as to who gets closest to Allah and look forward to His mercy and fear His punishment, for the punishment of your Lord is to be guarded against.

58. And there is no town which We will not destroy before the day of resurrection or punish severely, that is recorded in the book.

59. And nothing prevented us from sending signs except that the earliest communities denied them, and We gave Thamud the she-camel as a visible sign but they wronged her, and We only send signs as a warning.

60. And when We told you: your Lord has surrounded the people, and We only made the dream We showed you a test for the people, and the cursed tree in the Qur'an, and We frighten them but it only increases them in major transgression.

61. And when We said to the angels: Prostrate before Adam, they prostrated except for Iblis (the devil); he said: am I going to prostrate before someone You created from clay?

62. He said: Look at the one You have favoured above me, if You give me delay until the day of resurrection I will mislead his descendants except for a few.

63. He said: Go, then whoever follows you among them, hell is your reward, an ample reward!

64. And incite whoever you can among them with your voice and impress on them with your horses and men and share in their wealth and children and promise them, and the devil only promises them an illusion.

65. As for My servants, you have no authority over them, and your Lord is sufficient as protector.

66. Your Lord is the One who makes the ship move on the sea for you so you seek of His favours, for He is merciful to you.

67. And when harm afflicts you on sea, all whom you call upon besides Him disappear, then when He rescues you on to land, you renounce, and man is ungrateful.

68. Are you then safe from Him subjecting you to a landslide or sending a storm against you? Then you will not find a protector for yourselves.

69. Or are you safe that He returns you to it another time and sends against you a raging wind, then drowns you because you rejected (the truth), then you will not find anyone to assist you against Us.

70. And We have honoured the children of Adam and carried them on land and sea and provided well for them and favoured them greatly above many of those We created.

71. On the day We call every people with their leader, then who is given his book in his right hand, those will read their book and will not be wronged the least.

72. And whoever was blind in this world, he will be blind in the hereafter and most astray from the way.

73. And they were about to tempt you away from what We revealed to you so that you would invent something else against us, and then they would have taken you as a friend.

74. And had We not made you firm you would have inclined to them a little.

75. Then We would have made you taste double (the punishment) in life and double in death, then you would not have found for yourself a helper against Us.

76. And they were about to drive you out from the land in order to expel you from it, and then they would not have stayed behind after you except a little.

77. This was the custom for whoever We sent as messenger before you, and you will not find an alteration in Our custom.

78. Keep up prayer from the lowering of the sun to the darkness of night and recite the Qur'an at daybreak, for the recitation of the Qur'an at daybreak is witnessed.

79. And spend some of the night in prayer as an additional effort for you, your Lord might raise you to a recognised position.

80. And say: my Lord, provide me an honourable entrance and an honourable exit, and give me authority and assistance from You.

81. And say: the truth has come and falsehood has vanished, for falsehood always vanishes.

82. And We have revealed of the Qur'an that which is a healing and mercy for the believers, and it only increases the wrongdoers in loss.

83. And when We give blessings to man, he rebels and keeps aside, and when harm afflicts him, he is despondent.

84. Say: let everyone do as he sees fit, for your Lord knows best who is most guided on the way.

85. And they ask you about the Spirit. Say: the Spirit is from the command of my Lord and you were only given very little knowledge.

86. And if We pleased, We would take away that which We revealed to you, then you would not find for yourself a protector against Us.

87. Except by the mercy of your Lord, for His favours upon you are great.

88. And if men and jinn combined to bring similar to this Qur'an, they would not bring anything similar to it, even if they supported each other.

89. And We have explained to people in this Qur'an all kind of examples, but most people refuse anything but rejection.

90. And they say: we will not believe until you make a spring gush out of the earth for us.

91. Or you have a garden of palm trees and grapes and the rivers run through it.

92. Or you make the sky fall on us like you claimed or you bring Allah and the angels in front of us.

93. Or you have a house of gold or ascend in the sky, and we will not believe in your ascent until you bring down to us a book we can read. Say: Glorified is my Lord, am I anything but a man and messenger?

94. And nothing prevents people from believing when the guidance comes to them except that they say: did Allah raise a man as a messenger?

95. Say: if angels walked safely on earth, We would have send upon them from the sky an angel as a messenger.

96. Say: Allah is sufficient as a witness between me and you, for He knows and sees His servants.

97. And whomever Allah guides, he is guided, and whom He lets go astray, you will not find protectors besides Him for them, and We gather them on the day of resurrection on their faces, blind, dumb and deaf. Their abode is hell; whenever it dies out We increase the flame for them.

98. This is the punishment for having rejected Our signs. And they say: when we are bones and dust, are we going to be raised as a new creation?

99. Have they not considered that Allah, who created the heavens and the earth, is capable of creating the like of them? And He has appointed for them a fixed term in which there is no doubt, but the wrongdoers refuse anything but rejection.

100. Say: if you were to own the treasures of your Lord's mercy you would withhold out of fear of poverty, and man is always stingy.

101. We gave Musa (Moses) seven clear signs, so ask the Children of Israel, when he came to them and Pharaoh said to him: Oh Musa (Moses), I think you are deranged.

102. He said: you already know that these were sent by the Lord of the heavens and the earth as clear evidence, and oh Pharaoh, I think you are doomed.

103. And he wanted to drive them out of the land, so We drowned him and all those with him.

104. And after that We said to the Children of Israel: live on the land, then when the final promise comes, We bring you herded together.

105. And We revealed it in truth and in truth it came down, and We only sent you as a bringer of good news and warner.

106. And it is a Qur'an which We have divided so that you recite it to people gradually, and We have sent it down successively.

107. Say: believe in it or do not believe in it, those who were given knowledge before fall prostrate on their faces when it is recited to them.

108. And they say: glorified is our Lord, the promise of our Lord will come to pass.

109. And they fall prostrate on their faces crying, and it increases them in humility.

110. Say: call on Allah or call on the Merciful, whatever you call on, His are the most beautiful names. And do not be loud in your prayer nor hide it, and seek a way between that.

111. And say: Allah is praised who did not adopt a son nor does He have a partner in the kingdom nor does He have an ally from beneath Him, and proclaim His greatness.

Surah 18: *Al-Kahf*
(The Cave)

In the name of Allah, the Owner and Giver of Mercy

1. Allah is praised who revealed to His servant the book and did not place any deviation in it.

2. Upright as a warning of severe harm from Him and good news to the believers who do good work that they will have a beautiful reward.

3. In which they will remain forever.

4. And as a warning to those who say Allah has adopted a son.

5. They have no knowledge of it nor have their fathers, grave is the word that comes out of their mouths, they only speak a lie.

6. So you almost kill yourself with worry pursuing them as they do not believe in this word.

7. For We have placed everything on earth as an adornment for it to test them who of them is best in deeds.

8. And We will turn what is on it into barren soil.

9. Or do you consider the companions of the cave and the inscription amongst Our amazing signs?

10. When the youths sought refuge in the cave and said: our Lord, give us mercy from You and grant us righteousness in our affair.

11. So We sealed their ears in the cave for a number of years.

12. Then We raised them in order to know which of the two groups would best count the duration they stayed.

13. We tell you their account in truth. They were youths who believed in their Lord and We increased them in guidance.

14. And We fortified their hearts when they rose and said: our Lord is the Lord of the heavens and the earth, we shall not call on any god besides Him or we would say something excessive.

15. These our people have adopted gods besides Him. Why do they not bring a clear authority for them? So who is more wrong than he who invents a lie against Allah?

16. And when you part from them and what they serve besides Allah, seek refuge in the cave, your Lord will spread out His mercy for you and grant you ease in your affair.

17. And you see the sun pass to the right of their cave when it rises and avoid them on the left when it sets whilst they are in a gap between. This is from the signs of Allah. Whom Allah guides, he is guided, and whom

He lets go astray, you will not find a guardian for him to lead him right.

18. And you consider them awake whilst they are asleep, and We turn them to the right and the left, and their dog stretches out its paws at the entrance. If you were to stumble across them, you would have run away and been filled with fear of them.

19. And likewise We raised them so that they would ask each other. One of them said: how long did you stay? They said: we stayed a day or part of a day. They said: your Lord knows best how long you stayed, so send one of you with these coins of yours to the town and let him see which food is purest and bring you provision from it, and let him be discrete, so nobody notices you.

20. For if they discover you, they will stone you or return you to their religion and you will never succeed.

21. And like this We had them found out so that they would know that Allah's promise is true and that there is no doubt about the hour when they argued amongst each other about their affair and said: construct a building over them. Your Lord knows best about them. Those who won the argument said: we will erect a prayer place over them.

22. They will say (they were) three and their dog the fourth, and they say five and their dog the sixth, guessing the unseen, and they say seven and their dog the eighth. Say: my Lord knows their number best, only few know about them, so do not openly dispute about them regarding anything that is not apparent nor ask any of them their opinion about them.

23. And do not say about anything that I will do this tomorrow,

24. Except if Allah pleases. And remember your Lord if you forgot and say: maybe my Lord will guide me to greater righteousness than this.

25. And they stayed in their cave for three hundred years, to which they add nine.

26. Say: Allah knows best how long they stayed, His is the unseen of the heavens and the earth, He sees and hears all; they have no protector besides Him nor does He share His judgement with anyone.

27. And recite to them what has been revealed to you from the book of your Lord, there is no changing His words and you will not find a refuge besides Him.

28. And be yourself patient together with those who call their Lord in the mornings and evenings seeking His presence, and do not avert your eyes from them seeking the adornment of this world, and do not obey the one whose heart We have made careless about remembering Us and he follows his desire and his effort is wasted.

29. And say: the truth from your Lord, so whoever pleases, let him believe, and whoever pleases, let him reject, for We have prepared a fire for the wrongdoers which surrounds them completely, and when they ask for drink, they are given to drink water like lava which roasts their faces - what a bad drink and what a bad resting place.

30. Those who believe and do good work, We do not waste the reward of anyone with good deeds.

31. For them are the gardens of Eden through which rivers flow, they are adorned there with bracelets of gold and wear green clothes from silk and brocade, reclining there on couches - what a blessed reward and what a beautiful resting place.

32. And coin for them the likeness of two men: one of them We gave two gardens of grapes and surrounded them with palm trees and placed between them land for cultivation.

33. Each of the gardens produced its fruit without any reduction and We made a river emerge between them.

34. And he had abundance, so he said to his companion, challenging him, I have more wealth than you and stronger numbers.

35. And he entered his garden, doing wrong to himself, saying: I don't think this will ever disappear.

36. And I don't think the hour will happen, and if I were to be brought back to my Lord, I would find even better than this in its place.

37. His companion said to him, challenging him, do you reject the One who created you from soil, then from a sperm, then shaped you into a man?

38. But He is Allah, my Lord, and I do not associate anyone with my Lord.

39. Why did you not say, when you entered your garden, whatever pleases Allah! There is no power except in Allah, if you look at me, I have less wealth and children than you.

40. But maybe my Lord will give me better than your garden and send against it a torrent from the sky so that it becomes washed away soil.

41. Or its water recedes, so you will not be able to find it.

42. And his abundance was rounded up and he wrung his hands regarding what he had spent on it whilst it was abandoned in ruins and said: if only I did not associate anyone with my Lord.

43. And he had no party to help him besides Allah and was not going to be helped.

44. There the only true protection is with Allah, with Him is the best reward and the best outcome.

45. And coin for them the likeness of the worldly life as water which We send down from the sky and the plants of the earth absorb it, then they become dry stalks which the winds carry off, and Allah has power over all things.

46. Wealth and children are the adornment of the worldly life, and the lasting good deeds have a better reward with your Lord and give better rise to hope.

47. And on the day We move the mountains and you see the earth exposed, and We gather them and leave not any of them out.

48. And they will be presented before your Lord in ranks; you have come to Us as We created you the first time, but you claimed We would not have an appointment for you.

49. And the book will be placed and you see the sinners anxious about what it contains and they say: woe to us, this book does not leave anything small or big without counting it. And they find present what they had done and your Lord does not wrong anyone.

50. And when We said to the angels: prostrate before Adam, they prostrated except Iblis (the devil) who was from among the Jinn and deviated from the command of his Lord - are you then going to take him and his descendants as protecting friends besides Me when they are an enemy to you? A bad swap for the wrongdoers.

51. I did not let them witness the creation of the heavens and the earth nor the creation of themselves and I did not take the support of those who lead astray.

52. And on the day He says: call whom you claim to be My associates, then they call them but they do not respond to them and We place a barrier between them.

53. And the sinners see the fire and think that they will be thrown in it and will not find an escape from it.

54. We have explained to people in this Qur'an all kind of examples but man argues about most things.

55. And nothing prevented people from believing when the guidance came to them and to seek forgiveness from their Lord except (that they waited) for the example of the earliest communities to reach them or the punishment to face them.

56. And We only send the messengers as bringers of good news and warners, and those who reject (the truth) argue with falsehood in order to refute the truth with it and take My signs and their warnings as a joke.

57. And who is more wrong than he who has been reminded by the signs of his Lord and turns away from them and forgets what he has sent ahead for himself. We have placed a cover over their hearts, so they do not understand it, and a weight upon their ears, and if you call them to the guidance they will never be guided.

58. And your Lord is forgiving, full of mercy; if He overtook them on account of what they have earned, He would hasten the punishment for them, but there is a fixed term for them which they cannot avoid.

59. As for the towns We have destroyed when they did wrong, We decreed a fixed term for their destruction.

60. And when Musa (Moses) said to his male servant: I will not stop until I have reached the crossing between the two seas even if it takes a very long time.

61. And when they reached the crossing between them they forgot their fish and it quickly made its way into the sea.

62. And when they had passed beyond he said to his male servant: bring us our food, we have earned our share from this journey.

63. He said: see, when we went towards the rock I forgot the fish, and only the devil made me forget to mention it, and it amazingly made its way into the sea.

64. He said: this is what we were looking for, so they retraced their steps.

65. Then they found one of Our servants whom We had given mercy from Us and taught him knowledge from Us.

66. Musa (Moses) said to him: may I follow you so you will teach me of the righteousness you have been taught?

67. He said: you cannot bear patience with me.

68. And how can you bear patience with what you do not understand?

69. He said: if Allah wills you will find me patient and I will not disobey you in anything.

70. He said: then if you follow me, do not ask me about anything until I mention it to you.

71. So they set off until they boarded a boat in which he made a hole. He said: did you make a hole in it to drown its people? You've done a strange thing.

72. He said: did I not say that you cannot bear patience with me?

73. He said: do not take me to account for having forgotten and do not make the matter difficult for me.

74. So they set off until they met a boy and he killed him. He said: did you kill someone pure other than in retaliation, you have done something unacceptable.

75. He said: did I not tell you that you cannot bear patience with me?

76. He said: if I ask you anything after that, then do not accompany me; you will have found an excuse with me.

77. So they set off until when they reached the inhabitants of a town they asked them for food but they refused to entertain them. Then they found a wall there which was about to fall, so he strengthened it. He said: if you wanted, you could have taken a reward for it.

78. He said: this is the parting between me and you. I will inform you of the interpretation of what you could not bear patience with.

79. As for the boat, it belonged to poor people who worked on the sea, and I intended to damage it because there was a king after them who took every boat by force.

80. And as for the boy, his parents were believers and we feared that he would overpower them with transgression and rejection.

81. So we intended that their Lord replaced him for them with someone purer and more merciful.

82. And as for the wall, it belonged to two orphans in the town and there was a treasure for them under it and their father was a righteous man, so your Lord intended that they should reach their full strength and take out their

treasure as a mercy from your Lord. And I did not do it on my own accord. That is the interpretation of what you could not bear patience with.

83. And they ask you about the one with two horns. Say: I will recite to you a reminder about him.

84. We established him on earth and gave him the means for everything.

85. So he pursued a matter.

86. Until when he reached the setting point of the sun he found it set in a muddy spring and found near it a people. We said: oh two-horned one, you can punish them or you can treat them well.

87. He said: whoever does wrong, we will punish him, then he will be returned to his Lord who will punish him severely.

88. And whoever believes and does good, he will have a good reward and we will make it easy for him.

89. Then he pursued a matter.

90. Until when he reached the rising point of the sun he found it rising near a people whom We had not given any screening from it.

91. This is how it was, and We knew all about him.

92. Then he pursued a matter.

93. Until when he reached between the two extremes, he found another people who hardly understood any speech.

94. They said: Oh two-horned one, Ya'juj and Ma'juj (Gog and Magog) are spreading corruption on earth, so

shall we give you a tribute for you to place between us and them a barrier?

95. He said: what my Lord has established me with is better, so help me with labour, I will place between you and them a structure.

96. Bring me blocks of iron, then when he levelled the two ends he said: blow, until he made it glow, then he said: bring me the melted mass to pour on it.

97. And they could not climb over it nor could they cut through it.

98. He said: this is of the mercy of my Lord, but when my Lord's promise comes to pass He will make it crumble, and my Lord's promise is true.

99. And on that day We let some of them mingle with others, and the horn is blown and We gather them all.

100. And We present hell to those who rejected (the truth) on that day.

101. Those whose eyes were closed to My remembrance and who could not listen.

102. Do those who reject (the truth) count on taking My servants as protectors besides Me? We have prepared hell as a gift for those who reject (the truth).

103. Say: Shall I inform you whose work is most useless?

104. Those whose effort went astray in the life of the world and they reckon that they have done well.

105. Those are the ones who reject the signs of their Lord and the meeting with Him, so their deeds are wasted

and We assign no weight to them on the day of resurrection.

106. This is their reward: hell, on account of having rejected (the truth) and taken My signs and My messengers for a joke.

107. Those who believe and do good work, the gardens of paradise are their gift.

108. They remain there and will not want it to change.

109. Say: if the sea was the ink for the words of my Lord, the sea would run out before the words of my Lord would run out even if We brought a similar measure once more.

110. Say: I am only a human like you to whom has been revealed that your god is a single god, so whoever looks forward to meeting his Lord, let him do good work and not associate in the service to my Lord anyone.

Surah 19: *Maryam* (Mary)

In the name of Allah, the Owner and Giver of Mercy

1. Kaf, Ha, Ya, 'Ayn, Sad.

2. A mention of the mercy of your Lord upon His servant Zakariya (Zacharias).

3. When he secretly called out to his Lord.

4. Saying: my Lord, my strength is leaving me and my head has turned grey and I have never been disappointed when calling to You.

5. And I fear about my succession, and my wife is barren, so grant me from Yourself a successor.

6. To inherit from me and the family of Ya'qub (Jacob) and, oh Lord, make him pleasing (to You).

7. Oh Zakariya (Zacharias), We are giving you good news of a boy whose name is Yahya (John), We have not issued this name to anyone before.

8. He said: oh my Lord, how can I have a boy when my wife is barren and I have reached the end of my life.

9. He said: this is what your Lord states: it is easy for Me, I previously created you out of nothing.

10. He said: my Lord, assign me a sign. He said: your sign is that you shall not talk to people for three nights consecutively.

11. So he went out to his people from the prayer niche and gestured to them to glorify (Allah) in the mornings and evenings.

12. Oh Yahya (John), adopt the book with strength, and We gave him sound judgement as a young boy.

13. And (he was given) compassion and purity from Us, and he was aware (of Allah).

14. And devoted to his parents, and he was not oppressive or rebellious.

15. And peace is with him on the day he was born and the day he dies and the day he is brought to life again.

16. And mention in the book Maryam (Mary) when she retreated from her family to a place facing East.

17. Then she separated herself from them and We sent to her Our spirit and he appeared to her like a real man.

18. She said: I seek refuge in the Merciful from you if you beware (of Allah).

19. He said: I am a messenger of your Lord to grant you a pure boy.

20. She said: How can I have a boy when no man has touched me and I have not been immoral.

21. He said: this is what your Lord states: it is easy for Me, and in order for Us to make you a sign for people and a mercy from Us, and it was a decided matter.

22. So she carried him and retreated with him to a far off place.

23. Then going into labour drove her to a palm trunk. She said: woe to me, if only I died before this and would be completely forgotten.

24. Then he called her from beneath her: do not worry, your Lord has placed a stream beneath you.

25. And shake the palm tree towards you, ripe fresh dates will fall on you.

26. So eat and drink and rest your eyes, and if you see any person, say: I promised a fast to the Merciful and will therefore not speak to anyone today.

27. So she brought him to her people. They said: oh Maryam (Mary), you have brought something unacceptable.

28. Oh sister of Harun (Aaron), your father was not a bad man and your mother was not immoral.

29. Then she pointed to him. They said: how can we talk to someone who is a child in a cradle?

30. He said: I am the servant of Allah, He gave me the book and made me a prophet.

31. And He made me a blessing wherever I am and He instructed me with prayer and Zakat as long as I live.

32. And to be devoted to my mother and He did not make me oppressive or rebellious.

33. And peace is with me on the day I was born and the day I die and the day I am brought to life again.

34. That is 'Isa (Jesus), the son of Maryam (Mary), the statement of truth in which they have doubt.

35. It is not befitting for Allah to adopt a son. Glorified is He. When He decides a matter, then He says to it: Be, then it is.

36. And Allah is my Lord and your Lord, so serve Him. This is a straight path.

37. Then the allies differed amongst themselves, so woe to those who reject (the truth) from the assembly on a tremendous day.

38. Hear and see them on the day they come to Us, but the wrongdoers are in clear error today.

39. And warn them of the day of loss when the matter is decided, whilst they are careless and do not believe.

40. We will indeed inherit the earth and whoever is on it and they will return to Us.

41. And mention in the book Ibrahim (Abraham), he was a truthful prophet.

42. When he said to his father: oh my father, why do you serve that which does not hear nor see nor benefit you in any way?

43. Oh my father, I have received knowledge you did not receive, so follow me, I will guide you to a level path.

44. Oh my father, do not serve the devil, for the devil was disobedient to the Merciful.

45. Oh my father, I fear that a punishment from the Merciful will afflict you and you will be a friend to the devil.

46. He said: do you dislike my gods, oh Ibrahim (Abraham)? If you do not stop, I will curse you and you better get out of my way.

47. He said: peace be with you, I will ask my Lord for forgiveness for you, for He is always kind to me.

48. I will move away from you and what you serve besides Allah and call on my Lord, hopefully I will not be disappointed when calling to my Lord.

49. Then when he moved away from them and what they served besides Allah, We gave him Ishaq (Isaac) and Ya'qub (Jacob) and made each of them a prophet.

50. And We granted them of Our mercy and gave them a truthful and elevated reputation.

51. And mention in the book Musa (Moses), he was sincere and was a messenger and prophet.

52. And We called him from the mountain on the right and brought him near in direct communication.

53. And We gave him of Our mercy his brother Harun (Aaron) as a prophet.

54. And mention in the book Isma'il (Ishmael), he was the one to fulfil the promise and was a messenger and prophet.

55. And he instructed his family to pray and give Zakat and was accepted by His Lord.

56. And mention in the book Idris (Enoch), he was a truthful prophet.

57. And We raised him to a high status.

58. Those are the ones Allah has favoured of the prophets and the descendants of Adam and of those whom We carried with Nuh (Noah) and of the descendants of Ibrahim (Abraham) and Isra'il (Israel) and of those whom We guided and chose; when the signs of the Merciful were recited to them, they fell prostrate in tears.

59. And after them came a succession (of people) who neglected prayer and followed desires, and they will soon meet their downfall.

60. Except he who repents and believes and does good, for those will enter the garden and will not be wronged at all.

61. The gardens of Eden which the Merciful has promised to those who serve Him without seeing Him, for His promise will come to pass.

62. They will not hear any idle talk there, only peace, and they will have their provision in the mornings and evenings.

63. This is the garden which those of Our servants who bewared will inherit.

64. And we (the angels) only descend by the command of your Lord. To Him belongs what lies before us and what lies behind us and what is in between, and your Lord does not forget.

65. The Lord of the heavens and the earth and what is in between, so serve Him and persist in His service. Do you know anyone else like Him?

66. And man says: when I die, am I going to be brought back to life?

67. Does man not remember that We created him before when he was nothing?

68. So by your Lord, We shall gather them and the devils, then We shall present them kneeling down around hell.

69. Then We shall pick out from every faction those who were most obstinate against the Merciful.

70. Then We will know best those who are most deserving to burn in it.

71. And all of you will approach it, this is a final decision of your Lord.

72. Then We rescue those who bewared (of Allah) and abandon the wrongdoers kneeling down in it.

73. And when Our clear signs are recited to them, those who reject (the truth) say to those who believe: which of the two groups is more settled and better represented?

74. And how many generations have We destroyed before them who were better in luxury and appearance?

75. Say: whoever is in error, the Merciful will give him space until when they see what they were promised, either the punishment or the hour, then they will know who is worse off and weaker in support.

76. And Allah increases those who are guided in guidance, and the lasting good deeds have a better reward with your Lord and are better in return.

77. Have you considered him who rejects Our signs and says: I will be given wealth and children.

78. Does he access the unseen or has he entered into an agreement with the Merciful?

79. No way, We write down what he says and extend the punishment for him.

80. And We inherit what he says was his and he comes to Us alone.

81. And they adopt gods besides Allah to be a strength for them.

82. No way, they will reject their service and be hostile to them.

83. Have you not considered that We sent the devils to those who reject (the truth) to stir them up.

84. So be not in a hurry about them, We have a count-down for them.

85. On the day We carry those who beware (of Allah) to the Merciful.

86. And We herd the sinners towards hell.

87. They have no power of intercession except for him who had an agreement with the Merciful.

88. And they say: the Merciful has adopted a son.

89. You have come up with something awful.

90. The heavens almost split from it and the earth shakes and the mountains crumble,

91. That they claim for the Merciful a son.

92. And it is not befitting for the Merciful to adopt a son.

93. For all who are in the heavens and on earth come to the Merciful as servants.

94. He has counted them and given them a number.

95. And each of them comes on the day of resurrection alone.

96. Those who believe and do good work, the Merciful will give them a welcome.

97. And We have made it easy on your tongue so that you give good news to those who beware (of Allah) and warn with it an obstinate people.

98. And how many generations have We destroyed before them; do you notice any of them or hear the slightest sound from them?

Surah 20: **Ta Ha**

In the name of Allah, the Owner and Giver of Mercy

1. Ta Ha.

2. We did not reveal the Qur'an to you to be distressed.

3. Only as a reminder to whoever fears (Allah).

4. A revelation from the One who created the earth and the elevated heavens.

5. The Merciful, who rose to the throne.

6. To Him belongs what is in the heavens and what is on earth and what is in between and what is below the ground.

7. And when you speak audibly, He knows the secrets and what is most hidden.

8. Allah, there is no god but Him, His are the most beautiful names.

9. And has the story of Musa (Moses) reached you?

10. When he saw a fire and said to his people: wait, I noticed a fire, maybe I can bring you a spark of it or find guidance by the fire.

11. Then when he came to it he was called: oh Musa (Moses).

12. I am your Lord, so take off your sandals, for you are in the sacred valley of Tuwa.

13. And I have chosen you, so listen to what is being revealed.

14. For I am Allah, there is no god except Me, so serve Me and keep up prayer to remember Me.

15. The hour will come, I hardly hide it, so that every soul is rewarded for what it strives for.

16. So let not one who does not believe in it and follows his desire divert you from it so that you are ruined.

17. And what is that in your right hand, oh Musa (Moses)?

18. He said: it is my staff, I lean on it and I round up my sheep with it and it has other uses for me.

19. He said: throw it, oh Musa (Moses).

20. So he threw it and it became a moving snake.

21. He said: take it and do not fear, We will return it to its original form.

22. And press your hand against your side, it will come out white without harm, another sign.

23. So that We show you of Our great signs.

24. Go to Pharaoh, he is transgressing.

25. He said: my Lord, expand my chest.

26. And make my task easy for me.

27. And untie the knot from my tongue.

28. So they understand my speech.

29. And give me a deputy from my family.

30. Harun (Aaron), my brother.

31. Increase with him my strength.

32. And give him a share in my task.

33. So that we glorify You a lot.

34. And remember You a lot.

35. For You watched over us.

36. He said: your request has been granted, oh Musa (Moses).

37. And We already favoured you another time.

38. When We revealed to your mother what was revealed:

39. Drop him into the basket and drop it into the river, then the river will carry it to the bank and an enemy to Me and to him will take it. And I poured love from Me on you so that you would grow up under My eyes.

40. When your sister went and said: shall I point you to someone who will care for him? So We returned you to your mother to comfort her eyes and so she would not worry. And you killed a person and We rescued you from the grief and tested you a great deal, then you stayed a few years with the people of Madyan (Midian), then you came as decreed, oh Musa (Moses).

41. And I have chosen you for Myself.

42. Go, you and your brother, with My signs and do not tire of My remembrance.

43. Go to Pharaoh, he is transgressing.

44. And talk to him gently so that he might reflect or fear.

45. He said: Our Lord, we fear that he will abuse us or transgress.

46. He said: do not fear, I am with you, listening and seeing.

47. So go to him and say: we are two messengers of your Lord, so send with us the Children of Israel and do not punish them. We have brought you a sign from your Lord, and peace be with him who follows the guidance.

48. It has been revealed to us that the punishment is upon him who denies and turns away.

49. He said: and who is your Lord, oh Musa (Moses).

50. He said: our Lord is the One who gave everything its origin then directed it.

51. He said: then what is the state of the earliest generations?

52. He said: knowledge about them is with my Lord in a book, my Lord neither errs nor forgets.

53. The One who gave you the earth as an expanse and cut paths in it for you and sent water from the sky by which We bring out various pairs of plants.

54. Eat and graze your cattle, for in this are signs for those with reason.

55. From it We created you and into it you return and from it We will bring you out once again.

56. And We showed him all Our signs, but he denied and refused.

57. He said: did you come to expel us from our land with your magic, oh Musa (Moses)?

58. So we will bring you similar magic. Set an appointed time between us and you that neither we nor you will miss, at an open place.

59. He said: your appointed time is the day of celebration and let people gather in the morning.

60. So Pharaoh turned away and agreed his plot, then he came.

61. Musa (Moses) said to them: woe to you, do not invent a lie against Allah so He afflicts you with punishment, and whoever invents (a lie) will be destroyed.

62. Then they discussed their situation secretly amongst themselves.

63. They said: these are two magicians who want to expel you from your land with their magic and take away your traditions.

64. So agree on your plot, then come in ranks, and today the one who comes out on top will be successful.

65. They said: oh Musa (Moses), either you throw or we throw first.

66. He said: no, you throw, then their ropes and sticks appeared to move with their magic.

67. So Musa (Moses) sensed fear in himself.

68. We said: do not fear, you will come out on top.

69. And throw what is in your right hand, it will take over the magician's plot they have constructed, and the magician does not succeed, wherever he goes.

70. Then the magicians fell prostrate, saying: we believe in the Lord of Harun (Aaron) and Musa (Moses).

71. He said: do you believe him before I have given you permission? He must be your chief who taught you magic, so I will cut your hands and feet from opposite sides and crucify you on palm trunks and you will know who of us is more severe and lasting in punishment.

72. They said: we will not give you priority over the clear proofs which have come to us and the One who originated us, so decide what you have to, you only decide about this worldly life.

73. For we believe in our Lord so that He forgives us our sins and the magic you compelled us to do, and Allah is better and more lasting.

74. Whoever comes to his Lord as a sinner, for him is hell where he will neither die nor live.

75. And whoever comes to Him as a believer who does good work, for them are the highest stages.

76. Gardens of Eden through which rivers flow where they will remain, and that is the reward for him who purifies himself.

77. And We revealed to Musa (Moses) to travel with My servants and strike a dry path in the sea for them without fearing to be overtaken or being afraid.

78. Then Pharaoh followed them with his soldiers and the sea completely surrounded them.

79. And Pharaoh led his people astray and did not guide them.

80. Oh Children of Israel, We rescued you from your enemy and had a meeting with you with the mountain on the right and sent to you honeydew and quails.

81. Eat from the good things We have provided you with and do not transgress in this state, so My anger becomes lawful on you, and on whom My anger becomes lawful, he has fallen.

82. And I am forgiving to him who repents and believes and does good work and then is guided.

83. And why have you hurried away from your people, oh Musa (Moses)?

84. He said: they are following behind me, and I hurried to you in order to please You, my Lord.

85. He said: We have tested your people after you and Samiri led them astray.

86. So Musa (Moses) returned to his people angry and sad, saying: oh my people, did not your Lord give you a good promise? Was this taking too long for you or did you want anger from you Lord to become lawful on you, so that you broke your promise to me?

87. They said: we did not break our promise to you on our own account, but we carried loads of the jewellery of the people and cast it (in the fire) just as Samiri told us to.

88. Then he brought the body of a calf out for them which had a mooing sound, so they said: this is your god and the god of Musa (Moses), but he forgot.

89. Do they not see that it does not talk back to them nor has any control over harm or good for them?

90. And Harun (Aaron) said to them before: oh my people, you are being tested by it and your Lord is

the Merciful, so follow me and obey my command.

91. They said: we will not stop being devoted to it until Musa (Moses) returns to us.

92. He said: oh Harun (Aaron), what prevented you, when you saw them go astray,

93. From following me? Did you disobey my command?

94. He said: oh son of my mother, do not grab me by the beard nor by the head, I feared that you would say: you divided the Children of Israel and did not heed my word.

95. He said: and what do you have to say, oh Samiri?

96. He said: I saw what they did not see and took hold of a handful of the trace of the messenger and threw it in, and this is what my soul suggested to me.

97. He said: so go and your destiny in life will be that you will say: I am untouchable, and you will have an appointed time which you will not miss, and look at your god that you were devoted to: we will burn it, then scatter it in the sea.

98. For your god is Allah, the One besides whom there is no god and whose knowledge extends to everything.

99. This is how We tell you of the information gone before and of which We have given you a reminder from Ourselves.

100. Whoever turns away from it, he will carry a burden on the day of resurrection.

101. They will remain there and what they carry on the day of resurrection will be bad for them.

102. On the day the horn is blown and We will gather the sinners on that day with their eyes turning white.

103. Whispering to each other: you have only stayed ten days.

104. We know best what they say when the one most reasonable of them says: you have only stayed a day.

105. And they ask you about the mountains, so say: my Lord will scatter them.

106. Then leave them as an empty space.

107. In which you will see neither contours nor protrusion.

108. On that day they will follow the caller without deviation and the voices will be subdued to the Merciful and you will not hear anything except a whisper.

109. On that day intercession will not benefit anyone unless the Merciful has given him permission and is pleased with what he says.

110. He knows what lies before them and behind them and they do not grasp Him in knowledge.

111. And the faces are humbled before the Living, the Eternal, and whoever is burdened with wrongdoing will be destroyed.

112. And whoever did good work and is a believer, he will not fear wrongdoing nor injustice.

113. And this is how We revealed it as an Arabic Qur'an and explained the promise in it so that they beware (of Allah) or are given a reminder.

114. Exalted, therefore, is Allah, the true king, and do not be in a hurry with the Qur'an before its revelation has been completed for you and say: my Lord, increase me in knowledge.

115. And We had an agreement with Adam before but he forgot and We did not find that he had resolve.

116. And when We said to the angels: "Prostrate before Adam", they prostrated except for Iblis (the devil); he refused.

117. So We said: oh Adam, this is an enemy to you and your wife, so let him not expel you from the garden, so you would be distressed.

118. For you are not hungry there nor are you exposed.

119. And you are not thirsty there nor are you hot.

120. Then the devil whispered to him, saying: oh Adam, shall I direct you to the tree of eternity and a kingdom which does not diminish?

121. So they both ate from it and their bodies became apparent to them and they began to cover themselves with leaves from the garden, and Adam disobeyed his Lord and went astray.

122. Then His Lord chose him and turned back to him and guided him.

123. He said: Get down from here, all of you, as enemies one to another. then when a guidance reaches you from Me, whoever then follows My guidance, he will not go astray nor be distressed.

124. And whoever turns away from My reminder, he will have a constrained life and on the day of resurrection We will gather him blind.

125. He will say: my Lord, why did You gather me blind when I could see?

126. He will say: likewise Our signs came to you but you forgot them, likewise you will be forgotten today.

127. And this is how We punish the one who is wasteful and does not believe in the signs of his Lord, and the punishment of the hereafter is more severe and more lasting.

128. Are they not guided by how many generations We destroyed before them in whose homes they walk? In this are signs for those with reason.

129. And if a word from your Lord had not gone before, it would be inevitable, but it is a limited term.

130. So have patience with what they say and glorify the praise of your Lord before sun rise and before it sets, and during part of the night glorify Him and at the ends of the day, so that you may be content.

131. And do not extend your eyes to the enjoyment We have given some couples of them as the splendour of this world in order to test them by it, and the provision of your Lord is better and more lasting.

132. And instruct your family to pray and be consistent in it; We do not ask provision from you, We provide for you, and the outcome is for those who beware (of Allah).

133. And they say: why does not a sign come to us from our Lord? Did not a clear proof reach them from the earlier records?

134. And had We destroyed them with a punishment before that, they would have said: our Lord, why did You not send a messenger to us so we would follow Your signs before being humiliated and disgraced?

135. Say: all are waiting, so wait, then you will know who are the companions on the level path and who is guided.

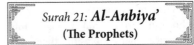

Surah 21: *Al-Anbiya'*
(The Prophets)

In the name of Allah,
the Owner and Giver of Mercy

1. People's reckoning is coming close and they are turning away carelessly.

2. Whenever a new reminder comes to them from their Lord, they listen to it whilst playing.

3. Their hearts are distracted and the wrongdoers meet secretly saying: is this not a human like you? Are you going to give in to the spell when you can see?

4. He said: my Lord knows what is spoken in the heaven and on earth and He listens and knows.

5. But they said: confused dreams, rather he invented it, rather he is a poet, so let him bring us a sign like the messengers sent before.

6. No town which We destroyed before them believed, so are they going to believe?

7. And before you We only sent men to whom We gave revelation, so ask those who keep the reminder if you don't know.

8. And We did not give them bodies which do not consume food nor were they immortal.

9. Then We fulfilled the promise and rescued whom We please and destroyed the wasteful.

10. We have revealed to you a book containing your reminder, so will you not understand?

11. How often did We crush a town who did wrong and brought into existence other people after them?

12. Then when they felt our adversity, they ran away from it.

13. Don't run away but return to the luxury you were in and your homes so you can be questioned!

14. They said: woe to us, we were wrongdoers.

15. And this call of theirs did not stop until We cut them down completely.

16. And We did not create the heaven and earth and what is between as a pastime.

17. Had We wanted to find amusement, We could have found that with Ourselves if We were to do so.

18. But We pour the truth over falsehood so it repels it and it vanishes,

and you will suffer for what you make out.

19. And to Him belongs what is in the heavens and on earth, and those near him are not too arrogant to serve Him and do not tire of it.

20. They glorify night and day without slowing down.

21. Or do they adopt gods from the earth who resurrect the dead?

22. If there were gods other than Allah in them (the heavens and the earth), they would have been corrupted, so glorified is Allah, the Lord of the throne, above what they make out.

23. He is not questioned about what He does, and they are questioned.

24. Or do they adopt gods besides Him? Say: bring your proof! This is the reminder for those who are with me and was the reminder for those before me, but most of them don't know the truth and turn away.

25. And whenever We sent a messenger before you We revealed to him that there is no god but I, so serve Me.

26. And they say: the Merciful has adopted a son; glorified is He, but they are honoured servants.

27. They do not precede Him in speech and carry out His command.

28. He knows what lies before them and behind them and they do not intercede except for whom it is accepted and they are anxious out of fear of Him.

29. And if any of them says: I am a god besides Allah, We will punish him with hell, this is how We punish the wrongdoers.

30. Do those who reject (the truth) not see that the heavens and the earth were a continuous canvas, then We separated them and made from water every living thing, do they then not believe?

31. And We placed stabilisers on earth to support it with and cut paths through them so that you are guided.

32. And We placed the sky as a protected ceiling whilst they turn away from Our signs.

33. And He is who created the night and the day and the sun and the moon, each travels in an orbit.

34. And We did not give eternity to any human before you, so when you die, will they live forever?

35. Every soul will taste death, and We test them with bad and good as a trial and they return to Us.

36. And when those who reject (the truth) see you, they only take you as a joke: is this the one who mentions your gods? And they reject the remembrance of the Merciful.

37. Man was created impatient; I will show you My signs, so do not be in a hurry.

38. And they say: when will this promise happen if you are truthful?

39. If those who reject (the truth) knew the time when they cannot keep the fire off their faces nor off their backs and they will not be helped.

40. But it will reach them suddenly and startle them, so they cannot avert it nor will they be given time.

41. And messengers before you were made fun of, and those who laughed at them were met with what they made fun of.

42. Say: who guards you night and day against the Merciful? But they turn away from the remembrance of their Lord.

43. Or do they have gods who protect them against Us? They cannot help themselves nor are they assisted by Us.

44. But We gave enjoyment to these and their fathers until they grew old. Do they not see that we reduce the earth from its ends, so will they be the winners?

45. Say: I only warn you with the revelation, and the deaf do not hear the call when they are warned.

46. And when a hint of the punishment of your Lord touches them, they say, woe to us, we were wrongdoers.

47. And We set down the scales of justice on the day of resurrection so that no soul will be wronged the least, and if it is the weight of a mustard seed We bring it out, and We are sufficient in counting.

48. And We gave Musa (Moses) and Harun (Aaron) the distinction (between right and wrong) and a light and reminder for those who beware (of Allah).

49. Those who fear their Lord in secret and are anxious about the hour.

50. And this is a blessed reminder which We have revealed, so do you dislike it?

51. And We gave Ibrahim (Abraham) his good sense before, and We knew all about him.

52. When he said to his father and his people: what are these images you are devoted to?

53. They said: we found our fathers serving them.

54. He said: you and your fathers were in clear error.

55. They said: did you bring us the truth or are you messing about?

56. He said: but your Lord is the Lord of the heavens and the earth, the One who originated you, and I am a witness to that.

57. And by Allah, I will plot against your idols after you have turned your backs.

58. Then he cut them into pieces except for their chief so that they would return to him.

59. They said: who did this to our gods, for he is a wrongdoer.

60. They said: we heard a youth mention them, he is called Ibrahim (Abraham).

61. They said: then bring him before the people so that they are witnesses.

62. They said: did you do this to our gods, oh Ibrahim (Abraham)?

63. He said: but this chief of theirs did it, so ask them if they speak.

64. Then they turned back to themselves and said: you yourselves are the wrongdoers.

65. Then they shook their heads; you know that these don't speak.

66. He said: do you then serve besides Allah what does not benefit you the least nor help you?

67. Worthless is what you serve besides Allah, do you not then understand?

68. They said: burn him and help your gods if you want to act.

69. We said: oh fire, be coolness and peace for Ibrahim (Abraham).

70. And they wanted to plot against him, but we made them the losers.

71. And We rescued him and Lut (Lot) to the land which We have blessed for all the world.

72. And We gave him Ishaq (Isaac) and Ya'qub (Jacob) in addition and made each of them righteous.

73. And We made them into leaders who guide by Our command and revealed to them to do good and to keep up prayer and give Zakat, and they served Us.

74. And Lut (Lot) We gave the ability to judge and knowledge and rescued him from the town which committed obscenities, for they were a bad and sinful people.

75. And We admitted him into Our mercy, for he is of the righteous.

76. And Nuh (Noah), when he called Us before and We responded to him and rescued him and his family from the tremendous distress.

77. And We helped him against the people who denied Our signs, for they were a bad people, so We downed them altogether.

78. And Dawud (David) and Sulayman (Solomon), when they judged about the harvest, when the sheep of the people strayed into it, and We witnessed their judgement.

79. And We let Sulayman (Solomon) understand it, and each of them We gave the ability to judge and knowledge, and We made the mountains and the birds subservient to glorify with Dawud (David), and this is what We did.

80. And We taught him the manufacture of armour for you to protect you against your harm, so will you be grateful?

81. And for Sulayman (Solomon) We made the strong wind travel by his command to the land the surroundings of which We have blessed, and We knew about everything.

82. And of the devils were those who dived for him and did other work, and We guarded them.

83. And Ayyub (Job), when he called his Lord: harm has befallen me and You are the most merciful of all.

84. So We responded to him and removed all harm from him and gave him his family and the like of it in addition as a mercy from Us and a reminder to those who serve.

85. And Isma'il (Ishmael) and Idris (Enoch) and Dhu-l-Kifl (Ezekiel), each were of the patient.

86. And We admitted them into Our mercy, for they are of the righteous.

87. And the one in the fish (Jonah), when he went angrily and thought that We had no control over him, then he called in the dark that there is no god but You, glorified are You, I was of the wrongdoers.

88. So We responded to him and rescued him from the grief, and this is how we rescue the believers.

89. And Zakariya (Zacharias), when he called his Lord: my Lord, do not leave me on my own, and you are the best of inheritors.

90. So We responded to him and gave him Yahya (John) and healed his wife for him, for they strived for good deeds and called Us in hope and in awe and were humble before Us.

91. And the one who guarded her chastity, so We blew into her of Our spirit and made her and her son a sign for all the world.

92. This is your community, a single community, and I am your Lord, so serve Me.

93. And they divided their affairs amongst them; each will return to Us.

94. Then whoever does good work and is a believer, his effort will not be rejected and We will write it down.

95. And it is forbidden for a town which We destroyed that they should come back.

96. Until Ya'juj and Ma'juj (Gog and Magog) are let loose and appear from everywhere.

97. And the true promise has come close, then the eyes of those who reject (the truth) will be glazed over: woe to us, we were careless about this, but we were wrongdoers.

98. You and what you serve besides Allah are the fuel of hell, you will be led to it.

99. If these were gods, they would not be led to it, and they will all remain in it.

100. There will be sighing for them in it, yet they will not hear in it.

101. Those whom We have given good before will be far removed from it.

102. They will not hear its hissing and will remain in what their souls long for.

103. The great terror will not worry them and the angels will welcome them: this is the day you were promised.

104. On the day We roll up the sky like a scroll for writing. As We began the first creation We will bring it back, a promise upon Us, We will do it.

105. And We previously wrote in the Psalms after the reminder that Our righteous servants will inherit the earth.

106. In that is a declaration for people who serve.

107. And We only sent you as a mercy for all the world.

108. Say: it has been revealed to me that your god is a single god, so will you submit?

109. Then if they turn away, say: I told you anyway, and I have no idea

whether what you have been promised is close or far off.

110. He knows what is said openly and knows what you hide.

111. And I have no idea whether it may be a trial for you and a provision for a while.

112. He said: Lord, judge with the truth! And our Lord is the Merciful, who is to be implored against what you make out.

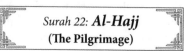

Surah 22: *Al-Hajj*
(The Pilgrimage)

In the name of Allah,
the Owner and Giver of Mercy

1. Oh people, beware of your Lord, for the trembling of the hour is a tremendous thing.

2. On the day when you see every nursing mother neglect what she nurses and every pregnant mother drop her burden and you see people as drunk when they are not drunk, but the punishment of Allah is severe.

3. And amongst people is he who argues about Allah without knowledge and follows every defiant devil.

4. It has been decreed for him that whoever befriends him, he will lead him astray and guide him to the punishment of the fire.

5. Oh people, if you are in doubt of the resurrection, then (consider that) We created you from soil, then from a sperm, then from an implant, then from a partly shaped piece of flesh in order to make it clear for you, and We retain in the wombs what We please until a fixed date, then We bring you out as a child, then let you reach your full strength, and amongst you is he who dies (early) and amongst you is he who ends up in the most feeble old age, so that he knows nothing after having had knowledge, and you see the earth lifeless, then when We send water onto it, it comes to life and swells and grows of every splendid species.

6. This is because Allah is the truth, and He revives the dead and He is able to do anything.

7. And the hour will come without doubt, and Allah will raise those in the graves.

8. And amongst people is he who argues about Allah without knowledge or guidance or enlightening book.

9. He turns away in order to lead away from the way of Allah. His is disgrace in this world and on the day of resurrection We make him taste the punishment of burning.

10. This is for the deeds you have sent ahead and that Allah does not wrong (His) servants.

11. And amongst people is he who serves Allah borderline, so if good befalls him, he is content with it, and if a trial befalls him, he turns away; he has lost the world and the hereafter - that is the clear loss.

12. He calls besides Allah on what does neither harm nor benefit him - that is the extensive error.

13. He calls on whose harm is more likely than his benefit - a bad protector and a bad friend.

14. Allah enters those who believe and do good work into gardens through which rivers flow, for Allah does what He pleases.

15. Whoever thinks that Allah will not help him (His messenger) in the world and the hereafter, let him find a means to ascend the heaven and try to cut off (the help), then see if his plot removes what enrages him.

16. And this is how We revealed clear signs and that Allah guides whom He pleases.

17. Those who believe and the Jews, the Sabeans, the Christians, the Zoroastrians and the idolaters, Allah will judge between them on the day of resurrection, for Allah is a witness to everything.

18. Do you not see that whoever is in the heavens and on earth prostrates to Allah, and the sun and the moon and the stars and the mountains and the trees and the creatures and many of the people? And many deserve the punishment, and whomever Allah humiliates, nobody can honour him, for Allah does what He pleases.

19. These are the two adversaries who dispute about their Lord, so those who reject (the truth), a garment of fire will be cut for them and boiling water will be poured over their heads.

20. It melts what is in their bellies and their skins.

21. And they will have iron chains.

22. Whenever they want to escape from it due to the distress, they will be returned to it: taste the punishment of burning.

23. Allah enters those who believe and do good work into gardens through which rivers flow; they are adorned there with bracelets of gold and pearls and their clothing there will be of silk.

24. And they are guided to good speech and are guided to the path of the Praiseworthy.

25. Those who reject (the truth) and divert from the way of Allah and the sacred mosque which We have placed for people, both the resident and the visitor - whoever wants to incline to wrongdoing there, We make him taste a painful punishment.

26. And when We provided Ibrahim (Abraham) with the location of the house: do not associate anything with Me and purify My house for those who go around, and those who stand (in prayer) and those who bow in prostration.

27. And announce to people the pilgrimage, they will come to you on foot and on every conveyance, they will come from every distant direction.

28. In order to witness benefits for them and remember the name of Allah on known days over the domestic cattle He has provided for them, so eat of it and feed the unfortunate poor.

29. Then they complete their rituals and fulfil their pledges and go round the ancient house.

30. This is how it is, and whoever honours the prohibitions of Allah, it is better for him with his Lord, and

you are permitted the cattle except that which has been revealed to you, so shun the abomination of idols and shun false speech.

31. Sincerely devoted to Allah without associating anything with Him, and whoever associates anything with Allah, it is as if he falls out of the sky and the birds snatch him or the wind blows him to a remote place.

32. This is how it is, and whoever honours the rites of Allah, it is from the awareness of the hearts.

33. They contain benefits for you until a fixed date, then they are delivered to the ancient house.

34. And to every community We have given a sacrifice to mention the name of Allah over that which We have provided them with from the domestic cattle, so your Lord is a single god, so submit to Him and give good news to those who are humble.

35. Those who when Allah is mentioned, their hearts become fearful, and those who bear patiently with what afflicts them, and those who keep up prayer and spend from what We have provided for them.

36. And We have made the fattened sacrificial animals signs of worship from Allah for you, you have (much) good in them, so mention the name of Allah over them when they are lined up. Then when their sides fall, eat from them and feed those who are content and those who ask; this is how We made them of service to you so that you would be grateful.

37. Neither their meat nor their blood reaches Allah, but your awareness reaches Him; this is how We made them of service to you so that you exalt Allah for having guided you, and give good news to those who do good.

38. For Allah defends the believers, for Allah does not love any faithless rejecter (of the truth).

39. Permission is given to those who have been fought because they have been wronged, and Allah is able to help them.

40. Those who were expelled from their homes without right only because they say: our Lord is Allah. And if Allah did not repel some people by others, the monasteries, churches, synagogues and mosques where Allah's name is mentioned a lot would have been destroyed, but Allah helps those who help Him, for Allah is strong and mighty.

41. Those who when We establish them on earth keep up prayer and give Zakat and command good conduct and forbid wrongdoing, and the outcome of affairs belongs to Allah.

42. And if they deny you, then the people of Nuh (Noah) and 'Ad and Thamud denied before them.

43. And the people of Ibrahim (Abraham) and the people of Lut (Lot).

44. And the inhabitants of Madyan (Midian), and Musa (Moses) was denied, so I gave time to those who rejected (the truth), then I overtook them, and how was My rebuttal!

45. And how many wrongdoing towns did We destroy, so they are abandoned in ruins, and how many dried up wells and elevated castles?

46. Do they not travel on the earth with hearts that understand or ears that hear? The eyes do not go blind, but the hearts inside go blind.

47. And they ask you to hasten the punishment, and Allah does not break His promise. And a day with your Lord is like a thousand years of what you count.

48. And how many wrongdoing towns did I give time, then I overtook them, and to Me is the journey.

49. Say: oh people, I am a clear warner for you.

50. So for those who believe and do good work will be forgiveness and generous provision.

51. And those who strive to undermine Our signs will be the inmates of hell-fire.

52. And whenever We sent a messenger or prophet before you, the devil interfered with his recitation when he recited, then Allah cancels the devil's interference, then Allah lays down His signs, and Allah is knowing and wise.

53. So that Allah makes the interference of the devil a test for those with a disease in their hearts and whose hearts are hardened, and the wrongdoers are far away (from the truth).

54. And so that those who have been given knowledge know that it is the truth from your Lord, so they believe in it and their hearts are humbled towards it, and Allah guides the believers to a straight path.

55. And those who reject (the truth) will remain in doubt about it until the hour comes upon them suddenly or the punishment of an endless day reaches them.

56. The kingdom on that day belongs to Allah, He judges between them, so those who believed and did good work will be in gardens of blessing.

57. And those who rejected (the truth) and denied Our signs, for those will be a humiliating punishment.

58. And those who migrated in the way of Allah and were then killed or died, Allah provides them with a good provision, for Allah is the best of providers.

59. We let them enter from an entrance they are pleased with, and Allah is knowing and gentle.

60. This is how it is, and whoever inflicts punishment comparable to what had been inflicted on him and is then overcome, Allah will help him, for Allah is lenient, forgiving.

61. This is because Allah blends the night into the day and blends the day into the night and Allah hears and sees.

62. This is because Allah is the truth, and whatever they call besides Him is falsehood and Allah is exalted and great.

63. Do you not see that Allah sends down water from the sky, then the earth becomes green, for Allah is kind and informed.

64. To Him belongs what is in the heavens and what is on earth, and Allah is the rich and praiseworthy.

65. Do you not see that Allah makes whatever is on earth of service to you, and the ship sails on the sea by His command, and He prevents the sky from falling onto the earth except by His permission, for Allah is lenient and merciful with mankind.

66. And He is who gave you life, then He lets you die, then He revives you, but man rejects (the truth).

67. To every community We have given a sacrifice to observe, so let them not challenge you in the matter and call to your Lord, for you are on straight guidance.

68. And if they dispute with you, say: Allah knows best what you do.

69. Allah judges between you on the day of resurrection with regard to what you used to differ in.

70. Don't you know that Allah knows what is in the heaven and on earth? All that is in a book, for that is easy for Allah.

71. And they serve besides Allah that which no authority has been sent to them for and which they have no knowledge about, and the wrongdoers have no helper.

72. And when Our clear signs are recited to them, you notice in the faces of those who reject (the truth) the dislike, they would almost attack those who are reciting Our signs to them. Say: Shall I inform you of worse than that? The fire, Allah has promised it to those who reject (the truth), and it is a bad destination.

73. Oh people, a likeness has been coined for you, so listen to it: those whom you call besides Allah cannot create a fly even if they combined their efforts to do so, and if the fly takes something off them, they cannot recover it from it; week is the seeker and the one sought.

74. They do not measure Allah's true ability, for Allah is strong and mighty.

75. Allah selects from the angels messengers and from people, for Allah hears and sees.

76. He knows what lies before them and behind them and to Allah return all things.

77. Oh you believers, bow down and prostrate and serve your Lord and do good in order to succeed.

78. And strive in the way of Allah with true effort, He has chosen you and did not place any hardship on you in the religion, the persuasion of your father Ibrahim (Abraham); he called you Muslims (those who submit) before, and in this case the messenger will be a witness against you and you will be witnesses against mankind, so keep up prayer and give Zakat and hold on to Allah, He is your protector, the best protector and the best helper.

Surah 23: *Al-Mu'minun*
(The Believers)

In the name of Allah,
the Owner and Giver of Mercy

1. Successful are the believers,

2. Who are humble in their prayers,

3. And who turn away from idle talk,

4. And who give Zakat,

5. And who guard their chastity,

6. Except with regard to their partners and those in their possession, for then they are not to blame.

7. Then if anyone desires beyond that, then those exceed the limits.

8. And who look after their trust and agreements,

9. And who guard their prayers,

10. Those are the inheritors,

11. Who inherit paradise where they will remain.

12. And We created man from an extract of clay.

13. Then We place it as sperm in a protective location.

14. Then We shaped the sperm into an implant and shaped the implant into a piece of flesh and shaped the piece of flesh into bones and covered the bones with meat, then We bring it out as a different creation, so exalted is Allah the best of creators.

15. Then after that you will die.

16. Then on the day of resurrection you will be raised.

17. And We created above you seven passages and We were not careless with the creation.

18. And We sent water in measure from the sky and let it settle on earth, and We are able to make it disappear.

19. Then We produce with it gardens of palm trees and grapes in which you have plenty of fruit and from which you eat.

20. And a tree which emerges from mount Sinai, which grows oil and seasoning for those who eat.

21. And there is a lesson for you in the cattle: We give you to drink from what is in their bellies and you have plenty of uses in them and you eat of them.

22. And you are carried on them and on the ship.

23. And We previously sent Nuh (Noah) to his people, saying: oh my people, serve Allah, you have no god other than Him, do you not beware (of Him)?

24. Then the leaders of his people who rejected (the truth) said: this is only a human like you who wants to be better than you, and if Allah pleased, He would have sent angels, we never heard of this amongst our forefathers.

25. He is only a man who is possessed, so wait with him for a while.

26. He said: my Lord, help me against their denial.

27. So We revealed to him to construct the ship before Our eyes and with Our revelation, then when Our command comes and the earth bursts open, lead into it a pair of each kind together with your family, except those of them on whom the word has gone before, and do not address Me regarding the wrongdoers, for they will be drowned.

28. Then when you and those with you have boarded the ship say: praised is Allah who rescued us from the wrongdoing people.

29. And say: my Lord, grant me a blessed landfall, and You are the best to grant it.

30. In this are indeed signs, and We did test them as always.

31. Then We raised another generation after them.

32. And We sent amongst them a messenger of their own: serve Allah, you have no god other than Him, do you not beware (of Him)?

33. And the leaders of his people who rejected (the truth) and denied the meeting of the hereafter and whom We had made comfortable in this life said: this is only a human like you who eats of what you eat and drinks of what you drink.

34. And if you were to obey a human like you, you would be losers.

35. Does he promise you that when you die and are dust and bones, you will be brought out again?

36. Most shocking is what you are promised.

37. There is only this worldly life of ours, we live and we die and we will not be resurrected.

38. He is only a man who has invented a lie against Allah and we do not believe him.

39. He said: my Lord, help me against their denial.

40. He said: Soon they will come to regret.

41. So the roar rightfully overtook them and We scattered them, so away with the wrongdoing people.

42. Then We raised other generations after them.

43. No community precedes its fixed term nor do they delay it.

44. Then We send Our messengers in succession. Each time their messenger came to a community they denied him and We made them follow one another and made them history, so away with people who do not believe.

45. Then We sent Musa (Moses) and his brother Harun (Aaron) with Our signs and a clear authority.

46. To Pharaoh and his leaders, but they were arrogant and were proud people.

47. So they said: are we going to believe two humans like us when their people serve us?

48. So they denied the two and were of those to be destroyed.

49. And We gave Musa (Moses) the book, so that they would be guided.

50. And We made the son of Maryam (Mary) and his mother a sign and lead them towards a hill with shelter and springs.

51. Oh messengers, eat from the good things and do good work, I know what you do.

52. And this your community is a single community, and I am your Lord, so beware of Me.

53. Then they split their affairs amongst them into doctrines, each party rejoicing in what they have.

54. So leave them in their misery for a while.

55. Do they reckon that when We expand wealth and children for them,

56. We hasten the good for them? But they don't realise.

57. Those who are humble out of fear of their Lord,

58. And those who believe in the signs of their Lord,

59. And those who do not associate anything with their Lord,

60. And those who give what they were given and their hearts are fearful that they will return to their Lord,

61. Those are racing towards the good and they are the first to achieve it.

62. And We do not burden a soul beyond its capacity, and We have a record which speaks the truth and they will not be wronged.

63. But their hearts are sealed against it and they have other work which they busy themselves with.

64. Until when We overtake the affluent ones amongst them with the punishment, then they pray.

65. Don't pray today, for you will not be helped.

66. You previously denied Our signs when they were recited to you and turned away on your heels.

67. Arrogant with it, talking boldly at night.

68. Do they not understand speech, or has something come to them which did not come to their forefathers?

69. Or don't they know their messenger and dislike him?

70. Or do they say he is mad? But he brought them the truth, and most of them resent the truth.

71. And if the truth were to follow their desires the heavens and the earth and whoever is in them would be corrupted, but We brought them their reminder and they turn away from their reminder.

72. Or do you ask them for a contribution, but the contribution of your Lord is better and He is the best of providers.

73. And you do call them to a straight path.

74. And those who do not believe in the hereafter deviate from the path.

75. And if We were to have mercy on them and take away any hardship they face, they would continue to get lost in their rebellion.

76. And We previously overtook them with the punishment, and they did not give in to their Lord nor humble themselves.

77. Until when We open for them a door full of severe punishment, then they are left with nothing.

78. And He is who arranged hearing, and eyesight and hearts for you, little thanks you give.

79. And He is who spread you out on earth, and to Him will you be gathered.

80. And He is who gives life and death, and His is the alternation of night and day, so will you not understand?

81. But they say things similar to what the earliest communities said.

82. They said: when we have died and are dust and bones, are we going to be raised again?

83. We and our fathers were promised this before, these are only stories of old.

84. Say: to whom belongs the earth and whoever is on it, if you know?

85. They will say: to Allah. Say: so will you not take heed?

86. Say: who is the Lord of the seven heavens and the Lord of the great throne?

87. They will say: (it belongs) to Allah. Say: so will you not beware (of Him)?

88. Say: in whose hand is the ownership of everything and He gives protection and there is no protection against Him, if you know?

89. They will say: (it belongs) to Allah. Say: so how are you conceited?

90. But We brought them the truth, and they deny.

91. Allah did not adopt a son and there is no other god with Him, otherwise every god would take what he created and they would exalt one above the other; glorified is Allah above what they make out.

92. The One who knows the unseen and the apparent, so exalted is He above what they associate.

93. Say: my Lord, if you show me what they have been promised,

94. Then, my Lord. do not place me amongst the wrongdoing people.

95. And We are able to show you what We promise them.

96. Repel bad with what is better, We know best what they make out.

97. And say: my Lord, I seek refuge in You from the suggestions of the devils.

98. And I seek refuge in you, my Lord, that they should be present.

99. Until when death reaches any of them, he says: my Lord, send me back.

100. So that I do good work in what I left behind; no way, it is only something he says, and behind them is a barrier until the day of resurrection.

101. Then when the horn is blown, there will be no connection between them on that day and they will not ask each other.

102. So whose weight is heavy, those will be successful.

103. And whose weight is light, those will have lost themselves, they will remain in hell.

104. The fire will burn their faces and they will be eaten away in it.

105. Were not My signs recited to you but you denied them?

106. They will say: our Lord. our misfortune has overtaken us and we were people who went astray.

107. Our Lord, take us out from here, then if we return, we will be wrongdoers.

108. He will say: Off with you in there and do not talk to Me.

109. For there a group of My servants saying: our Lord, we believe, so forgive us and have mercy on us, and You are the best of those who have mercy.

110. So you ridiculed them until they made you forget to remember Me and you laughed about them.

111. Today I reward them for having had patience, for they are the winners.

112. He will say: how many years did you stay on earth?

113. They will say: we stayed a day or part of a day; ask those who keep count.

114. He will say: you stayed only a little while if you had known.

115. Did you then reckon that We created you without purpose and that you would not be brought back to Us?

116. So exalted is Allah, the true king, there is no god but Him, the Lord of the noble throne.

117. And whoever calls on another god alongside Allah for whom he has no proof, his reckoning is with his Lord, for those who reject (the truth) do not succeed.

118. And say: my Lord, forgive and have mercy, and you are the best of those who have mercy.

Surah 24: *An-Nur*
(Light)

In the name of Allah,
the Owner and Giver of Mercy

1. A Surah which We have revealed and made obligatory and revealed in it clear signs so you pay heed.

2. The female and the male fornicator, beat each one of them with a hundred beatings and let not pity for both overcome you regarding the religion of Allah if you are believers in the last day, and let a group of the believers witness their punishment.

3. The male fornicator may not marry except a female fornicator or idolatress, and the female fornicator may not be married except by a male fornicator or idolater, and it is forbidden for the believers.

4. And those who accuse innocent women and then do not bring four witnesses, beat them with eighty beatings and do not ever accept evidence from them, and those are the sinful.

5. Except those who repent afterwards and make amends, for Allah is forgiving, merciful.

6. And those who accuse their partners and have no witnesses but themselves, the evidence of any of them will be to witness four times by Allah that he is truthful.

7. And a fifth time that the curse of Allah shall be upon him if he is a liar.

8. And the punishment is averted from her if she witnesses four times by Allah that he is a liar.

9. And a fifth time that the anger of Allah shall be upon her if he is truthful.

10. And you depend on Allah's favour and mercy upon you and that Allah is accepting and wise.

11. Those who brought the falsehood are a large group amongst you; do not consider it bad for you, it is good for you; for every man amongst them is the sin he has earned, and for the one amongst them who owns the greatest share of it is a severe punishment.

12. Why, when you heard it, did not the believing men and women think good within themselves and say: this is a clear falsehood?

13. Why did they not bring four witnesses for it? So if they did not bring the witnesses, then they are liars before Allah.

14. And if it were not for the favours and mercy of Allah upon you in this world and the hereafter, a severe punishment would have afflicted you for having spread it.

15. When your tongues uttered it and your mouths said things of which you had no knowledge and you considered it trivial, but with Allah it is serious.

16. And why, when you heard it, did you not say: it is not for us to say this, glorified are You, this is a serious slander.

17. Allah admonishes you not to return to something similar ever if you are believers.

18. And Allah explains to you His signs, and Allah is knowing and wise.

19. Those who love indecency to spread amongst the believers, for them is a painful punishment in this world and the hereafter, and Allah knows and you don't know.

20. And you depend on Allah's favour and mercy upon you and that Allah is lenient and merciful.

21. Oh you believers, do not follow in the footsteps of the devil; whoever follows in the footsteps of the devil, he commands indecency and wrongdoing, and if it were not for the favour and mercy of Allah upon you, none of you would ever be purified, but Allah purifies whom He pleases, and Allah listens and knows.

22. And let not the generous and affluent amongst you stop giving to relatives and the poor and the emigrants in the way of Allah - let them be lenient and pardon; don't you love that Allah forgives you? And Allah is forgiving and merciful.

23. Those who accuse unaware innocent believing women are cursed in this world and the hereafter and for them is a severe punishment.

24. On the day their tongues, hands and feet will witness against them as to what they used to do.

25. On that day Allah repays them their rightful dues and they know that Allah is the clear truth.

26. Bad women are for bad men and bad men for bad women, and good women are for good men and good men for good women - these are innocent of what they say, theirs is forgiveness and generous provision.

27. Oh you believers, do not enter houses other than your own houses until you have asked for permission and greeted their inhabitants, that is better for you, so you pay heed.

28. And if you do not find anyone there, then do not enter unless permission has been given to you, and if you are told to go back, go back, it is purer for you, and Allah knows what you do.

29. It is no sin for you to enter uninhabited houses where there is provision for you, and Allah knows what you let on and what you hide.

30. Tell the believing men to lower their eyes and guard their chastity, that is purer for them, for Allah is informed of what they get up to.

31. And tell the believing women to lower their eyes and guard their chastity and not to display their beauty except of what is apparent, and to throw their head coverings over their chests and not to display their beauty except to their husbands or their sons or their husband's sons or their brothers or their brothers' sons or their sisters' sons or their womenfolk or those in their possession or the incapable amongst their male attendants or the children who are not aware of women's nakedness, and not to stamp their feet to attract attention in spite of hiding their beauty; and repent to Allah altogether, oh you believers, in order to be successful.

32. And marry those who are single from amongst you and the righteous from amongst your male and female servants; if they are poor, Allah will enrich them from His favours, and Allah is generous and knows.

33. And let those who cannot find a marriage opportunity abstain until Allah enriches them from His favours. And those who want freedom of those in your possession, set them free if you know of good in them and give them of the wealth of Allah that He gave you, and do not compel your female servants to transgress if they want to be chaste, desiring the offering of this world, and if anyone compels them, then Allah is forgiving and merciful after they have been compelled.

34. We have revealed to you clear signs and the example of those who went before you and an admonition for those who beware (of Allah).

35. Allah is the light of the heavens and the earth; the example of His light is that of a niche in which there is a lamp; the lamp is within a glass; the glass is as if it were a bright star set ablaze by a blessed olive tree whose oil is neither from the East nor the West; its oil almost glows without fire having touched it; light upon light; Allah guides to His light whom He pleases, and Allah coins examples for people, and Allah knows everything.

36. In houses where Allah has permitted His name to be elevated and remembered, where He is glorified in the mornings and the evenings,

37. By men whom neither trade nor business distracts from the remembrance of Allah and from keeping up prayer and giving Zakat; they fear a day when the hearts and eyesight will be overturned.

38. So that Allah rewards them the best of their deeds and increases them from His favour, and Allah provides for whom He pleases without counting.

39. And those who reject (the truth), their deeds are like a mirage on empty flat land which the thirsty thinks is water, until when he reaches it he finds nothing and finds Allah present who pays him his account in full, and Allah is swift in counting.

40. Or like darknesses in the deep sea covered by waves with waves above, above which are clouds, darkness layered on top of each other, if he takes out his hand he can hardly see it, and to whom Allah does not give any light, he has no light.

41. Do you not see that everyone in the heavens and on earth glorifies Allah, and the birds in flocks? Each know their prayers and glorifications, and Allah knows what they do.

42. And to Allah belongs the kingdom of the heavens and the earth, and to Allah is the journey.

43. Do you not see that Allah makes clouds move, then combines them, then turns them into stacks, then you see the precipitation emerge from within, and He sends it down from the sky from towering clouds containing hailstone and afflicts with it whom He pleases and withholds it from whom

He pleases; its flash of lightning almost blinds the eyes.

44. Allah alternates the night and day, for in that is a lesson for those who see.

45. And Allah created every creature from water; amongst them are those who crawl on their bellies, and amongst them are those who walk on two legs, and amongst them are those who walk on four. Allah creates what He pleases, for Allah is able to do anything.

46. We have already revealed clear signs, and Allah guides whom He pleases to a straight path.

47. And they say: we believe in Allah and the messenger and obey, then a group of them turns away after that, and they are not believers.

48. And when they are called to Allah and His messenger to judge between them, a group of them are opposed to it.

49. And if the right is in their favour they come to him voluntarily.

50. Is there a disease in their hearts or are they in doubt or do they fear that Allah and His messenger would do them injustice? But they are the wrongdoers.

51. The statement of the believers, whenever they are called to Allah and His messenger to judge between them, is that they say: we listen and we obey, and those are the successful.

52. And whoever obeys Allah and His messenger and fears Allah and bewares of Him, those are the winners.

53. And they swear by Allah their utmost oaths that if you commanded them, they would move out; say: don't swear, (show) appropriate obedience, for Allah knows what you do.

54. Say: obey Allah and obey the messenger, then if you turn away, then upon him is what he has been tasked with and upon you is what you have been tasked with, and if you obey him you are guided, and the duty of the messenger is only to convey clearly.

55. Allah has promised the believers who do good work amongst you to make them successors on earth like He made those before you successors and to establish their religion for them, which He is content with for them, and to exchange their fear for hope. They serve Me and do not associate anything with Me. And whoever rejects (the truth) after that, those are the sinful.

56. And keep up prayer and give Zakat and obey the messenger in order to receive mercy.

57. Don't think that those who reject (the truth) will escape on earth. Their abode is the fire, and it is a bad destination.

58. Oh you believers, let those in your possession and those who of you who have not yet reached puberty ask your permission (to enter) on three occasions: before the prayer at daybreak and when you take off your outer garments during the mid-day heat and after the night prayer; three times of privacy for you. There is no sin for them or you outside those times if they move amongst you and you mingle. This is how Allah explains the signs to you, and Allah is knowing and wise.

59. And once your children have reached puberty, they should ask permission as those before them did. This is how Allah explains His signs to you, and Allah is knowing and wise.

60. And the elderly women who have no hope of marriage, it is no sin for them to take off their outer garments without displaying their beauty, and to refrain from it is better for them, and Allah listens and knows.

61. There is no harm for the blind, nor is there harm for the lame, nor is there harm for the sick nor for yourselves that you eat from your houses or the houses of your fathers or the houses of your mothers or the houses of your brothers or the houses of you sisters or the houses of you paternal uncles or the houses of your maternal uncles or the houses of your paternal aunts or the houses of your maternal aunts or of which you hold the keys or of a friend of yours; there is no sin for you to eat together or apart; so if you enter houses, offer their inhabitants a blessed good greeting from Allah; this is how Allah explains the signs for you to consider.

62. For the believers are those who believe in Allah and His messenger and when they are gathered with him for some matter they do not leave until they ask his permission; those who ask your permission are the ones who believe in Allah and His messenger,

so if they ask for your permission on account of some affair of theirs, then give permission to whom you please from them and ask Allah to forgive them, for Allah is forgiving and merciful.

63. Do not address the messenger amongst you like you address each other. Allah knows those of you who sneak away secretly, so let those who deviate from His command watch out for a trial or painful punishment to afflict them.

64. For sure to Allah belongs whatever is in the heavens and on earth; He knows your situation and on the day they are returned to him He will inform them of what they did, and Allah knows everything.

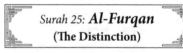

Surah 25: *Al-Furqan*
(The Distinction)

In the name of Allah,
the Owner and Giver of Mercy

1. Exalted is He who revealed the distinction (between truth and falsehood) to His servant for him to be a warner to all the world.

2. He to whom belongs the kingdom of the heavens and the earth and who did not adopt a son nor does He have any partner to share in the kingdom, and He created everything and arranged it in measure.

3. And they take gods besides Him who do not create anything and are themselves created, and they have no power over harm or benefit for themselves and are not in charge of death, life or the resurrection.

4. And those who reject (the truth) say: this is only a falsehood he invented and other people helped him with it; what they have come up with is wrong and dishonest.

5. And they say: stories of old which he has written down, and they are recited to him in the mornings and evenings.

6. Say: it has been revealed by Him who knows the secrets of the heavens and the earth, for He is forgiving and merciful.

7. And they say: what is the matter with this messenger that he eats food and walks in the market? Why was not an angel sent to him to be a warner with him?

8. And why was he not given a treasure or owns a garden to eat from it. And the wrongdoers say: you only follow a deranged man.

9. See how they coin likenesses for you and go astray and can't find a way.

10. Exalted is He who, if He pleases, will give you better than that: gardens through which rivers flow, and will give you castles.

11. But they deny the hour, and We have promised for one who denies the hour a fire.

12. When it sees them from afar, they hear its fury and hissing.

13. And when they are thrown into a tight place there in which they are tied together, then they call for destruction.

14. Do not call for a single destruction today, but call for many destructions.

15. Say: is this better or the garden of eternity those who beware (of Allah) have been promised as their reward and destination?

16. They have there whatever they please, being immortal, a promise your Lord will make good.

17. And on the day He gathers them and what they serve besides Allah and says: did you lead these servants of Mine astray or did they lose the way?

18. They will say: glorified are You, it was not befitting for us to take protectors besides You, but You gave them and their fathers provision until they forgot the reminder and were ruined as people.

19. So they deny what you say and you can neither bring about change nor help, and whoever does wrong amongst you, We make him taste a great punishment.

20. And whenever We sent messengers before you they ate food and walked in the markets, and We made some of you a test for others as to whether you are patient, and your Lord is watching.

21. And those who do not look forward to meet Us say: why are not the angels sent down to us or do we see our Lord? They are arrogant in themselves and highly insulting.

22. On the day they see the angels there will be no good news for the sinful and they will order them to stay put.

23. And We turn to the work they did and turn it into dispersed dust.

24. The inhabitants of the garden will be in the best outcome that day and the most beautiful place of rest.

25. And on the day the sky, with the clouds, will be split open and the angels will come down in a descent;

26. On that day the true kingdom will belong to the Merciful, and it will be a difficult day for those who rejected (the truth).

27. And on the day the wrongdoer will bite his hands and say: woe to me, if only I had chosen a way with the messenger.

28. Woe upon woe to me, if only I did not choose this fellow for a friend.

29. He lead me astray from the reminder after it came to me, and the devil always abandons man.

30. And the messenger will say: oh my Lord, my people turned away from this Qur'an.

31. And likewise We arranged for every prophet an enemy from amongst the sinful, and your Lord is sufficient as a guide and helper.

32. And those who reject (the truth) say: why is not the Qur'an revealed to him in one go? In this manner We strengthen your heart and recite it gradually.

33. And whenever they bring you an example We bring instead the truth and best explanation.

34. Those who are gathered into hell on their faces, they are worst off and most astray from the way.

35. And We gave Musa (Moses) the book and made his brother Harun (Aaron) a deputy with him.

36. And We said: go both to the people who deny Our signs, then We annihilated them completely.

37. And the people of Nuh (Noah), when they denied the messengers, We drowned them and made them a sign for mankind, and We promised the wrongdoers a painful punishment.

38. And 'Ad and Thamud and the people around the waterhole (ar-Rass) and many generations between them.

39. For each of them We coined likenesses, and each of them We destroyed completely.

40. And they have come across the town on which an evil rain fell - did they not see it? But they did not hope for the resurrection.

41. And when they see you, they only make fun of you: is this the one whom Allah sent as a messenger?

42. He almost made us stray from our gods if we did not hold on to them. And soon will they know, when they see the punishment, who is most astray from the way.

43. Have you considered him who takes as his god his desire? Are you going to protect him?

44. Or do you think that most of them listen or understand? They are like the cattle; rather they are more astray from the way.

45. Do you not see how your Lord extends the shadow, and if He pleased He could have made it stationary? Then We made the sun a pointer for it.

46. Then We gradually reduce it towards Us.

47. And He is who made the night a cover for you and sleep for rest and made the day for rising.

48. And He is who sent the winds as good news in advance of His mercy, and We send clean water down from the sky.

49. To revive a dead land with it, and We give it to drink to many animals and people We have created.

50. And We have circulated it amongst them so that they would take heed, but most people refuse anything but rejection.

51. And if We pleased, We would have raised a warner in every town.

52. So do not obey those who reject (the truth) and fight them with it in a major effort.

53. And He is who mingled the two bodies of water, one sweet and palatable, the other salty and unpalatable, and He placed a barrier and impassable border between them.

54. And He is who created a human being from water and gave him lineage and relationships, and your Lord is powerful.

55. And they serve besides Allah what neither benefits nor harms them, and the one who rejects (the truth) is openly rebellious against his Lord.

56. And We only sent you as a bringer of good news and a warner.

57. Say: I do not ask you for a reward for it, but whoever pleases may choose a way towards his Lord.

58. And rely on the One who lives and does not die and glorify His praise, and He is sufficiently informed about the sins of His servants.

59. The One who created the heavens and the earth and what is between them in six days, then He rose onto the throne, the Merciful, so ask anyone informed about Him.

60. And if they are told to prostrate to the Merciful, they say: who is the Merciful, are we to prostrate to whom you command us to? and it increases their disagreement.

61. Exalted is He who placed constellations in the sky and placed amongst them a light and a radiant moon.

62. And He is who made the night and day alternate for anyone who wishes to take heed or give thanks.

63. And the servants of the Merciful are those who walk gentle on the earth and when the ignorant address them, they say: peace.

64. And those who spend the night prostrating to their Lord and standing (in prayer).

65. And those who say: our Lord, avert from us the punishment of hell, for its punishment is unbearable.

66. It is a bad outcome and abode.

67. And those who when they spend are neither wasteful nor stingy, and the right balance is between the two.

68. And those who do not call on any other god alongside Allah and do not kill anyone whom Allah has forbidden except in justice and do not fornicate, and whoever does this commits a crime.

69. The punishment will be multiplied for him on the day of resurrection and he will remain in it disgraced.

70. Except for him who repents and believes and does good work, for those Allah replaces their bad deeds with good deeds, and Allah is forgiving and merciful.

71. And whoever repents and does good, he truly repents to Allah.

72. And those who do not witness falsehood and when they pass by idle talk, they pass by dignified.

73. And those who when they are reminded of the signs of their Lord do not ignore them deaf and blind.

74. And those who say: our Lord, make our partners and offspring pleasing to look at and make us leaders for those who beware (of You).

75. Those will be rewarded a high station on account of their patience and will meet there greetings and peace.

76. They will remain there, a good outcome and abode.

77. Say: my Lord would not pay attention to you but for your prayer, yet you denied, so soon the inevitable will happen.

Surah 26: **Ash-Shu'ara'**
(The Poets)

In the name of Allah,
the Owner and Giver of Mercy

1. Ta, Sin, Mim.

2. These are the signs of the clear book.

3. You almost kill yourself with worry that they are not believers.

4. If We please, We would send a sign from the sky down to them and their necks would remain humbled by it.

5. And whenever a new reminder comes to them from the Merciful, they tend to turn away from it.

6. So they denied, then the news of what they used to make fun of will reach them.

7. Do they not look at the earth, how many a precious species We grew on it.

8. For in that is a sign, and most of them are not believers.

9. And your Lord is the mighty and merciful.

10. And when your Lord called Musa (Moses) to go to the wrongdoing people.

11. The people of Pharaoh, as to why they do not beware (of Allah).

12. He said: my Lord, I fear that they deny me.

13. And my chest tightens and my tongue does not loosen, so send for Harun (Aaron).

14. And they hold a crime against me, so I fear that they will kill me.

15. He said: no way, go both with My signs, We are with you listening.

16. So they both came to Pharaoh and said: we are a messenger from the Lord of all worlds.

17. That you should send with us the Children of Israel.

18. He said: did we not look after you amongst us as a child and you stayed amongst us some years of your life?

19. And you did the deed you did and were of the ungrateful.

20. He said: I did it when I was astray.

21. Then I fled from you when I feared you, and my Lord granted me the ability to judge and made me of the messengers.

22. And is this the favour you hold against me, that you enslaved the Children of Israel?

23. Pharaoh said: and who is the Lord of all worlds?

24. He said: the Lord of the heavens and the earth and what is between them, if you are certain.

25. He said to those around him: are you not listening?

26. He said: your Lord and the Lord of your forefathers.

27. He said: your messenger who has been sent to you is possessed.

28. He said: the Lord of the East and the West and what is between them, if you understand.

29. He said: if you take a god other than me, I will certainly imprison you.

30. He said: even if I bring you something clear?

31. He said: then bring it if you are truthful.

32. So he threw down his staff and it became a real snake.

33. And he pulled out his hand and it could be seen as white.

34. The leaders around him said: this is a knowledgeable magician.

35. He wants to expel you from your land with his magic, so what do you command?

36. They said: defer him and his brother and dispatch mobilisers to the cities,

37. To bring you every knowledgeable magician.

38. Then the magicians were gathered for an appointment on a specified day.

39. And the people were told: are you going to gather?

40. So we can follow the magicians if they are the winners?

41. And when the magicians came they said to Pharaoh: will we have a reward if we are the winners?

42. He said: yes, and you will then be of the inner circle.

43. Musa (Moses) said to them: throw what you can throw.

44. So they threw their ropes and sticks and said: by the might of Pharaoh, we will be the winners.

45. Then Musa (Moses) threw his stick, then it took over what they invented.

46. Then the magicians fell prostrate.

47. They said: we believe in the Lord of all worlds.

48. The Lord of Musa (Moses) and Harun (Aaron).

49. He said: do you believe in him before I have given you permission? For sure he is your chief who taught you magic, so soon you will know: I will cut your hands and feet from opposite sides and will crucify you all.

50. They said: no harm, we will turn to our Lord.

51. For we hope that our Lord will forgive us our sins because we are the first amongst the believers.

52. And We revealed to Musa (Moses) to travel with My servants, for you will be followed.

53. Then Pharaoh sent mobilisers to the cities.

54. These are a small group.

55. And they have angered us.

56. And we are force to be reckoned with.

57. So We drove them out of gardens and springs.

58. And treasures and honoured dwellings.

59. This is what happened, and We made the Children of Israel inherit them.

60. So they pursued them in the morning.

61. And when the two groups faced each other the companions of Musa (Moses) said, we have been overtaken.

62. He said: no way, for my Lord is with me, He will guide me.

63. Then We revealed to Musa (Moses) to strike the sea with your stick, then it parted and each part was like a great mountain.

64. Then We made the others advance after that.

65. And We rescued Musa (Moses) and all who were with him.

66. Then We drowned the others.

67. For in that is a sign, and most of them are not believers.

68. And your Lord is the mighty and merciful.

69. And recite to them the news about Ibrahim (Abraham).

70. When he said to his father and his people: what do you serve?

71. They said: we serve idols and remain devoted to them.

72. He said: do they hear you when you call?

73. Or benefit you or do harm?

74. They said: but we found our fathers do the same.

75. He said: then look at what you serve;

76. You and your forefathers:

77. They are an enemy to me, except for the Lord of all worlds.

78. The One who created me then guided me.

79. And the One who feeds me and gives me to drink.

80. And if I am ill, He heals me.

81. And the One who makes me die, then brings me to life.

82. And the One of whom I hope that He forgives me my sins on the day of repayment.

83. My Lord, grant me the ability to judge and make me join the righteous.

84. And give me a truthful reputation amongst those to come.

85. And make me of those who inherit the garden of blessings.

86. And forgive my father, for he was of those astray.

87. And do not humiliate me on the day they will be raised.

88. On the day when neither wealth nor children are of benefit.

89. Except for him who comes to Allah with a clean heart.

90. And the garden will be brought near to those who beware (of Allah).

91. And hell-fire will be presented to the transgressors.

92. And they will be told: where is what you used to serve?

93. Besides Allah, are they going to help you or help themselves?

94. So they and the transgressors will be dumped into it.

95. And all the soldiers of Iblis (the devil).

96. They will say, whilst they argue there:

97. By Allah, we were in clear error.

98. When we equated you with the Lord of all worlds.

99. And only the sinful lead us astray.

100. So we have no intercessors.

101. And no dear friend.

102. If only we could return and be of the believers.

103. For in that is a sign, and most of them are not believers.

104. And your Lord is the mighty and merciful.

105. The people of Nuh (Noah) denied the messengers.

106. When their brother Nuh (Noah) said to them: will you not beware (of Allah)?

107. For I am a reliable messenger to you.

108. So beware of Allah and obey me.

109. And I do not ask you for a reward for it, for my reward is only with the Lord of all worlds.

110. So beware of Allah and obey me.

111. They said: should we believe in you when the down and out follow you?

112. He said: I have no knowledge of what they used to do.

113. For their reckoning is upon my Lord, if only you realised.

114. And I am not going to drive away the believers.

115. For I am only a clear warner.

116. They said: if you do not stop, oh Nuh (Noah), you will be stoned.

117. He said: my Lord, my people deny me.

118. So decide clearly between me and them and rescue me and the believers with me.

119. So We rescued him and those with him in the loaded ship.

120. Then We drowned the remainder.

121. For in that is a sign, and most of them are not believers.

122. And your Lord is the mighty and merciful.

123. 'Ad denied the messengers.

124. When their brother Hud said to them: will you not beware (of Allah)?

125. For I am a reliable messenger to you.

126. So beware of Allah and obey me.

127. And I do not ask you for a reward for it, for my reward is only with the Lord of all worlds.

128. Do you pointlessly construct a marker on every elevated place?

129. And adopt fortified buildings as if you lived forever?

130. And when you strike out you strike out as tyrants?

131. So beware of Allah and obey me.

132. And beware of the One who furnished you with what you know.

133. Furnished you with cattle and children.

134. And gardens and springs.

135. For I fear for you the punishment of a tremendous day.

136. They said: It is the same for us whether you caution us or do not caution us.

137. For there is only the first creation.

138. And we will not be resurrected.

139. So they denied him and We destroyed them, for in that is a sign, and most of them are not believers.

140. And your Lord is the mighty and merciful.

141. Thamud denied the messengers.

142. When their brother Salih said to them: will you not beware (of Allah)?

143. For I am a reliable messenger to you.

144. So beware of Allah and obey me.

145. And I do not ask you for a reward for it, for my reward is only with the Lord of all worlds.

146. Are you going to be left safe here?

147. In gardens and springs?

148. And plantations and palm trees with packed date clusters?

149. And you carve out strong homes from the mountains?

150. So beware of Allah and obey me.

151. And do not obey the command of the wasteful.

152. Those who cause corruption on earth and do not reform.

153. They said: you are deranged.

154. You are only a human like us, so bring a sign if you are truthful.

155. He said: this is a she-camel, she will drink and you will drink on a known day.

156. And do not touch her with harm so that the punishment of a tremendous day overtakes you.

157. So they bled her to death, then came to regret.

158. Then the punishment overtook them, for in that is a sign, and most of them are not believers.

159. And your Lord is the mighty and merciful.

160. The people of Lut (Lot) denied the messengers.

161. When their brother Lut (Lot) said to them: will you not beware (of Allah)?

162. For I am a reliable messenger to you.

163. So beware of Allah and obey me.

164. And I do not ask you for a reward for it, for my reward is only with the Lord of all worlds.

165. Do you go for males amongst everyone?

166. And leave the wives your Lord has created for you? But you are outrageous people.

167. They said: if you do not stop, oh Lut (Lot), you will be expelled.

168. He said: I am only describing your deeds.

169. My Lord, rescue me and my family from what they do.

170. So We rescued him and his family altogether.

171. Except an old woman who stayed behind.

172. Then We destroyed the others.

173. And We let it rain on them, and it was an evil rain for those who had been warned.

174. For in that is a sign, and most of them are not believers.

175. And your Lord is the mighty and merciful.

176. And the inhabitants of the woodlands (al-Ayka) denied the messengers.

177. When Shu'ayb (Jethro) said to them: will you not beware (of Allah)?

178. For I am a reliable messenger to you.

179. So beware of Allah and obey me.

180. And I do not ask you for a reward for it, for my reward is only with the Lord of all worlds.

181. Give full measure and do not reduce it.

182. And weigh with a level scale.

183. And do not withhold from people their belongings and do not spread corruption on earth.

184. And beware of the One who created you and the earlier creation.

185. They said: you are deranged.

186. And you are only a human like us, and we consider you a liar.

187. So drop on us a piece of the sky if you are truthful.

188. He said: my Lord knows best what you do.

189. So they denied him, then the punishment of the day of obscuration overtook them, and it was the punishment of a tremendous day.

190. For in that is a sign, and most of them are not believers.

191. And your Lord is the mighty and merciful.

192. And it is a revelation from the Lord of all worlds

193. He sent with it the trusted Spirit.

194. Unto your heart, so that you would be of the warners.

195. In a clear Arabic language.

196. And it is in the earlier scriptures.

197. Is it not a sign for them that the scholars of the Children of Israel know it?

198. And had We revealed it to some foreigners,

199. Then he would have read it to them, they would not have believed in it.

200. This is how We let it pass through the hearts of the sinful.

201. They do not believe in it until they see the painful punishment.

202. And it reaches them suddenly when they are not aware.

203. Then they will say: will we be given time?

204. Do they hasten Our punishment?

205. Have you considered that if We give them provision for some years,

206. Then what they were promised reaches them,

207. The provision they were given will not benefit them?

208. And We never destroyed a town unless there was a warner for it.

209. A reminder, and We were not oppressors.

210. And the devils do not descend with it.

211. And it is not befitting for them, and they are unable to.

212. For they are cut off from listening.

213. So do not call on any other god with Allah, then you would be of those to be punished.

214. And warn your immediate relatives.

215. And give comfort to the believers who follow you.

216. And if they disobey you, then say: I am free of what you do.

217. And rely on the mighty and merciful.

218. Who sees you when you stand up.

219. And when you bend amongst the prostrate.

220. For He listens and knows.

221. Shall I inform you on whom the devils descend?

222. They descend on every sinful liar.

223. They listen out, but most of them are liars.

224. And the poets, the misguided follow them.

225. Do you not see that they wander about in every valley,

226. And that they say what they don't do.

227. Except those who believe and do good and remember Allah a lot and defend themselves after having been wronged, and the wrongdoers will soon know which way they will turn.

Surah 27: *An-Naml*
(Ants)

In the name of Allah,
the Owner and Giver of Mercy

1. Ta Sin. These are the signs of the reading (Qur'an) and a clear book.

2. A guidance and good news for the believers.

3. Those who keep up prayer and give Zakat and are certain about the hereafter.

4. Those who do not believe in the hereafter, We make their deeds appeal to them, so they get lost.

5. For those is the worst punishment and they will be the losers in the hereafter.

6. And you have received the Qur'an from One wise and knowing.

7. When Musa (Moses) said to his family: I noticed a fire, I will bring you news from there or will bring you a glowing ember so you can warm yourselves.

8. Then when he reached it, he was called: blessed is who is in the fire and who surrounds it and glorified is Allah, the Lord of all worlds.

9. Oh Musa (Moses), I am Allah the mighty and wise.

10. And throw your stick, then when he saw it move as if it was a snake, he turned away and did not turn around; oh Musa (Moses): do not fear, the messengers have no fear in My presence.

11. Except he who has done wrong, then replaces bad with good, for I am forgiving and merciful.

12. And place your hand on your chest, it will come out white without harm amongst seven signs for Pharaoh and his people, for they were sinful people.

13. And when Our signs reached them clearly visible they said: this is plain magic.

14. And they disputed them sinfully and arrogantly whilst their own souls acknowledged them, so see what the outcome was like for the corrupters.

15. And We gave Dawud (David) and Sulayman (Solomon) knowledge and they said: praised is Allah who favoured us over many of His believing servants.

16. And Sulayman (Solomon) inherited from Dawud (David) and said: oh people, we were taught the speech of birds and have been given of everything, this is indeed a clear favour.

17. And his soldiers from the Jinn and humans and birds were gathered before Sulayman (Solomon) and arranged into divisions.

18. Until when they came upon the valley of the ants, an ant said: oh ants, enter your homes so that Sulayman (Solomon) and his soldiers do not crush you without realising.

19. Then he smiled amused at her words and said: my Lord, grant me that I am grateful for Your blessing which You have blessed me and my parents with and that I do good work which You will be pleased with and enter me by Your mercy amongst Your righteous servants.

20. Then he inspected the birds and said: how come I don't see the hoopoe (Hudhud) or is he absent?

21. I shall punish him severely or slaughter him unless he brings a clear authority.

22. But he wasn't far off and said: I discovered what you had not discovered and brought you from Sheba (Saba') reliable information.

23. I found a woman ruling over them who has been given of everything and has a mighty throne.

24. And I found her people prostrate to the sun instead of Allah, and the devil made their deeds appeal to them so he diverted them from the way and they are not guided.

25. That they do not prostrate to Allah who brings out what is hidden in the heavens and the earth and knows what you conceal and what you disclose.

26. Allah, there is no god but Him, the Lord of the mighty throne.

27. He said: we shall see whether you are truthful or a liar.

28. Go with this letter of mine and deliver it to them, then turn away from them and see what they come back with.

29. She said: oh leaders, an honourable letter has been delivered to me.

30. It is from Sulayman (Solomon) and is in the name of Allah, the Owner and Giver of Mercy.

31. Do not exalt above me and come to me in submission (as Muslims).

32. She said: oh leaders, advise me in the matter, I do not decide a matter unless you are witnesses.

33. They said: we possess power and terrifying strength, and the matter is for you to decide, so see what you will command.

34. She said: when kings enter a town they ruin it and make the most respected of it the most humiliated, and that is what they do.

35. And I shall sent a gift to them, then wait what the messengers return with.

36. And when it reached Sulayman (Solomon) he said: are you providing me with wealth when what Allah has given me is better than what He has given you? But you rejoice in your gift.

37. Return to them, for we will come to them with soldiers they cannot face up to and will expel them humiliated and conquered.

38. He said: oh leaders, who of you will bring me her throne before they come to me in submission?

39. A cunning Jinn said: I will bring it to you before you get up from your seat and I am certainly able to do that.

40. The one who had knowledge of the book said: I will bring it to you in the wink of an eye; then when he saw it positioned near him he said: this is of the favour of my Lord to test me whether I am grateful or ungrateful, and whoever is grateful, he is grateful for his own good, and whoever is ungrateful, my Lord is rich and generous.

41. He said: we will alter her throne for her to see if she is guided or of those who are not guided.

42. Then when she came, she was told: is your throne like this? She said: as if it was the one. And we were given knowledge before her and had submitted (as Muslims).

43. And what she used to serve besides Allah diverted her, for she belonged to people who rejected (the truth).

44. She was told: enter the palace. Then when she saw it, she thought it was water and bared her legs. He said: it is a palace made of crystal. She said: my Lord, I have wronged myself and submit with Sulayman (Solomon) to Allah, the Lord of all worlds.

45. And to Thamud We sent their brother Salih, (saying) serve Allah, then they became two arguing factions.

46. He said: oh my people, why do you hasten the bad before the good? Why don't you ask Allah for forgiveness in order to receive mercy?

47. They said: we see a bad omen in you and those with you. He said: your bad omen is with Allah, but you are being tried as a people.

48. And there were nine clans in the town who caused corruption on earth and did not reform.

49. They said: let's swear by Allah that we will attack him and his family at night then say to his protector that we did not witness the destruction of his family and that we are truthful.

50. And they schemed their scheme and We schemed Our scheme, and they did not realise.

51. So see what the outcome of their scheme was like: We destroyed them and their people altogether.

52. And these their houses are deserted because of their wrongdoing. In that is a sign for people who know.

53. And We rescued those who believed and constantly bewared (of Allah).

54. And Lut (Lot) when he said to his people: do you visibly go for indecency?

55. Do you come to men with lust instead of women? But you are an ignorant people.

56. And the reply of his people was merely that they said: expel the family of Lut (Lot) from your town for they are people who want to keep clean.

57. So We rescued him and his family except his wife whom We decreed to stay behind.

58. And We let it rain on them, and it was an evil rain for those who had been warned.

59. Say: Allah is praised and peace upon His servants whom He has chosen. Is Allah better or what you assign as partners?

60. Or who created the heavens and the earth and sent water for you from the sky, so that We grow with it gardens full of splendour? You could not grow its trees! Is there a god with Allah? But they are people who turn away.

61. Or who made the earth firm and made rivers run through it and made stabilisers for it and placed a barrier between the two bodies of water? Is there a god with Allah? But most of them don't know.

62. Or who responds to the distressed when he calls Him and removes the harm and makes you successors on earth? Is there a god with Allah? Little do you reflect.

63. Or who guides you in the darkness on land and on sea and who sends the wind as a bringer of good news before His mercy? Is there a god with Allah? Exalted is Allah above what they assign as partners.

64. Or who originates the creation then repeats it and who provides from you from the sky and the earth? Is there a god with Allah? Say: bring your proof if you are truthful.

65. Say: nobody in the heavens and the earth knows the unseen except Allah and they have no idea when they will be raised.

66. But does their knowledge extend to the hereafter? No, they are in doubt of it. No, they are blind to it.

67. And those who reject (the truth) say: when we are dust as well as our fathers, are we going to be brought back?

68. We and our fathers were promised this before, these are only stories of old.

69. Say: travel on the earth, then see what the outcome was like for the sinful.

70. And do not worry about them nor be uptight about what they are scheming.

71. And they say: when will this promise happen if you are truthful?

72. Say: maybe some of what you hasten will befall you quickly.

73. And your Lord is full of generosity towards people, but most of them give no thanks.

74. And your Lord knows what they hide inside and what they disclose.

75. And there is nothing hidden in the sky or on earth but it is in a clear record.

76. This Qur'an relates to the Children of Israel most of what they differ in.

77. And it is a guidance and mercy for the believers.

78. Your Lord decides between them by His judgement and He is the mighty and knowing.

79. So rely on Allah, for you are upon the clear truth.

80. For you cannot make the dead hear and cannot make the deaf hear when they turn away.

81. And you will not guide the blind away from their error. You can only make those hear who believe in Our signs and submit (as Muslims).

82. And when the word against them comes to pass We bring out a creature from the earth for them to speak to them that mankind were not sure about Our signs.

83. And on the day We gather a portion from each community of those who denied Our signs and arrange them into divisions.

84. Until when they come, He will say: did you deny My signs without grasping them in knowledge, or what did you do?

85. And the word against them comes to pass on account of their wrongdoing, so they cannot speak.

86. Do they not see that We made the night for them to rest in and the day to see? In that are signs for people who listen.

87. And on the day the horn is blown, whoever is in the heavens and on earth is terrified except whom Allah pleases, and all come to Him in submission.

88. And you will see the mountains, which you consider solid, disperse like the clouds. This is the design of Allah who perfected everything, for He knows what you do.

89. Whoever brings a good deed will have better than it, and they will be safe from the terror of that day.

90. And whoever brings a bad deed, their faces will be thrown into the fire. Are you being punished except for what you did?

91. I have only been commanded to serve the Lord of this land which He has made sacred, and everything belongs to Him, and I have been commanded to be the first to submit (as Muslim).

92. And to recite the Qur'an; so whoever wants to be guided, is guided for his own good, and to whoever goes astray say: I am only a warner.

93. Say: Allah is praised, He will show you His signs so that you know them, and my Lord is not unaware of what you do.

Surah 28: *Al-Qasas*
(The Story)

In the name of Allah,
the Owner and Giver of Mercy

1. Ta, Sin, Mim.

2. These are the signs of the clear book.

3. We recite to you in truth of the information about Musa (Moses) and Pharaoh for people who believe.

4. Pharaoh exalted on earth and turned its people into factions, a group of whom he oppressed, slaughtering their sons and sparing their women, for he was of the corrupters.

5. And We wanted to show favour to those who were oppressed on earth and make them leaders and make them the inheritors.

6. And to establish them on earth and show Pharaoh and Haman and their soldiers from them what they were afraid of.

7. And We revealed to the mother of Musa (Moses) to suckle him, then when you fear for him, throw him into the river and do not fear nor worry, for We will return him to you and make him of the messengers.

8. Then the family of Pharaoh picked him up so he would be an enemy and worry for them, for Pharaoh and Haman and their soldiers were guilty.

9. And the wife of Pharaoh said: a comfort for my eyes and yours, do not kill him, maybe he will benefit us or we will adopt him as a son, and they did not realise.

10. And the heart of the mother of Musa (Moses) became empty and she almost disclosed him had We not made her heart firm so that she would be of the believers.

11. So she said to his sister, go after him, then she saw him from the side-lines whilst they did not realise.

12. And We had forbidden to him wet-nurses before, so she said: shall I point you to the people of a house who will take care of him for you and be sincere to him?

13. So We returned him to his mother so that her eyes would be comforted and she would not worry and would know that the promise of Allah is true, but most of them don't know.

14. And when he attained his full strength and stature We gave him the ability to judge and knowledge and this is how We reward those who do good.

15. And he entered the town when its inhabitants were unaware and found there two men fighting, one from his faction and one from his enemies; then the one from his faction asked for his assistance against the one from his enemies, so Musa (Moses) hit him and finished him off. He said: this is from the devil's work, for he is a clear misleading enemy.

16. He said: my Lord, I have wronged myself, so forgive me. Then He forgave him, for He is forgiving and merciful.

17. He said: my Lord, because you have favoured me I will not support the sinful.

18. Then he became fearful and apprehensive in the town when the one who had sought his help the day before called out for his help. Musa (Moses) said to him: you are a clear hothead.

19. Then when he wanted to strike the one who was an enemy to them both he said: oh Musa (Moses), do you want to kill me like you killed someone yesterday? You only want to be a tyrant on earth and don't want to be of the reformers.

20. And a man came running from the other end of town, saying: oh Musa (Moses), the leaders are commanding to kill you, so leave, I am sincere to you.

21. So he left from there fearful and apprehensive and said: my Lord, rescue me from the wrongdoing people.

22. Then when he faced towards Madyan (Midian) he said: maybe my Lord will guide me to the level way.

23. And when he arrived at the water of Madyan (Midian) he found a community of people there who watered (their flocks) and found besides them two women staying away. He said: what is the matter with you? They said: we will not water (our flock) until the shepherds have gone, and our father is an old man.

24. So he watered them for them, then turned towards the shade and said: my Lord, I am in need of any good you may send to me.

25. Then one of them came walking shyly and said: my father calls you to pay you a reward for having watered (our flock) for us. Then when he came and related to him the story he said: do not fear, you have been rescued from the wrongdoing people.

26. One of them said: oh my father, hire him, for the best you can hire is the strong and trusted.

27. He said: I want to marry one of these two daughters of mine to you on condition that you work for me for eight seasons, but if you complete ten then that is up to you, and I do not want to overburden you, you will, if Allah pleases, find me of the righteous.

28. He said: that is between me and you, whichever of the two terms I complete, there shall be no enmity against me, and Allah is a guardian over what we say.

29. Then when Musa (Moses) had completed the term and travelled with his family, he noticed on the side of the mountain a fire. He said to his family: wait, I noticed a fire, maybe I bring you news from there or a burning log from the fire so you can warm yourselves.

30. Then when he reached it he was called from the right side of the valley at the blessed location of the tree: oh Musa (Moses), I am Allah, the Lord of all worlds.

31. And throw your stick, then when he saw it move as if it was a snake, he turned away and did not turn around; oh Musa (Moses): come close and do not fear, for you are safe.

32. Insert your hand onto your chest, it will come out white without harm, and bring your arms together (over your chest) to calm your fear. So these are two proofs from your Lord for Pharaoh and his leaders, for they are sinful people.

33. He said: my Lord, I killed someone from them and fear that they will kill me.

34. And my brother Harun (Aaron) is more eloquent in speech than me, so send him with me in support to confirm me, for I fear that they will deny me.

35. He said: We will strengthen your support with your brother and give you both authority, so they will not get to you; with Our signs you both and those who follow you will be the winners.

36. Then when Musa (Moses) came to them with Our clear signs they said: this is only invented magic and we have not heard this from our forefathers.

37. And Musa (Moses) said: my Lord knows best who comes with the guidance from Him and to whom belongs the final abode, for the wrongdoers do not succeed.

38. And Pharaoh said: oh leaders, I do not know any other god for you than myself, so supply me, oh Haman, with clay and build me a structure from which to ascend to the god of Musa (Moses), for I consider him a liar.

39. And he and his soldiers were arrogant on earth without right and thought that they would not return to Us.

40. So We overtook him and his soldiers and threw them into the sea, then see what the outcome of the wrongdoers was like.

41. And We made them leaders calling to the fire and on the day of resurrection they will not be helped.

42. And We had them followed by a curse, and on the day of resurrection they are amongst the despised.

43. And We gave Musa (Moses) the book, after having destroyed the earlier generations, as clear evidence for mankind and a guidance and mercy so that they might reflect.

44. And you were not on the Western side when We decided the matter for Musa (Moses) and you were not of the witnesses.

45. But We raised generations until the time seemed too long for them; and you did not live amongst the inhabitants of Madyan (Midian) to recite to them Our signs, but We sent others.

46. And you were not on the side of the mountain when We called, but it is a mercy from your Lord in order for you to warn a people to whom no warner has come before you, so that they reflect.

47. So that when an affliction befalls them on account of what they have sent ahead they cannot say: our Lord, why did You not send a messenger to us so we could follow Your signs and be of the believers?

48. Then when the truth from Us came to them they said: why hasn't he been given the like of what Musa (Moses) was given? Did they not reject what Musa (Moses) had been given before, saying: two magicians supporting each other, and saying: we reject each of them.

49. Say: then bring a book from Allah which is more guided than those two, and I will follow it, if you are truthful.

50. Then if they do not respond to you, then know that they only follow their desires, and who is more astray than he who follows his desire without guidance from Allah, for Allah does not guide the wrongdoing people.

51. And We made the word reach them continuously so that they might reflect.

52. Those to whom We gave the book before believe in it.

53. And when it is recited to them they say: we believe in it, for it is the truth from our Lord, we submitted (as Muslims) before.

54. Those will be given their reward twice on account of having had patience and warding off bad with good and spending of what We provided them with.

55. And if they hear idle talk, they turn away from it and say: our work is for us and your work is for you, peace be with you, we do not seek the ignorant.

56. For you do not guide whom you love but Allah guides whom He pleases, and He knows best who is guided.

57. And they say: if we follow the guidance with you we will be forced out from our land. Did We not establish for them a safe sanctuary where fruit of all kinds arrives as provision from Us, but most of them don't know.

58. And how many a town have We destroyed which took pride in its living standards, so these are their homes which were not inhabited after them except a little, and We were the inheritors.

59. And your Lord never destroys a town until he raises in its midst a messenger who recites to them Our signs, and We never destroy towns unless their inhabitants are wrongdoers.

60. And whatever you have been given is the provision of the life of the world and its adornment, and what is with Allah is better and more lasting, do you not then understand?

61. Is he whom We have given a good promise and he achieves it like the one whom We have given provision in the life of the world, then on the day of resurrection he is of those summoned?

62. And on the day He calls them and says: where are My associates whom you claimed?

63. Those against whom the word comes to pass will say: our Lord, these are the ones whom we lead astray, we lead them astray just as we were astray, we disown them before You, they did not serve us.

64. And it will be said: call your associates, so they call them but they will not respond to them, and they see the punishment - if only they were guided.

65. And on the day He calls them, then will say: how did you respond to the messengers?

66. And they will be blind to any information on that day and will not ask each other.

67. So whoever repents and believes and does good, he will likely be successful.

68. And your Lord creates what He pleases and chooses, they do not have a choice, glorified is Allah and exalted above what they associate.

69. And your Lord knows what they hide inside and what they disclose.

70. And He is Allah, there is no god but Him, He is praised in this world and the next, and His is the judgement and to Him you will return.

71. Say: have you considered if Allah made the night continuous for you until the day of resurrection, what god other than Allah would bring you light? Do you not then listen?

72. Say: have you considered if Allah made the day continuous for you until the day of resurrection, what god other than Allah would bring you a night to rest in? Do you not then see?

73. And of His mercy He made for you the night and the day so that you rest in it and seek of His favours and so that you are grateful.

74. And on the day He calls them and says: where are My associates whom you claimed?

75. And We take a witness from each community, then say: bring your proof, then they know that the truth belongs to Allah and what they used to invent deserts them.

76. Qarun (Korah) was of the people of Musa (Moses) but transgressed against them, and We gave him treasures whose keys weighed down a strong camel, when his people said to him: do not show off, Allah does not love the show-offs.

77. And seek with that what Allah has given you the abode of the hereafter and do not forget your share of this world and do good like Allah has done good to you and do not seek corruption on earth, for Allah does not love the corrupters.

78. He said: I was given it on account of my own knowledge. Did he not know that Allah destroyed generations before him who had greater strength and larger numbers than him? And the sinful will not be questioned about their sins.

79. So he came out to his people in his adornments. Those who wanted the life of the world said: if only we had like what Qarun (Korah) has been given, for he is full of good fortune.

80. Those who were given knowledge said: woe to you, the reward of Allah

is better for those who believe and do good, and only the patient achieve it.

81. Then We made the earth collapse with him and his house, and there was no detachment to help him besides Allah and he was not being helped.

82. And those who wished for his place the day before started saying: wow, Allah expands the provision for whom He pleases of His servants and tightens it, and if Allah had not bestowed favours on us, He would have made (the earth) collapse with us, wow, those who reject (the truth) do not succeed.

83. This is the abode of the hereafter which We made for those who do not seek arrogance nor corruption on earth, and the outcome is for those who beware (of Allah).

84. Whoever brings a good deed, he will receive better than it, and whoever brings a bad deed, those who do bad will only be punished for what they did.

85. The One who prescribed the Qur'an for you will return you to the promised place. Say: my Lord knows best who brings the guidance and who is in clear error.

86. And you could not hope that the book would be given to you except as a mercy from your Lord, so do not provide support to those who reject (the truth).

87. And let them not divert you from the signs of Allah after they were revealed to you and call upon your Lord and do not be of the idolaters.

88. And do not call with Allah on any other god, there is no god but Him, everything will be destroyed except His presence, His is the judgement and to Him you will return.

Surah 29: *Al-Ankabut* (The Spider)

In the name of Allah, the Owner and Giver of Mercy

1. Alif, Lam, Mim.

2. Do people think that they will be left alone saying: we believe, and will not be tested?

3. We tested those before them, so that Allah knows those who are truthful and knows the liars.

4. Or do those who do bad think that they will precede Us? Bad is how they judge.

5. Whoever hopes to meet Allah, Allah's appointed time will come, and He listens and knows.

6. And whoever makes an effort, makes an effort for his own good, for Allah is independent of all the worlds.

7. And those who believe and do good work, We cancel their bad deeds and reward them for the best of what they used to do.

8. And We instructed man to be kind to his parents, and if they argue with you to associate with Me what you have no knowledge of, then do not obey them. To Me is your return, then I will inform you of what you used to do.

9. And those who believe and do good work, We will enter them amongst the righteous.

10. And amongst people is he who says: we believe in Allah, then when he is harmed because of Allah he makes out the trials of people as the punishment of Allah, and if a victory comes from your Lord, he will say: we were with you. Does not Allah know best what everyone keeps inside?

11. And Allah will surely know those who believe and will surely know those who pretend.

12. And those who reject (the truth) say to the believers: follow our way and we will carry your shortcomings, yet they carry none of their shortcomings, for they are liars.

13. And they will carry their burdens and other burdens with them, and they will be asked on the day of resurrection about what they used to invent.

14. And We sent Nuh (Noah) to his people, then he stayed amongst them a thousand years minus fifty years, then the floods took them whilst they were wrongdoers.

15. And We rescued him and his companions in the ship and made it a sign for all the worlds.

16. And Ibrahim (Abraham), when he said to his people: serve Allah and beware of Him, that is better for you if you knew.

17. For you serve besides Allah idols and create a falsehood; those whom you serve besides Allah do not control provision for you, so seek provision with Allah and serve Him and thank Him; to Him you will return.

18. And if you deny, then communities before you already denied, and the duty of the messenger is only to convey clearly.

19. Do they not see how Allah initiates the creation then repeats it? For that is easy for Allah.

20. Say: travel on earth and see how He initiated the creation, then Allah brings about the final existence, for Allah is able to do anything.

21. He punishes whom He pleases and has mercy on whom He pleases, and to Him will you be brought back.

22. And you will not escape on earth nor the sky, and you have besides Allah no protector nor helper.

23. And those who reject Our signs and the meeting with Him, those despair of My mercy and for those is a painful punishment.

24. But the answer of his people was only that they said: kill him or burn him, so Allah rescued him from the fire, for in that are signs for people who believe.

25. He said: you have between yourselves adopted idols besides Allah in this world whom you love, then on the day of resurrection you will reject each other and curse each other, and your abode is the fire and you will not be helped.

26. Then Lut (Lot) believed in him and said: I will migrate towards my Lord, for He is the mighty and wise.

27. And We bestowed on him Ishaq (Isaac) and Ya'qub (Jacob) and placed amongst his descendants the prophethood and the book and gave him his reward in this world, and in the hereafter he is amongst the righteous.

28. And Lut (Lot) when he said to his people: you bring an indecency no-one in the whole world has preceded you with!

29. For you come to men and cut off the way and come up with what is objectionable in your meetings, but the answer of his people was only that they said: bring us Allah's punishment if you are truthful.

30. He said: my Lord, help me against the corrupt people.

31. And when Our messengers came to Ibrahim (Abraham) with the good news, they said: we will destroy the inhabitants of this town, for its inhabitants are wrongdoers.

32. He said: but Lut (Lot) is in there. They said: we know best who is in there, we will rescue him and his family except his wife who is of those who stay behind.

33. And when Our messengers came to Lut (Lot), he was concerned and uneasy about them. They said: do not fear nor worry, for we will rescue you and your family except your wife who is of those who stay behind.

34. We shall send down on the inhabitants of this town a punishment from the sky because of their excesses.

35. And We left a clear sign of it for people who understand.

36. And to Madyan (Midian) (We sent) their brother Shu'ayb (Jethro) who said: oh my people, serve Allah and hope for the last day and do not spread corruption on earth.

37. But they denied, so the earthquake overtook them and they were found face down in their houses in the morning.

38. And 'Ad, and Thamud, as is apparent to you from their homes, and the devil made their deeds appeal to them, so he diverted them from the way whilst they were aware of it.

39. And Qarun (Korah) and Pharaoh and Haman, and Musa (Moses) came to them with clear proofs but they were arrogant on earth but did not get ahead.

40. And each did We overtake due to his sin, so of them is on whom We sent a storm, and of them is whom the roar overtook, and of them is with whom We made the earth collapse, and of them is whom We drowned, and Allah did not wrong them, but they wronged themselves.

41. The likeness of those who adopt protectors besides Allah is that of the spider adopting a dwelling, and the most feeble of dwellings is the dwelling of the spider if they only knew.

42. Allah knows whatever they call upon besides Him, and He is mighty and wise.

43. And these are the likenesses We coin for people, and only those with knowledge understand them.

44. Allah created the heavens and the earth in truth, for in that is a sign for the believers.

45. Recite what has been revealed to you of the book and keep up prayer, for prayer prevents indecency and wrongdoing, and the remembrance of Allah is greater, and Allah knows what you do.

46. And do not argue with the people of the book except with what is better, except for the wrongdoers amongst them, and say: we believe in that which has been revealed to us and which has been revealed to you, and our Lord and your Lord is one, and we submit to Him (as Muslims).

47. And this is how We revealed to you the book, and the ones to whom we gave the book believe in it, and of those there is who believes in it, and only those who reject (the truth) object to Our signs.

48. And you did not recite from a book before nor write it with your own hand, otherwise the ignorant would have doubted.

49. But they are clear signs in the hearts of those who were given knowledge, and only the wrongdoers object to Our signs.

50. And they say: why were not signs sent down to him from his Lord? Say: the signs are with Allah, and I am only a plain warner.

51. Is it not sufficient for them that We revealed to you the book which is recited to them, for in that is indeed a mercy and reminder for people who believe.

52. Say: Allah is sufficient as a witness between me and you, He knows what is in the heavens and on earth, and those who believe in falsehood and reject Allah, those are the losers.

53. And they ask you to hasten the punishment, and if it was not a fixed date, the punishment would have reached them, and it will reach them suddenly when they are not aware.

54. They ask you to hasten the punishment, and hell surrounds those who reject (the truth).

55. On the day the punishment covers them from above and from below them and He will say: taste what you were used to do.

56. Oh My servants who believe, My earth is spacious, so serve Me.

57. Every soul will taste death, then you will return to Us.

58. And those who believe and do good, We will arrange chambers for them in the garden (of paradise) through which rivers flow where they will remain; blessed is the reward of those who work.

59. Those who were patient and relied on their Lord.

60. And how many a creature does not carry its provision; Allah provides for it and for you, and He listens and knows.

61. And if you were to ask them who created the heavens and the earth and made the sun and the moon of service, they would say: Allah. So where to are they diverted?

62. Allah expands the provision for whom He pleases and tightens it, for Allah knows everything.

63. And if you were to ask them who sent down water from the sky to revive with it the earth after its death, they would say: Allah. Say: Allah is praised. But most of them do not understand.

64. And this worldly life is only pastime and play, and the abode of the hereafter is the real life, if only they knew.

65. And when they board the ship they call Allah making their religion sincere for Him, then when We rescue them to land, they associate (others with Him).

66. So that they reject that which We gave them and in order to enjoy it for a while, but they will soon know.

67. Do they not see that We have made a safe sanctuary whilst people are attacked all around them? Do they then believe in falsehood and reject the blessings of Allah?

68. And who is more wrong than he who invents a lie against Allah or denies the truth when it reaches him? Is not in hell a home for those who reject (the truth)?

69. And those who strive for Us, We will guide them Our ways, and Allah is with those who do good.

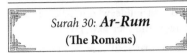

Surah 30: *Ar-Rum*
(The Romans)

In the name of Allah,
the Owner and Giver of Mercy

1. Alif, Lam, Mim.

2. The Romans have been defeated.

3. In the nearside land, and they will after their defeat be victorious.

4. In a few years. To Allah belongs the matter before and after, and on that day the believers will rejoice.

5. In the victory of Allah. He gives victory to whom He pleases and He is mighty and merciful.

6. A promise from Allah. Allah does not break His promise, but most people don't know.

7. They know the apparent of the life of this world and are careless of the hereafter.

8. Do they not reflect about themselves? Allah did not create what is in the heavens and on earth and what is between them except with truth and for a fixed term, but many people reject the meeting with their Lord.

9. Do they not travel on earth and see what the outcome of those before them was? They were stronger than them in power and made their mark on the earth and cultivated it more than these cultivated it, and their messengers came to them with clear proofs, so Allah did not wrong them but they wronged themselves.

10. Then the outcome of those who did bad was bad for that they denied the signs of Allah and made fun of them.

11. Allah initiates the creation, then repeats it, then you will return to Him.

12. And on the day the hour happens, the sinful will despair.

13. And they will have no mediator from their associates and will reject their associates.

14. And on the day the hour happens, on that day they will be separated.

15. As for those who believed and did good work, they will be settled happily in the garden.

16. And as for those who rejected (the truth) and denied Our signs and the meeting of the hereafter, those will be presented for punishment.

17. So glorified is Allah when you enter the night and when you get up in the morning.

18. And He is praised in the heavens and on earth and in the afternoon and when you reach mid-day.

19. He brings out the living from the dead and brings out the dead from the living and revives the earth after its death, and likewise you will be brought out.

20. And of His signs is that He created you from soil, then you spread out as humans.

21. And of His signs is that he created for you partners from amongst yourselves to find rest in them, and He placed love and mercy between you, for in that are signs for people who reflect.

22. And of His signs is the creation of the heavens and the earth and the difference in your languages and colours, for in that are signs to those who know.

23. And of His signs is your sleep at night and in the day and that you seek of His favours, for in that are signs for people who listen.

24. And of His signs He shows you the lightning in fear and hope and sends down from the sky water, then revives with it the earth after its death, for in that are signs for people who understand.

25. And of His signs is that the sky and the earth function by His command, then when He calls you with a call from the earth, you will be brought out.

26. And to Him belongs what is in the heavens and on earth, everything is submissive to Him.

27. And He is who initiates the creation, then repeats it, and this is most easy for Him, and His are the most exalted attributes in the heavens and on earth and He is the mighty and wise.

28. Allah coins a likeness for you of yourselves: do those in your possession share what We have provided you with to the extent that you are equal in it and you fear them as you fear each other? This is how Allah explains the signs for people who understand.

29. But the wrongdoers follow their own desires without knowledge, so

who will guide whom Allah lets go astray? And they have no helpers.

30. So turn your face to this religion sincerely devoted; the natural disposition upon which Allah created people. There is no changing the creation of Allah. That is the upright religion, but most people do not know.

31. Repent to Him and beware of Him and keep up prayer and do not be of the idolaters.

32. Of those who divide their religion and are factions, each party rejoicing in what they have.

33. And when harm befalls people, they call their Lord, repenting to Him, then when He lets them taste mercy from Him, a group of them associate (others) with Allah.

34. So that they reject that which We gave them, then enjoy it for a while, you will soon know.

35. Or did We send an authority to them, someone who tells them of that which they associate?

36. And when We let people taste mercy, they rejoice in it, and when something bad afflicts them on account of what they have sent ahead, they are depressed.

37. Do they not see that Allah expands the provision for whom He pleases and tightens it, for in that are signs for people who believe.

38. So give the relatives their due and the poor and the traveller, that is better for those who want to please Allah, and those are the successful.

39. And whatever you give in interest to increase the wealth of people, it does not increase with Allah, and whatever you give in Zakat, seeking to please Allah, those are the ones who achieve growth.

40. Allah is who created you, then provided for you, then lets you die, then revives you. Is there any of your associates who does anything of that? Glorified and exalted is He above what they associate.

41. Corruption is becoming apparent on land and on sea on account of what people have brought about, so that He makes them taste some of what they have done so that they return.

42. Say: travel on earth and see what the outcome was like for those before, most of them were idolaters.

43. So turn your face to the upright religion before a day comes when there is no turning back from Allah. On that day they will be parted.

44. Who rejected (the truth), his rejection is upon him, and who did good, they paved the way for themselves.

45. So that Allah rewards those who believe and do good work from His favours, for He does not love those who reject (the truth).

46. And of His signs is that He sends the winds as bringers of good news and to let you taste of His mercy and for the ship to sail by His command and for you to seek of His blessings and so that you would be grateful.

47. And We sent messengers before you to their people and they brought them clear proofs, then We took revenge on those who sinned, and it is a duty upon Us to help the believers.

48. Allah is who sends the winds, then they promote the clouds, then He spreads them in the sky as He pleases, and He darkens them and you see precipitation emerge from within, then when He afflicts with it whom He pleases of His servants, they rejoice.

49. When before it was sent down on them they were in despair.

50. So look at the effects of the mercy of Allah, how He revives the earth after its death, for likewise the dead will be revived, and He is able to do anything.

51. And if We send a wind and they see it turn yellow, they will still reject (the truth) after that.

52. For you cannot make the dead hear and cannot make the deaf hear when they turn away.

53. And you will not guide the blind away from their error. You can only make those hear who believe in Our signs and submit (as Muslims).

54. Allah is who created you weak, then gave strength after weakness, then gave weakness and grey hair after strength, and He creates what He pleases and He is the knowing and powerful.

55. And on the day the hour happens, the sinful will swear that they did not stay longer than an hour, this is how they were diverted.

56. And those who were given knowledge and belief will say: you stayed in accordance with the decree of Allah until the day of resurrection, so this is the day of resurrection, but you did not know.

57. So on that day their excuses do not benefit the wrongdoers nor will they be allowed redress.

58. And We have coined in this Qur'an all kinds of likenesses for people, and if you were to bring them a sign, those who reject (the truth) would say: you are only making it up.

59. This is how Allah imprints on the hearts of those who do not know.

60. So have patience, for the promise of Allah is true, and let not those who are unsure distract you.

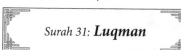

Surah 31: **Luqman**

In the name of Allah, the Owner and Giver of Mercy

1. Alif, Lam, Mim.

2. These are the signs of the wise book.

3. A guidance and mercy for those who do good.

4. Those who keep up prayer and give Zakat and are certain about the hereafter.

5. They are the ones who follow the guidance from their Lord, and they are the ones who will succeed.

6. And among people is he who acquires idle talk to divert from the way of Allah without knowledge

and makes fun of it; for those is a humiliating punishment.

7. And when Our signs are recited to him he turns away arrogantly as if he didn't hear them, as if there was a weight upon his ears, so announce to him a painful punishment.

8. Those who believe and do good work, for them are gardens of blessing.

9. They remain there, a true promise of Allah, and He is the mighty and wise.

10. He created the heavens without supports that you can see and placed stabilisers on earth so it doesn't shake you up and spread on it all kinds of creatures, and We send water from the sky, then We grow on it every precious species.

11. This is the creation of Allah, so show me what those besides Him created! But the wrongdoers are in clear error.

12. And We gave Luqman the wisdom to be grateful to Allah, and whoever is grateful to Allah is grateful to himself, and whoever is ungrateful, Allah is rich and praiseworthy.

13. And when Luqman said to his son, admonishing him: my dear son, do not associate anything with Allah, for this association is a great wrongdoing.

14. And We instructed man regarding his parents - his mother carried him with increasing weakness, and his weaning took two years: be grateful to Me and to your parents, to Me is the journey.

15. And if they argue with you to associate with Me what you have no knowledge of, then do not obey them, and accompany them in this world with good conduct and follow the way of whoever turns to Me, then your return is to Me and I will inform you of what you did.

16. Oh my dear son, if there is the weight of a mustard seed inside a rock or in the heavens or on earth, Allah will bring it out, for Allah is kind and informed.

17. Oh my dear son, keep up prayer and command good conduct and forbid wrongdoing and be patient with what befalls you, for that is one of the firmest things (to do).

18. And do not brush off people and do not walk carelessly on earth, for Allah does not love an arrogant show-off.

19. And be measured in your walk and subdue your voice, for the most disliked of voices is the voice of the donkey.

20. Do you not see that Allah made subservient to you what is in the heavens and what is on earth and showered upon you His blessings openly and secretly? And among people is who argues about Allah without knowledge or guidance or enlightening book.

21. And when they are told to follow what Allah has revealed they say: No, we follow what we found our ancestors doing. What if the devil calls them to the punishment of the fire?

22. And whoever submits his orientation towards Allah and does

good, he has held on to a reliable link, and to Allah belongs the outcome of things.

23. And whoever rejects (the truth), do not worry about his rejection; their return is to Us, then We inform them about what they did, for Allah knows what is kept inside.

24. We give them provision for a while, then force them towards an unrelenting punishment.

25. And if you were to ask them who created the heavens and the earth, they would say: Allah. Say: praised is Allah, but most of them don't know.

26. To Allah belongs what is in the heavens and on earth, for Allah is the rich and praiseworthy.

27. And if all the trees on earth were pens and he would expand the sea with another seven seas (as ink), the words of Allah would not run out, for Allah is mighty and wise.

28. Your creation and resurrection is only like that of a single soul, for Allah hears and sees.

29. Do you not see that Allah blends the night into the day and blends the day into the night and made subservient the sun and the moon, each floats up to a fixed term, and that Allah is informed of what you do?

30. This is because Allah is the truth, and whatever they call besides Him is falsehood and Allah is exalted and great.

31. Do you not see that the ship sails on the sea with the blessings of Allah so that He shows you of His signs, for

in that are signs for everyone patient and grateful.

32. And when the waves cover them like darkness, they call Allah, making their religion sincere for Him, then when He rescues them onto land, there is the wavering among them, and only every faithless rejecter objects to Our signs.

33. Oh people, beware of your Lord and fear a day when a father cannot save his son nor a son save his father in the least, for the promise of Allah is true, so let not the life of the world mislead you nor let passing provisions mislead you about Allah.

34. For with Allah is the knowledge of the hour, and He sends down the rain, and He knows what is in the wombs, and no soul has an idea what it will earn the next day, and no soul has an idea on which land it will die, for Allah knows and is informed.

Surah 32: **As-Sajdah** (Prostration)

In the name of Allah, the Owner and Giver of Mercy

1. Alif, Lam, Mim.

2. A revelation of the book without doubt from the Lord of all worlds.

3. Or do they say he has invented it? But it is the truth from your Lord in order for you to warn a people to whom no warner has come before you, for them to be guided.

4. Allah is who created the heavens and the earth and what is between them in six days, then He rose onto

the throne, you have neither protector nor mediator besides Him, do you not then reflect?

5. He directs the command from the heaven to the earth, then it ascends to Him within a day whose measure is a thousand years of your counting.

6. That is the One who knows the unseen and the apparent, the mighty, the merciful.

7. The One who beautified everything He created and originated the creation of man from clay.

8. Then He made his descendants from an extract of insignificant fluid.

9. Then He shaped him and breathed into him of His spirit and gave you hearing and eyesight and hearts, little thanks do you give.

10. And they say: once we got lost in the earth, are we going to be in a new creation? But they reject the meeting with their Lord.

11. Say: the angel of death who has been entrusted with you will take you away, then you will return to your Lord.

12. And if you could see when the sinful will hang their heads low before their Lord: our Lord, look at us and listen to us and send us back, we will do good, for we are certain.

13. And if We pleased, We would give each soul its own guidance, but the word from Me has come to pass that I will fill hell with the Jinn and humans altogether.

14. So taste (it) on account of having forgotten the meeting of this day of yours, for We have forgotten you, and taste the punishment of eternity on account of what you did.

15. Those believe in Our signs who when they are reminded by them fall prostrate and glorify the praise of their Lord and are not arrogant.

16. They abstain from resting to call their Lord in fear and hope and spend of what We have provided them with.

17. For no soul knows what comfort is hidden for them as reward for what they used to do.

18. Is then the believer like the sinful? They are not the same.

19. As for those who believe and do good work, their accommodation is in gardens as a gift for what they used to do.

20. And as for those who were sinful, their accommodation is the fire; each time they want to leave it they are returned to it and are told: taste the punishment of the fire that you used to deny.

21. And We will let them taste the lesser punishment before the greater punishment so that they turn back.

22. And who is more wrong than he who is reminded of the signs of his Lord, then turns away from them, for We will take revenge on the sinful.

23. And We gave the book to Musa (Moses), so have no doubt about the meeting with him, and made it a guidance for the Children of Israel.

24. And We made from them leaders to guide by Our command as they

were patient and were certain about Our signs.

25. For your Lord will judge between them on the day of resurrection regarding what they used to differ in.

26. Are they not guided by how many generations We destroyed before them in whose homes they walk? In this are signs, will they then not listen?

27. Do they not see that We give the dry earth water to drink, then We bring out vegetation with it from which their cattle and they themselves eat, so do they not look?

28. And they say: when will this victory happen if you are truthful?

29. Say: on the day of victory their belief will not benefit those who rejected (the truth) and they will not be given time.

30. So turn away from them and wait, for they are waiting.

Surah 33: *Al-Ahzab*
(The Allies)

In the name of Allah,
the Owner and Giver of Mercy

1. Oh prophet, beware of Allah and do not obey those who reject (the truth) and the pretenders, for Allah is knowing and wise.

2. And follow that which has been revealed to you from your Lord, for Allah is informed of what you do.

3. And rely on Allah, and Allah is sufficient as a protector.

4. And Allah did not give any man two hearts inside him, and He did not make the wives whom you divorce by likening them to your mothers your mothers, and He did not make your adopted children your children; that is what you say with your mouths, and Allah tells the truth and He guides the way.

5. Call them after their fathers, it is more just before Allah, and if you don't know their fathers, then they are your brothers in religion and your protégés, and there is no sin upon you in your mistakes but in what your hearts intend, and Allah is forgiving and merciful.

6. The prophet is more protective of the believers than they are themselves and his wives are their mothers, and relatives are mutual protectors of each other in the book of Allah, before the believers and the emigrants, but you should treat your protégés well; this is laid down in the book.

7. And when We took of the prophets their promise and of you and Nuh (Noah), Ibrahim (Abraham), Musa (Moses), 'Isa (Jesus) the son of Maryam (Mary), and We took a binding promise of them.

8. So that He will ask the truthful about their truthfulness, and He has promised to those who reject (the truth) a painful punishment.

9. Oh you believers, remember the blessings of Allah upon you when fighters reached you and We sent against them a wind and fighters you did not see, and Allah sees what you do.

10. When they came upon you from above and below and when your eyesight faded and you lost heart and had second thoughts about Allah.

11. There the believers were tested and shaken severely.

12. And when the pretenders and those with a disease in their hearts said: Allah and His messenger only promised us an illusion.

13. And when a party from them said: oh inhabitants of Yathrib, you have no foothold so turn back, and a group from them asked the prophet to be excused saying: our houses are unprotected, but they were not unprotected, they only wanted to flee.

14. And if they had been overrun and been asked into temptation (to rebel), they would have done so and hesitated only little.

15. And they had previously promised Allah that they would not turn their backs, and the promise to Allah will be asked about.

16. Say: fleeing will not benefit you when you flee from death or fighting and then only enjoy it a little.

17. Say: who will protect you against Allah if He wants harm for you or mercy? And they will not find besides Allah any protector or helper.

18. Allah already knows those of you who cause a hindrance and those who say to their brothers: come, join us, when they rarely show courage themselves.

19. They are jealous of you, and at times of fear you see them look at you, their eyes turning like one whom death has overtaken; then when the fear passes, they scald you with a harsh tongue, greedy for the benefit. Those do not believe, so Allah has frustrated their efforts, and that is easy for Allah.

20. They think that the allies had not gone, and if the allies came, they wish they could hide amongst the desert Arabs asking for news about you, and if they were amongst you, they would not fight much.

21. You have in the messenger of Allah a beautiful example for whoever hopes for Allah and the last day and remembers Allah a lot.

22. And when the believers saw the allies, they said: this is what Allah and His messenger promised us, and Allah and His messenger were truthful, and it only increases them in belief and submission.

23. Amongst the believers are men who are true to what they promised Allah, and amongst them is he who has discharged his obligation, and amongst them is he who waits, and they did not change the least.

24. So that Allah rewards the truthful for their truthfulness and punishes the pretenders if He pleases or turns back to them, for Allah is forgiving and merciful.

25. And that Allah turns back those who reject (the truth) with their anger, not having gained any benefit, and Allah is sufficient for the believers in battle, and Allah is strong and mighty.

26. And He made those of the people of the book who had assisted them come down from their fortresses and cast terror into their hearts; you killed a group and took a group captive.

27. And He made you inherit their land and homes and wealth as well as land you never passed before, and Allah is able to do anything.

28. Oh prophet, say to your wives: if you desire the life of this world and its ornaments, then come, I will give you provision and let you go in a nice way.

29. And if you desire Allah and His messenger and the abode of the hereafter, then Allah has promised those who do good among you an immense reward.

30. Oh women of the prophet, whoever of you commits a clear indecency, the punishment will be doubled for her, and that is easy for Allah.

31. And whoever of you is content with Allah and His messenger and does good, We give her her reward twice and have promised her a dignified provision.

32. Oh women of the prophet, you are not like any other woman, if you beware (of Allah), then be not too accommodating in speech so that he in whose heart there is a disease takes hope, and speak appropriately.

33. And remain in your homes and do not show off like in the early days of ignorance and keep up prayer and give Zakat and obey Allah and His messenger. Allah wants to avert any disgrace from you, oh members of the household, and purify you completely.

34. And remember what is being recited in your homes of the signs of Allah and the wisdom, for Allah is kind and informed.

35. For men and women who submit (as Muslims), and men and women who believe, and men and women who are humble, and men and women who are truthful, and men and women who are patient, and men and women who are devote, and men and women who are charitable, and men and women who fast, and men and women who guard their chastity, and men and women who remember Allah often, Allah has promised them forgiveness and a tremendous reward.

36. And it is not befitting for a believing man or woman that, when Allah and His messenger have decided a matter, they should have a choice in the matter; and whoever disobeys Allah and His messenger has clearly gone astray.

37. And when you said to him whom Allah had favoured and whom you had favoured: hold on to your wife and beware of Allah, and you concealed within you what Allah will disclose and feared people when Allah has more right to be feared; so when Zayd had parted from her, We married her to you so that there would be no sin upon the believers regarding the wives of their adopted sons when they have parted from them, and Allah's command comes to pass.

38. There is no blame on the prophet in what Allah has prescribed for him, the custom of Allah amongst those who went before, and Allah's command is a firm decree.

39. Those who convey the messages of Allah and fear Him and fear nobody except Allah, and Allah is sufficient for keeping count.

40. Muhammad is not the father of any of your men but the messenger of Allah and the seal of the prophets, and Allah knows all things.

41. Oh you believers, remember Allah often.

42. And glorify Him in the mornings and evenings.

43. He is who sends blessings on you, and so do His angels, in order to bring you out of darkness to the light, and He is merciful with the believers.

44. Their greeting on the day they meet Him will be peace, and He has promised them a generous reward.

45. Oh prophet, We have sent you as a witness, bringer of good news and warner.

46. And one who calls to Allah and a radiant light.

47. And give good news to the believers that they will have great favours from Allah.

48. And do not obey those who reject (the truth) and the pretenders and ignore their harm and rely on Allah, and Allah is sufficient as a protector.

49. Oh you believers, if you marry believing women and then divorce them before touching them, then there is no waiting period for them to count, so give them provision and release them in a nice way.

50. Oh prophet, We have made permissible for you your wives whom you have given their dues and those in your possession from the captives Allah has given you, and the daughters of your paternal uncles and paternal aunts and the daughters of your maternal uncles and maternal aunts who migrated with you, and any believing woman who wants to give herself to the prophet if the prophet wants to marry her - exclusively for you and not the believers, We know what We have prescribed for them regarding their wives and those in their possession - so that there will be no blame on you, and Allah is forgiving and merciful.

51. Let be whom you please and draw close to you whom you please, and if you desire one whom you have set aside, it is no sin for you; that is more likely to give them comfort and not to make them worry and let them be content with what you have given each of them, and Allah knows what is in your hearts, and Allah is knowing and gentle.

52. No further women are permitted to you after that, nor that you replace them with other wives, even if you like their beauty, except for those in your possession, and Allah watches over everything.

53. Oh you believers, do not enter the homes of the prophet except after having been given permission for food and without waiting around for it, but if you have been called, then enter, and once you have eaten, then disperse without socialising in talk, for that troubles the prophet but he is shy of you, yet Allah is not shy of the truth. And if you ask them (his wives) for provision, then ask them from behind a curtain, that is purer for your hearts and their hearts. And it is not befitting for you to trouble the prophet nor to ever marry his wives after him, for that would be a serious matter with Allah.

54. If you disclose something or hide it, Allah knows everything.

55. There is no sin upon them regarding their fathers, sons, brothers, brothers' sons, sisters' sons nor their womenfolk and those in their possession; and beware of Allah, for Allah is a witness to everything.

56. Allah and His angels send blessings upon the prophet; oh you believers, send blessings upon him and abundant peace.

57. Those who insult Allah and the prophet, Allah has cursed them in this world and the hereafter and prepared for them a humiliating punishment.

58. And those who insult the believing men and women without cause are guilty of slander and clear sin.

59. Oh prophet, tell your wives, daughters and the women of the believers to draw their outer garments around them, that makes it more likely for them to be recognised and not molested, and Allah is forgiving and merciful.

60. If the pretenders and those with a disease in their hearts and those who spread rumours in Madinah do not stop, We will let you deal with them, then they will not remain in your neighbourhood for long.

61. They will be cursed, wherever they are found they will be captured and killed.

62. The custom of Allah with those who went before, and you will not find a change in the custom of Allah.

63. People ask you about the hour, say: knowledge of it is with Allah, and how can you tell whether the hour might be near.

64. Allah has cursed those who reject (the truth) and prepared a flame for them.

65. They will remain in it forever; they will not find a protector nor helper.

66. On the day their faces will be flung into the fire they will say: woe to us, we should have obeyed Allah and obeyed the messenger.

67. And they will say: our Lord, we obeyed our masters and chiefs, so they lead us astray from the path.

68. Our Lord, give them twice the punishment and curse them with a mighty curse.

69. Oh you believers, do not be like those who insulted Musa (Moses), so Allah cleared him of what they said and he was respected before Allah.

70. Oh you believers, beware of Allah and talk within limits.

71. He will improve your work and forgive you your sins, and whoever obeys Allah and His messenger has achieved ultimate success.

72. We presented the trust to the heavens and the earth and the mountains, and they refused to bear it and were apprehensive about it, and man bore it, for he was transgressing and foolish.

73. In order for Allah to punish the male and female pretenders and idolaters and for Allah to turn in acceptance to the male and female believers, and Allah is forgiving and merciful.

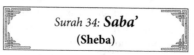

Surah 34: **Saba'**
(Sheba)

In the name of Allah, the Owner and Giver of Mercy

1. Praised is Allah to whom belongs what is in the heavens and what is on earth, and He is praised in the hereafter and He is wise and informed.

2. He knows what enters the earth and what emerges from it and what descends from the sky and what ascends through it, and He is merciful and forgiving.

3. And those who reject (the truth) say: the hour will not come upon us. Say: but no, by my Lord, it will come upon you. He knows the unseen; not the weight of a tiny speck escapes Him in the heavens and on earth, nor what is smaller than that nor what is bigger, but it is in a clear record.

4. So that He rewards those who believe and do good work, theirs will be forgiveness and generous provision.

5. And those who strive to obscure Our signs, theirs is a punishment of painful affliction.

6. And those who were given knowledge see that what has been revealed to you from your Lord is the truth and guides to the path of the mighty and praiseworthy.

7. And those who reject (the truth) say: shall we direct you to a man who informs you that once you are totally disintegrated you will be in a new creation.

8. Has he invented a lie against Allah or is he mad? But those who do not believe in the hereafter are in punishment and extensive error.

9. Do they not see the sky and earth before and behind them? If We pleased, We could make the earth swallow them up or drop a piece of the sky on them. In that is a sign for every repenting servant.

10. And We gave Dawud (David) favours from Us: oh mountains, and oh birds, echo his worship; and We made the iron pliable for him.

11. So that you make (protective) garments and design them well; and do good work, for I see what you do.

12. And to Sulayman (Solomon) (We subjected) the wind - it took a month to go and a month to return - and We let a spring of brass flow for him, and (subjected) of the Jinn who worked in front of him with the permission of his Lord, and any of them who defies Our command, We make him taste the punishment of the fire.

13. They make for him whatever he wants of elevated structures, statues, large watering basins and permanent cooking vessels: be grateful, oh family of Dawud (David), and few of My servants are grateful.

14. Then when We decreed death for him, only the earth worms who ate his staff pointed them to his death, so when it fell apart, it became clear to the Jinn that if they had known the unseen, they would not have remained in the humiliating punishment.

15. There was a sign for Saba' (Sheba) in their homes: gardens both on the right and the left, eat from the provision of your Lord and thank Him, a good land and a forgiving Lord.

16. But they turned away, so We sent against them a flood from the dam and replaced both their gardens with gardens of bitter food and tamarisk and some cedar trees.

17. This is how We punished them for having been ungrateful, and do We not only punish the ungrateful?

18. And We placed between them and the towns We had blessed clearly visible towns and facilitated travel between them: travel there night and day safely.

19. But they said: our Lord, extend our journeys, and they wronged themselves, so We made them history and scattered them completely; for in this are signs for everyone who is patient and grateful.

20. And Iblis (the devil) made his thought about them come true and they followed him except a group of the believers.

21. And he had no authority over them other than that We would tell apart who believes in the hereafter from who is in doubt of it, and your Lord is keeper of everything.

22. Say: call those whom you claim besides Allah, they do not own the weight of a tiny speck in the heavens nor on earth and they have no share in them and He does not take any support from them.

23. And intercession does not benefit with Him except for whom permission has been given, until when their hearts have calmed down they say: what did your Lord say? They say: the truth, and He is the exalted and great.

24. Say: who provides for you from the heavens and the earth? Say: Allah, and we or you are either upon guidance or in clear error.

25. Say: you will not be asked about what we have committed and we will not be asked about what you do.

26. Say: our Lord will bring us together, then He will judge between us in truth, and He is the knowing judge.

27. Say: show me those you have attached to Him as partners, but no, He is Allah the mighty and wise.

28. And We have only sent you as a bringer of good news and warner

to all of mankind, but most people don't know.

29. And they say: when will this promise happen if you are truthful?

30. Say: you have an appointed day which you cannot hold back by an hour nor bring forward.

31. And those who reject (the truth) say: we will not believe in this Qur'an nor that which came before it, and if you saw the wrongdoers standing before their Lord, some of them responding to others, with those who were weak saying to those who were arrogant: if it had not been for you we would have been believers.

32. Those who were arrogant will say to those who were weak: did we prevent you from the guidance after it reached you? But you were sinners.

33. And those who were weak will say to those who were arrogant: but the (constant) scheming night and day when you commanded us to reject Allah and set up partners for Him. And they start regretting when they see the punishment, and We have placed cuffs around the necks of those who reject (the truth), are they punished for anything other than what they did?

34. And never have We sent a warner to a town but its affluent people said: we reject what you were sent with.

35. And they said: we have more wealth and children and we will not be punished.

36. Say: my Lord expands the provision for whom He pleases and tightens it, but most people don't know.

37. And it is not your wealth or children which bring you closer to Us, but whoever believes and does good work, those will be rewarded twice for what they did and will be safe in chambers.

38. And those who strive to undermine Our signs will be presented for punishment.

39. Say: my Lord expands the provision for whom of His servants He pleases and tightens it, and whatever you spend, He replaces it, and He is the best provider.

40. And on the day He gathers them all, He will then say to the angels: did these serve you?

41. They will say: glorified are You, You are our protector without them, but they served the Jinn, most of them believed in them.

42. So today they cannot benefit nor harm each other, and We will say to the wrongdoers: taste the punishment of the fire which you used to deny.

43. And when Our clear signs are recited to them they say: this is only a man who wants to divert you from what your forefathers served. And they say: this is only a falsehood he invented. And those who reject the truth say when it comes to them: this is only plain magic.

44. And We did not give them a book which they study nor did We send a warner to them before you.

45. And those before them denied, and they did not even achieve a tenth of what We had given them, so they denied My messenger, and how was My rebuttal!

46. Say: I only admonish you with one thing: that you stand before Allah together or alone and reflect: there is no madness in your companion, for he is only a warner to you of a pending severe punishment.

47. Say: I did not ask any reward from you, but it is for you, for my reward is only upon Allah and He is a witness to everything.

48. Say: my Lord pronounces the truth, He knows the unseen.

49. Say: the truth has come and falsehood does not bring about or confirm anything.

50. Say: if I go astray, then I go astray at my own loss, and if I am guided, then due to what my Lord has revealed to me, for He listens and is near.

51. And if you saw when they are terror-stricken without escape and taken from nearby.

52. And they say: we believe in it, and to where will they return from afar?

53. And they rejected it before and made predictions about the unseen from afar.

54. And they are prevented from what they wanted just like it happened to their kind before, for they were in severe doubt.

Surah 35: **Fatir**
(The Originator)

In the name of Allah,
the Owner and Giver of Mercy

1. Allah is praised, the originator of the heavens and the earth who made the angels messengers with two, three and four wings. He increases in creation what He pleases, for Allah is able to do anything.

2. When Allah opens up mercy for people, nobody can withhold it, and when He withholds it, nobody after Him can send it, and He is mighty and wise.

3. Oh people, remember the blessings of Allah upon you. Is there a creator other than Allah who provides for you from the sky and the earth? There is no god but Him, so where to are you diverted?

4. And if they deny you, then messengers before you were previously denied, and to Allah return all things.

5. Oh people, Allah's promise is true, so let not the life of the world mislead you and let not passing provisions mislead you about Allah.

6. For the devil is an enemy to you, so treat him as an enemy, for he calls his party to be amongst the inmates of the fire.

7. Those who reject (the truth) will have a severe punishment, and those who believe and do good work will have forgiveness and a great reward.

8. So what about him whose bad work appeals to him and he regards it as good? For Allah lets go astray whom He pleases and guides whom He pleases. So do not trouble yourself about them, for Allah knows what they get up to.

9. And Allah is who sends the winds, then they promote the clouds, then We direct them to a dead land and revive the earth with it after its death; like that will be the resurrection.

10. Whoever seeks strength, all strengths belongs to Allah, He supports the good word and elevates the righteous deed. And those who scheme bad deeds, for them is a severe punishment and their scheme is ruined.

11. And Allah created you from soil, then from a sperm, then made you into pairs; and no female carries nor gives birth but with His knowledge, and nobody grows old or has his age reduced but it is in a record, for that is easy for Allah.

12. And the two bodies of water are not the same: this one is sweet and palatable and can be drunk, and this is salty and unpalatable. And of each you eat fresh meat and extract jewellery which you wear. And you see the ship cut through them so that you seek of His bounty and that you would be grateful.

13. He blends the night into the day and blends the day into the night and made subservient the sun and the moon, each floats for a fixed term. That is Allah your Lord, His is the kingdom, and those you call besides

Him do not own even the skin on a date stone.

14. When you call them, they do not hear your call, and if they heard it, they would not respond to you, and on the day of resurrection they will reject your idolatry, and only one who is informed can give you information.

15. Oh people, you are the poor in the sight of Allah, and Allah is rich and praiseworthy.

16. If He pleases, He can remove you and bring a new creation.

17. And that is not difficult for Allah.

18. And no-one burdened will carry another's burden, and if someone weighed down asks for it to be lifted, nothing of it will be lifted, not even by a relative; for you warn only those who fear their Lord in secret and keep up prayer, and whoever purifies himself, purifies himself for his own good, and to Allah is the journey.

19. And the blind and the seeing are not the same.

20. Nor the darkness and the light.

21. Nor the shade and the full heat.

22. Nor are the living and the dead the same, for Allah makes whom He pleases listen, and you cannot make those in the graves listen.

23. For you are only a warner.

24. For We have sent you with the truth as a bringer of good news and a warner, and there has not been a community without a warner amongst them.

25. And if they deny you, then those before them already denied; their messengers came to them with clear proofs and with the scriptures and with the enlightening book.

26. Then I overtook those who rejected (the truth), and how was My rebuttal!

27. Do you not see that Allah sends down water from the sky, then We make fruit of different colours grow with it. And of the mountains there are white and red streaks, of different colours, and raven black.

28. And of the people and the animals and the cattle there are also different colours. Only those with knowledge amongst His servants fear Allah, for Allah is mighty and forgiving.

29. Those who recite the book of Allah and keep up prayer and spend of what We have provided them with secretly and openly hope for a trade which does not diminish.

30. So that Allah will repay them their reward and give them increase from His bounty, for He forgives and appreciates.

31. And what We have revealed to you of the book is the truth, confirming what came before, for Allah is informed of and sees His servants.

32. Then We gave the book as an inheritance to those of Our servants We chose, but amongst them is he who wrongs himself, and amongst them is he who is half-hearted, and amongst them is he who moves forward with good deeds by the permission of Allah - that is the great blessing.

33. The gardens of Eden which they will enter, where they will be adorned with bracelets of gold and pearls, and their clothing there will be of silk.

34. And they will say: praised is Allah who took the worry from us, for our Lord forgives and appreciates.

35. Who permitted us the lasting abode by His blessing, no hardship afflicts us there and no exhaustion afflicts us there.

36. And those who reject (the truth), theirs is the fire of hell, it will not be terminated for them so that they die, and its punishment will not be lightened for them - this is how We reward every rejecter (of the truth).

37. And they will scream there: our Lord, take us out, we will do good work other than what we used to do. Did We not give you enough life to reflect, should anybody have wanted to, and the warner came to you? So taste, for there is no helper for the wrongdoers.

38. For Allah knows the secrets of the heavens and the earth, for He knows what is kept inside.

39. He is who made you successors on earth, so whoever rejects (the truth), his rejection is upon himself, and their rejection only increases those who reject in being detestable before their Lord, and their rejection only increases those who reject in loss.

40. Say: Look at your associates whom you call besides Allah; show me what they have created of the earth, or do they have a share in the heavens, or have We given them a book and they follow evidence from it? But the wrongdoers only promise each other an illusion.

41. Allah prevents the heavens and the earth from disintegrating, and if they disintegrated, nobody after Him could stop them, for He is gentle and forgiving.

42. And they swear by Allah their utmost oaths that if a warner came to them they would be better guided than any other community, then when a warner comes to them, it only increases their disagreement.

43. Arrogant on earth and scheming evil, and evil scheming only overtakes its owners; so do they wait but for the example of the earliest communities? For you will not find in the custom of Allah any change, and you will not find in the custom of Allah any alteration.

44. Do they not travel on earth and see what the outcome was like for those before them, and they were stronger than them in power? And nothing escapes Allah in the heavens nor on earth, for He is knowing and able.

45. And if Allah held people to account for what they committed (on earth), He would not leave a single creature on its back, but He gives them time until a fixed date, then when their date comes, then Allah did watch His servants.

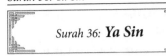

Surah 36: **Ya Sin**

In the name of Allah, the Owner and Giver of Mercy

1. Ya Sin.

2. By the wise Qur'an.

3. You are one of the messengers.

4. On a straight path.

5. A revelation from the mighty and merciful.

6. To warn people whose fathers had not been warned and they were careless.

7. The word has already come to pass against most of them, so they don't believe.

8. For We have placed cuffs around their necks and they reach up to their chins so they are stiffened.

9. And We placed a barrier before them and a barrier behind them and sealed them in, so they don't see.

10. It makes no difference to them whether you warn them or warn them not, they will not believe.

11. For you warn only who follows the reminder and fears the Merciful in secret, so give him good news of forgiveness and a generous reward.

12. For We revive the dead and record what they have sent ahead and their traces, and We list everything in a clear ledger.

13. And coin for them the likeness of the inhabitants of the town when the messengers came to it.

14. When We sent two to them but they denied them, so We added a third, and they said: we have been sent to you.

15. They said, you are only humans like us, and the Merciful has not sent anything, for you are only lying.

16. They said: our Lord knows that we were indeed sent to you.

17. And our duty is only to convey clearly.

18. They said: we see a bad omen in you, if you do not stop we will stone you and a painful punishment from us will afflict you.

19. They said: your bad omen is with you once you have been reminded, but you are wasteful people.

20. And a man came running from the far end of the town saying: oh my people, follow the messengers.

21. Follow those who do not ask you for a reward and are guided.

22. And how should I not serve the One who originated me and you return to Him?

23. Should I take gods besides Him? If the Merciful wants harm for me, their intercession does not benefit me the least and they don't save me.

24. I would then be in clear error.

25. I surely believe in your Lord, so listen to me.

26. He was told: enter the garden (of paradise); he said: if only my people knew.

27. How my Lord has forgiven me and made me of the honoured.

28. And We did not send soldiers from the sky against his people after him, and We never send them.

29. For it was only a single scream and they were extinct.

30. What loss for My servants: never does a messenger reach them but they make fun of him.

31. Do they not see how many towns We destroyed before them and that they do not return to them?

32. And that they will altogether be presented before Us?

33. And a sign for them is the dead earth. We revive it and grow from it seed crops from which they eat.

34. And We place gardens of palm trees and grapes on it and make springs gush out from it.

35. So that they eat from its fruit whilst they did not produce it themselves. Will they not be grateful?

36. Glorified is He who created all pairs of that which the earth grows and of themselves and of what they do not (yet) know.

37. And a sign for them is the night. We remove the day from it and they are in darkness.

38. And the sun travels to its destination, that is the arrangement of the mighty and knowing.

39. And for the moon We have arranged phases until it returns like a withered palm leaf.

40. It is not befitting for the sun to overtake the moon nor for the night to precede the day, and each travels in an orbit.

41. And a sign for them is that We carried their descendants on the laden ship.

42. And created something similar for them which they board.

43. And if We please, We drown them, and there will be no one to call for help and they will not be saved.

44. Except by a mercy from Us and as a provision for a while.

45. And when they are told: beware of what is ahead of you and what is behind you so that you find mercy;

46. And whenever one of the signs of their Lord comes to them, they tend to turn away from it.

47. And when they are told: spend of what Allah has provided you with, those who reject (the truth) say to those who believe: should we feed whom Allah would have fed if He pleased? You are surely in clear error.

48. And they say: when will this promise happen if you are truthful?

49. They are only waiting for a single scream to overtake them, yet they argue.

50. Then they cannot raise a warning nor return to their families.

51. And the horn will be blown and they will stream to their Lord from the graves.

52. They will say: woe to us, who has dispatched us from our resting place? This is what the Merciful did promise and the messengers were truthful.

53. For it was only a single scream and they all are presented before Us.

54. Then today no soul will be wronged the least and you will only be rewarded for what you did.

55. The inhabitants of the garden will be happily busy today.

56. They and their partners will be reclining on couches in the shade.

57. They will have fruit there and have whatever they ask for.

58. Peace offered by a merciful Lord.

59. And keep away today oh sinners.

60. Did I not take your promise, oh children of Adam, not to serve the devil, for he is a clear enemy to you?

61. And to serve Me, that is a straight path?

62. And he had already led astray a large group of you, so did you not understand?

63. This is hell which you were promised.

64. Enter it today on account of having rejected (the truth).

65. Today We seal their mouths, and their hands will talk to Us and their feet will give evidence of what they used to commit.

66. And if We pleased We would have obliterated their eyesight, so they search for a path but how can they see?

67. And if We pleased We would have frozen them on the spot, so they could neither go forward nor back.

68. And whomever We give long life, We reverse his development, so do they not understand?

69. And We did not teach him poetry, nor would it befit him, for it is only a reminder and a clear reading (Qur'an).

70. To warn whoever is alive and so that the word comes to pass against those who reject (the truth).

71. Do they not consider that We created for them from Our handiwork cattle, so they own it?

72. And We made them submissive to them, and they are carried by them and they eat from them.

73. And they have benefits and drink from them, so are they not grateful?

74. And they adopt gods besides Allah so they would help them.

75. They cannot help them but they are ever ready to defend them.

76. So do not worry about what they say, for We know what they conceal and what they disclose.

77. Does man not see that We created him from a sperm, then he argues openly.

78. And he coins a likeness for Us and forgets his creation; he says: who will revive the bones when they decayed?

79. Say: the One who brought them into existence the first time will revive them, and He knows all creation.

80. The One who gave you fire from a green tree, so that you kindle with it.

81. Is not the One who created the heavens and the earth able to create

the like of them? For sure, He is the knowing creator.

82. For His command whenever He wants something is to say to it: Be, then it is.

83. So glorified is the One in whose hand rests the kingdom of everything and to whom you will return.

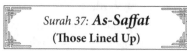

Surah 37: **As-Saffat**
(Those Lined Up)

In the name of Allah,
the Owner and Giver of Mercy

1. By those lined up in rows.

2. And those holding back.

3. And those reciting the reminder.

4. Your god is indeed one.

5. The Lord of the heavens and the earth and what is between them and the Lord of the sunrises.

6. We have adorned the heaven of this world with the adornment of stars.

7. And a protection against every rebellious devil.

8. They cannot listen to the highest counsel and are pelted from every side.

9. Chased away, and theirs is a lasting punishment.

10. Except for one who tries to do so by stealth, then a bright shooting star pursues him.

11. So ask them, are they stronger in creation or whom else We created, for We created them from sticky clay.

12. Yet you are amazed and they make fun.

13. And when they are reminded they do not remember.

14. And when they see a sign they belittle it.

15. And say: this is only plain magic.

16. When we have died and are dust and bones, are we going to be raised again?

17. Or our forefathers?

18. Say: yes, and you will be submissive.

19. For it will be a single shout and they will see.

20. And they will say: woe to us, this is the day of repayment.

21. This is the day of division which you used to deny.

22. Gather the wrongdoers and their partners and all that they served,

23. Besides Allah, and guide them to the path of hell-fire.

24. And arrest them, for they will be questioned.

25. What is the matter with you that you don't help each other?

26. But today they have surrendered.

27. And some of them approach others, asking each other,

28. Saying: you came to us (claiming to be) from the right.

29. They say: but you were not believers.

30. And we had no authority over you, but you were transgressing people.

31. So the word of our Lord came to pass for us that we had to taste it.

32. And we led you astray for we were astray.

33. So today they will share in the punishment.

34. For this is how We deal with the sinners.

35. When they are told that there is no god but Allah they are arrogant.

36. And they say: are we going to abandon our gods for a possessed poet?

37. But he brought the truth and the messengers were right.

38. You will taste the painful punishment.

39. And you will only be punished for what you did.

40. Except the sincere servants of Allah.

41. For them is a known provision.

42. Fruit, and they will be honoured.

43. In gardens of blessings.

44. They will face each other happily.

45. They will be waited upon with a cup of flowing beverage.

46. White (in colour), delicious to drink.

47. With no harmful effect in it nor will they be drained by it.

48. And with them will be exclusive women of rare beauty.

49. As if they were hidden white pearls.

50. Then some of them approach others, asking each other.

51. A speaker amongst them says: I had a friend.

52. Who said: are you confirming the truth of this?

53. That when we have died and are dust and bones, are we going to be judged?

54. He says: do you want to take a look?

55. Then he looks and sees him in the midst of hell-fire.

56. He says: by Allah, he almost ruined me.

57. And had it not been for the favour of my Lord, I would have been called to account.

58. So we will not die?

59. Except for our first death, and we will not be punished.

60. For this is the ultimate success.

61. For the like of this should everybody work.

62. Is this a better reward or the tree of Zaqqum?

63. For We made it a trial for the wrongdoers.

64. It is a tree which grows from the base of hell-fire.

65. Its fruit is like the heads of devils.

66. Then they will be eating from it and filling their stomachs with it.

67. Then they will have a cocktail of boiling water on top of it.

68. Then they will be returned to hell-fire.

69. For they found their fathers astray.

70. Then they eagerly followed into their footsteps.

71. And most of the earliest communities before them went astray.

72. And We did send warners amongst them.

73. So see what the outcome of those warned was like.

74. Except the sincere servants of Allah.

75. And We previously called Nuh (Noah), and he responded well.

76. And We rescued him and his family from the tremendous distress.

77. And We made his descendants the survivors.

78. And We left him to be remembered by those afterwards.

79. Peace be with Nuh (Noah) in all the worlds.

80. For this is how We reward those who do good.

81. For he is of Our believing servants.

82. Then We drowned the others.

83. And of his faction is Ibrahim (Abraham).

84. When he came to his Lord with a clean heart.

85. When he said to his father and his people: what do you serve?

86. Do you want invented gods besides Allah?

87. So what do you think of the Lord of all worlds?

88. Then he took a look at the stars.

89. Then he said: I feel sick.

90. Then they turned away from him.

91. So he turned to their gods and said: don't you eat?

92. What is the matter with you that you don't speak?

93. Then he struck them with his right hand.

94. Then they hurried towards him.

95. He said: do you serve what you carve yourselves?

96. When Allah created you and what you do?

97. They said: build a structure for him and throw him into the fire.

98. So they wanted to plot against him, but We made them the lowest.

99. And he said: I will go towards my Lord, He will guide me.

100. My Lord, make me from amongst the righteous.

101. Then We gave him good news of a gentle son.

102. Then when he was old enough to go out with him, he said, oh my son, I saw in my dream that I should sacrifice you, so see what you think. He said: oh my father, do what you have been commanded, you will find me if Allah pleases of the patient.

103. So when they had both submitted and he turned him face down,

104. We called him: oh Ibrahim (Abraham)!

105. You have already fulfilled the dream; for this is how we reward those who do good.

106. For this is the clear test.

107. And We ransomed him with a great sacrifice.

108. And We left him to be remembered by those afterwards.

109. Peace be upon Ibrahim (Abraham).

110. This is how We reward those who do good.

111. For he is of Our believing servants.

112. And We gave him good news of Ishaq (Isaac) as a prophet from amongst the righteous.

113. And We blessed him and Ishaq, and of their descendants are those who do good and those who clearly wrong themselves.

114. And We already favoured Musa (Moses) and Harun (Aaron).

115. And We rescued them and their people from the tremendous distress.

116. And We helped them and they were the victorious.

117. And We gave them the clarifying book.

118. And We guided them on the straight path.

119. And We left them to be remembered by those afterwards.

120. Peace be upon Musa (Moses) and Harun (Aaron).

121. For this is how We reward those who do good.

122. For they are of Our believing servants.

123. And Ilyas (Elijah) is one of the messengers.

124. When he said to his people: will you not beware (of Allah)?

125. Do you call on Baal and abandon the best of creators?

126. Allah, your Lord and the Lord of your forefathers.

127. But they denied him, so they will be presented.

128. Except the sincere servants of Allah.

129. And We left him to be remembered by those afterwards.

130. Peace be upon Ilyas (Elijah).

131. For this is how We reward those who do good.

132. For he is of Our believing servants.

133. And Lut (Lot) is one of the messengers.

134. When We rescued him and his family altogether.

135. Except an old woman who stayed behind.

136. Then We destroyed the others.

137. And you pass by them in the mornings.

138. And at night, so don't you understand?

139. And Yunus (Jonah) is one of the messengers.

140. When he ran away to the laden ship.

141. Then after drawing lots was defeated.

142. Then the fish swallowed him whilst he blamed himself.

143. And had he not been of those who glorify (Allah),

144. He would have stayed in its belly till the day when they are resurrected.

145. Then We flung him into the open whilst he was sick.

146. And We grew a marrow plant for him.

147. And We sent him to a hundred thousand (people) or more.

148. Then they believed and We gave them provision for a while.

149. So ask them: does your Lord have daughters whilst they have sons?

150. Or did We create the angels female whilst they were witnesses?

151. It is of their inventions that they say:

152. Allah has fathered children, and they are lying.

153. That he has chosen daughters over sons.

154. What is the matter with you, how do you judge?

155. Don't you reflect?

156. Or do you have a clear authority?

157. Then bring your letter (of authority) if you are truthful.

158. And they claimed a relationship between Him and the Jinn, when the Jinn already knew that they will be presented.

159. Glorified is Allah above what they make out.

160. Except the sincere servants of Allah.

161. For you and what you served,

162. You will not tempt anyone against Him,

163. Except him who enters the hell-fire.

164. And each of us has a known place.

165. And We are the ones lined up.

166. And We are the ones who glorify.

167. And they used to say:

168. If only we had a reminder from the earlier communities,

169. We would have been sincere servants of Allah.

170. But they rejected him, so they shall soon know.

171. And Our word has gone before regarding Our messengers,

172. That they will be helped,

173. And that Our forces will be victorious.

174. So turn away from them for a while.

175. And watch them, for soon they will see.

176. Do they hasten Our punishment?

177. Then when it comes down on their habitations, bad is the awakening of those who have been warned.

178. And turn away from them for a while.

179. And watch, for soon they will see.

180. Glorified is your Lord, the Lord of Might, above what they make out.

181. And peace be upon the messengers.

182. And Allah is praised, the Lord of all worlds.

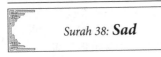

Surah 38: **Sad**

In the name of Allah,
the Owner and Giver of Mercy

1. Sad. By the Qur'an as the reminder.

2. But those who reject (the truth) are in arrogance and far away (from it).

3. How many generations have We destroyed before them, then they called out when it was too late to escape.

4. And they were astonished that a warner from amongst themselves came to them, and those who reject (the truth) said: this is a lying magician.

5. Does he make all the gods one god? This is a strange thing.

6. And their leaders urge them on: go and help your gods, this is what is needed.

7. We haven't heard of this in any other religion, this is an invention.

8. Has the reminder been revealed to him from amongst us? But they are in doubt about My reminder. But they have not yet tasted My punishment.

9. Do they own the treasures of the mercy of your Lord, the mighty and generous?

10. Or do they own the kingdom of the heavens and the earth and what is between them? Then let them ascend by any means.

11. The forces of the allies will be defeated in this.

12. The people of Nuh (Noah) and 'Ad and the Pharaoh with all his monuments denied before them.

13. And Thamud and the people of Lut (Lot) and the inhabitants of the woodlands (*al-Ayka*); those were the allies.

14. Each of them denied the messengers, so the punishment came to pass.

15. And these are only waiting for a single scream, which cannot be prevented.

16. And they said: our Lord, hasten our share for us before the day of reckoning.

17. Have patience with what they say and remember Our powerful servant Dawud (David) who was repentant.

18. For We made the mountains of service to glorify with him in the evenings and at sunrise.

19. And the assembled birds all returned to him.

20. And We strengthened his kingdom and gave him wisdom and the power of speech.

21. And has the information of the antagonists reached you when they climbed up to the secluded area?

22. When they entered upon Dawud (David) and he was startled by them. They said: don't be afraid, we are two antagonists one of whom has transgressed against the other, so judge between us with the truth and do not deviate and guide us to the level path.

23. For this brother of mine has ninety-nine sheep and I have one sheep, so he said: entrust it to me, and he overpowered me in speech.

24. He said: he has wronged you by asking for your sheep to be added to his sheep, and many partners transgress against each other except those who believe and do good work, and they are few. And Dawud (David) knew that We had tested him and asked his Lord for forgiveness and went down in prostration and repented.

25. So We forgave him that, and he will be close to Us and have a good return.

26. Oh Dawud (David), We have made you a representative on earth, so judge between people with the truth and do not follow desire to lead you astray from the way of Allah, for those who lead away from the way of Allah will have a severe punishment for having forgotten the day of reckoning.

27. And We did not create the heaven and the earth and what is between them without purpose. That is the assumption of those who reject (the truth), so woe to those who reject (the truth) from the fire.

28. Or did We make those who believe and do good work like those who spread corruption on earth? Or did We make those who beware (of Allah) like those immoral?

29. It is a blessed book We revealed to you so that they might understand its signs and so that those with understanding will reflect.

30. And We gave Dawud (David) Sulayman (Solomon), a blessed servant, for he was repentant.

31. When the best-bred horses were presented before him in the evening.

32. Then he said: I was overtaken with love for beautiful horses above the remembrance of my Lord until they disappeared out of sight.

33. Return them to me, then he began to pass (his hands) over their legs and necks.

34. And We tested Sulayman (Solomon) and placed a (mere) body onto his throne, then he repented.

35. He said: my Lord, forgive me and grant me a kingdom which will not befit anyone after me, for you are the generous.

36. Then We made the wind of service to him to travel by his command willingly wherever he directed it.

37. And the devils, all the builders and divers.

38. And others tied in cuffs.

39. This is Our gift, so give or withhold (of it) without counting.

40. And he will be close to Us and have a good return.

41. And remember Our servant Ayyub (Job) when he called his Lord that the devil has touched me with affliction and punishment.

42. Stir with your foot: there is cold water to wash and drink.

43. And We granted him his family and the like of it in addition as a mercy from Us and a reminder to those with understanding.

44. And take a bunch of leaves in your hand and strike with it and do not break your vow. We found him to be patient, a blessed servant, for he was repentant.

45. And remember Our servants Ibrahim (Abraham), Ishaq (Isaac) and Ya'qub (Jacob) full of strength and insight.

46. We chose them for their sincere remembrance of the (final) abode.

47. And they are amongst the chosen few with Us.

48. And remember Isma'il (Ishmael), Al-Yasa' (Elisha) and Dhu-l-Kifl (Ezekiel), and each was of the select.

49. This is a reminder, and for those who beware (of Allah) is the best destination.

50. Gardens of Eden with the doors opened for them.

51. They recline there asking for lots of fruit and drink.

52. And with them will be exclusive women companions.

53. This is what you were promised for the day of reckoning.

54. This is Our provision which will not deplete.

55. So it is, and for the transgressors will be the worst destination.

56. Hell, which they will enter, a bad place to be.

57. So it is, so they shall taste it with boiling water and freezing cold.

58. And other similar combinations.

59. Here is a group to join you, there is no welcome for them, for they will enter the fire.

60. They will say: but there is no welcome for you, you prepared this for us, and it is a bad place to stay.

61. They will say: our Lord, whoever prepared this for us, give them double punishment in the fire.

62. And they will say: how come we don't see men we counted amongst the worst?

63. We ridiculed them, but they have become invisible.

64. This arguing of the inhabitants of the fire is indeed true.

65. Say: I am only a warner, and there is no god but Allah the one and dominant.

66. The Lord of the heavens and the earth and what is between them, the mighty and forgiving.

67. Say: this is serious news.

68. You turn away from it.

69. I have no knowledge of the highest counsel when they argue.

70. It has only been revealed to me that I am a plain warner.

71. And when your Lord said to the angels: I am creating a human from clay.

72. Then when I have fashioned him and breathed into him of My spirit, fall prostate before him.

73. Then all the angels prostrated.

74. Except Iblis (the devil), he was arrogant and was of those who rejected (the truth).

75. He said: oh Iblis, what prevented you from prostrating to what I created with both My hands? Have you become arrogant or were you proud?

76. He said: I am better than him, You created me from fire and created him from clay.

77. He said: then get out of here, for you are cursed.

78. And My curse will be upon you until the day of repayment.

79. He said: my Lord, then give me time till the day when they are resurrected.

80. He said: then you are given time.

81. Till the day of the time known.

82. He said: then by Your power I will mislead them all.

83. Except Your sincere servants amongst them.

84. He said: let this be true, and I pronounce the truth.

85. I will fill hell-fire with you and all of them who follow you.

86. Say: I do not ask you for a reward for it and I do not impose.

87. It is only a reminder for all the world.

88. And you will soon know the news of it.

Surah 39: *Az-Zumar* (The Clusters)

In the name of Allah, the Owner and Giver of Mercy

1. The revelation of the book is from Allah the mighty and wise.

2. For We revealed to you the book with the truth, so serve Allah, making religion sincere for Him.

3. For sure to Allah belongs the sincere religion, and those who take protectors besides Him, (saying) we only serve them to bring us closer to Allah, Allah will judge between them regarding what they used to differ in, for Allah does not guide any liar and rejecter (of the truth).

4. If Allah wanted to adopt a son, He would have chosen what He pleased from what He created, glorified is He, He is Allah the one and dominant.

5. He created the heavens and the earth with truth, He makes the night cover the day and the day cover the night and made subservient the sun and the moon, each floats for a fixed term; for sure He is the mighty and forgiving.

6. He created you from a single soul, then made from it its partner and sent you from the cattle eight in pairs; He creates you in the wombs of your mothers in a successive creation in three layers of darkness; that is Allah your Lord, His is the kingdom, there is no god but Him, so where to are you diverted?

7. If you reject (the truth), then Allah is independent of you, yet He is not content with the rejection from His servants, and if you give thanks, He is content with you, and no-one burdened will carry another's burden, then your return is to your Lord and He will inform you what you used to do, for He knows what is kept inside.

8. And if harm befalls man, he calls his Lord, turning to Him, then when He grants him a favour from Him, he forgets what he called for before and sets up partners for Allah to be lead astray from His way. Say: enjoy your rejection for a while, for you are of the inmates of the fire.

9. Or what about him who is devoted throughout the night in prostration and standing (in prayer), concerned about the hereafter and hoping for the mercy of his Lord? Say: are those who know and those who do not know the same? For only those with understanding reflect.

10. Say: oh My servants who believe, beware of your Lord. For those who do good in this world will be good, and the earth of Allah is spacious, and the patient will be paid their reward without counting.

11. Say: I have been commanded to serve Allah, making religion sincere for Him.

12. And I have been commanded to be the first to submit (as Muslim).

13. Say: I fear, if I disobeyed my Lord, the punishment of a tremendous day.

14. Say: I serve Allah, making my religion sincere for Him.

15. So serve what you please besides Him. Say: the losers are those who have lost themselves and their families on the day of resurrection; for sure this is the clear loss.

16. They will be shut off by fire from above and from below, this is what Allah scares His servants with: oh My servants, beware of Me!

17. And those who shun the idols and do not serve them and turn to Allah, for them is good news, so give good news to My servants.

18. Those who listen to the speech and follow the best of it, those are the ones Allah has guided and those are the ones with understanding.

19. So he for whom the word about the punishment comes to pass, are you going to rescue him from the fire?

20. But for those who beware of their Lord will be chambers with chambers built above them and rivers flowing below them, a promise from Allah - Allah does not break His promise.

21. Do you not see how Allah sends water from the sky, then He makes it pass through springs, then He makes vegetation of different colour grow from it, then it dries out and you see it yellow, then He makes it crumble - in that is surely a reminder for those with understanding.

22. Consider then him whose chest Allah has expanded towards Islam and he follows a light from his Lord, and woe to those whose hearts are hardened against the remembrance of Allah, they are in clear error.

23. Allah has revealed the best account in a book replete with similarities from which the skins of those who fear their Lord shiver, then their skins and hearts incline to the remembrance of Allah. This is the guidance of Allah by which He guides whom He pleases, and whomever Allah lets go astray, there is no-one to guide him.

24. Consider then him who tries to keep the harm of the punishment off his face, and the wrongdoers will be told: taste what you have earned.

25. Those before them denied, then the punishment reached them from where they were not aware.

26. And Allah made them taste the humiliation in the life of this world, and the punishment of the hereafter is even greater if they only knew.

27. And We have coined for people every kind of likeness in this Qur'an so that they reflect.

28. An Arabic reading (Qur'an) without distortion, so that they beware (of Allah).

29. Allah coins the similitude of a man who is owned by quarrelling partners and a man who belongs exclusively to one man - are they alike? Allah is praised, but most of them don't know.

30. You will die, and they will die.

31. Then on the day of resurrection you will argue before your Lord.

32. And who is more wrong than he who lies about Allah or denies truthfulness when it reaches him? Is not in hell a home for those who reject (the truth)?

33. And he who brings truthfulness and confirms it, those are the ones who beware (of Allah).

34. They will have what they please with their Lord, that is the reward for those who do good.

35. So that Allah ignores from them the worst they did and gives them their reward for the best they used to do.

36. Is not Allah enough for His servant? And they try to scare you with those besides Him, and whomever Allah lets go astray, there is no-one to guide him.

37. And whomever Allah guides, there is no-one to lead him astray. Is not Allah mighty and vengeful?

38. And if you asked them who created the heavens and the earth, they would say: Allah. Say: consider then what you call on besides Allah, if Allah wanted harm for me, would they remove His harm, or if He wanted mercy for me, would they withhold His mercy? Say: Allah is sufficient for me, on Him let all those rely who want to rely on something.

39. Say: oh my people, act as you do, I also act, then soon you will know.

40. Whom a humiliating punishment will reach and who will deserve a lasting punishment.

41. We have revealed to you the book for mankind with truth, so whoever wants to be guided, does so for his own good, and who goes astray, goes astray against himself, and you are not a guardian over them.

42. Allah receives the souls when they die, and those which did not die in their sleep, then He retains those for whom death has been decreed and sends the others until a fixed term, for in that are signs for people who reflect.

43. Or do they take mediators besides Allah? Say: even though they do not have power over anything nor understand?

44. Say: to Allah belongs all mediation, his is the kingdom of the heavens and the earth, then you will return to Him.

45. And when he mentions Allah alone, the hearts of those who do not believe in the hereafter shudder, and when those besides Him are mentioned, then they rejoice.

46. Say: oh Allah, originator of the heavens and the earth who knows the unseen and the apparent, You judge between Your servants in what they used to differ in.

47. And if those who did wrong had all that is on earth and the like again, they would give it up to avert the harm of the punishment on the day of resurrection, and they become aware from Allah of what they did not count on.

48. And they become aware of what they committed and what they used to make fun of overcomes them.

49. And if harm befalls man, he calls Us, then when We grant him a favour from Us he says: I achieved this by knowledge, but it is a test and most of them don't know.

50. Those before them already said this but what they gathered did not benefit them.

51. Then the evil of what they committed afflicted them, and the wrongdoers amongst these, the evil of what they committed will afflict them and they will not escape.

52. Do they not know that Allah expands the provision for whom He pleases and tightens it, for in that are signs for people who believe.

53. Say: oh My servants who have been extravagant against themselves, do not despair of the mercy of Allah, for Allah forgives all sins, for He is the forgiving, merciful.

54. And turn to your Lord and submit to Him before the punishment reaches you - then you will not be helped.

55. And follow the best of what has been revealed to you from your Lord before the punishment reaches you suddenly when you are unaware.

56. When a soul will say: what a loss that I neglected the cause of Allah when I was of those who made fun.

57. Or will say: if only Allah had guided me I would have been of those who bewared (of Allah).

58. Or will say when it sees the punishment: if only I could return and would be of those who do good.

59. But no, My signs came to you before and you denied them and were arrogant and were of those who rejected (the truth).

60. And on the day of resurrection you will see those who denied Allah with

blackened faces - is not in hell a home for the arrogant?

61. And Allah will rescue those who bewared on account of their accomplishment, no harm will touch them and they will not worry.

62. Allah is the creator of everything and He is a guardian over everything.

63. To Him belong the keys of the heavens and the earth, and those who reject the signs of Allah, they are the losers.

64. Do you command me to serve other than Allah you fools?

65. And it has been revealed to me and to those before me that if you associate (anything with Allah) your work is wasted and you will be of the losers.

66. But serve Allah and be of the grateful.

67. And they do not measure Allah's true ability, and the whole earth will be in His grasp on the day of resurrection and the heavens rolled up in His right hand, glorified and exalted is He above what they associate.

68. And the horn will be blown and whoever is in the heavens and whoever is on earth will be struck down except whom Allah pleases; then it will be blown again and they will stand up and see.

69. And the earth will shine with the light of its Lord, and the book will be laid out, and the prophets and witnesses will be brought and it will be

decided between them with truth and they will not be wronged.

70. And every soul will be repaid what it did and He knows best what you do.

71. And those who rejected (the truth) will be driven to hell in clusters until when they reach it, its gates will be opened and its guards will tell them: did not messengers of your own reach you and recite to you the signs of your Lord and warn you about the meeting of this day of yours? They will say: sure, but the word about the punishment has come to pass about those who rejected (the truth).

72. They will be told: enter the gates of hell to remain there, and bad is the home of the arrogant.

73. And those who bewared of their Lord will be driven to the garden in clusters until when they reach it, its gates will have been opened and its guards will tell them: peace be with you, you were good, so enter it forever.

74. And they will say: praised is Allah who kept His promise and gave us the earth as an inheritance to settle in the garden where we please, so blessed is the reward of those who work.

75. And you will see the angels circling the throne, glorifying the praise of their Lord, and it has been decided between them with truth and it will be said: praised is Allah the Lord of all worlds.

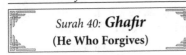

Surah 40: **Ghafir**
(He Who Forgives)

**In the name of Allah,
the Owner and Giver of Mercy**

1. Ha Mim.

2. The revelation of the book is from Allah the mighty and knowing.

3. He who forgives sin and accepts repentance, who has severe punishment and full power, there is no god but Him, to Him is the journey.

4. Only those who reject (the truth) argue about the signs of Allah, so be not deceived by how they move about in the land.

5. The people of Nuh (Noah) before them and the allies after them denied, and each community wanted to overtake their messenger and argued in ignorance in order to refute the truth, then I overtook them, and how was My punishment!

6. And this is how your Lord's word about those who reject (the truth) comes true that they are inmates of the fire.

7. Those who carry the Throne and those surrounding it glorify the praise of their Lord and believe in Him and ask for forgiveness for those who believe: our Lord, Your mercy and knowledge extends to everything, so forgive those who repent and follow Your way and safeguard them from the punishment of hell-fire.

8. Our Lord, and let them enter the gardens of Eden which you have promised them, and those who are righteous amongst their parents and partners and children, for you are the mighty and wise.

9. And safeguard them from (the punishment for) bad deeds, and whomever You safeguard (from the punishment for) bad deeds on that day You have already shown mercy, and that is the ultimate success.

10. Those who reject (the truth) will be called: Allah's aversion is greater than your own aversion when you were called to faith but rejected.

11. They will say: our Lord, you made us die twice and revived us twice, then we acknowledged our sins, so is there a way out?

12. This is your outcome because when Allah alone was called, you rejected, and when something was associated with Him, you believed, then the judgement belongs to Allah, the exalted and great.

13. He is who shows you His signs and sends for you from the sky provision, and only those who repent reflect.

14. So call Allah, making the religion sincere for Him, even if the rejecters resent it.

15. He is above all ranks and owns the throne, He sends the Spirit by His command to whom He pleases of His servants to warn of the day of meeting.

16. On the day they are exposed nothing of them will be hidden from Allah. To whom does the kingdom belong today? To Allah the one and dominant.

17. Today every soul will be repaid for what it has earned, there is no injustice today, for Allah is swift in counting.

18. And warn them of the day to come when the hearts will be stuck near the throats; the wrongdoers will have no close confidant nor mediator to be followed.

19. He knows every secret glance and what is hidden inside.

20. And Allah decides with the truth, and those they call besides Him cannot decide anything, for Allah listens and sees.

21. Do they not travel on earth and see what the outcome was like for those before them? They were greater in power and impact on earth than them, then Allah seized them on account of their sins, and they had no defence against Allah.

22. This is because their messengers came to them with clear proofs but they rejected, so Allah seized them, for He is strong and severe in punishment.

23. And We sent Musa (Moses) with Our signs and a clear authority.

24. To Pharaoh and Haman and Qarun (Korah), but they said: a lying magician.

25. Then when he brought them the truth from Us, they said: kill the children of those who believe with him and spare their women, and the plot of those who reject (the truth) is only in vain.

26. And Pharaoh said: let me kill Musa (Moses), then he can call his Lord, for

I fear that he will change your religion or bring about corruption on earth.

27. And Musa (Moses) said: I seek refuge in my Lord from every arrogant person who does not believe in the day of reckoning.

28. And a believing man from the family of Pharaoh who had hidden his belief said: are you going to kill a man for saying 'my Lord is Allah' whilst he has already brought you clear proofs from his Lord? And if he is a liar, then his lie is upon him, and if he is truthful, some of what he has promised you will afflict you, for Allah does not guide whoever is an exaggerating liar.

29. Oh my people, yours is the kingdom today and you dominate on earth, but who will help us against Allah's harm when it reaches us. Pharaoh said: I only show you what I see and I only guide you to the way of good conduct.

30. And the one who believed said: oh my people, I fear for you the like of the day of the allies.

31. The like of the fate of the people of Nuh (Noah), 'Ad, Thamud and those after them, and Allah does not want to wrong His servants.

32. And oh my people, I fear for you the day of being called.

33. The day when you will turn your backs, you will have no protector against Allah, and whomever Allah lets go astray, there is no-one to guide him.

34. And Yusuf (Joseph) already brought you clear proofs before, but you remained in doubt about what he brought you until when he passed away you said: Allah will not raise a messenger after him. This is how Allah lets the extravagant and doubtful go astray;

35. Those who argue about the signs of Allah without authority given by Him, which is highly offensive to Allah and those who believe. This is how Allah imprints on the heart of every arrogant tyrant.

36. And Pharaoh said: oh Haman, build me a structure so that I can reach the connections;

37. The connections to the heavens and take a look at the god of Musa (Moses), and I surely consider him a liar. And this is how his bad deeds appealed to Pharaoh and he was diverted from the way, and the plot of Pharaoh lead only to destruction.

38. And the one who believed said: oh my people, follow me, I will guide you to the way of good conduct.

39. Oh my people, this worldly life is only a provision, and the hereafter is the lasting abode.

40. Whoever does bad, he will only be rewarded with the like of it, and whoever does good, male or female, and is a believer, those will enter the garden where they will be provided for without counting.

41. And oh my people, how come I call you to the garden and you call me to the fire?

42. You call me to reject Allah and associate with Him what I have no

knowledge of, and I call you to the mighty and forgiving.

43. Without fail that which you call me to has no claim in this world and the next, and our return is to Allah, and the extravagant will be inhabitants of the fire.

44. Then you will remember what I said to you and I will entrust my affairs to Allah, for Allah sees His servants.

45. Then Allah protected him against the evil they were scheming whilst the family of Pharaoh was surrounded by the worst punishment.

46. The fire to which they will be presented in the mornings and evenings, and on the day the hour happens: let the family of Pharaoh enter the severest punishment.

47. And they dispute with each other in the fire, then the weak say to the arrogant: we followed you, so will you avert a portion of the fire from us?

48. The arrogant say: we are all in it, for Allah has already judged between His servants.

49. And those in the fire say to the guards of hell: call your Lord to reduce for us a day of the punishment.

50. They say: did not your messengers reach you with clear proofs? They say: sure. They say: then call, and the call of those who rejected (the truth) is only in vain.

51. For We help Our messengers and the believers in the worldly life and on the day the witnesses stand up.

52. On the day when their excuses will not benefit the wrongdoers and they will be cursed and theirs is a bad abode.

53. And We gave Musa (Moses) guidance and made the Children of Israel inherit the book.

54. A guidance and reminder for those with understanding.

55. So be patient, for the promise of Allah is true, and ask for forgiveness for your sin and glorify the praise of your Lord in the evenings and mornings.

56. Those who argue about the signs of Allah without authority given by Him, they are only filled with pride and will not win the argument, so seek refuge in Allah, for He listens and sees.

57. The creation of the heavens and the earth is greater than the creation of mankind, but most of mankind don't know.

58. And the blind and the seeing are not the same, nor those who believe and do good work and the evil-doer, little do you reflect.

59. The hour will come, there is no doubt in it, but most of mankind don't believe.

60. And your Lord says: call Me, I will respond to you, for those who are too arrogant to serve Me will enter hell in submission.

61. Allah is who made the light for you to rest in and the day to see, for Allah is full of favours for mankind, but most of mankind are ungrateful.

62. This is Allah for you, your Lord, the creator of everything, there is no god but Him, so where to are you diverted?

63. This is how those are diverted who dispute the signs of Allah.

64. Allah is who made the earth firm for you and the sky a cover and shaped you and made your shape beautiful and provided well for you, this is Allah for you, your Lord, so exalted is Allah the Lord of all worlds.

65. He is the living, there is no god but Him, so call Him, making the religion sincere for Him, praised is Allah the Lord of all worlds.

66. Say: I have been forbidden from serving those you call besides Allah when the clear proofs reached me from my Lord, and have been commanded to submit to the Lord of all worlds.

67. He is who created you from soil, then from a sperm, then from an implant, then He brings you out as a child in order for you to reach your strength, then you are going to age, and amongst you is he who dies before, and you will reach a fixed term so that you might understand.

68. He is who gives life and death, and when He decides a matter, He simply says to it "Be!", then it is.

69. Do you not consider how those who argue about the signs of Allah are diverted?

70. Those who deny the book and what We sent Our messengers with, but soon they will know.

71. When the cuffs will be on their necks and the chains, they will be dragged.

72. Through boiling water, then they will be heated in the fire.

73. Then they will be told: where is what you associated?

74. Besides Allah? They say: they have deserted us, but we did not call on anything before, that is how Allah leads those astray who reject (Him).

75. This is on account of you having rejoiced on earth without right and having been triumphant.

76. Enter the gates of hell to remain there, for bad is the home of the arrogant.

77. So be patient, for the promise of Allah is true, then whether We show you some of what We have promised them or take you away, to Us they will return.

78. We previously sent messengers, some of whom We related to you and some of whom We did not relate to you, and no messenger would bring a sign except with the permission of Allah, then when the command of Allah came, it was decided with truth and the followers of falsehood were the losers by then.

79. Allah is who gave you the cattle to ride on and to eat.

80. And you have benefits in them and can attain with them things you desire, and on them and on the ship you are carried.

81. And He shows you His signs, so which of the signs of Allah do you dislike?

82. Do they not travel on earth and see what the outcome was like for those before them? They were more numerous than them and stronger in

power and impact on earth, but what they gathered did not benefit them.

83. Then when their messengers came to them with clear proofs, they rejoiced in whatever knowledge they had, and what they made fun of overcame them.

84. Then when they saw Our affliction they said: we believe in Allah alone and reject what we associated with Him.

85. But their belief did not benefit them when they saw Our affliction. This is the custom of Allah which already came to pass amongst His servants, and those who reject (the truth) were the losers by then.

Surah 41: **Fussilat**
(Explained)

In the name of Allah,
the Owner and Giver of Mercy

1. Ha Mim.

2. A revelation from the Owner and Giver of Mercy.

3. A book whose verses have been explained, an Arabic reading (Qur'an) for people who know.

4. Good news and a warning, but most of them turn away and do not listen.

5. And they say: our hearts are covered against what you call us to and in our ears is a weight and between us and you is a barrier, so act, for we are acting.

6. Say: I am only a human like you whilst it has been revealed to me that your god is a single god, so go straight to Him and ask Him for forgiveness, and woe to the idolaters.

7. Those who do not give Zakat and reject the hereafter.

8. Those who believe and do good work, for them is a limitless reward.

9. Say: do you reject the One who created the earth in two days and you set up partners for Him? That is the Lord of all worlds.

10. And He placed stabilisers on it from above it and blessed it and arranged its provision in four days in fair measure for those who seek it.

11. Then He moved to the heaven which was smoke and said to it and to the earth: come obediently or reluctantly; they said: we come obediently.

12. Then He arranged it into seven heavens in two days and revealed to each heaven its affairs, and We adorned the lowest heaven with lights and protection, that is the arrangement of the mighty and knowing.

13. Then if they turn away, say: I have warned you of being struck down like 'Ad and Thamud.

14. When their messengers came to them continuously (saying:) do not serve anything but Allah, they said: if our Lord pleased He would have sent angels, so we reject what you have been sent with.

15. Then as for 'Ad, they were arrogant on earth without right and said: who is stronger in power than us? Did they not consider that Allah who created

them is stronger in power than them? And they disputed Our signs.

16. Then We sent against them an icy wind over days of disaster to make them taste the punishment of humiliation in the worldly life, and the punishment of the hereafter is even more humiliating and they will not be helped.

17. And as for Thamud, We guided them but they preferred blindness to guidance, so the humiliating punishment struck them down on account of what they committed.

18. And We rescued those who believed and constantly bewared (of Allah).

19. And on that day the enemies of Allah will be gathered to the fire and arranged into divisions.

20. Until when they reach it, their hearing and eyesight and skins will witness against them as to what they did.

21. And they will say to their skins: why did you witness against us? They will say: Allah has given us speech, He who gives speech to everything, and He created you the first time and to Him you return.

22. And you did not expect that your hearing and eyesight and skins would witness against you, but you thought that Allah did not know much of what you did.

23. And this thought you held about your Lord has ruined you so you became losers.

24. So if they are patient, the fire is their home, and if they ask for reprieve, they will not be reprieved.

25. And We assigned them friends so that they made appealing to them what lay before them and what lay behind them, and the word came true for them which had gone before in communities of the Jinn and mankind that they would be losers.

26. And those who reject (the truth) say: do not listen to this Qur'an and belittle it so that you will prevail.

27. So We will make those who reject (the truth) taste a severe punishment and will reward them in line with the worst they did.

28. That is the punishment of the enemies of Allah, the fire, they will have an eternal home in it as a reward for having disputed Our signs.

29. And those who reject (the truth) say: our Lord, show us those of the Jinn and mankind who lead us astray so that we trample them under our feet so that they are the lowest.

30. Those who say: our Lord is Allah, then uphold it, the angels descend on them, saying: fear not and worry not and look forward to the garden which you have been promised.

31. We are your protectors in this world and the hereafter and you will have there whatever your souls desire and you will have there whatever you ask for.

32. A gift from One who is forgiving and merciful.

33. And who is better in speech than him who calls to Allah and does good and says: I am of those who have submitted (as Muslims).

34. And the good deed and the bad deed are not the same; repel with that which is better, then the one with enmity between you and him will become like a dear friend.

35. And only those who are patient achieve this and only those with good fortune achieve this.

36. And if you are in any way provoked by the devil then seek refuge in Allah, for He is who listens and knows.

37. And of His signs are the night and the day and the sun and the moon; do not prostrate to the sun nor to the moon but prostrate to Allah who created them if you serve Him.

38. And if they are arrogant, then those near your Lord glorify Him night and day and do not grow weary.

39. And of His signs is that you see the earth bare, then when We send water upon it, it comes to life and swells. For sure, the One who gives life to it will revive the dead, for He is able to do anything.

40. Those who dispute Our signs are not hidden from Us. Is then he better who is thrown in the fire or he who arrives safe on the day of resurrection? Do as you please, for He sees what you do.

41. Those who reject the reminder when it comes to them: it is certainly a mighty book.

42. Falsehood does not reach it from before or behind, it is a revelation from One who is wise and praiseworthy.

43. You are only told what messengers before you were told, for your Lord is full of forgiveness and full of painful punishment.

44. And had We made it a foreign reading (Qur'an) they would have said: why have its verses not been explained? Foreign and Arab? Say: it is a guidance and healing for those who believe, and those who do not believe, there is a weight upon their ears and they are blind to it, those will be called from a distant place.

45. And We already gave Musa (Moses) the book, then they differed about it, and had not a word gone before from your Lord, it would have been decided between them, and they are indeed in severe doubt about it.

46. Whoever does good, it is for himself, and who does bad, it is against himself, and your Lord does not wrong His servants.

47. To Him is the knowledge of the hour referred, and no fruit emerges from its shell and no female is pregnant or gives birth but with His knowledge, and on the day they will be asked: where are your associates? They will say: let us be, we have no evidence.

48. And what they called on before deserted them, and they realise they have no escape.

49. Man does not grow weary of calling for good, and when harm afflicts him, he is weary and depressed.

50. And if We make him taste mercy from Us after harm afflicted him, he is likely to say: this is for me and I don't think the hour will happen, and if I were to return to my Lord, I would find even better with Him, then We will inform those who rejected (the truth) of what they did and will make them taste an unrelenting punishment.

51. And when We give blessings to man, he rebels and keeps aside, and when harm afflicts him, he prays excessively.

52. Say: have you considered that if it is from Allah and then you reject it, who is more astray than him who is far away (from the truth)?

53. We will show them Our signs in the cosmos and in themselves until it becomes clear to them that it is the truth. Is it not sufficient that your Lord is a witness to everything?

54. But they are in doubt about meeting their Lord, yet He surrounds everything.

Surah 42: *Ash-Shura* (Consultation)

In the name of Allah, the Owner and Giver of Mercy

1. Ha Mim.

2. 'Ayn Sin Qaf.

3. This is how Allah reveals to you and those before you, Allah, the mighty and wise.

4. To Him belongs what is in the heavens and what is on earth, and He is the exalted and great.

5. The heavens almost break up from above and the angels glorify the praise of their Lord and ask forgiveness for those on earth, for sure Allah is the forgiving and merciful.

6. And those who adopt protectors besides Him, Allah is their keeper and you are not their guardian.

7. And this is how We revealed to you an Arabic reading (Qur'an) to warn the leading township and those around it and warn of the day of gathering in which there is no doubt; a group will be in the garden and a group will be in the fire.

8. And if Allah pleased He would have made you a single community, but He enters whom He pleases into His mercy, and the wrongdoers have neither protector nor helper.

9. Or do they take protectors besides Allah? But Allah is the protector and He revives the dead and He is able to do anything.

10. And whatever you differ in, the judgement about it belongs to Allah, that is Allah your Lord, on Him I rely and to Him I repent.

11. The originator of the heavens and the earth who gave you partners from amongst yourselves and the cattle in pairs, thus He made you spread out, there is nothing like Him, and He listens and sees.

12. To Him belong the keys of the heavens and the earth, He expands the provision for whom He pleases and tightens it, for He knows everything.

13. He has ordained for you in the religion what He instructed Nuh (Noah) with and what He revealed to you and what We instructed Ibrahim (Abraham) with and Musa (Moses) and 'Isa (Jesus): that you uphold the religion and do not break up regarding it. It is a big deal for the idolaters what you call them to. Allah chooses whom He pleases to come to Him and guides to Him who repents.

14. And they only broke up after the knowledge had reached them out of transgression amongst each other, and had not a word from your Lord gone before until a fixed term, it would have been decided between them, and those who inherited the book after them are in severe doubt about it.

15. So call to that and be steadfast as you have been commanded and do not follow their desires and say: I believe in any book Allah has revealed and have been commanded to deal justly with you, Allah is our Lord and your Lord, our deeds are for us and your deeds are for you, there is no dispute between us and you, Allah will gather us and to Him is the journey.

16. And those who dispute about Allah after He has been responded to, their argument is void before their Lord and upon them is (His) anger and theirs is a severe punishment.

17. Allah is who revealed the book with truth and (set up) the balance, and how can you tell whether the hour might be near.

18. Those are in a hurry for it who do not believe in it, and those who believe are anxious about it and know that it is the truth. For sure, those who are in doubt about the hour are in extensive error.

19. Allah is kind to His servants; He provides for whom He pleases and He is the strong and mighty.

20. Whoever wants the fruit of the hereafter, We increase its fruit for him, and whoever wants the fruit of this world, We give him of it and he has no share in the hereafter.

21. Or do they have partners who ordain for them in the religion what Allah did not permit? And if it had not been for the promise of judgement, it would have been decided between them, and for the wrongdoers is a painful punishment.

22. You will see the wrongdoers anxious about what they committed and it will fall upon them, and those who believe and do good work will be in the greenery of the gardens (of paradise) where they will have what they please with their Lord, that is the great favour.

23. This is the good news Allah gives to His servants who believe and do good work. Say: I do not ask you for a reward for it except love towards relatives, and whoever performs a good deed, We increase good for him through it, for Allah forgives and appreciates.

24. Or do they say he invented a lie against Allah? But if Allah pleased, He would seal your heart, and Allah eradicates falsehood and verifies the truth with His words, for He knows what is kept inside.

25. And He is who accepts repentance from His servants and overlooks bad deeds and knows what you do.

26. And He responds to those who believe and do good work and increases them of His favours, and for those who reject (the truth) is a severe punishment.

27. And if Allah expanded the provision for His servants, they would transgress on earth, but He sends in measure what He pleases, for He is informed of and sees His servants.

28. And He is who sends down the rain after they despair and spreads out His mercy, and He is the praiseworthy protector.

29. And of His signs is the creation of the heavens and the earth and all the creatures He spread on it, and He is able to gather them when He pleases.

30. And whatever affliction befalls you, it is due to what you yourselves have brought about, and He overlooks a lot.

31. And you will not escape on earth, and you have besides Allah no protector nor helper.

32. And of His signs are the towering ships traversing the sea.

33. If He pleases, He makes the wind stop and they remain motionless on top of it.

34. Or He destroys them on account of what they committed, and He overlooks a lot.

35. And those who argue about Our signs will know that they have no escape.

36. For whatever you have been given is the provision of the life of the world, and what is with Allah is better and more lasting for those who believe and rely on their Lord.

37. And those who shun the major sins and indecencies, and whenever they are angry, they forgive.

38. And those who respond to their Lord and keep up prayer and decide their affairs in consultation between them and spend of what We have provided them with.

39. And those who when they are afflicted by transgression help each other.

40. And the punishment for harm is a similar harm, but whoever lets it be and does good, his reward is with Allah, for He does not love the wrongdoers.

41. And whoever takes revenge after having been wronged, they should not be prevented.

42. Only those should be prevented who wrong people and transgress on earth without right, for those is a painful punishment.

43. And whoever is patient and forgives, that is one of the firmest things (to do).

44. And whomever Allah lets go astray, He has no protector after that, and you see the wrongdoers, when they see the punishment, say: is there a way of preventing it?

45. And you see them presented before it, fearful in humiliation, cautiously looking around, and the believers will say: the losers today are those who lost themselves and their families on the day of resurrection, for sure the wrongdoers will be in a lasting punishment.

46. And they had no protectors to help them besides Allah, and whomever Allah lets go astray, there is no way for him.

47. Respond to your Lord before a day arrives when there is no avoiding Allah; on that day you will have no refuge and you will have no defence.

48. And if they turn away, then We have not sent you as a guardian over them, for your duty is only to convey, and when We let man taste a mercy from Us, he rejoices in it, and when harm afflicts them on account of what they have sent ahead, then man is ungrateful.

49. To Allah belongs the kingdom of the heavens and the earth, He creates what He pleases, He grants whom He pleases females, and grants whom He pleases males.

50. Or He pairs them up as males and females, and He makes whom He pleases barren, for He is knowing and powerful.

51. And it is not befitting for a human that Allah should talk to him except by revelation or from behind a barrier, or He sends a messenger to pass on of the revelation what He pleases by His permission, for He is knowing and wise.

52. And this is how We revealed to you through a Spirit We command, you had no idea what the book was or the faith, but We made it a light to guide with it whom We please of Our servants, and you certainly guide towards a straight path.

53. The path of Allah to whom belongs what is in the heavens and what is on earth, for sure to Allah return all matters.

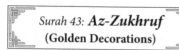

Surah 43: *Az-Zukhruf* (Golden Decorations)

In the name of Allah, the Owner and Giver of Mercy

1. Ha Mim.

2. By the clear book.

3. We made it an Arabic reading (Qur'an) so that you might understand.

4. And in the original book with Us it is exalted and wise.

5. Should We then withdraw the reminder from you entirely because you are wasteful people?

6. And how many a prophet have We sent to the earliest communities.

7. And whenever a prophet came to them, they made fun of him.

8. So We destroyed those with a grip stronger than theirs and the example of the earliest communities came to pass.

9. And if you asked them who created the heavens and the earth, they will say: the mighty and knowing has created them.

10. The One who gave you the earth as an expanse and cut paths in it for you so that you might be guided.

11. And the One who sent water from the sky in measure, then We revive with it a dead land; likewise you will be brought out.

12. And the One who created all pairs and gave you the ship and the cattle which you mount.

13. So that you are well established on them, then remember the blessings of your Lord when you are established on them and say: glorified is He who made this subservient to us, we could not have subjected them.

14. And we will turn to our Lord.

15. And they assign for Him a portion of His (own) servants, for man is clearly ungrateful.

16. Has He then taken daughters from what He created and chosen for you sons?

17. And when any of them is given news of what they coin as a likeness for the Merciful, his face darkens and he is upset:

18. Someone brought up amongst pleasantries - and he cannot sustain the argument.

19. And they make the angels who are amongst the servants of Allah female. Did they witness their creation? Their evidence will be recorded and they will be asked.

20. And they say: if the Merciful pleased, we would not serve them besides Him. They have no knowledge of this, for they only guess.

21. Or did We give them a book before so that they hold on to it?

22. But they say: we found our fathers upon a practice and we are guided by their traditions.

23. And this is how We never sent a warner before you to a town but its affluent people said: we found our fathers upon a practice and we emulate their traditions.

24. He said: what if I brought you something better guided than what you found your fathers doing? They said: we reject what you have been sent with.

25. So We took revenge on them, then see what the outcome of those who denied was like.

26. And when Ibrahim (Abraham) said to his father and his people: I am free of what you serve.

27. Except for the One who originated me, for He will guide me.

28. And He made this into a lasting word amongst his descendants so they would return.

29. But I have given provision to those and their fathers until the truth reaches them and a clearly spoken messenger.

30. And when the truth reached them, they said: this is magic and we reject it.

31. And they said: why was not this Qur'an revealed to a man of the two great towns?

32. Do they divide the mercy of your Lord? We divide amongst them their livelihood in the worldly life and raised some of them above others in stages so that some of them take others in service, and the mercy of your Lord is better than what they amass.

33. And if it wouldn't turn mankind into a single community We would have granted those who reject the Merciful silver roofs on their houses and stairs on which they ascend.

34. And (silver) doors for their houses and couches on which they recline.

35. And golden decorations, but all of that would only be the provision of this world, and the hereafter with your Lord is for those who beware.

36. And whoever is blind to the reminder of the Merciful, We assign for him a devil who will be a friend for him.

37. And they divert them from the way but they think that they are guided.

38. Until when he comes to Us he says: if only there was the distance of the two Easts between me and you, what a bad friend.

39. And today it will not benefit you, if you did wrong, that you will share the punishment.

40. Can you then make the deaf hear or guide the blind or who is in clear error?

41. And if We take you away, We will take revenge on them.

42. Or if We show you what We have promised them, We have power over them.

43. So hold on to that which has been revealed to you, for you are on a straight path.

44. And it is a reminder for you and your people, and you will soon be asked.

45. And ask the messengers whom We sent before you, did We allow gods besides the Merciful to be served?

46. And We sent Musa (Moses) with Our signs to Pharaoh and his leaders and he said: I am a messenger of the Lord of all worlds.

47. Then when he came to them with Our signs, they made fun of them.

48. And every sign We showed them was greater than the previous one, and We overtook them with the punishment so that they might turn back.

49. And they said: oh you magician, call your Lord for us on account of what He has promised to you, for we will be guided.

50. Then when We removed the punishment from them, they broke their promise.

51. And Pharaoh announced amongst his people, saying: oh my people, do I not own the kingdom of Egypt and these rivers which flow before me? Don't you see?

52. Am I not better than him who is a low cast and can hardly speak clearly?

53. Then why have not golden bracelets been given to him or did the angels come in tow with him?

54. So he fooled his people and they obeyed him, for they were sinful people.

55. Then when they provoked Us We took revenge on them and drowned them altogether.

56. Then We made them a precedent and an example for those to come.

57. And when the son of Maryam (Mary) is given as an example, your people protest against it.

58. And they say: are our gods better or he? They only present it to you as a contradiction, for they are argumentative people.

59. For he is only a servant whom We have favoured and made him an example for the Children of Israel.

60. And if We pleased, We could replace you with angels to be successors on the earth.

61. And there is sure knowledge of the hour, so do not doubt it, and follow me, that is a straight path.

62. And let not the devil divert you, for he is a clear enemy to you.

63. And when 'Isa (Jesus) came with clear proofs he said: I have brought you wisdom and am to clarify to you some of that in which you differed, so beware of Allah and obey me.

64. For Allah is my Lord and your Lord, so serve Him. This is a straight path.

65. Then the allies differed amongst themselves, so woe to those who do wrong from the punishment of a painful day.

66. Do they just wait that the hour reaches them suddenly when they are not aware?

67. Close friends will be enemies to each other on that day, except those who beware (of Allah).

68. Oh My servants, you shall not fear today nor shall you worry.

69. Those who believe in Our signs and did submit (as Muslims).

70. Enter the garden, you and your partners, happily.

71. They will be waited upon with golden plates and cups and it will contain whatever the souls desire and what the eyes delight in, and you will remain there forever.

72. And this is the garden which you have inherited on account of what you did.

73. You have lots of fruit in it and eat from it.

74. For the sinful remain in the punishment of hell-fire.

75. It will not be lightened for them and they will be left with nothing.

76. And We did not wrong them, but they were the wrongdoers.

77. And they will call: oh angel, let your Lord finish us off. He will say: you will stay.

78. We previously brought you the truth, but most of you disliked the truth.

79. Or do they decide any matter? We decide.

80. Or do they think that We do not hear their secrets and secret meetings? But no, Our messengers are with them, recording.

81. Say: if the Merciful had a son, then I would be the first to serve (him).

82. Glorified is the Lord of the heavens and the earth, the Lord of the throne, above what they make out.

83. So leave them to busy themselves and play until they meet their promised day.

84. And He is god in the heaven and god on earth, and He is the wise and knowing.

85. Exalted is He to whom belongs the kingdom of the heavens and the earth and what is between them, and He has knowledge of the hour and to Him you return.

86. And those whom they call besides Him have no power of intercession except for him who is a witness to the truth and with knowledge.

87. And if you were to ask them who created them, they would say: Allah. So where to are they diverted?

88. And his saying (will be): oh my Lord, these people did not believe.

89. So ignore them and say: peace, for they will soon know.

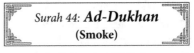

Surah 44: **Ad-Dukhan**
(Smoke)

In the name of Allah,
the Owner and Giver of Mercy

1. Ha Mim.

2. By the clear book.

3. We revealed it during a blessed night, for We continually issued warnings.

4. During it every matter to be judged is decided.

5. A command from Us, for We continually sent (messengers).

6. As mercy from your Lord, for He listens and knows.

7. The Lord of the heavens and the earth and what is between them, if you are certain.

8. There is no god but He, He gives life and death, your Lord and the Lord of your forefathers.

9. But they play whilst in doubt.

10. So look out for a day when the sky brings clear smoke.

11. Which surrounds people, that is a painful punishment.

12. Our Lord, remove the punishment from us, for we believe.

13. How can they have a reminder (now), when a clear messenger came to them before?

14. Then they turned away and said: he has been taught and is possessed.

15. We will remove the punishment a little, for you will return.

16. On the day We take a major grip, for We take revenge.

17. And We tested before them the people of Pharaoh and an honourable messenger came to them.

18. (Saying): Return to me the servants of Allah, for I am a reliable messenger to you.

19. And do not exalt against Allah, for I have brought you a clear authority.

20. And I seek refuge in my Lord and your Lord that you would abuse me.

21. And if you do not believe me then leave me alone.

22. Then he called his Lord that these people are sinful.

23. So travel with My servants at night, for you will be followed.

24. And leave through the sea calmly, for they are forces to be drowned.

25. How many gardens and springs did they leave behind.

26. And plantations and honoured dwellings.

27. And blessings which they enjoyed.

28. This is what happened, and We made others inherit them.

29. And the sky and the earth did not cry for them, and they were not spared.

30. And We did rescue the Children of Israel from the humiliating punishment.

31. From Pharaoh, for he was extravagantly wasteful.

32. And We knowingly chose them above everybody else.

33. And We gave them signs which contained a clear test.

34. For these say:

35. There is only our first death, and we will not be raised.

36. Then bring our forefathers, if you are truthful.

37. Are they better or the people of Tubba' (in Yemen) and those before them, We destroyed them, for they were sinful.

38. And We did not create the heavens and earth and what is between as a pastime.

39. We only created them with the truth, but most of them don't know.

40. The day of division is the appointment for all of them.

41. The day when no protector will benefit his protégée the least and they will not be helped.

42. Except for the one on whom Allah has mercy, for he is the mighty and merciful.

43. For the tree of Zaqqum,

44. Is the food of the sinner,

45. Like lava bubbling in the bellies,

46. Like the bubbling of boiling water.

47. Take him and carry him into the midst of hell-fire.

48. Then pour the punishment of boiling water over his head.

49. Taste it, for you are the mighty and honourable.

50. For this is what you doubted.

51. Those who beware (of Allah) will be in a safe place.

52. In gardens and springs.

53. They will wear silk and brocade, facing each other.

54. This is how it is, and We will marry them to women of rare beauty.

55. They will ask there for any kind of fruit in safety.

56. They will not taste death there after the first death, and He will protect them from the punishment of hell-fire.

57. A favour from your Lord, that is the ultimate success.

58. And We have made it easy (to recite) in your language so that they might reflect.

59. So watch out, for they will watch out.

Surah 45: *Al-Jathiyah* (Kneeling)

In the name of Allah, the Owner and Giver of Mercy

1. Ha Mim.

2. The revelation of the book is from Allah the mighty and wise.

3. In the heavens and the earth there are signs for the believers.

4. And in your creation and in the creatures He spread out are signs for people who are certain.

5. And in the alternation of night and day and the provision Allah has sent from the sky to revive with it the earth after its death and the turning of the winds are signs for people who understand.

6. These are the signs of Allah which We recite to you in truth, so in what tale after Allah and His signs do they believe?

7. Woe to every sinful liar.

8. Who hears the signs of Allah recited to him, then he arrogantly persists as if he did not hear them, so announce to him a painful punishment.

9. And if he comes to know of any of Our signs he makes fun of them; for those is a humiliating punishment.

10. Hell will follow them and what they have gathered will not benefit them nor that they took protectors besides Allah, and theirs is a severe punishment.

11. This is a guidance, and for those who reject the signs of their Lord is a punishment of painful affliction.

12. Allah is who made of service to you the sea so that the ship sails on it by His command and you seek of His favours in order to be grateful.

13. And He made of service to you what is in the heavens and what is on earth, entirely from Him, these are signs for people who reflect.

14. Tell those who believe to forgive those who do not hope for the days of Allah, so that He may reward people in line with what they did.

15. Whoever does good, it is for himself, and who does bad, it is against himself, then you return to your Lord.

16. And We gave the Children of Israel the book and the judgement and the prophethood and provided them with good food and favoured them over everybody else.

17. And We gave them clear proofs by way of the commandments, then they did not differ except after the knowledge had reached them out of transgression amongst each other, for your Lord will decide between them on the day of resurrection with regard to what they used to differ in.

18. Then We placed you upon a code of conduct by way of commandments, so follow them and do not follow the desires of those who don't know.

19. For they will not benefit you the least with Allah, and the wrongdoers are protectors of each other, and Allah is the protector of those who beware (of Him).

20. This is an eye-opener for mankind and a guidance and a mercy for people who are certain.

21. Or do those who commit bad think that We make them equal to those who believe and do good during their lives and after death? They judge badly.

22. And Allah created the heavens and the earth with truth and so that every soul will be rewarded for what it committed and they will not be wronged.

23. Have you considered the one who takes his desire as god and Allah lets him go astray knowingly and seals his hearing and heart and places a blindfold over his eyes, so who will guide him after Allah, don't you reflect?

24. And they say: there is only our worldly life, we die and live, and only time destroys us, and they have no knowledge about it, they only presume.

25. And when Our clear signs are recited to them, their argument is only that they say: bring our forefathers if you are truthful.

26. Say: Allah gives you life, then He makes you die, then He gathers you to the day of resurrection in which there is no doubt, but most people don't know.

27. And to Allah belongs the kingdom of the heavens and the earth, and on the day the hour happens, on that day the followers of falsehood are losers.

28. And you will see every community kneeling down; every community will be called towards its record: today you will be rewarded for what you used to do.

29. This is Our record which speaks to you with the truth, for We used to write down what you used to do.

30. Then as for those who believed and did good, their Lord will enter them into His mercy, that is the clear success.

31. And as for those who rejected (the truth): were not My signs recited to you but you were arrogant and were sinful people?

32. And when it was said that the promise of Allah is true and there is no doubt about the hour you said: we have no idea what the hour is, we follow only assumptions and we are not sure.

33. And they become aware of the bad they had committed and what they used to make fun of overcame them.

34. And it is said: today We forget you just as you forgot the meeting of this day of yours and your abode is the fire and you have no helpers.

35. This is because you made fun of the signs of Allah and the worldly life deceived you, so today they will not emerge from it and they will not be allowed redress.

36. So Allah is praised, the Lord of the heavens and the Lord of the earth, the Lord of all worlds.

37. And to Him belongs greatness in the heavens and on earth, and He is the mighty and wise.

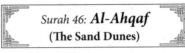

Surah 46: **Al-Ahqaf**
(The Sand Dunes)

In the name of Allah,
the Owner and Giver of Mercy

1. Ha Mim.

2. The revelation of the book is from Allah the mighty and wise.

3. We did not create the heavens and the earth and what is between them except with truth and for a fixed term, and those who reject (the truth) turn away from what they have been warned of.

4. Say: have you considered that which you call on besides Allah? Show me what they created of the earth, or do they have a share in the heavens? Bring me a book preceding this one or a trace of knowledge if you are truthful.

5. And who is more astray than who calls besides Allah on those who will not respond to him until the day of resurrection and who are unaware of their prayers?

6. And when mankind is gathered, they will be enemies to them and will reject their service.

7. And when Our clear signs are recited to them, those who reject (the truth) say about the truth when it reaches them: this is plain magic.

8. Or do they say he invented it? Say: if I invented it, then you are powerless to help me against Allah, He knows best what you engage in, He is sufficient as witness between me and you and He is the forgiving and merciful.

9. Say: I am not the first of the messengers, and I don't know what will happen to me nor to you, I only follow what has been revealed to me and I am only a clear warner.

10. Say: have you considered that if it is from Allah and you reject it - whereas a witness from the Children of Israel gives evidence to something similar, then he believes - that you are arrogant? For Allah does not guide wrongdoing people.

11. And those who reject (the truth) say to those who believe: if it was good, they would not have got it before us. And as they are not guided by it they will say: this is an ancient falsehood.

12. And before it came the book of Musa (Moses) as a guide and mercy, and this book is a confirmation in the Arabic language to warn those who do wrong and give good news to those who do good.

13. Those who say: our Lord is Allah, then uphold it, they shall have no fear nor worry.

14. Those are the inhabitants of the garden in which they remain as a reward for what they used to do.

15. And We admonished man to be good to his parents. His mother carried him in discomfort and gave birth to him in discomfort, and

carrying and weaning him takes thirty months, then finally when he reaches full strength and reaches forty years he says: my Lord, grant me that I am grateful for your blessings which You have blessed me with and my parents and that I do good work which You will be pleased with, and make my children good for me, for I turn to You and am of those who have submitted (as Muslims).

16. Those are the ones of whom We will accept the best of what they did and whose bad deeds We disregard from amongst the inhabitants of the garden, a true promise that they were given.

17. And he who says to his parents: get off, are you promising me that I will be raised when generations before me have gone by? And they implore Allah, (saying) woe to you, believe, for the promise of Allah is true, but he says: these are only stories of old.

18. Those are the ones upon whom the word has come true (as it did) amongst the communities of Jinn and mankind who have passed before them, for they were losers.

19. For all there are stages on account of what they did, and He will repay them their deeds and they will not be wronged.

20. On the day those who reject (the truth) are presented to the fire: you spent all the good you had in your worldly life and enjoyed it, so today you will be rewarded with a humiliating punishment for having been arrogant on earth without right and for having been corrupt.

21. And remember the brother of 'Ad when he warned his people in the sand dunes, and there have been warnings before him and after him, that you should not serve anyone but Allah, for I fear for you the punishment of a tremendous day.

22. They said: did you come to us to divert us from our gods? Then bring us what you promise us if you are truthful.

23. He said: knowledge rests with Allah, and I convey to you what I was sent with, but I see you are ignorant people.

24. Then when they saw clouds approaching their valleys they said: these are clouds to bring us rain. But it is what you were in a hurry for: a wind containing a painful punishment.

25. It destroys everything by the command of its Lord, so they ended up with only their homes left to be seen; this is how we punish the sinful people.

26. And We had established them more than We established you and gave them hearing and eyesight and hearts, but neither their hearing nor their eyesight nor their hearts benefited them the least when they disputed the signs of Allah, and what they used to make fun of overcame them.

27. And We destroyed towns around you before and explained the signs so that they might turn back.

28. Then why did not those whom they adopted as gods to endear them to Allah help them? But they deserted them, and that is their falsehood and what they used to invent.

29. And when We dispatched to you a group of the Jinn to listen to the Qur'an, then when they were in its presence they said: be quiet, then when it was completed, they went back to their people as warners.

30. They said: oh our people, we have listened to a book which has been revealed after Musa (Moses), confirming what came before it, which guides to the truth and to a straight path.

31. Oh our people, respond to the invitation of Allah and believe in Him, He will forgive you of your sins and protect you from a painful punishment.

32. And whoever does not respond to the invitation from Allah, he will not escape on earth and will have no protectors besides Him, those are in clear error.

33. Do they not consider that Allah, the One who created the heavens and the earth and did not tire of their creation, is able to revive the dead, for sure He is able to do anything.

34. And on the day those who rejected (the truth) are presented to the fire (it is said): is this not true? They will say: Sure, by our Lord. So taste the punishment because you used to reject (the truth).

35. So be patient like those firm amongst the messengers were patient, and do not be in a hurry for them; on the day they see what they were promised it is as if they will not have stayed except an hour of the day. This is a declaration, so will anyone but the sinful people be destroyed?

Surah 47: **Muhammad**

In the name of Allah, the Owner and Giver of Mercy

1. Those who reject (the truth) and divert from the way of Allah, their work is lost.

2. And those who believe and do good work and believe in what has been revealed to Muhammad, which is the truth from your Lord, He will cancel their bad deeds and improve their situation.

3. That is because those who reject (the truth) follow falsehood and those who believe follow the truth from their Lord; this is how Allah coins their examples for mankind.

4. So when you meet those who reject (the truth) - until the war settles -, strike their necks until you have weakened them, then tie them up firmly, after which you may be generous or ransom them; that is how it is, and if Allah pleased, He could have struck them down, but it is for Him to test some of you through others, and those who are killed in the way of Allah, their work will not be lost.

5. He will guide them and improve their situation.

6. And enter them into the garden which He has made known to them.

7. Oh you believers, if you help Allah, Allah helps you and makes your foothold firm.

8. And those who reject (the truth), they will be ruined and their work is lost.

9. That is because they disliked what Allah revealed, so He wastes their work.

10. Do they not travel on earth and see what the outcome was like for those before them? Allah brought destruction upon them, and for those who reject (the truth) is a similar fate.

11. This is because Allah is the protector of the believers and those who reject (the truth) have no protector.

12. Allah enters those who believe and do good work into gardens through which rivers flow, and those who reject (the truth) will have enjoyment and eat like the cattle eat, and the fire is their home.

13. And how many towns which were stronger than your town, which threw you out, did We destroy and they had no helper.

14. Is then one who follows clear proof from his Lord like one to whom his bad deeds appeal and they follow their desires?

15. The likeness of the garden, those who beware (of Allah) have been promised: there are rivers of water which is not polluted and rivers of milk which does not change its taste and rivers of wine which is pleasant for those who drink it and rivers of pure honey, and they will have all kinds of fruit there and forgiveness from their Lord; unlike those who remain in the fire and are given boiling water to drink, so it cuts their intestines.

16. And amongst them is he who listens to you until when they emerge from your presence they say to those who were given knowledge: what did he just say? Those are the ones whose hearts Allah has sealed and they follow their desires.

17. And those who follow the guidance, He increases them in guidance and gives them their awareness.

18. Are they then only waiting that the hour is upon them suddenly, whilst its signs have already come? So what reminder will they have when it reaches them?

19. Know then that there is no god but Allah and seek forgiveness for your sins and for the believing men and women, and Allah knows your movements and your abode.

20. And the believers say: why is no Surah being revealed? Then when a decisive Surah is revealed and fighting is mentioned in it, you see those in whose hearts is a disease looking at you as if surrounded by death - more befitting for them would be:

21. Obedience and appropriate words, then, once the matter has been decided, if they were true to Allah it would be better for them.

22. Would you not, if you turn away, cause corruption on earth and cut off your family ties?

23. Those are the ones whom Allah has cursed and whom He makes deaf and blinds their eyesight.

24. Do they not reflect on the Qur'an? Or are there locks upon their hearts?

25. Those who turn their backs after the guidance has been made clear to them, the devil gives them suggestions and hope.

26. That is because they say to those who dislike what Allah has sent: we obey you in some matters, and Allah knows their secrets.

27. So how will it be when the angels take them away and strike their faces and backs?

28. That is because they followed what displeases Allah and dislike His pleasure, so He wastes their work.

29. Or do those with a disease in their hearts think that Allah will not expose their grudges?

30. And if We pleased, We would show them to you so that you know them by their mark, but you will know them from the way they talk, and Allah knows your work.

31. We shall test you until We know those who strive amongst you and those who have patience, and We shall test your intelligence.

32. Those who reject (the truth) and divert from the way of Allah and break away from the messenger after the guidance has been made clear to them, they will not harm Allah the least, and He will waste their work.

33. Oh you believers, obey Allah and obey the messenger and do not spoil your work.

34. Those who reject (the truth) and divert from the way of Allah and then die in rejection, Allah will not forgive them.

35. So do not lose heart and call for a truce when you will come out on top, and Allah is with you and will not deprive you of your work.

36. For the life of this world is only play and pastime, and if you believe and beware, He will give you your reward and will not ask you for your wealth.

37. If He asked you for it and persisted you would withhold and He would expose your grudges.

38. You are the ones called to spend in the way of Allah, but amongst you is he who withholds - and whoever withholds only withholds from himself, and Allah is rich and you are poor; and if you turn away He will replace you with a different people who will not be like you.

Surah 48: **Al-Fath** (Victory)

In the name of Allah, the Owner and Giver of Mercy

1. We have given you a clear victory.

2. So that Allah forgives you any sin that has been and that is to come and completes His favours upon you and guides you on a straight path.

3. And so that Allah helps you with mighty support.

4. He is who sent tranquillity into the hearts of the believers to increase them further in their faith, and to Allah belong the forces of the heavens and the earth, and Allah is knowing and wise.

5. So that He enters the believing men and women into gardens through which rivers flow, where they will remain, and cancels their bad deeds, and this is the ultimate success with Allah.

6. And punishes the pretending men and women and idolatrous men and women who thought bad of Allah - the bad turns back on them, and Allah is angry with them and curses them and promises them hell, a bad destination.

7. And to Allah belong the forces of the heavens and the earth, and Allah is mighty and wise.

8. We sent you as a witness and bringer of good news and a warner.

9. So that you would believe in Allah and His messenger and strengthen him and defend him and glorify Him in the mornings and evenings.

10. Those who pledged allegiance to you have pledged allegiance to Allah; Allah's hand was above their hands. Then if someone falls short, he falls short against himself, and if someone keeps what he promised to Allah, He will give him a tremendous reward.

11. Those desert Arabs who stayed behind will say to you: our wealth and families kept us busy, so forgive us.

They say with their mouths what is not in their hearts. Say: then who has any power for you over Allah if He wants harm or benefit for you? But Allah is informed of what you do.

12. But you thought that the messenger and the believers would never return to their families, and that appealed to you in your hearts and you thought bad and were ruined as people.

13. And whoever does not believe in Allah and His messenger, We have promised a flame for those who reject (the truth).

14. And to Allah belongs the kingdom of the heavens and the earth; He forgives whom He pleases and punishes whom He pleases, and Allah is forgiving and merciful.

15. Those who stayed behind say when you leave to acquire booty: allow us to follow you. They want to change the word of Allah. Say: you will not follow us; this is what Allah said before. Then they will say: you only envy us - but they hardly understand.

16. Say to the desert Arabs who stayed behind: you will be called against a people with terrifying strength whom you will fight unless they surrender, then if you obey, Allah will give you a good reward, and if you turn away as you turned away before, He will punish you with a painful punishment.

17. There is no blame on the blind, nor is there blame on the lame, nor is there blame on the sick, and whoever obeys Allah and His messenger, He enters him into the gardens through

which rivers flow, and whoever turns away, He punishes him with a painful punishment.

18. Allah was content with the believers when they pledged allegiance to you under the tree, and He knew what was in their hearts and sent tranquillity upon them and rewarded them with a near victory.

19. And much booty for them to acquire, and Allah is mighty and wise.

20. And Allah promised you that you would acquire much booty and sped this up for you and kept the people's hands off you, to make it a sign for the believers and to guide you on a straight path.

21. And more which you have not yet obtained but which Allah has full knowledge of, and Allah is able to do anything.

22. And if those who reject (the truth) fought you, they would turn their backs and then not find any protector or helper.

23. The custom of Allah which has gone before, and you will not find a change in the custom of Allah.

24. And He is who kept their hands off you and your hands off them in the valley of Makkah after He had given you victory over them, and Allah saw what you did.

25. They are the ones who reject (the truth) and prevent you from the sacred mosque and the intercepted offering from reaching its destination, and if there were not believing men and believing women whom you don't know and whom you would pass over and for whom you would unknowingly be to blame - for Allah enters into His mercy whom He pleases -, if those had left We would have punished those who reject (the truth) amongst them with a painful punishment.

26. When those who reject (the truth) placed rage into their hearts, the rage of ignorance, Allah sent His tranquillity upon His messenger and upon the believers and held them to the word of awareness (that there is no god but Allah), which they had most right to and which belonged to them, and Allah knows everything.

27. Allah has verified His messenger's vision with the truth that you will enter the sacred mosque, if Allah pleases, safe, with shaved and cropped heads, without fear, for He knew what you did not know and gave a near victory besides that.

28. He is who sent His messenger with the guidance and the religion of truth to make it manifest over all religion, and Allah is sufficient as a witness.

29. Muhammad is the messenger of Allah, and those with him are stern against those who reject (the truth) and merciful amongst themselves. You see them bowing and prostrating, seeking favours from Allah and approval. Their marks are on their faces from the traces of prostration. That is their likeness in the Torah, and their likeness in the Gospel is that of a seed from which a shoot emerges, then strengthens, then rises straight from its stalk to please the planter and

to annoy those who reject (the truth). Allah has promised those of them who believe and do good forgiveness and an immense reward.

Surah 49: *Al-Hujurat* (The Private Rooms)

In the name of Allah, the Owner and Giver of Mercy

1. Oh you believers, do not put yourselves before Allah and His messenger and beware of Allah, for Allah listens and knows.

2. Oh you believers, do not raise your voices above the voice of the prophet and do not talk loudly with him like you do with each other so that your work would be wasted whilst you don't realise.

3. Those who subdue their voices near the messenger of Allah, they are those whose hearts Allah has purified towards awareness; for them is forgiveness and a tremendous reward.

4. Those who call you from behind your private rooms, most of them don't understand.

5. And if they had patience until you come out to them, it would be better for them, and Allah is forgiving and merciful.

6. Oh you believers, if a sinner comes to you with information, verify it before you afflict people in ignorance and then regret what you have done.

7. And know that the messenger of Allah is amongst you. If he followed you in many matters, you would be in trouble, but Allah made faith dear to you and made it appealing in your hearts and made you dislike rejection and sin and transgression - those are the righteous.

8. As a favour and blessing from Allah, and Allah is knowing and wise.

9. And if two groups of believers fight, make peace between them, then if one of them transgresses against the other, fight the one which transgresses until it returns to the command of Allah, then when it returns, make peace between them with impartiality and be just, for Allah loves the just.

10. For the believers are brothers, so make peace between your brothers and beware of Allah in order to receive mercy.

11. Oh you believers, let not one people make fun of another people, perhaps they are better than them, nor let some women make fun of other women, perhaps they are better than them, and do not talk bad of each other nor call each other derogatory names - bad is a name of immorality after faith -, and those who do not repent are the wrongdoers.

12. Oh you believers, greatly shun assumptions, for some assumptions are sinful, and do not spy nor backbite about each other. Would any of you want to eat the flesh of his dead brother? No, you dislike it. And beware of Allah, for Allah is accepting and merciful.

13. Oh mankind, We have created you from male and female and made you into clans and tribes so that you know each other. The most honoured

amongst you before Allah is the most aware (of Him) amongst you, for Allah is knowing and informed.

14. The desert Arabs say: we believe. Say: you don't believe yet, but say: we submit, and faith has not yet entered your hearts. And if you obey Allah and His messenger He will not deprive you of any of your work, for Allah is forgiving and merciful.

15. For the believers are those who believe in Allah and His messenger and then have no doubt and strive with their wealth and their lives in the way of Allah, those are the truthful.

16. Say: are you teaching Allah your religion? And Allah knows what is in the heavens and what is on earth, and Allah knows everything.

17. They consider it as a favour to you that they have submitted. Say: don't consider your submission a favour to me, but Allah did you a favour that He guided you to faith if you are truthful.

18. For Allah knows the secrets of the heavens and the earth, and Allah sees what you do.

Surah 50: **Qaf**

In the name of Allah,
the Owner and Giver of Mercy

1. Qaf. By the glorious Qur'an.

2. But they are astonished that a warner from amongst themselves came to them, so those who reject (the truth) say: this is a strange thing.

3. That when we have died and are dust, we will be brought back from beyond.

4. We know what the earth takes of them, and with Us is a protected record.

5. But they deny the truth when it reaches them and they are in a state of confusion.

6. Don't they look at the sky above them how We constructed it and ornamented it and it has no cracks?

7. And We expanded the earth and placed on it stabilisers and made grow on it of every splendid species.

8. As an enlightenment and reminder for every repenting servant.

9. And We sent water as a blessing from the sky and grow with it gardens and crops from seed.

10. And tall date trees with layered date clusters.

11. As a provision for the servants (of Allah), and We revive with it a dead land. Likewise will be the resurrection.

12. The people of Nuh (Noah) and the people around the waterhole (*ar-Rass*) and Thamud denied before them.

13. And 'Ad and Pharaoh and the brothers of Lut (Lot).

14. And the inhabitants of the woodlands (*al-Ayka*) and the people of Tubba' (in Yemen); they all denied the messengers, so the promise came true.

15. Are We then exhausted by the first creation? But they are uncertain about the new creation.

16. And We created man and know what his soul suggests to him and We are closer to him than his jugular vein.

17. When the two who keep meeting (him) sit on the right and the left.

18. He does not utter a word but there is an observer present with him.

19. And the delirium of death comes in truth, that is what you tried to avoid.

20. And the horn is blown, that is the promised day.

21. And every soul comes with a driver and a witness.

22. You were unaware of this, then We removed your covering from you and your eyesight today is firm.

23. And his companion will say: this is what I have brought.

24. Throw every obstinate rejecter (of the truth) into hell.

25. Who forbids what is good in transgression and doubt.

26. Who placed another god with Allah, so throw him into the severe punishment.

27. His companion will say: our Lord, I did not cause him to be excessive, but he was in extensive error.

28. He will say: do not argue before Me, I have already advanced My promise to you.

29. The word will not be changed before Me, and I do not wrong My servants.

30. On the day We will say to hell: are you full? and it will say: is there more?

31. And the garden will be brought near to those who beware (of Allah), without distance.

32. This is what you were promised for every one who repents and is mindful.

33. Who fears the Merciful in secret and comes with a repentant heart.

34. Enter it with peace, that is the day of eternity.

35. They will have what they please there, and with Us is more.

36. And how many generations have We destroyed before them with a stronger grip than theirs, so search the land, is there an escape?

37. In this is a reminder for whoever has a heart or listens and is a witness.

38. And We created the heavens and the earth and what is between them in six days, and no exhaustion afflicted Us.

39. So have patience with what they say and glorify the praise of your Lord before the rising of the sun and before its setting.

40. And glorify Him during the night and after your prostrations.

41. And listen out on the day the caller calls from a nearby place.

42. On the day they hear the roar in truth, that is the day of resurrection.

43. We give life and give death and to Us is the journey.

44. On the day the earth will rapidly spit them out, that will be an easy assembly for Us.

45. We know best what they say, and you are no tyrant over them, so remind with the Qur'an those who fear the promise.

Surah 51: **Adh-Dhariyat**
(Those Dispersing)

In the name of Allah,
the Owner and Giver of Mercy

1. By those dispersing (winds).

2. And those load-carrying (clouds).

3. And those (ships) travelling with ease.

4. And those (angels) arranging affairs.

5. What you have been promised is true.

6. And the repayment will take place.

7. By the well-textured sky.

8. You differ in your claims.

9. Those are diverted from it who are avert.

10. Death to the liars.

11. Who are carelessly inattentive.

12. They ask: when will the day of repayment be?

13. The day when they will be tried on the fire.

14. Taste your trial, this is what you were in a hurry for.

15. Those who beware (of Allah) will be in gardens and springs.

16. They will take what their Lord gives them, for they did good before then.

17. They slept little at night.

18. And at dawn they asked for forgiveness.

19. And in their wealth those who asked and the destitute had a right.

20. And on the earth are signs for those who are certain.

21. And in yourselves, so don't you see?

22. And in the heaven is your provision and what you have been promised.

23. So by the Lord of the heaven and the earth, it is the truth just as you are able to speak.

24. Has the story of the honoured guests of Ibrahim (Abraham) reached you?

25. When they entered upon him and said: peace. He said: Peace, oh unfamiliar people.

26. Then he went back to his family and brought a well-fed calf.

27. Then he put it before them and said: won't you eat?

28. Then he felt afraid of them. They said: fear not, and they gave him good news of a knowledgeable boy.

29. Then his wife approached with a shriek and struck her face and said: a barren old woman?

30. They said: this is what your Lord said, for He is wise and knowing.

31. He said: So what have you come for, oh messengers?

32. They said: we were sent to the sinful people.

33. To send upon them stones of clay.

34. Embossed by your Lord for the wasteful.

35. So We took out all the believers who were there.

36. And We did not find there except one household of those who submitted (as Muslims).

37. And We left in it a sign for those who fear the painful punishment.

38. And in Musa (Moses) when We send him to Pharaoh with a clear authority.

39. Then he turned away with his support and said: a magician or possessed.

40. So We overtook him and his forces and flung them into the sea whilst he blamed himself.

41. And in 'Ad when We sent against them the relentless wind.

42. It leaves nothing that it comes upon without turning it rotten.

43. And in Thamud when they were told enjoy yourselves for a while.

44. So they violated the command of their Lord and the lightning struck them whilst they looked on.

45. And they could neither stand up nor were they helped.

46. And the people of Nuh (Noah) before, for they were sinful people.

47. And We constructed the heaven with support and We are expanding it.

48. And We spread out the earth and how well did We level it.

49. And of everything We created pairs so that you would reflect.

50. So flee to Allah, for I am a clear warner from Him to you.

51. And do not place with Allah any other god, for I am a clear warner from Him to you.

52. Likewise no messenger came to those before them but they said: a magician or possessed.

53. Is this their legacy? But they are transgressing people.

54. So turn away from them and you are not to blame.

55. And remind, for the reminder benefits the believers.

56. And I did not create Jinn and mankind except to serve Me.

57. I do not want provision from them and don't want them to feed Me.

58. For Allah is the provider with firm strength.

59. And the wrongdoers will have their share just like the share of their companions, so let them not be in a hurry.

60. And for those who reject (the truth) the day they have been promised will prove a calamity.

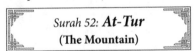

Surah 52: *At-Tur*
(The Mountain)

In the name of Allah,
the Owner and Giver of Mercy

1. By the mountain.

2. And the book with the record.

3. In spread-out scrolls.

4. And the constantly visited house.

5. And the raised canopy.

6. And the overflowing sea.

7. The punishment of your Lord will take place.

8. It cannot be averted.

9. On the day the sky will sway.

10. And the mountains will move.

11. Woe on that day to those who deny.

12. Who play in a bubble.

13. The day they will be forced into the fire of hell.

14. This is the fire you used to deny.

15. Is this magic or don't you see?

16. Enter it, then have patience or don't have patience, it will be the same for you, for you are rewarded for what you used to do.

17. Those who beware (of Allah) will be in gardens and blessings.

18. Enjoying what their Lord gave them, and their Lord guarded them from the punishment of hell-fire.

19. Eat and drink legitimately on account of what you used to do.

20. They will recline on couches arranged in rows, and We will marry them to women of rare beauty.

21. And those who believed and their descendants followed them in faith, We unite them with their descendants and will not deprive them of any of their work; everyone will secure what he has earned.

22. And We give them abundance of the fruit and meat they desire.

23. They will pass on a cup there which gives rise to neither idle talk nor sin.

24. And boy servants of their own will wait on them as if they were hidden pearls.

25. And some of them approach others, asking each other,

26. Saying: we were anxious amongst our families before.

27. Then Allah bestowed favours on us and guarded us from the punishment of scorching heat.

28. For we called Him before, as He is the charitable and merciful.

29. So remind, for by the blessing of your Lord you are neither a fortune teller nor possessed.

30. Or do they say: a poet, we will wait until his luck runs out.

31. Say: wait, I shall wait with you.

32. Or does their imagination dictate this to them, or are they transgressing people?

33. Or do they say: he made it up? But they don't believe.

34. So let them bring a statement comparable to it if they are truthful.

35. Or were they created from nothing, or are they the creators?

36. Or did they create the heavens and the earth? But they are not certain.

37. Or do they have the treasures of your Lord, or are they in charge?

38. Or do they have a ladder (to access heaven) from which they listen? Then let the one of them who listens bring some clear authority.

39. Or are daughters for Him and sons for you?

40. Or do you ask them for a reward and they are burdened by debt?

41. Or do they have access to the unseen so they write it down?

42. Or do they want to plot? But those who reject (the truth) are the ones plotted against.

43. Or do they have a god other than Allah? Glorified is Allah above what they associate.

44. And if they saw a piece of the sky fall down, they would say: a heap of clouds.

45. So leave them until they meet the day on which they will be struck down.

46. The day when their plot will not benefit them the least and they will not be helped.

47. And for the wrongdoers will be a punishment beyond that, but most of them don't know.

48. And have patience with the judgement of Allah, for you are in Our eyes, and glorify the praise of your Lord when you get up.

49. And during the night, then glorify Him when the stars fade.

Surah 53: **An-Najm**
(The Star)

In the name of Allah,
the Owner and Giver of Mercy

1. By the star when it came down.

2. Your companion is not in error nor mislead.

3. And he does not speak from desire.

4. It is only a revelation given.

5. Taught to him by the One strong in power.

6. Then he rose in full splendour.

7. And he was on the highest horizon.

8. Then he approached and came down.

9. And was at a distance of two bow lengths or less.

10. Then He revealed to His servant what He revealed.

11. The heart did not belie what it saw.

12. Do you then doubt him in what he sees?

13. And he saw him another time.

14. Near the sacred cedar tree.

15. Where the garden of home is.

16. When the cedar tree was completely covered.

17. The eyes looked neither aside nor beyond.

18. He saw of the greatest signs of his Lord.

19. Have you considered Al-Lat and Al-'Uzza?

20. And Manat, the other third one?

21. Do you have males and He has females?

22. This would be an unfair division.

23. They are only names you and your fathers have given. Allah has not sent any authority for it. They only follow assumptions and what their souls desire, when guidance has already reached them from their Lord.

24. Or does man get what he wishes for?

25. But to Allah belongs the hereafter and this world.

26. And how many angels are there in the heavens whose intercession does not benefit the least except after Allah has given permission to whom He pleases and is content with.

27. Those who do not believe in the hereafter name the angels by female names.

28. They have no knowledge of this. They only follow assumptions, and assumptions do not have any value in the face of truth.

29. So leave whoever turns away from Our remembrance and only wants the life of this world.

30. That is the extent of their knowledge, for your Lord knows best who has strayed from His way, and He knows best who is guided.

31. And to Allah belongs what is in the heavens and what is on earth, so that He will reward those who did bad on account of what they did, and rewards those who did good with the best.

32. Those who stay away from major sins and indecencies, but for the unintentional, for your Lord is far-reaching in forgiveness and knew best about you when He originated you on the earth and when you were embryos in the wombs of your mothers, so do not declare yourselves pure, He knows best who bewares.

33. Have you considered him who turns away.

34. And gives little and withholds.

35. Does he have knowledge of the unseen, so he sees?

36. Or has he not been informed of what is in the books of Musa (Moses),

37. And Ibrahim (Abraham), who gave in full?

38. That no-one burdened will carry another's burden.

39. And that man only gets what he strives for.

40. And that what he strives for will soon be seen.

41. Then he will be given his full reward.

42. And that the final destination is to your Lord.

43. And that He makes him laugh and cry.

44. And that He makes him die and live.

45. And that He created male and female in pairs.

46. From a sperm when it is ejaculated.

47. And that upon Him is the second creation.

48. And that He gives independence and contentment.

49. And that He is the Lord of Sirius.

50. And He destroyed 'Ad of old.

51. And Thamud, so they did not last.

52. And the people of Nuh (Noah) before, for they were most sinful and transgressing.

53. And those who were turned upside down.

54. And completely covered.

55. Then which of the blessings of your Lord do you doubt?

56. This is a warning like the earlier warnings.

57. The imminent has come close.

58. Nobody besides Allah can prevent it.

59. Are you then astonished about this statement?

60. And laugh and do not cry?

61. And you are stuck up?

62. But prostrate to Allah and serve Him.

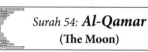

Surah 54: *Al-Qamar*
(The Moon)

In the name of Allah,
the Owner and Giver of Mercy

1. The hour has come close and the moon has split.

2. And if they were to see every sign, they would turn aside and say: fleeting magic.

3. And they deny and follow their desires, and everything has its time and place.

4. And information has already reached them to prove them wrong.

5. Far-reaching wisdom, but the warnings will be of no use.

6. So turn away from them; on the day the caller calls to something abhorrent,

7. They will emerge from the graves with downcast eyes as if they were swarming locusts.

8. Rushing towards the caller. Those who rejected (the truth) will say: this is a difficult day.

9. The people of Nuh (Noah) denied before them, so they denied Our servant and said: he is possessed, and he was rejected.

10. So he called his Lord: I have been overcome, so help me.

11. Then We opened the gates of heaven with water pouring down.

12. And We caused springs to gush out of the earth, and the water met in accordance with a pre-arranged command.

13. And We carried him on a construction from planks and nails,

14. To float under Our eyes; a punishment for those who reject (the truth).

15. And We left it as a sign, so does anyone pay heed?

16. And how was My punishment and warning!

17. And We made the Qur'an easy to remember, so does anyone pay heed?

18. 'Ad denied, so how was My punishment and warning!

19. We sent against them an icy wind on a final day of disaster.

20. It uprooted people as if they were the stumps of cut down palm trees.

21. And how was My punishment and warning!

22. And We made the Qur'an easy to remember, so does anyone pay heed?

23. Thamud denied the warnings.

24. So they said: are we to follow a single human from amongst us? This would be error and madness for us.

25. Did he receive the reminder amongst us? But he is an impertinent liar.

26. Tomorrow they will know who is the impertinent liar.

27. We will send them the she-camel as a trial for them, so watch them and be patient.

28. And inform them that the water is to be shared between them, each drink will be apportioned.

29. Then they called their companion, so he grabbed her and bled her to death.

30. And how was My punishment and warning!

31. We sent against them a single scream, then they were like dried up fencing twigs.

32. And We made the Qur'an easy to remember, so does anyone pay heed?

33. The people of Lut (Lot) denied the warnings.

34. We sent against them a storm, except for the family of Lut (Lot), We rescued them at dawn.

35. As a blessing from Us; this is how We reward the grateful.

36. And he had warned them of Our grip, but they doubted the warnings.

37. And they desired his guests, so We blinded them, then taste Our punishment and warnings.

38. And the next morning the inevitable punishment greeted them.

39. So taste My punishment and warning!

40. And We made the Qur'an easy to remember, so does anyone pay heed?

41. And the warnings came to the family of Pharaoh.

42. But they denied all of Our signs, so We overtook them in a mighty and powerful way.

43. Are your rejecters (of the truth) better than those, or do you have an exemption in the scriptures?

44. Or do they say: we are a victorious crowd?

45. The crowd will be defeated and they will turn their backs.

46. But they have been promised the hour, and the hour is worse and more bitter.

47. The sinners are in error and madness.

48. On the day they will be dragged on their faces into the fire: taste the touch of hell.

49. For We created everything in measure.

50. And Our command is (given) just once, like a quick glance.

51. And We destroyed your factions, so does anyone pay heed?

52. And everything they did is in the record.

53. And everything small or big is recorded.

54. Those who beware (of Allah) will be in gardens and rivers.

55. In a position of sincerity with a powerful king.

Surah 55: *Ar-Rahman*
(The Owner of Mercy)

In the name of Allah,
the Owner and Giver of Mercy

1. The Owner of mercy.

2. He taught the Qur'an.

3. He created man.

4. He taught him speech.

5. The sun and the moon are set on a course.

6. And the stars and the trees prostrate.

7. And He has raised the sky and placed the balance.

8. So that you do not upset the balance.

9. And uphold equity in justice and do not fall short of the balance.

10. And He placed the earth for living creatures.

11. On it are fruit and palms with protected fruit stalks.

12. And seed crop with leaves and scented herbs.

13. Then which of the blessings of your Lord do you both deny?

14. He created man from a cement like in pottery.

15. And He created Jinn from an extract of fire.

16. Then which of the blessings of your Lord do you both deny?

17. The Lord of the two Easts and the Lord of the two Wests.

18. Then which of the blessings of your Lord do you both deny?

19. He allowed the two seas to flow and meet.

20. Between them is a barrier they do not transgress.

21. Then which of the blessings of your Lord do you both deny?

22. He makes pearls and corals emerge from them.

23. Then which of the blessings of your Lord do you both deny?

24. And His are the towering ships spread across the sea like mountains.

25. Then which of the blessings of your Lord do you both deny?

26. All that is on (earth) will vanish.

27. And the presence of Allah will remain full of glory and dignity.

28. Then which of the blessings of your Lord do you both deny?

29. Whoever is in the heavens and on earth implores Him; every day He is busy.

30. Then which of the blessings of your Lord do you both deny?

31. We will deal with you, you two burdensome creations.

32. Then which of the blessings of your Lord do you both deny?

33. Oh congregation of Jinn and Mankind, if you are able to penetrate the distances of the heavens and the earth, then do it, you will not penetrate them except with an authority.

34. Then which of the blessings of your Lord do you both deny?

35. You will be bombarded with flames of fire and copper and will not help each other.

36. Then which of the blessings of your Lord do you both deny?

37. Then when the sky breaks up and is like red tanned leather.

38. Then which of the blessings of your Lord do you both deny?

39. On that day neither Mankind nor Jinn will be asked about their sins.

40. Then which of the blessings of your Lord do you both deny?

41. The sinners will be known by their mark and taken by their forelocks and feet.

42. Then which of the blessings of your Lord do you both deny?

43. This is hell which the sinners denied.

44. They will move between it and boiling water.

45. Then which of the blessings of your Lord do you both deny?

46. And whoever fears standing before his Lord will have two gardens.

47. Then which of the blessings of your Lord do you both deny?

48. Full of diversity.

49. Then which of the blessings of your Lord do you both deny?

50. Two springs emerge in them.

51. Then which of the blessings of your Lord do you both deny?

52. In them are all kinds of fruit in pairs.

53. Then which of the blessings of your Lord do you both deny?

54. They will recline on cushions whose lining will be of brocade, and the harvest of the two gardens is close-by.

55. Then which of the blessings of your Lord do you both deny?

56. In them will be exclusive women companions whom neither man nor jinn has touched before them.

57. Then which of the blessings of your Lord do you both deny?

58. As if they were pearls and coral.

59. Then which of the blessings of your Lord do you both deny?

60. Is the reward of goodness anything but goodness?

61. Then which of the blessings of your Lord do you both deny?

62. And there are two gardens beyond them.

63. Then which of the blessings of your Lord do you both deny?

64. With dense vegetation.

65. Then which of the blessings of your Lord do you both deny?

66. Two springs spill out in them.

67. Then which of the blessings of your Lord do you both deny?

68. In them are fruit and palms and pomegranates.

69. Then which of the blessings of your Lord do you both deny?

70. In them are women of goodness and beauty.

71. Then which of the blessings of your Lord do you both deny?

72. Exclusive beauties in tents.

73. Then which of the blessings of your Lord do you both deny?

74. Neither man nor jinn has touched them before them.

75. Then which of the blessings of your Lord do you both deny?

76. They will recline on green cushions and splendid carpets.

77. Then which of the blessings of your Lord do you both deny?

78. Exalted is the name of your Lord full of glory and dignity.

Surah 56: **Al-Waqi'ah**
(The Event)

In the name of Allah, the Owner and Giver of Mercy

1. When the event happens.

2. There is no denying its happening.

3. Subduing, elevating.

4. When the earth trembles.

5. And the mountains crumble.

6. And are like scattered dust.

7. And you will be three types.

8. So the companions on the right, who are the companions on the right?

9. And the companions on the left, who are the companions on the left?

10. And those going ahead, they go ahead.

11. They are the ones brought close.

12. In gardens of blessings.

13. A multitude of the early ones.

14. And a few of the later ones.

15. On decorated couches.

16. They recline on them facing each other.

17. Eternal youths wait on them.

18. With tumblers and glasses and cups of flowing beverage.

19. They will not get a headache from it nor be drained by it.

20. And fruit of their choosing.

21. And meat of birds they desire.

22. And women of rare beauty.

23. Like hidden pearls.

24. A reward for what they used to do.

25. They will hear neither idle nor sinful talk.

26. Only the saying: peace, peace.

27. And the companions on the right, who are the companions on the right?

28. Amongst cedar trees without thorns.

29. And layered banana plants.

30. And extensive shade.

31. And flowing water.

32. And plenty of fruit.

33. Neither in short supply nor forbidden.

34. And raised cushions.

35. We recreated them.

36. And made them virgins.

37. Loving and young.

38. For the companions on the right.

39. A multitude of the early ones.

40. And a multitude of the later ones.

41. And the companions on the left, who are the companions on the left?

42. In scorching heat and boiling water.

43. And shaded by black smoke.

44. Neither cool nor gentle.

45. For they were affluent before.

46. And persisted in great sin.

47. And said: when we have died and are dust and bones, are we going to be raised again?

48. Or our forefathers?

49. Say: the early ones and the late ones,

50. They will be gathered for an appointment on a specified day.

51. Then, oh you stray deniers,

52. You will eat from the tree of Zaqqum.

53. And fill your bellies with it.

54. And drink boiling water after it.

55. And drink mad with thirst.

56. This is their share on the day of repayment.

57. We created you, so why don't you confirm it?

58. Have you considered your issue?

59. Do you create it, or are We the creators?

60. We apportion death amongst you, and We will not be stopped,

61. To replace you with the like of you and bring you into an existence you don't know.

62. And you know about the first creation, so why don't you reflect.

63. Have you considered your harvest?

64. Do you grow the seed, or do We grow it?

65. If We pleased, We could make it crumble, so you would be left exclaiming:

66. We are broke.

67. No, we are destitute.

68. Have you considered your drinking water?

69. Do you send it down from the rain clouds, or do We send it down?

70. If We pleased We could make it brackish, so why are you not grateful?

71. Have you considered the fire you kindle?

72. Did you create its trees, or did We create them?

73. We made it a reminder and a comfort for the weary.

74. So glorify the name of your mighty Lord.

75. But I swear by the locations of the stars,

76. And this is a mighty oath, if you knew:

77. This is a distinguished reading (Qur'an).

78. In a preserved book.

79. Only the pure touch it.

80. A revelation from the Lord of all worlds.

81. Do you reject this statement?

82. And repay your provision with denial?

83. So why, when it (the soul of a dying person) reaches the throat,

84. And you look on,

85. And We are closer to him than you, but you don't see,

86. Why, if you are not accountable,

87. Don't you bring it back, if you are truthful?

88. So if he was of those brought close,

89. Then it is rest and provision and a blessed garden.

90. And if he was of the companions on the right,

91. Then it is "peace with you" from the companions on the right.

92. And if he was of the deniers gone astray,

93. Then it is a gift of boiling water,

94. And entry to hell.

95. For this is the certain truth.

96. So glorify the name of your mighty Lord.

Surah 57: *Al-Hadid* (Iron)

In the name of Allah, the Owner and Giver of Mercy

1. What is in the heavens and on earth glorifies Allah, and He is the mighty and wise.

2. To Him belongs the kingdom of the heavens and the earth, He gives life and death, and Allah is able to do anything.

3. He is the first and the last, the apparent and the concealed, and He knows everything.

4. He is who created the heavens and the earth in six days, then He rose onto the throne, He knows what enters the earth and what emerges from it and what descends from the sky and what ascends through it, and He is with you wherever you are, and Allah sees what you do.

5. To Him belongs the kingdom of the heavens and the earth, and to Allah return all affairs.

6. He blends the night into the day and blends the day into the night, and He knows what is kept inside.

7. Believe in Allah and His messenger and spend of what He has allowed to be passed on to you, so for those of you who believe and spend is a great reward.

8. And what is the matter with you that you don't believe in Allah and His messenger who calls you to believe in your Lord, when He has already taken a promise from you, if you are believers?

9. He is who sent down clear proofs to His servant to take you out of darkness into the light, and Allah is lenient and merciful with you.

10. And what is the matter with you that you don't spend in the way of Allah when to Allah belongs the inheritance of the heavens and the earth? Those of you who spent and fought before the victory are not alike but are of a higher level than those who spent and fought afterwards, and to all has Allah promised good, and Allah is informed of what you do.

11. Who will lend to Allah an excellent loan so that He multiplies it for him and he has a generous reward?

12. On the day you see the believing men and women with their light racing before them and on their right - good news for you today: gardens through which rivers flow where they will remain, that is the ultimate success.

13. On the day the pretending men and women will say to those who believed: look at us so that we can borrow some of your light. They will be told: turn back to what you left behind and look for light. Then a wall will be stuck between them with a door which has mercy on the inside and outside of it is the punishment.

14. They will call them: were we not with you? They will say: sure, but you corrupted yourselves and waited and doubted, and hopes mislead you until Allah's command came to pass, and passing provisions mislead you about Allah.

15. So today no compensation will be taken from you nor from those who rejected (the truth), your abode is the fire, it is your master, a bad destination.

16. Has not the time come for the believers that their hearts humble towards the remembrance of Allah and what He has revealed of the truth and that they should not be like those who were given the book before them, but time went too slowly for them and their hearts hardened, and many of them were sinful?

17. Know that Allah revives the earth after its death; We have already explained the signs to you so that you might understand.

18. The truthful men and women who lend an excellent loan to Allah, He multiplies it for them and they have a generous reward.

19. And those who believe in Allah and His messengers, those are the truthful and the witnesses before their Lord, they will have their reward and their light; and those who reject (the truth) and deny Our signs, those are the inmates of hell-fire.

20. Know that the life of this world is only play and pastime and adornment and boasting amongst you and amassing of wealth and children - like the rain when those who reject (the truth) like its vegetation, then it dries out and you see it yellow, then it crumbles, and in the hereafter there is severe punishment and forgiveness and contentment from Allah, and the life of this world is only a passing provision.

21. Strive for the forgiveness of your Lord and a garden whose width is like the width of the heavens and the earth which has been prepared for those who believe in Allah and His messengers. That is the favour of Allah which He gives to whom He pleases, and Allah possesses immense favours.

22. No affliction strikes on earth nor within yourselves but it is in a record before We discharge it, for that is easy for Allah.

23. So that you don't worry about what has passed you by nor rejoice in

what you were given, and Allah does not love an arrogant show-off.

24. Those who are mean and command people to be mean, and whoever turns away, Allah is the rich and praiseworthy.

25. We sent Our messengers with clear proofs and sent the book with them and the balance so that mankind upholds justice, and We sent iron which contains severe harm and benefits for mankind and so that Allah knows who helps Him and His messengers in secret, for Allah is strong and mighty.

26. And We sent Nuh (Noah) and Ibrahim (Abraham) and placed the prophethood and the book amongst their descendants, yet amongst them are those who are guided, and many of them are sinful.

27. Then We let Our messengers follow into their footsteps and made 'Isa (Jesus), the son of Maryam (Mary), follow and gave him the Injil and placed in the hearts of those who followed him kindness and mercy, and monasticism they invented, We did not prescribe it for them except that they should seek the contentment of Allah, and they did not observe it properly, so We gave those who believed amongst them their reward, and many of them were sinful.

28. Oh you believers, beware of Allah and believe in His messenger, He will give you double measure of His mercy and give you a light by which you walk and forgive you, and Allah is forgiving and merciful.

29. Let the people of the Book know that they have no power whatsoever over the favours of Allah and that all favours are in Allah's hand, He gives them to whom He pleases, and Allah possesses immense favours.

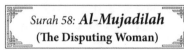

Surah 58: *Al-Mujadilah*
(The Disputing Woman)

In the name of Allah,
the Owner and Giver of Mercy

1. Allah has heard the speech of her who disputed with you about her husband and complained to Allah, and Allah hears your discussion, for Allah listens and sees.

2. Those of you who divorce their women by likening them to their mothers, they are not their mothers, their mothers are only those who gave birth to them, and they say something unacceptable and false, and Allah is lenient and forgiving.

3. And those who divorce their women by likening them to their mothers and go back on their word, they must free a slave before the two touch, that is what you are admonished with, and Allah is informed of what you do.

4. And who is unable, he must fast two consecutive months before the two touch, and he who does not find (the means) must feed sixty poor, that is in order for you to believe in Allah and His messenger, and these are the limits of Allah, and for those who reject (the truth) is a painful punishment.

5. Those who transgress the limits of Allah and His messenger will be defeated just like those before them were defeated, and We have already sent clear proofs, and for those who reject (the truth) is a humiliating punishment.

6. On the day Allah raises them all and informs them of what they did, Allah counted it and they forgot it, and Allah is a witness to everything.

7. Don't you see that Allah knows what is in the heavens and on earth, and there is not a secret meeting of three, but He is the fourth with them, nor of five, but He is the sixth with them, nor of less or more than that but He is with them wherever they are, then He informs them of what they did on the day of resurrection, for Allah knows everything.

8. Don't you see how those who were forbidden from secret meetings returned to what they were forbidden from and conspired to sin and rebellion and disobedience to the messenger, and when they came to you they greeted you in a way Allah does not have you greeted and say to themselves: why does Allah not punish us for what we say? Hell is enough for them, they will enter it, and it is a bad journey.

9. Oh you believers, when you meet in secret, do not conspire to sin and rebellion and disobedience to the messenger, but conspire to righteousness and awareness (of Allah), and beware of Allah to whom you will be gathered.

10. For secret meetings are from the devil so that he worries the believers, and he will not harm them at all except by the permission of Allah, and on Allah let the believers rely.

11. Oh you believers, when you are told to make room in gatherings, make room, Allah will make room for you, and when you are told to get up, get up, Allah will elevate those of you who believe and who were given knowledge in rank, and Allah is informed of what you do.

12. Oh you believers, when you have a private meeting with the messenger, give charity in advance of your private meetings, that is better and purer for you, and if you don't find (the means), then Allah is forgiving and merciful.

13. Do you hesitate to give charity before your private meetings? If you don't do it and Allah has turned to you in forgiveness, then keep up prayer and give Zakat and obey Allah and His messenger, and Allah is informed of what you do.

14. Don't you see those who befriend a people whom Allah is angry with, they are neither part of you nor them and knowingly swear upon a lie.

15. Allah has promised them a severe punishment, for bad is what they used to do.

16. They adopt their faith by way of protection then divert from the way of Allah, so theirs is a humiliating punishment.

17. Neither their wealth nor children will help them the least against Allah; those are the inmates of the fire where they will remain.

18. On the day Allah raises all of them and they swear to Him like they swore to you and think that they have a case, but no, they are liars.

19. The devil has taken possession of them and made them forget the remembrance of Allah; those are the party of the devil, for sure the party of the devil are the losers.

20. Those who transgress the limits of Allah and His messenger, those are the lowest.

21. Allah has decreed that I and My messengers will win, for Allah is strong and mighty.

22. You will not find people who believe in Allah and the last day showing love to those who transgress the limits of Allah and His messenger, even if they were their fathers or sons or brothers or families; for those, Allah has written faith in their hearts and helps them with a spirit from Him and enters them into gardens through which rivers flow where they will remain. Allah is content with them and they are content with Him. Those are the party of Allah, for sure the party of Allah are the successful.

Surah 59: *Al-Hashr*
(The Gathering)

In the name of Allah,
the Owner and Giver of Mercy

1. What is in the heavens and what is on earth glorifies Allah, and He is the mighty and wise.

2. He is who expelled those who rejected (the truth) from the people of the Book from their homes for a first gathering. You did not think that they would come out, and they thought that their strongholds would keep Allah out, so Allah came to them from where they did not expect and cast fear into their hearts. They destroyed their houses with their own hands and the hands of the believers, so take a lesson oh you who see.

3. And if Allah had not written expulsion for them, He would have punished them in this world and in the hereafter the punishment of the fire would be theirs.

4. This is because they break away from Allah and His messenger, and whoever breaks away from Allah, then Allah is severe in punishment.

5. You did not cut down a tree or leave it standing on its roots but with the permission of Allah and so that He would humiliate the sinful.

6. And whatever Allah gave to His messenger from them, you did not spur on any horses or camels for it, but Allah gives His messengers control over what He pleases, and Allah is able to do anything.

7. And whatever Allah gave to His messenger from the inhabitants of the towns, it belongs to Allah and His messenger and the relatives and the orphans and the poor and the traveller, so that it does not just circulate amongst the rich of you, and what the messenger gives you, take it, and what he forbids you, leave it, and beware of Allah, for Allah is severe in punishment.

8. For the poor of the emigrants who left their homes and wealth to seek favour from Allah and contentment and help Allah and His messenger, those are the truthful.

9. And those who prepared the home and had faith before they came, loving those who migrated to them and not finding within themselves any desire for what they were given and preferring them over themselves even if they were in poverty, and whoever is protected from the greed of his own soul, those are the successful.

10. And those who came after them saying: our Lord forgive us and our brothers who preceded us in faith and do not place in our hearts any spite towards those who believe, our Lord, for you are lenient and merciful.

11. Have you not seen those who pretend, saying to their brothers who reject (the truth) from the people of the Book: if you are expelled, we will migrate with you and we will not obey anybody against you ever, and if you are fought, we will help you, and Allah is a witness that they are liars.

12. If they are expelled, they do not migrate with them, and if they are fought, they do not help them, and if they were to help them, they would turn their backs, then they will not be helped.

13. They have more fear in their hearts of you than of Allah, that is because they are people who do not understand.

14. They will not fight you all out except from fortified towns or from behind walls, their adversity amongst themselves is strong, you think they are together, but their hearts are apart, that is because they are people who do not think.

15. Like those before them nearby, they tasted the evil outcome of their affairs and a painful punishment is theirs.

16. Like the devil when he says to man: reject (the truth), then when he rejects (it) he says: I am free of you, for I fear Allah the Lord of all worlds.

17. So the outcome of both is that they will be forever in the fire, and that is the punishment of the wrongdoers.

18. Oh you believers, beware of Allah and let each soul mind what it sends ahead for tomorrow, and beware of Allah, for Allah is informed of what you do.

19. And be not like those who forgot Allah, so He made them forget themselves, those are the sinful.

20. The inhabitants of the fire and the inhabitants of the garden are not alike, the inhabitants of the garden are the successful.

21. Had We sent this Qur'an onto a mountain you would see it break down out of fear of Allah, and these are the examples We coin for mankind so that they reflect.

22. He is Allah the One besides whom there is no god, who knows the unseen and the apparent, He is the owner and giver of mercy.

23. He is Allah the One besides whom there is no god, the king, the holy, the origin of peace, the safeguard, the controller, the mighty, the compelling, the elevated, glorified is Allah above what they associate.

24. He is Allah the creator, the originator, the artist, to him belong the most beautiful names, whatever is in the heavens and on earth glorifies Him, and He is the mighty, the wise.

> *Surah 60:* **Al-Mumtahinah**
> **(The Woman Being Tested)**

In the name of Allah,
the Owner and Giver of Mercy

1. Oh you believers, do not take My enemy and your enemy as protectors, showing love towards them when they have rejected the truth you have received and expelled the messenger and you because you believe in Allah, your Lord, when you go out striving in My way and seeking My contentment, but you secretly show love towards them, and I know best what you conceal and what you disclose, and whoever amongst you does that, he has strayed from the level way.

2. When they get hold of you they are enemies to you and stretch their hands out against you and talk bad of you and love that you would reject (the truth).

3. Your family ties and children will not benefit you on the day of resurrection when He will judge between you, and Allah sees what you do.

4. There is a beautiful example for you in Ibrahim (Abraham) and those with him when they said to their people: we are free of you and what you serve besides Allah, we reject you, and enmity and hatred will forever exist between us until you believe in Allah alone; except for Ibrahim (Abraham) saying to his father: I will ask forgiveness for you, and I cannot avail you the least before Allah; our Lord, on You we rely and to You we repent and to You is the journey.

5. Our Lord, do not make us a target for those who reject (the truth), and forgive us, our Lord, for You are the mighty and wise.

6. There is a beautiful example for you in them for whoever hopes for Allah and the last day, and whoever turns away, Allah is rich and praiseworthy.

7. Perhaps Allah will place love between you and your enemies, and Allah is capable, and Allah is forgiving and merciful.

8. Allah does not stop you from doing good and being just to those who did not fight you due to religion and did not expel you from your houses, for Allah loves the just.

9. Allah only stops you from befriending those who fought you and expelled you from your houses and helped in your expulsion, and whoever befriends them, those are the wrongdoers.

10. Oh you believers, when emigrating believing women come to you, test them. Allah knows best about their faith. Then when you find them to be believers, do not return them to those who reject (the truth) - they are not permitted for each other. And give them what they have spent, and it is no sin for you to marry them if you give them their dues, and do not hold on to the bonds with those who reject (the truth), but ask for what you have spent and let them ask for what they have spent, that is the judgement of Allah who judges between you, and Allah is knowing and wise.

11. And if you have lost wives to those who reject (the truth), and you have obtained booty, then give those who have lost their wives the measure of what they have spent and beware of Allah in whom you believe.

12. Oh prophet, when the believing women come to you, let them give allegiance to you that they will not associate anything with Allah and will not steal nor fornicate nor kill their children nor come up with some false invented claim regarding the parentage of their children nor disobey you in anything appropriate. So let them give allegiance and ask forgiveness from Allah for them, for Allah is forgiving and merciful.

13. Oh you believers, do not befriend a people with whom Allah is angry, they despair of the hereafter like those who reject (the truth) despair of the inhabitants of the graves.

Surah 61: **As-Saff**
(Ranks)

In the name of Allah, the Owner and Giver of Mercy

1. What is in the heavens and what is on earth glorifies Allah, and He is the mighty and wise.

2. Oh you believers, why do you say what you don't do?

3. It is highly offensive to Allah that you say what you don't do.

4. Allah loves those who fight in His way in ranks as if they were a tight-fitting structure.

5. And when Musa (Moses) said to his people, oh my people, why do you give me troubles when you know that I am the messenger of Allah to you, then when they turned aside, Allah turned their hearts, and Allah does not guide sinful people.

6. And when 'Isa (Jesus) the son of Maryam (Mary) said: oh children of Israel, I am the messenger of Allah to you, confirming what came before me of the Torah and giving you good news of a messenger to come after me whose name is Ahmad, then when he came to them with clear proofs they said: this is plain magic.

7. And who is more wrong than he who invents against Allah a lie when he is called to submission (Islam), and Allah does not guide wrongdoing people.

8. They want to extinguish the light of Allah with their mouths, and Allah

will complete His light even if those who reject (the truth) resent it.

9. He is who sent His messenger with the guidance and the religion of truth to make it manifest over all religion even if the idolaters resent it.

10. Oh you believers, shall I point you to a trade which will rescue you from a painful punishment?

11. Believe in Allah and His messenger and strive in the way of Allah with your wealth and your lives, that is better for you if you knew.

12. He will forgive you your sins and enter you into gardens through which rivers flow and good accommodation in the gardens of Eden, that is the ultimate success.

13. And other things which you love, help and victory from Allah are near, and give good news to the believers.

14. Oh you believers, be helpers of Allah like 'Isa (Jesus) the son of Maryam (Mary) said to the disciples: who will be my helpers towards Allah? The disciples said: we are the helpers of Allah, then a group of the Children of Israel believed and a group rejected (the truth), so We strengthened those who believed against their enemies and they became dominant.

Surah 62: **Al-Jumu'a**
(The Friday Congregation)

In the name of Allah, the Owner and Giver of Mercy

1. What is in the heavens and what is on earth glorifies Allah, the king, the holy, the mighty, the wise.

2. He is who raised amongst the gentiles a messenger from amongst them who recites to them His signs and purifies them and teaches them the book and the wisdom, when before that they were in clear error.

3. And others of them whom they have not yet met, and He is the mighty and wise.

4. This is the favour of Allah which He gives to whom He pleases, and Allah possesses immense favours.

5. The likeness of those who were entrusted with the Torah and then did not act on it is like the donkey who carries scrolls, bad is the likeness of people who deny the signs of Allah, and Allah does not guide wrongdoing people.

6. Say: oh you Jews, if you claim that you are protected friends of Allah besides (the rest of) mankind, then wish for death if you are truthful.

7. And they never wish for it because of the deeds they have sent ahead, and Allah knows the wrongdoers.

8. Say: death, which you run away from, will catch up with you, then you will be returned to the One who knows the unseen and the apparent and He will inform you of what you used to do.

9. Oh you believers, if you are called to prayer on Friday, hurry to the remembrance of Allah and leave your business, that is better for you if you knew.

10. Then when the prayer has finished spread out on earth and seek the favours of Allah and remember Allah a lot in order to be successful.

11. And when they see trade or pastime, they disperse towards it and leave you standing; say: what is with Allah is better than pastime and trade, and Allah is the best of providers.

Surah 63: *Al-Munafiqun*
(The Pretenders)

In the name of Allah,
the Owner and Giver of Mercy

1. When the pretenders come to you they say: we witness that you are the messenger of Allah, and Allah knows that you are indeed His messenger, and Allah witnesses that the pretenders are lying.

2. They adopt their faith by way of protection then divert from the way of Allah, bad is what they used to do.

3. That is because they believed, then rejected, so their hearts were sealed so that they do not understand.

4. And when you see them, their physique amazes you, and when they speak, you listen to their speech as if they were towering trees; they think that every shout is against them, they are the enemy, so be wary of them, may Allah destroy them, where to are they diverted?

5. And when they are told: come so that the messenger of Allah asks for forgiveness for you, they turn their heads aside and you see them arrogantly moving away.

6. It is the same for them whether you ask forgiveness for them or don't ask forgiveness for them - Allah will not forgive them, for Allah does not guide sinful people.

7. They are the ones who say: don't spend on those who are with the messenger of Allah until they break away, and to Allah belong the treasures of the heavens and the earth, but the pretenders don't understand.

8. They say: when we return to Madinah the stronger will drive the weaker out of it, and to Allah belongs all strength and to His messenger and to the believers, but the pretenders don't know.

9. Oh you believers, let not your wealth and children distract you from the remembrance of Allah, and whoever does so, those are the losers.

10. And spend of what Allah has provided you with before death comes to any of you and he will say: my Lord, if only You delayed me for a little longer, so that I can give charity and be of the righteous.

11. And Allah will not delay any soul when its term has come, and Allah is informed of what you do.

Surah 64: **At-Taghabun**
(Dispossession)

In the name of Allah,
the Owner and Giver of Mercy

1. Whatever is in the heavens and what is on earth glorifies Allah, His is the kingdom and His is the praise and He is able to do anything.

2. He is who created you, and amongst you is he who rejects (the truth) and

he who believes, and Allah sees what you do.

3. He created the heavens and the earth with truth and shaped you and made your shape beautiful, and to Him is the journey.

4. He knows what is in the heavens and on earth and knows what you conceal and what you disclose, and Allah knows what is kept inside.

5. Did not the information of those who rejected (the truth) before reach you, so they tasted the evil outcome of their affairs and theirs is a painful punishment.

6. That is because their messengers came to them with clear proofs but they said: are we to be guided by a human? So they rejected (the truth) and turned away, and Allah does not need them, and Allah is rich and praiseworthy.

7. Those who reject (the truth) claim that they will not be resurrected, say: sure, by my Lord, you will be resurrected, then you will be informed of what you did, that is easy for Allah.

8. So believe in Allah and His messenger and the light which We have sent down, and Allah is informed of what you do.

9. On the day He will gather you to the day of congregation, that is the day of dispossession, and whoever believes in Allah and does good, He will cancel his (minor) bad deeds and enter him into gardens through which rivers

flow where they will remain forever, that is the ultimate success.

10. And those who reject (the truth) and deny Our signs, those are the inmates of the fire where they will remain, and it is a bad destination.

11. No affliction strikes except with the permission of Allah, and whoever believes in Allah, He will guide his heart, and Allah knows everything.

12. And obey Allah and the messenger, but if you turn away, then the duty of Our messenger is only to convey clearly.

13. Allah, there is no god but Him, so on Allah shall the believers rely.

14. Oh you believers, there are enemies of you amongst your partners and children, so be wary of them, and if you are lenient and forgive and seek forgiveness, then Allah is forgiving and merciful.

15. For your wealth and children are a test and with Allah is a tremendous reward.

16. So beware of Allah as much as you can and listen and obey and spend for the good of yourselves, and whoever is protected from the greed of his own soul, those are the successful.

17. If you lend Allah an excellent loan, He will multiply it for you and forgive you, and Allah is appreciative and gentle.

18. The One who knows the unseen and the apparent, the mighty, the wise.

Surah 65: **At-Talaq**
(Divorce)

In the name of Allah, the Owner and Giver of Mercy

1. Oh prophet, when you divorce women, then divorce them for their waiting period and observe the waiting period and beware of Allah your Lord. Do not expel them from their houses and let them not leave unless they have come up with a clear indecency, and these are the limits of Allah, and whoever transgresses the limits of Allah has wronged himself. You don't know if Allah might bring about a different situation after that.

2. Then when they have reached their term, keep them honourably or part from them honourably, and let two just people amongst you be witnesses and let them uphold the evidence before Allah. That is the admonition for whoever believes in Allah and the last day, and who bewares of Allah, He will find him a way out.

3. And He provides for him from where he does not expect it, and whoever relies on Allah, He is sufficient for him, for Allah enforces His command; Allah has given a measure to everything.

4. And for those of your women who have the menopause and you are unsure, their waiting period is three months as for those who missed a period, and those who are pregnant, their waiting period is until they have given birth, and whoever bewares of

Allah, He will make his affairs easy for him.

5. This is the command of Allah He revealed to you, and whoever bewares of Allah, He cancels his bad deeds and increases his reward.

6. Accommodate them where you accommodate yourselves and do not harm them to constrain them, and if they are pregnant, then spend on them until they have given birth, and if they breast-feed for you, then give them their reward, and consult each other appropriately, and if you disagree, then let someone else breast-feed for him.

7. Let the one with abundance spend of his abundance, and whose provision is tightened, let him spend of what Allah gave him, Allah does not burden a soul beyond what He has given it. Allah will grant ease after hardship.

8. And how many towns disobeyed the command of their Lord, so We subjected them to a severe reckoning and punished them severely?

9. Then they tasted the evil outcome of their affairs, and the outcome of their affairs was a loss.

10. Allah has promised them severe punishment, so beware of Allah oh you who have understanding and believe; Allah has already sent you a reminder.

11. A messenger who recites the clear signs of Allah to you in order to take those who believe and do good out of darkness into the light, and whoever believes in Allah and does good, He will enter him into gardens through

which rivers flow where they will remain forever; Allah has already prepared the best provision for him.

12. Allah is who created seven heavens and likewise of the earth. The command comes down between them so that you know that Allah is able to do anything and that Allah has full knowledge of everything.

Surah 66: *At-Tahrim*
(The Prohibition)

In the name of Allah, the Owner and Giver of Mercy

1. Oh prophet, why do you prohibit what Allah has permitted to you, seeking the contentment of your wives, and Allah is forgiving and merciful.

2. Allah has already prescribed for you the expiation of your oaths, and Allah is your protector and He is knowing and wise.

3. And when the prophet talked in confidence to one of his wives, then when she announced it and Allah disclosed it to him, he made known some of it and withheld some, so when he informed her of it she said: who told you this? He said: the Knowing and Informed has told me.

4. If both of you repent to Allah, your hearts will have deviated, and if you support each other against him, then Allah is his protector, and Jibril (Gabriel) and the righteous of the believers, and the angels will support him also.

5. If he divorced you, his Lord might replace you with better wives who submit (as Muslims), believe, are humble, repent, serve (Allah), fast, were previously married or are virgins.

6. Oh you believers, protect yourselves and your families from a fire whose fuel is people and stones, guarded over by stern and strong angels who do not disobey Allah in what He commands them and do what they have been commanded.

7. Oh you who reject (the truth), don't make excuses today, for you are rewarded on account of what you did.

8. Oh you believers, turn in sincere repentance to Allah, maybe Allah will cancel your bad deeds and enter you into gardens through which rivers flow on the day when Allah will not humiliate the prophet and those who believed with him; their light will race before them and on their right, they will say: our Lord, perfect our light for us and forgive us, for You are able to do anything.

9. Oh prophet, fight the rejecters and the pretenders and be tough with them, and their abode is hell, a bad destination.

10. Allah coins as similitude for those who reject (the truth) the wife of Nuh (Noah) and the wife of Lut (Lot): they were in the care of two righteous servants of Ours but deceived them, so they did not avail them the least against Allah and they will be told: enter the fire with those who enter.

11. And Allah coins as a similitude for those who believe the wife of Pharaoh when she said: my Lord, build me a house with You in the garden and rescue me from Pharaoh and his deeds and rescue me from the wrongdoing people.

12. And Maryam (Mary), the daughter of 'Imran, who guarded her chastity, so We blew into her of Our spirit, and she confirmed the words and books of her Lord and was of the humble.

Surah 67: *Al-Mulk* (The Kingdom)

In the name of Allah, the Owner and Giver of Mercy

1. Exalted is He in whose hand is the kingdom and He is able to do anything.

2. The One who created death and life to test you as to who does the best deeds, and He is the mighty and forgiving.

3. The One who created seven heavens in layers; you don't see any neglect in the creation of Allah. Look again, do you see any gaps?

4. Then look yet another time, your gaze will return to you weak and exhausted.

5. And We have adorned the heaven of this world with lights and made them a repellent for the devils and promised them the punishment of the fire.

6. And for those who reject their Lord is the punishment of hell, a bad destination.

7. When they are thrown in it they hear it gulping and bubble up.

8. It almost bursts with anger, whenever a group is thrown into it, its guards ask them: did not a warner reach you?

9. They will say: sure, a warner reached us, but we denied and said: Allah has not revealed anything, you are just in a great delusion.

10. And they will say: if we listened or pondered, we would not be inmates of the fire.

11. So they acknowledge their sins, so away with the inmates of the fire.

12. For those who fear their Lord in secret is forgiveness and a great reward.

13. So conceal your speech or disclose it, He knows what is kept inside.

14. Does not He who created know? And He is the kind and informed.

15. He is who made the earth stretch out for you, so walk on its back and eat of His provision, and towards Him is the resurrection.

16. Are you safe that He who is in the heaven will not make the earth swallow you up and it will quake?

17. Or are you safe that He who is in the heaven will not send a storm against you, then you will know what My warning means?

18. And those before them denied, then how was My rebuttal!

19. Don't they look at the birds above them extending and retracting their wings? None but the Owner of Mercy holds them up, for He sees everything.

20. Or who will be a force to help you besides the Owner of Mercy?

Those who reject (the truth) deceive themselves.

21. Or who will provide for you if He withholds His provision? But they persist in insolence and resentment.

22. Is he who walks with his face stuck to the ground better guided or who walks upright on a straight path?

23. Say: He is who brought you into existence and gave you hearing and eyesight and hearts, little thanks you give.

24. Say: He is who spread you out on earth, and to Him will you be gathered.

25. And they say: when will this promise happen if you are truthful?

26. Say: the knowledge is with Allah, and I am only a clear warner.

27. Then when they see it close by, the faces of those who reject (the truth) will be gloomy and they are told: this is what you asked for.

28. Say: have you considered if Allah destroyed me and those with me, or has mercy on us, who will protect those who reject (the truth) from a painful punishment?

29. Say: He is the Owner of Mercy, we believe in Him and rely on Him, then you will soon know who is in clear error.

30. Say: have you considered if your water would turn brackish, who will bring you flowing water?

Surah 68: **Al-Qalam**
(The Pen)

In the name of Allah,
the Owner and Giver of Mercy

1. Nun. By the pen and what they write.

2. By the grace of your Lord, you are not possessed.

3. And you will have a limitless reward.

4. And you are of great character.

5. So you will see and they will see.

6. Who of you has been tempted.

7. For your Lord knows best who has strayed from His way and He knows best those who are guided.

8. So do not obey the deniers.

9. They want you to compromise, so they compromise.

10. And do not obey anyone who makes empty promises.

11. Who incites and spreads dissent.

12. Who forbids what is good in transgression and sin.

13. A demagogue and a low-life.

14. Though he has wealth and children.

15. When Our signs are recited to him he says: stories of old.

16. We will brand him on the snout!

17. We tested them like We tested the inhabitants of the garden when they swore: we will harvest it in the morning.

18. And they did not have any reservations.

19. Then, a delegation from your Lord encircled it whilst they were asleep.

20. And it became as if depleted.

21. Then they called each other in the morning:

22. Let's go to your plantation if you want to cut it down.

23. So they set off, urging each other to keep out of view,

24. So that no poor person would enter it against your will.

25. And they set out determined and strong.

26. Then, when they saw it, they said: we have been mistaken.

27. No, we are destitute.

28. The most level-headed amongst them said: did I not tell you to glorify (Allah)?

29. They said: glorified is our Lord, we did wrong.

30. Then they turned to each other, complaining.

31. They said: woe to us, we did wrong.

32. Maybe our Lord will replace it with something better for us, for We look in hope to our Lord.

33. This is what the punishment is like, and the punishment of the hereafter is greater if they only knew.

34. Those who beware (of Allah) will have gardens of blessings with their Lord.

35. Do We equate those who submit with the sinful?

36. What is the matter with you, how do you judge?

37. Or do you have a book which you study?

38. Does it give you what you want?

39. Or do you have an oath from Us which extends to the day of resurrection that you will have your own judgement?

40. Ask them, who of them claims this.

41. Or do they have associates? Then let them bring their associates if they are truthful.

42. On the day He will manifest Himself and they will be called to prostrate but can't do it.

43. Their eyes downcast, covered in humiliation, and they were previously called to prostrate when they were sound.

44. So leave Me and those who deny this statement, We will gradually lead them on from where they don't know.

45. And I give them some space, for My plot is firm.

46. Or do you ask them for a reward and they are burdened by debt?

47. Or do they have access to the unseen so they write it down?

48. So have patience for the judgement of your Lord and do not be like the one inside the fish when he called in distress.

49. If a favour from your Lord had not reached him, he would have stayed in the hollow condemned.

50. But his Lord chose him and made him of the righteous.

51. And those who reject (the truth) would like to kill you with their eyes when they hear the reminder and say: he is possessed.

52. Yet it is only a reminder for all the world.

Surah 69: *Al-Haqqah*
(The True Event)

In the name of Allah,
the Owner and Giver of Mercy

1. The true event.

2. What is the true event?

3. And how do you know what the true event is?

4. Thamud and 'Ad denied the calamity.

5. As for Thamud, they were destroyed by their transgression.

6. And as for 'Ad, they were destroyed by a raging icy wind.

7. He directed it against them for seven nights and eight days consecutively, then you saw the people thrown to the ground as if they were stumps of cut down palm trees.

8. So do you see any remnant of them?

9. And Pharaoh and those before him and the overturned towns produced sinful acts.

10. So they disobeyed the messenger of their Lord, then He overtook them in a powerful way.

11. When the water breached its boundaries, We carried you in the ship.

12. To make it a reminder for you and to be retained by attentive ears.

13. Then, when the horn will be blown once,

14. And the earth and the mountains will be lifted and levelled in one go.

15. On that day the event happens.

16. And the sky will break up and be fragile that day.

17. And the angels will be in the vicinity and eight will carry the throne of your Lord above them that day.

18. That day you will be presented, nothing will be hidden of you.

19. Then who is given his record in his right hand, he will say: come and read my record.

20. I thought I would meet my reckoning.

21. And he will be in a life of contentment.

22. In an elevated garden.

23. Its pickings will be close by.

24. Eat and drink legitimately on account of what you left behind in the days gone by.

25. And who is given his record in his left hand, he will say: woe to me, if only I wasn't given my record.

26. And wouldn't know my reckoning.

27. If only this was the end.

28. My wealth did not help me.

29. My authority has departed from me.

30. Take him and shackle him.

31. Then throw him into hell-fire.

32. Then lock him into a chain measuring seventy arms' length.

33. For he did not believe in Allah, the mighty.

34. And did not encourage the feeding of the poor.

35. So he will not have any dear friend here today.

36. And no food except waste product.

37. Only the sinners eat it.

38. But I swear by what you see,

39. And by what you don't see,

40. It is the speech of an honourable messenger,

41. And it is not the speech of a poet, little do you believe,

42. Nor the speech of a fortune-teller, little to you reflect,

43. A revelation from the Lord of all worlds.

44. And if he made up some sayings against Us,

45. We would take his right hand,

46. Then cut his arteries,

47. And none of you could save him.

48. And it is a reminder for those who beware (of Allah).

49. And We know that there are deniers amongst you.

50. And it is a loss for those who reject (the truth).

51. And it is the certain truth.

52. So glorify the name of your mighty Lord.

Surah 70: *Al-Ma'arij*
(Connections)

***In the name of Allah,
the Owner and Giver of Mercy***

1. A questioner asks about the punishment to befall,

2. Those who reject (the truth), which cannot be averted,

3. From Allah, who owns all connections.

4. The angels and the Spirit ascend to Him on a day the measure of which is fifty thousand years.

5. So have beautiful patience.

6. They see it far off.

7. And We see it close by.

8. On the day the sky will be like sludge.

9. And the mountains will be like wool.

10. And dear friends will ask another.

11. They see them, and the sinful would like to be ransomed from the punishment on that day by his children,

12. And his spouse and his brother,

13. And his family, which shelters him,

14. And all who are on earth, so he could be rescued.

15. But no, it is ablaze,

16. It tears away the flesh,

17. It calls whoever turned away and turned his back,

18. And hoarded and accumulated.

19. For man has been created impatient,

20. When harm afflicts him, he is anxious,

21. And when good afflicts him, he withholds,

22. Except those who pray,

23. Who are constant in their prayers,

24. And in whose wealth there is a known share,

25. For those who ask and are deprived,

26. And who confirm the day of repayment,

27. And who fear the punishment of their Lord,

28. For nobody is safe from the punishment of their Lord,

29. And who guard their chastity,

30. Except with regard to their partners or those in their possession, for then they are not to blame.

31. Then if anyone desires beyond that, then those exceed the limits.

32. And who look after their trust and agreements,

33. And who uphold their testimony,

34. And who guard their prayers,

35. They will be honoured in gardens.

36. So what is the matter with those who reject (the truth) that they run towards you,

37. In scattered groups from the right and the left?

38. Does every one of them hope to enter a garden of blessings?

39. But no, We created them from what they know.

40. But I swear by the Lord of the sunrises and sunsets that we are able,

41. To replace them with better than them, and We will not be outdone.

42. So leave them to busy themselves and play until they meet their promised day.

43. The day they will rapidly emerge from the graves as if they were racing towards a goal.

44. Their eyes downcast, covered in humiliation, that is the day they were promised.

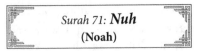

Surah 71: *Nuh*
(Noah)

In the name of Allah,
the Owner and Giver of Mercy

1. We sent Nuh (Noah) to his people: warn your people before a painful punishment reaches them.

2. He said: oh my people, I am a clear warner to you,

3. That you must serve Allah and beware of Him and obey me.

4. He will forgive you of your sins and give you time until a fixed date, for when the date of Allah comes, it cannot be delayed, if only you knew.

5. He said: my Lord, I called my people night and day.

6. But my call only made them avoid me more.

7. And each time I call them so You forgive them, they place their fingers in their ears and pull their clothes over themselves and persist and are arrogant.

8. Then I called them openly.

9. Then I talked to them frankly and in private.

10. And I said: seek forgiveness from your Lord, for He is forgiving.

11. He will send abundant rain from the sky for you,

12. And will expand wealth and children for you and give you gardens and give you rivers.

13. What is the matter with you that you don't have any hope for the greatness of Allah?

14. When He created you in stages.

15. Don't you see how Allah created seven heavens in layers?

16. And He placed the moon in them as a light and placed the sun as a lamp.

17. And Allah made plants grow for you from the earth.

18. Then He returns you to it and brings you out again.

19. And Allah spread the earth out for you.

20. So that you follow its cut-out paths.

21. Nuh (Noah) said: my Lord, they disobey me and follow those whose wealth and children only increase them in loss.

22. And they schemed a grand scheme.

23. And said: don't abandon your gods and don't abandon Wadd, Suwa', Yaghuth, Ya'uq and Nasr.

24. And they mislead many and only increase the wrongdoers in error.

25. On account of their sins they were drowned and entered the fire, and you will not find a helper for them against Allah.

26. And Nuh (Noah) said: my Lord, do not leave a single house of those who reject (the truth) on earth.

27. For if you leave them, they will mislead your servants and only give birth to those who are immoral and reject (the truth).

28. My Lord, forgive me and my parents and those who enter my home as believers, and the believing men and women, and only increase the wrongdoers in ruin.

Surah 72: *Al-Jinn*
(Jinn)

In the name of Allah,
the Owner and Giver of Mercy

1. Say: it has been revealed to me that a group of the Jinn listened and said: we have heard an amazing reading (Qur'an).

2. It guides to righteousness, so we believe in it and will not associate anyone with our Lord.

3. And, exalted is the greatness of our Lord, He did not adopt a spouse or son.

4. And our fools said excessive things about Allah.

5. And we thought mankind and the Jinn would not say lies about Allah.

6. And men from mankind used to seek assistance from men from the Jinn and they increased their rebellion.

7. And they thought, like you thought, that Allah would not resurrect anyone.

8. And We searched out the heaven and found it filled with stern guards and shooting stars.

9. And we sat on listening posts there, but whoever listens now, he finds a shooting star waiting for him.

10. And we don't know whether bad is intended for those on earth or whether their Lord wants righteousness for them.

11. And there are righteous ones and others amongst us, our ways differ.

12. And we figured that we cannot outwit Allah on earth and cannot outwit Him by fleeing.

13. And when we heard the guidance, we believed it, and who believes in his Lord, he will not fear loss nor oppression.

14. And there are those who submit (as Muslims) amongst us and there are those who are unjust, and those who submit, they aspire to righteousness.

15. And the unjust, they are fuel for hell.

16. And if they stayed on the path, We would give them water to drink in abundance.

17. To test them with it, and whoever turns away from the remembrance of his Lord, He will lead him into heavy punishment.

18. And the mosques are for Allah, so do not call on anyone with Allah.

19. And when the servant of Allah stood up to call Him, they almost clung to him.

20. Say: I call on my Lord and I do not associate anyone with Him.

21. Say: I have no power to harm or guide you.

22. Say: nobody will protect me from Allah, and I have no refuge besides Him.

23. It is only a declaration from Allah and His message, and whoever disobeys Allah and His messenger, the fire of hell is for him where they will remain forever.

24. Then when they see what they have been promised, they will know whose help is the weakest and smallest in numbers.

25. Say: I have no idea whether what you have been promised is close by or whether my Lord prolongs it.

26. He knows the unseen, and He does not disclose His secret to anyone.

27. Except for a messenger He is content with, then He dispatches a guard before and behind him.

28. So that He knows that he has conveyed the message of his Lord, and He has full knowledge of them and takes full account of everything.

Surah 73: **Al-Muzammil**
(The One Invested
(with the mission))

In the name of Allah,
the Owner and Giver of Mercy

1. Oh you invested (with the mission),

2. Stand (in prayer) most of the night,

3. Half of it, or a little less,

4. Or more, and recite the Qur'an in measure,

5. We shall entrust you with a heavy statement.

6. The night-time has greater impact and speech is more pronounced in it.

7. During the day you have a busy schedule.

8. And remember the name of your Lord and devote yourself to Him.

9. The Lord of the East and the West, there is no god but Him, so take Him as a protector.

10. And have patience with what they say and part from them nicely.

11. And leave the deniers in their comfort to Me and give them some time.

12. We have shackles and hell-fire.

13. And food which causes choking and a painful punishment.

14. On the day the earth and mountains will tremble, and the mountains will be a pile of rubble.

15. We sent a messenger to you as a witness against you like We sent a messenger to Pharaoh.

16. But Pharaoh disobeyed the messenger, so We overtook him with a strong grip.

17. So how, if you reject (the truth), can you guard yourselves against a day which will turn children grey-haired?

18. The sky will break up then, His promise will be accomplished.

19. This is a reminder, so let whoever pleases take a way towards his Lord.

20. Your Lord knows that you stand (in prayer) almost two thirds of the night, or half of it, or a third of it, and a party of those with you also, and Allah measures the night and the day. He knows that you don't count it, so He turned to you in forgiveness. So read what comes easy of the Qur'an. He knows that some of you will be ill, and others travelling on earth to seek of the favours of Allah, and others who strive in the way of Allah, so read what comes easy of it, and keep up prayer and give Zakat and lend Allah an excellent loan, and whatever good you send ahead for yourselves, you will find it with Allah even better and of greater reward. And ask Allah for forgiveness, for Allah is forgiving and merciful.

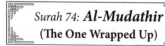

Surah 74: **Al-Mudathir**
(The One Wrapped Up)

In the name of Allah,
the Owner and Giver of Mercy

1. Oh you wrapped up,

2. Get up and warn,

3. And exalt your Lord,

4. And keep clean,

5. And shun filth,

6. And do not grant just to get more,

7. And have patience for your Lord,

8. Then when the horn is blown,

9. That will be a difficult day,

10. Not easy for those who reject (the truth),

11. Leave Me and whom I alone created,

12. And gave him wealth in abundance,

13. And children as witnesses,

14. And gave him comfort,

15. Then he hopes for more.

16. But no, he resisted Our signs.

17. I will make him suffer hardship.

18. He pondered and evaluated,

19. But how badly he evaluated,

20. Again, how badly he evaluated,

21. Then he looked,

22. Then he frowned and showed displeasure,

23. Then he turned away and became arrogant,

24. And said: this is only handed down magic,

25. It is only the speech of a human.

26. We will enter him into a fire.

27. And how do you know what fire it is?

28. It does not leave anything nor desist.

29. It disfigures humans.

30. Nineteen are set over it.

31. And We only appointed angels as wardens of the fire, and We only made their number a test for those who reject (the truth), so that those who were given the book would be certain and the believers would increase in faith and those who were given the book and the believers would not doubt, but those with a disease in their hearts and those who reject (the truth) would say: what does Allah want by this similitude? This is how We let go astray whom We please and guide whom We please, and nobody knows the forces of your Lord but He, and it is only a reminder for mankind.

32. But no, by the moon,

33. And the night when it recedes,

34. And the morning when it turns bright,

35. It is one of the great signs,

36. A warning to mankind,

37. For whoever of you wants to go ahead or stay behind,

38. Every soul is liable for what it commits,

39. Except for the companions of the right,

40. They ask each other in gardens,

41. About the sinful,

42. What lead you to the fire?

43. They will say: we were not of those who pray,

44. And we did not feed the poor,

45. And we joked with those who joked,

46. And we denied the day of repayment,

47. Until certainty reached us.

48. So the intercession of those who intercede will not benefit them.

49. So what is the matter with them that they turn away from the reminder?

50. As if they were frightened donkeys,

51. Running away from the whip,

52. But each man amongst them wants to be given his own scripture.

53. But no, they do not fear the hereafter.

54. No, it is a reminder.

55. So whoever pleases can remember it.

56. And they will only remember it if Allah pleases, He is in charge of awareness and of forgiveness.

Surah 75: *Al-Qiyamah* (Resurrection)

In the name of Allah, the Owner and Giver of Mercy

1. I swear by the day of resurrection.

2. And I swear by the self-depreciating soul.

3. Does man count on Us not gathering his bones?

4. For sure, We are able to restore his fingertips.

5. But man wants to contradict what lies before him.

6. He asks: when will the day of resurrection be?

7. Then when the eyes are dazed,

8. And the moon has disappeared,

9. And the sun and the moon have collided,

10. Man says that day: where is the escape?

11. But no, no shelter!

12. To your Lord is the destination that day.

13. That day man will be told what he sent ahead and what he left behind.

14. But man is observant of himself.

15. Even if he offers excuses.

16. Do not pronounce it (the Qur'an) in a hurry,

17. Upon Us is to collate and recite it,

18. Then once We have recited it, follow its recitation.

19. Then Upon Us is its explanation.

20. But no, you love the immediate life,

21. And abandon the hereafter.

22. Faces will shine on that day,

23. Looking towards their Lord,

24. And faces will be gloomy that day,

25. Suspecting that the worst will happen to them.

26. But no, when it (the soul of the dying person) reaches the collarbone,

27. And it is said: who will carry it up?

28. And He knows that it is the departure.

29. And agony will be heaped upon agony.

30. To your Lord is the journey that day.

31. Yet he did not confirm the truth nor pray.

32. But he denied and turned away.

33. Then he went proudly to his family.

34. Woe to you and woe again.

35. Once more, woe to you and woe again.

36. Does man count on being left to his own devices?

37. Was he not a sperm in an ejaculated fluid?

38. Then he was an implant, then He created and shaped (it),

39. And produced from it male and female in pairs.

40. Is He then not able to revive the dead?

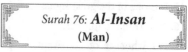

Surah 76: *Al-Insan*
(Man)

In the name of Allah,
the Owner and Giver of Mercy

1. Has man heard of a period of time when he wasn't even mentioned?

2. We created man from sperm made up of cells We put to the test, then We gave him hearing and eyesight.

3. We guided him the way, so he may be grateful or reject it.

4. We have promised those who reject (the truth) chains and cuffs and a fire.

5. The righteous will drink from a cup containing a mixture of camphor,

6. A spring of which the servants of Allah will drink, whose flow they direct.

7. They kept their promises and feared a day the harm of which is overpowering.

8. And they fed food out of love for Him to the poor and orphans and their relatives.

9. We only feed you to please Allah, we don't want any reward or thanks from you.

10. For we fear from our Lord an extensive gloomy day.

11. So Allah protected them from the harm of that day and granted them luxury and happiness.

12. And rewarded them for their patience with a garden and silk.

13. They recline there on couches and do not face the (heat of the) sun or freezing cold.

14. Its shade is close over them and its pickings hang low.

15. They will be waited upon with silver dishes and crystal glasses,

16. Crystal made of silver, which they will measure out.

17. And they will be given to drink there from a cup containing a mixture of ginger,

18. A spring there which is called Salsabil (Delicious Flow).

19. And they will be waited upon by eternal youth, if you saw them, you would consider them scattered pearls.

20. And if you looked again, you would see blessings and a vast kingdom.

21. They wear clothes of green silk and brocade and are adorned with bracelets of silver, and their Lord gives them a pure drink.

22. This is a reward for you and your effort is appreciated.

23. For We revealed to you the Qur'an in succession.

24. So wait for the judgement of your Lord and do not obey any sinner or rejecter (of the truth) amongst them.

25. And remember the name of your Lord in the mornings and evenings.

26. And at night, then prostrate to Him and glorify Him throughout the night.

27. For these love the immediate life and leave a grave day behind them.

28. We created them and strengthened their physique, and if We pleased, We could replace them with others like them.

29. This is a reminder, so let whoever pleases take a way towards his Lord.

30. And it will not please you unless Allah pleases, for Allah is knowing and wise.

31. He enters whom he pleases into His mercy, and for the wrongdoers He has promised a painful punishment.

Surah 77: *Al-Mursalat*
(Those Dispatched)

In the name of Allah,
the Owner and Giver of Mercy

1. By those dispatched repeatedly,

2. And those blowing violently,

3. And those scattering and propagating,

4. And those parting and dividing,

5. And those bringing the reminder,

6. By way of excuse or warning,

7. What you have been promised will take place.

8. Then when the stars fade,

9. And the sky breaks up,

10. And the mountains crumble,

11. And the messengers are gathered on time,

12. For which has this been reserved?

13. For the day of division.

14. And how do you know what the day of division is?

15. Woe on that day to those who deny.

16. Did We not destroy the earlier communities?

17. Then made the others follow them?

18. This is how We deal with the sinners.

19. Woe on that day to those who deny.

20. Did We not create you from an insignificant fluid?

21. And placed it in a protective location?

22. For a known term?

23. For We arrange it all in an excellent manner.

24. Woe on that day to those who deny.

25. Did We not make the earth a container,

26. For the living and the dead,

27. And placed on it tall stabilisers and gave you potable water to drink.

28. Woe on that day to those who deny.

29. Go away to what you denied.

30. Go away to a shadow dividing into three branches.

31. It does not grant shade nor benefit against the flame.

32. It throws out enormous sparks.

33. Like brass cables.

34. Woe on that day to those who deny.

35. On that day they will not speak.

36. Nor be given permission to make excuses.

37. Woe on that day to those who deny.

38. This is the day of division, We gathered you and the earlier communities.

39. Then plot, if you have a plot.

40. Woe on that day to those who deny.

41. Those who beware (of Allah) will be in shade and springs.

42. And fruit of what they desire.

43. Eat and drink legitimately on account of what you used to do.

44. For this is how We reward those who do good.

45. Woe on that day to those who deny.

46. Eat and enjoy a little, for you are sinful.

47. Woe on that day to those who deny.

48. And when they are told to bow down, they don't bow down.

49. Woe on that day to those who deny.

50. So what statement will they believe after this?

Surah 78: **An-Naba'**
(The News)

In the name of Allah,
the Owner and Giver of Mercy

1. What do they ask each other about?

2. About the serious news,

3. About which they differ.

4. But no, they will soon know,

5. Again no, they will soon know.

6. Did We not make the earth an abode,

7. And the mountains fixtures,

8. And created you in pairs?

9. And We made your sleep for rest,

10. And made the night a cover,

11. And made the day for livelihood.

12. And We built above you seven strong structures,

13. And placed a glowing light.

14. And We sent from the clouds driven by wind streaming rain,

15. To bring out greenery and plants with it,

16. And lush gardens.

17. For the day of division is an appointment.

18. On the day the horn is blown, then you come like swarms.

19. And the heavens will be opened and have gates.

20. And the mountains will be moved and become a mirage.

21. For hell lies in wait,

22. As a destination for the transgressors.

23. They will stay trapped in it.

24. They will neither taste coolness there nor a drink,

25. Except boiling water and freezing liquid.

26. A befitting reward.

27. For they did not hope for the reckoning,

28. And denied Our signs outright.

29. And We have preserved everything in a record.

30. Taste then, We will only increase your punishment.

31. For those who beware (of Allah) is accomplishment,

32. Enclosed gardens and grapes,

33. And youthful maidens,

34. And filled cups.

35. They will hear neither idle talk nor lies there.

36. A reward from your Lord, a measured gift.

37. The Lord of the heavens and the earth and what is between them, the Owner of mercy, they cannot speak before Him.

38. On the day the Spirit and the angels stand in rows nobody will speak except whom the Owner of mercy has given permission and he says what is right.

39. That is the day of truth, so let whoever pleases set his destination towards his Lord.

40. We warn you of a close-by punishment on the day a man will look at what he has sent ahead and the one who rejected (the truth) will say: if only I was dust.

Surah 79: **An-Nazi'at**
(The Collectors)

In the name of Allah,
the Owner and Giver of Mercy

1. By the collectors (of the soul),

2. Who tie it down,

3. And travel (with it),

4. Then move ahead,

5. Then organise affairs.

6. On the day of trembling,

7. Followed by another,

8. Hearts will be pounding that day,

9. With eyes downcast.

10. They will say: are we to be returned to our prior state,

11. When we were decayed bones?

12. They will say: this return would be a loss.

13. But it is only a single shout.

14. Then they are in wakefulness.

15. Has the story of Musa (Moses) reached you?

16. When his Lord called him in the sacred valley of Tuwa:

17. Go to Pharaoh, he is transgressing.

18. And say: are you willing to purify yourself,

19. And I guide you to your Lord, so you fear (Him)?

20. And he showed him the great sign.

21. But he denied and disobeyed.

22. Then he turned away hastily,

23. And gathered and announced,

24. And said: I am your highest Lord.

25. Then Allah overtook him with punishment in the hereafter and this world.

26. In this is a lesson for those who fear.

27. Are you stronger in creation or the sky which He built?

28. He raised its canopy and made it well-proportioned,

29. And made its night dark and brought out its morning light.

30. And after that He spread out the earth,

31. Brought out its water from it and its pasture,

32. And anchored the mountains.

33. A provision for you and for your cattle.

34. Then, when the great calamity comes,

35. That day man will remember what he strove for.

36. And hell-fire will be presented to those who see.

37. So whoever transgressed,

38. And preferred the life of this world,

39. Hell-fire is his home.

40. And whoever feared standing before his Lord and prevented his soul from desire,

41. The garden is his home.

42. They ask you about the hour, when it will happen.

43. How could you know about it?

44. Its conclusion is up to your Lord.

45. You only warn those who fear it.

46. On the day they see it, it will be as if they had only stayed an evening or a morning.

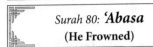

Surah 80: 'Abasa
(He Frowned)

**In the name of Allah,
the Owner and Giver of Mercy**

1. He frowned and turned away,

2. When the blind man came to him.

3. And how can you tell that he might have purified himself,

4. Or remembered, so the remembrance benefited him?

5. As for him who is arrogant,

6. You busy yourself with him,

7. And it is not up to you whether he purifies himself.

8. And as for him who hurries towards you,

9. And fears,

10. You pay no attention to him,

11. No, it is a reminder.

12. So whoever pleases can remember it.

13. On distinguished pages,

14. Elevated and purified,

15. In the hands of ambassadors,

16. Dignified and dutiful.

17. So man is destroyed when he rejects it.

18. From what did He create him?

19. From a sperm He created him and shaped him.

20. Then He made the way easy for him.

21. Then He made him die and be buried.

22. Then, when He pleases, He resurrects him.

23. But no, he does not comply with what He ordered him.

24. So let man look at his food:

25. We made the water pour out,

26. Then We made the earth split open,

27. And grew greenery on it,

28. And grapes and fresh dates,

29. And olive trees and date palms,

30. And abundant enclosed gardens,

31. And fruit and fodder.

32. A provision for you and for your cattle.

33. Then, when the scream comes,

34. That day man will run away from his brother,

35. And his mother and his father,

36. And his spouse and his children.

37. Every one of them will have something to keep him busy that day.

38. Faces will be bright on that day,

39. Laughing and happy,

40. And faces will be covered in dust that day,

41. Impurity will cover them,

42. Those are the immoral ones who rejected (the truth).

Surah 81: At-Takwir
(The Collapse)

**In the name of Allah,
the Owner and Giver of Mercy**

1. When the sun collapses,

2. And when the stars darken,

3. And when the mountains move,

4. And when heavily pregnant camels are neglected,

5. And when the wild beasts are gathered,

6. And when the seas overflow,

7. And when the souls are paired up,

8. And when the buried infant is asked,

9. For what sin she was killed,

10. And when the pages are opened,

11. And when the sky is torn away,

12. And when hell-fire is lit,

13. And when the garden is brought near,

14. Each soul will know what it has brought.

15. But I swear by the persisting stars,

16. As they move along,

17. And the night when it darkens,

18. And the morning when it gains strength,

19. It is the speech of an honourable messenger,

20. Powerful and established in the presence of the owner of the throne.

21. Obeyed and trusted.

22. And your companion is not possessed.

23. And he saw him clearly on the horizon.

24. And he is not holding back any secrets.

25. And it is not the speech of a cursed devil.

26. What are you claiming!

27. It is only a reminder for all the world.

28. For whoever of you pleases to go straight.

29. And it won't please you unless Allah pleases, the Lord of all worlds.

Surah 82: *Al-Infitar*
(The Rupture)

In the name of Allah,
the Owner and Giver of Mercy

1. When the sky ruptures,

2. And when the stars disperse,

3. And when the seas break out,

4. And when the graves are overturned,

5. Each soul will know what it has sent ahead and left behind.

6. O man, what deceived you about your generous Lord?

7. Who created you and shaped you and proportioned you.

8. He made you into any shape He pleased.

9. But no, you deny the debt.

10. And there are guardians set over you.

11. Dignified scribes.

12. They know what you do.

13. The righteous will be in blessings.

14. And the immoral will be in hell-fire.

15. They will enter it on the day of repayment.

16. And they will not be able to keep away from it.

17. And how do you know what the day of repayment is?

18. Again, how do you know what the day of repayment is?

19. The day when no soul will be able to help another soul and the matter that day belongs to Allah.

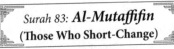

Surah 83: *Al-Mutaffifin*
(Those Who Short-Change)

In the name of Allah,
the Owner and Giver of Mercy

1. Woe to those who short-change,

2. Who, when they take measure from people, take it in full,

3. And when they measure and weigh up for them, reduce it.

4. Don't these know that they will be resurrected?

5. On a tremendous day.

6. The day people will stand before the Lord of all worlds.

7. But no, the record of the immoral is in (the vault of) Sijjin.

8. And how do you know what Sijjin is?

9. A sealed record.

10. Woe on that day to those who deny.

11. Who deny the day of repayment,

12. And only a sinful transgressor denies it.

13. When Our signs are recited to him he says: stories of old.

14. But no, what they committed has taken possession of their hearts.

15. No, on that day they will be barred from their Lord.

16. Then they will enter hell-fire.

17. Then they will be told: this is what you denied.

18. But no, the record of the righteous is in (the lofty place of) 'Illiyin.

19. And how do you know what 'Illiyin is?

20. A sealed record.

21. Those brought close witness it.

22. The righteous will be in blessings.

23. Looking on on couches.

24. You can tell the radiance of blessings on their faces.

25. They are given to drink from a sealed nectar.

26. Its seal is musk, and that is what all who compete should strive for.

27. Its mixture is of Tasnim.

28. A spring from which those who are brought close drink.

29. For the sinful used to make fun of the believers.

30. And when they passed them by, they winked at each other.

31. And when they returned to their families, they returned joking.

32. And when they saw them, they said: these are misled.

33. Yet they were not sent as guardians over them.

34. So today the believers make fun of those who rejected (the truth).

35. Looking on on couches.

36. Did those who rejected (the truth) get the reward for what they did?

Surah 84: *Al-Inshiqaq*
(The Splitting)

In the name of Allah,
the Owner and Giver of Mercy

1. When the sky splits up,

2. And listens to its Lord and obeys,

3. And when the earth is flattened,

4. And throws out what is in it and is depleted,

5. And listens to its Lord and obeys,

6. Oh man, you will work hard to (meet) your Lord, and you will meet Him.

7. Then, who is given his record in his right hand,

8. He will soon be given an easy reckoning,

9. And return to his family happy.

10. And who is given his record from behind his back,

11. He will soon call for destruction,

12. And enter the fire,

13. For he was happy amongst his family.

14. He thought he would not return,

15. But no, your Lord used to watch him.

16. But I swear by the twilight,

17. And the night and what it covers,

18. And the moon when it grows full,

19. You will travel stage by stage.

20. So what is the matter with them that they don't believe?

21. And when the Qur'an is recited to them they don't prostrate.

22. But those who reject (the truth) deny (it).

23. And Allah knows best what they conceal.

24. So announce to them a painful punishment.

25. Except those who believe and do good work, for them is a limitless reward.

Surah 85: *Al-Buruj*
(Constellations)

In the name of Allah,
the Owner and Giver of Mercy

1. By the sky with its constellations,

2. And the promised day,

3. And the witness and the evidence,

4. Death to the companions of the ditch,

5. The well-fuelled fire,

6. When they sat around it,

7. And witnessed what they did to the believers.

8. And they only held against them that they believed in Allah the mighty and praiseworthy.

9. The One to whom belongs the kingdom of the heavens and the earth and Allah is a witness to everything.

10. Those who persecute the believing men and women and then do not repent, the punishment of hell is theirs and they will have the punishment of burning.

11. Those who believe and do good work, theirs are gardens through which rivers flow, that is the great success.

12. For the grip of your Lord is strong.

13. He initiates and repeats.

14. And He is the forgiving and loving.

15. Owner of the glorious throne.

16. Who does what He wants.

17. Has the story of the forces reached you?

18. Of Pharaoh and Thamud?

19. But those who reject (the truth) are in denial.

20. And Allah catches them from behind.

21. But it is a glorious reading (Qur'an).

22. In a tablet kept safe.

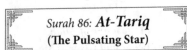

Surah 86: *At-Tariq*
(The Pulsating Star)

In the name of Allah,
the Owner and Giver of Mercy

1. By the sky and the pulsating (star).

2. And how do you know what the pulsating (star) is?

3. The luminous star.

4. Each soul has a guardian set over it.

5. So let man look from what he was created:

6. He was created from a gushing fluid.

7. Which emerges from between the loins and the chest.

8. He is able to bring him back.

9. On the day the secrets will be exposed,

10. And he has neither strength nor helper.

11. By the sky with its returning objects,

12. And the earth with its crevices,

13. This is a distinguished statement,

14. And it is not a joke.

15. For they plot a plot,

16. And I plot a plot,

17. So give those who reject (the truth) time and leave them for a while.

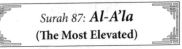

Surah 87: *Al-A'la*
(The Most Elevated)

In the name of Allah,
the Owner and Giver of Mercy

1. Glorify the name of your Lord, the most elevated.

2. Who created and shaped,

3. And proportioned and guided,

4. Who brings out the vegetation,

5. Then makes it darkened chaff.

6. We will make you recite, so you don't forget,

7. Except what Allah pleases, for He knows what is spoken openly and what is concealed.

8. And We will make it easy for you.

9. So remind where the reminder is of benefit.

10. He who fears will pay heed.

11. And the most unfortunate will avoid it,

12. Who enters the greatest fire,

13. Then he will neither die nor live there.

14. Successful is who purifies himself,

15. And remembers the name of his Lord and prays.

16. But you prefer the life of this world,

17. Whereas the hereafter is better and more lasting.

18. This is found in the earliest records,

19. The records of Ibrahim (Abraham) and Musa (Moses).

Surah 88: *Al-Ghashiyah*
(The Disaster)

In the name of Allah,
the Owner and Giver of Mercy

1. Has the story of the disaster reached you?

2. Faces will be downcast that day,

3. Struggling, exhausted,

4. They will enter a scorching fire.

5. They will be given to drink from a hot spring.

6. They will not have food except thorns,

7. Which do not nourish nor benefit against hunger.

8. Faces will be happy that day,

9. Content with their effort,

10. In an elevated garden.

11. They do not hear idle talk there.

12. In it is a flowing spring.

13. In it are raised couches,

14. And cups put in place,

15. And cushions lined up,

16. And spread-out carpets.

17. Don't they look at the camel, how it has been created?

18. And at the sky, how it has been raised?

19. And at the mountains, how they have been erected?

20. And at the earth, how it has been made smooth?

21. So remind, for you are a reminder.

22. You don't control them.

23. But for those who turn away and reject (the truth),

24. Allah will punish them with the greatest punishment.

25. For to Us is their return,

26. Then upon Us is their reckoning.

Surah 89: *Al-Fajr*
(Daybreak)

In the name of Allah,
the Owner and Giver of Mercy

1. By the Daybreak,

2. And the ten nights,

3. And the even and the odd,

4. And the night when it recedes,

5. Does this contain an oath for those of understanding?

6. Did you not see how your Lord dealt with 'Ad?

7. (The clan of) Iram with their tall buildings,

8. The like of which had not been created on the land.

9. And Thamud who carved out rocks in the valley.

10. And Pharaoh with his monuments,

11. Who all transgressed in the land,

12. And increased corruption in it,

13. So your Lord poured severe punishment over them.

14. For your Lord is watchful.

15. So when his Lord tries man by honouring and blessing him, he says: my Lord has honoured me.

16. And when He tries him by tightening is provision, he says: my Lord has humiliated me.

17. But no, you do not honour the orphan,

18. And do not encourage the feeding of the poor,

19. And   devour   the inheritance completely,

20. And love wealth greatly.

21. But no, when the earth will be shaken to the ground again and again,

22. And your Lord and the angels will come in ranks,

23. And hell will be brought that day - that day man remembers, but what use is the remembrance for him?

24. He will say: woe to me, if only I had sent (something) ahead for my life.

25. But today, nobody will punish like He does,

26. And nobody will restrain like He does.

27. Oh agreeable soul!

28. Return to your Lord, content and accepted,

29. And enter amongst My servants,

30. And enter My garden.

Surah 90: **Al-Balad**
(The City)

In the name of Allah,
the Owner and Giver of Mercy

1. I swear by this city.

2. And you are entitled to this city.

3. And by the father and his child,

4. We created man in (a state of) suffering.

5. Does man count on nobody having power over him?

6. He says: I have blown lots of money.

7. Does he count on nobody having seen him?

8. Did We not give him two eyes,

9. And a tongue and two lips,

10. And guided him the two pathways.

11. But he did not embark on the steep path.

12. And how do you know what the steep path is?

13. The setting free of a slave,

14. Or feeding on a day of famine,

15. Of   an   orphan   from amongst relatives,

16. Or someone poor from amongst the destitute,

17. Then to be of those who believe and encourage each other to patience and encourage each other to mercy.

18. Those are the companions of the right.

19. And those who reject Our signs, they are the companions of the left.

20. A fire will close in on them.

Surah 91: **Ash-Shams**
(The Sun)

In the name of Allah,
the Owner and Giver of Mercy

1. By the sun and its light,

2. And the moon when it follows it,

3. And the day when it makes it shine,

4. And the night when it hides it,

5. And the sky and how it is structured,

6. And the earth and how it is spread out,

7. And the soul and how it has been balanced,

8. And instinctively knows both immorality and awareness (of Allah).

9. Successful is who purifies it,

10. And failed has he who allows it to transgress,

11. Thamud denied in its transgression,

12. When they sent their worst,

13. And their messenger of Allah said to them: this is the she-camel of Allah and her drinking place,

14. But they denied him and bled her to death, then their Lord came over them on account of their sin and levelled them,

15. And did not fear the outcome.

Surah 92: *Al-Lail*
(The Night)

In the name of Allah,
the Owner and Giver of Mercy

1. By the night when it covers,

2. And the day when it exposes,

3. And the creation of male and female,

4. Your effort is diverse.

5. So whoever gives and bewares (of Allah),

6. And trusts in goodness,

7. We will make it easy for him.

8. And whoever is stingy and arrogant,

9. And denies goodness,

10. We will make it hard for him,

11. And his wealth will not benefit him when he dies.

12. For upon Us is the guidance,

13. And Ours is the hereafter and this life.

14. I warn you therefore of a raging fire.

15. Only the worst will enter it.

16. The one who denied and turned away.

17. And the pious will be kept away from it.

18. The one who gives his wealth to purify himself.

19. And he does not ask anyone for reward for a blessing,

20. But seeks the presence of his Lord the most elevated.

21. And soon he will be content.

Surah 93: **Ad-Duha**
(The Morning Light)

In the name of Allah,
the Owner and Giver of Mercy

1. By the morning light,

2. And the night when it is still,

3. Your Lord neither abandoned you nor hated you.

4. And the hereafter is better for you than the first part.

5. And soon your Lord will give to you and you will be content.

6. Did He not find you an orphan and sheltered you?

7. And found you lost and guided you?

8. And found you in need and enriched you?

9. So do not overpower the orphan,

10. And do not brush off the one who asks,

11. And talk of the favours of your Lord.

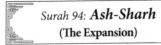

Surah 94: **Ash-Sharh**
(The Expansion)

In the name of Allah,
the Owner and Giver of Mercy

1. Did We not expand your chest,

2. And relieved you of your burden,

3. Which weighed down your back,

4. And elevated your mention?

5. So with hardship comes ease,

6. With hardship comes ease.

7. Then when you are done, rise,

8. And place your hope in your Lord.

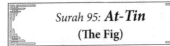

Surah 95: **At-Tin**
(The Fig)

In the name of Allah,
the Owner and Giver of Mercy

1. By the fig and the olive,

2. And by mount Sinai,

3. And this safe city,

4. We created man in the best stature.

5. Then We return him to the lowest of states.

6. Except those who believe and do good work, for them is a limitless reward.

7. So what makes you deny after that the debt?

8. Is not Allah the wisest of judges?

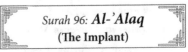

Surah 96: **Al-'Alaq**
(The Implant)

In the name of Allah,
the Owner and Giver of Mercy

1. Recite in the name of your Lord who created,

2. Created man from an implant.

3. Recite, and your Lord is the most generous,

4. Who taught with the pen,

5. Taught man what he did not know.

6. But man transgresses,

7. When he considers himself independent,

8. For to your Lord is the return.

9. Have you considered him who prevents,

10. A servant from praying?

11. Have you considered whether he is upon guidance,

12. Or orders awareness (of Allah)?

13. Have you considered whether he denies and turns away?

14. Does he not know that Allah sees?

15. But no, if he does not stop, We shall grab him by the forelock,

16. The lying, sinful forelock,

17. Then let him call his supporters,

18. We will call the enforcers.

19. Oh no, don't obey him; prostrate and draw close (to Allah).

Surah 97: **Al-Qadr**
(The Destiny)

In the name of Allah,
the Owner and Giver of Mercy

1. We revealed it during the night of destiny.

2. And how do you know what the night of destiny is?

3. The night of destiny is better than a thousand months.

4. The angels and the Spirit descend during it by the permission of their Lord with all affairs.

5. It means peace until the start of daybreak.

Surah 98: **Al-Bayyinah**
(Clear Proof)

In the name of Allah,
the Owner and Giver of Mercy

1. Those who reject (the truth) amongst the people of the Book and the idolaters will not give up until the clear proof reaches them.

2. A messenger from Allah who recites to them from purified pages.

3. Containing lasting statements.

4. Nor did those who were given the book differ except after the clear proof reached them.

5. And they were only ordered to serve Allah, making religion sincere for Him and devoted, and to keep up prayer and give Zakat, and that is the lasting religion.

6. Those who reject (the truth) amongst the people of the Book and the idolaters are in the fire of hell where they will remain; they are the worst creatures.

7. Those who believe and do good work, they are the best creatures.

8. Their reward with their Lord is the gardens of Eden through which rivers flow where they will remain forever. Allah is content with them and they are content with Him; that is for him who is fearful of his Lord.

Surah 99: **Al-Zalzalah**
(The Shaking)

In the name of Allah,
the Owner and Giver of Mercy

1. When the earth shakes its last,

2. And the earth expels its burden,

3. And man says: what is the matter with it?

4. That day it will tell its story,

5. Because your Lord inspired it.

6. That day mankind will proceed in groups to have their deeds inspected.

7. Then who did a tiny speck's weight of good, will see it.

8. And who did a tiny speck's weight of bad, will see it.

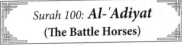

Surah 100: *Al-'Adiyat*
(The Battle Horses)

In the name of Allah,
the Owner and Giver of Mercy

1. By the snorting battle horses,

2. Who strike up sparks,

3. And attack in the morning,

4. Stirring up dust,

5. And breaking through the crowd,

6. Man is ungrateful of his Lord,

7. And he is a witness to that,

8. And he loves affluence greatly.

9. Does he not know that when what is in the graves will be overturned,

10. And what is kept inside will be exposed,

11. Your Lord will be informed about him that day?

Surah 101: *Al-Qari'ah*
(The Calamity)

In the name of Allah,
the Owner and Giver of Mercy

1. The Calamity.

2. What is the calamity?

3. And how do you know what the calamity is?

4. That day mankind will be like scattered moths,

5. And the mountains will be like puffed up wool.

6. Then he whose scales are heavy,

7. Will be in a life of contentment.

8. And he whose scales are light,

9. The pit will take care of him,

10. And how do you know what it is?

11. A scorching fire.

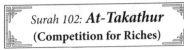

Surah 102: *At-Takathur*
(Competition for Riches)

In the name of Allah,
the Owner and Giver of Mercy

1. Competition for riches keeps you busy,

2. Until you enter your graves.

3. But no, you will soon know,

4. But no again, you will soon know,

5. For sure, if you had knowledge of the inevitable,

6. You would see hell-fire,

7. Then you will see it with your own eyes,

8. Then you will be asked that day about blessings.

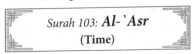

Surah 103: *Al-'Asr*
(Time)

In the name of Allah,
the Owner and Giver of Mercy

1. By Time,

2. Man is at a loss,

3. Except those who believe and do good work, admonish each other with the truth and encourage each other to patience.

Surah 104: **Al-Humazah**
(The Slanderer)

In the name of Allah,
the Owner and Giver of Mercy

1. Woe to every mocking slanderer.

2. Who gathers wealth and counts it.

3. He thinks his wealth will let him live forever.

4. But no, he will be flung into the shredder.

5. And how do you know what the shredder is?

6. Allah's lit fire,

7. Which engulfs the hearts.

8. It closes in on them,

9. In extensive columns.

Surah 105: **Al-Fil**
(The Elephant)

In the name of Allah,
the Owner and Giver of Mercy

1. Did you not see how your Lord dealt with the companions of the elephant?

2. Did He not make their plot go astray,

3. And sent against them flocks of birds,

4. Who pelted them with hardened stones,

5. So He made them like eaten up stalks?

Surah 106: **Quraysh**
(Quraysh)

In the name of Allah,
the Owner and Giver of Mercy

1. For the unity of Quraysh,

2. Their unity during the winter and summer journey,

3. Let them serve the Lord of this house,

4. Who fed them against hunger and protected them against fear.

Surah 107: **Al-Maun**
(Assistance)

In the name of Allah,
the Owner and Giver of Mercy

1. Have you considered him who denies his (religious) debt?

2. He is who snubs the orphan,

3. And does not encourage the feeding of the poor.

4. Woe then to those who pray,

5. Who are negligent of their prayers,

6. Who show off,

7. And refuse assistance.

Surah 108: **Al-Kauthar**
(Abundance)

In the name of Allah,
the Owner and Giver of Mercy

1. We have given you abundance.

2. So pray to your Lord and sacrifice,

3. For your adversary is bereft.

Surah 109: **Al-Kafirun**
(Those Who Reject the Truth)

In the name of Allah,
the Owner and Giver of Mercy

1. Say: Oh you who reject (the truth),

2. I do not serve what you serve,

3. And you are no servants of what I serve,

4. And I am no servant of what you used to serve,

5. And you are no servants of what I serve,

6. You have your religion and I have mine.

Surah 110: *An-Nasr*
(The Help)

In the name of Allah,
the Owner and Giver of Mercy

1. When help and victory come from Allah,

2. And you see people entering in the religion of Allah in large groups,

3. Then glorify the praise of your Lord and ask His forgiveness, for He is accepting.

Surah 111: *Al-Masad*
(Palm Fibre)

In the name of Allah,
the Owner and Giver of Mercy

1. May the hands of the father of flame perish, and may he perish.

2. His wealth and what he earned will not benefit him.

3. He will enter a fire full of flames.

4. And his wife, the carrier of gossip,

5. Will have a rope of palm fibre around her neckline.

Surah 112: *Al-Ikhlas*
(Sincerity)

In the name of Allah,
the Owner and Giver of Mercy

1. Say: He is Allah alone,

2. Allah the everlasting,

3. He does not reproduce nor has been reproduced,

4. And nobody is a match for Him.

Surah 113: *Al-Falaq*
(Dawn)

In the name of Allah,
the Owner and Giver of Mercy

1. Say: I seek refuge in the Lord of dawn,

2. From the harm of what He created,

3. And from the harm of darkness when it sets in,

4. And from the harm of women blowing on knots,

5. And from the harm of the envious when he shows envy.

Surah 114: *An-Nas*
(Mankind)

In the name of Allah,
the Owner and Giver of Mercy

1. Say: I seek refuge in the Lord of mankind,

2. The king of mankind,

3. The god of mankind,

4. From the harm of the secret whisperer,

5. Who whispers within people,

6. From amongst Jinn and mankind.

Brief Index of Subjects

A

'Ad, people of 7:65-74; 9:70; 11:50-60; 14:9; 22:42; 25:38; 26:123-140; 29:38; 38:12; 40:31; 41:13-16; 46:21-26; 50:13; 51:41-42; 53:50; 54:18-21; 69:4; 69:6-8; 89:6

Ablution, 4:43; 5:6

Abu Lahab (Father of Flame), 111:1-5

Adam, 2:31; 2:33-35, 2:37, 3:33, 3:59, 5:27, 7:11, 7:19, 7:26-27, 7:31, 7:35, 7:172, 17:61, 17:70, 18:50, 19:58, 20:115-117, 20:120-122, 36:60

Ahmad (Praised One), 61:6

Adultery, *see Zina*

Alcohol (narcotic drugs), 2:219; 5:90-91

Allah*,

accepts repentance, 2:54; 2:160; 9:104; 9:118; 40:3; 42:25

all beings in the Heavens and Earth glorify Him, 17:44; 21:19-20; 24:41; 57:1; 59:1; 59:24; 61:1; 62:1; 64:1

all benefit is in His hand, 3:73

all faces shall be humbled before Him, 20:111

all good is from Him, 4:78-79; 16:30; 16:53

all things are from Him, 4:78

begets not, nor is He begotten, 112:3

belief in, 2:62; 2:177; 2:256; 3:179; 3:193; 4:38-39; 4:59; 4:136; 4:152; 4:162; 4:171; 4:175; 7:158; 9:18-19; 9:44-45; 24:2; 24:62; 36:25; 40:84; 48:13; 49:15; 57:7-8; 57:19; 58:22; 60:4; 60:11; 61:11; 64:8; 64:11; 65:2; 67:29; 72:13; 85:8

believers love Him, 2:165; 2:177; 3:31; 5:54; 76:8

call upon Him, 6:52; 6:63; 7:29; 7:55-56; 7:180; 13:36; 18:28; 40:14; 40:60; 40:65

creates what He pleases/ will, 3:47; 5:17; 24:45; 28:68; 30:54; 35:1; 42:49; 82:8

does not change the condition of a people until they change, 13:11

does not waste the work of a worker, 3:195; 9:120; 12:56; 12:90; 18:30; 21:94; 52:21

does what He will, 2:253; 3:40; 11:107; 14:27; 22:14-18; 85:16

do not associate anything with him, 3:64; 4:36; 4:48; 4:116; 5:72; 6:14; 6:81; 6:88; 6:136; 6:148; 6:151; 9:31; 10:28-29; 13:16; 13:33; 13:36; 16:51-57; 16:73; 16:86; 17:22; 17:39-40; 17:56-57; 18:110; 22:31; 23:59; 23:117; 24:55; 25:68; 28:87-88; 29:8; 30:31; 31:13; 35:13-14; 39:64-65; 40:41-43; 40:66; 41:6; 43:45; 46:4-6; 50:26; 51:51; 60:12; 72:2; 72:18

exalted is He, 7:54; 23:14; 25:1; 25:10; 25:61; 43:85; 55:78;

expands provision and tightens it, 13:26; 17:30; 28:82; 29:62; 30:37; 34:36; 34:39; 39:52; 42:12; 42:27; 89:15-16

feeds but is not fed, 6:14; 51:57-58

forgives sins, 2:284; 3:31; 3:195; 4:116; 5:18; 5:39-40; 7:161; 8:29; 8:70; 12:92; 13:6; 14:10; 26:82; 28:16; 33:71; 36:27; 39:53; 40:3; 42:25; 42:30; 42:34; 46:31; 48:14; 67:28; 61:12; 64:17; 71:4

gives life to the dead, 2:28; 2:243; 2:259-260; 3:27; 6:36; 7:57; 10:31; 22:6; 30:19; 30:40; 30:50; 36:12; 36:79; 41:39; 42:9; 46:33; 50:11; 75:40; 80:22; 86:8

gives provisions, 2:57; 2:126; 2:172; 3:27; 3:37; 3:169; 5:114; 6:151; 7:50; 7:160; 8:26; 10:31; 10:93; 11:88; 14:37; 16:72; 16:75; 17:31; 17:70; 20:81; 20:132; 27:64; 29:60; 30:40; 34:24; 35:3; 40:13; 40:40; 40:64; 42:19; 45:5; 45:16; 50:11; 65:3; 67:15; 67:21; 106:4

* Due to the recurrence of the mention of the name of Allah throughout the Qur'an, only verses containing specific information on the given subjects have been included for reference

Allah, *(cont'd.)*

glory be to Him, 2:32; 2:116; 3:191; 4:171; 5:116; 6:100; 7:143; 9:31; 10:10; 10:18; 10:68; 12:108; 16:1; 17:43-44; 17:108; 21:22; 21:26; 21:87; 24:16; 24:36; 25:18; 27:8; 28:68; 30:17; 30:40; 33:42; 34:41; 36:83; 37:159; 37:180; 39:4; 39:67; 40:64; 43:13; 43:82; 59:23; 68:28-29; 69:52; 76:26; 87:1

guides whom He wills, 2:213; 2:272; 10:25; 13:27; 13:31; 14:4; 16:93; 22:16; 24:35; 24:46; 28:56; 35:8; 39:23; 42:52; 74:31

has no partner, 6:163; 7:191-198; 9:31; 10:66; 17:111; 23:91; 25:2; 35:40; 42:21; 68:41; 72:3

has no son, 2:116; 4:171; 6:101; 9:30; 10:68; 17:111; 18:4; 19:35; 19:88-92; 21:26; 23:91; 25:2; 37:152; 39:4; 43:81-82; 72:3

is enough, 2:137; 3:173; 4:6; 4:45; 4:70; 4:79; 4:81; 4:132; 4:166; 4:171; 8:62; 8:64; 9:59; 9:129; 10:29; 13:43; 17:17; 17:65; 17:96; 25:31; 25:58; 29:52; 33:3; 33:48; 39:38; 46:8; 48:28; 65:3

is not unaware of what you do, 2:74; 2:85; 2:140; 2:144; 2:149; 3:99; 6:132; 11:123; 14:42; 22:68; 23:17; 27:93

is the best of schemers, 3:54; 8:30; 13:42

knows all you let on and hide, 2:33; 2:77; 2:284; 3:29; 5:99; 6:3; 11:5; 14:38; 16:19; 16:23; 21:110; 27:25; 27:74; 28:69; 33:54; 36:76; 60:1; 64:4; 87:7

knows best who is guided, 6:117; 16:125; 17:84; 28:56; 53:30; 68:7

knows the Unseen, 2:33; 5:109; 5:116; 6:59; 6:73; 9:78; 9:94; 9:105; 10:20; 11:123; 13:9; 16:77; 18:26; 20:7; 23:92; 25:6; 27:65; 32:6; 34:3; 34:48; 49:18; 72:26; 84:23

manages affairs, 10:3; 10:31; 13:2; 32:5

meeting with Him, 2:46; 2:223; 2:249; 6:154; 10:11; 10:15; 10:45; 13:2; 18:110; 25:21; 29:5; 29:23; 30:8; 32:10; 33:44; 41:54; 84:6

nearness to Him, 2:186; 7:206; 11:61; 34:37; 34:50; 39:3; 50:16; 83:21; 83:28; 96:19

never breaks His promise, 3:9; 3:194; 13:31; 14:47; 30:6

no affliction strikes except with His permission, 64:11

no God but Him (One God), 2:133; 2:163; 2:255; 3:2; 3:6; 3:18; 3:62; 4:87; 5:73; 6:102; 6:106; 7:59; 7:65; 7:85; 7:158; 9:31; 9:129; 11:14; 11:50; 11:61; 11:84; 16:2; 20:8; 20:14; 20:98; 20:14; 20:98; 21:22; 21:25; 21:87; 23:23; 23:32; 23:116-117; 27:26; 27:60-64; 28:70; 28:88; 35:3; 38:65; 39:6; 40:3; 40:62; 40:65; 44:8; 47:19; 52:43; 59:22-23; 64:13

no power except in Him, 18:39

no refuge from Him except towards Him, 9:118; 72:22

obey Him, 3:132; 4:59; 4:69; 8:1; 8:20-21; 8:46; 9:71; 24:51-54; 33:33; 33:71; 47:33; 48:16-17; 49:14; 58:13; 64:12; 64:16

Praise be to Him, 1:2; 6:1; 6:45; 10:10; 14:39; 15:98; 16:75; 17:111; 18:1; 23:28; 25:58; 27:15; 27:59; 27:93; 28:70; 29:63; 30:18; 31:25; 34:1; 35:1; 35:34; 37:182; 39:29; 39:74-75; 40:55; 40:65; 50:39-40; 52:48-49; 64:1; 110:3

prostration to Him, 15:98; 16:49; 19:58; 20:70; 22:77; 25:64; 32:15; 39:9; 48:29; 50:40; 53:62; 76:26; 96:19

responds to the distressed, 27:62

says "Be!" and it is, 2:117; 3:47; 3:59; 6:73; 16:40; 19:35; 36:82

seek His forgiveness, 2:285-286; 3:16; 3:135; 3:147; 3:193; 4:64; 5:74; 7:155; 11:3; 11:52; 11:61; 11:90; 12:29; 12:98; 14:41; 19:47; 23:109; 23:118; 24:62; 28:16; 40:55; 41:6; 47:19; 51:18; 60:5; 71:10; 71:28; 73:20; 110:3

seek His help, 1:5; 2:45; 2:153

seek refuge in Him, 7:200-201; 16:98; 19:18; 23:97-98; 40:56; 41:36; 113:1; 114:1

D

E

G

H

Brief Index of Subjects

M

N

S

T

U